Published by
Fortune Favours LTD.

First published in September 2020.

ASIN B087CP84JG

All rights reserved. No part of this publication may be reproduced, stored in a retrieval system, or in any form or by any means, without the prior permission in writing of the publisher, nor be otherwise circulated in any form of binding or cover other than that in which it is published and without a similar conditions including this condition being imposed on the subsequent publisher.

British Library Cataloguing-in-Publication Data:
A catalogue record for this book is available from the British Library.

© Text copyright Tava O'Halloran
Tava O'Halloran asserts the moral right to be identified as the author of this work, except for the cover design, copyright © Rich Pack

The story, the experiences, and the words in this book are the author's alone. Although the author and publisher have made every effort to ensure that the information in this book was correct at the time of publication, the author and publisher do not assume and hereby disclaim any liability to any party for any loss, damage, or disruption caused by errors or omissions, whether such errors or omissions result from negligence, accident, or any other cause.

Queen of Clubs

A MEMOIR

dedications

Devoted to
My triangle of love.
I don't exist without you both.

Written for
You.
My dear beautiful friend. I am eternally grateful to you for reading these words.

Thank You
Lana Del Ray.
I listened to your Spotify 'Complete' playlist for two years while I wrote every word of this story. In a weird, hypnotised trance. Although I think the world could take a break from me absent-mindedly singing My pussy tastes like Pepsi Cola, as I do the grocery shopping.

And my last, but most necessary dedication.
To my fellow underdog creatives and the 107 agents who told me 'No' (or generally, an implied 'no' with their silence, because quite often they don't even bother to reply to our elaborate pitches and polished proposals).

Don't wait for them to 'allow' you to tell your story: show your art, pursue your creative vision or launch your big wild idea. Do it yourself. The days of them deciding which 'ideas' get to live and breathe, and which don't, are numbered. With their outdated methods of 'financially driven - what's commercially hot today - how big is their social platform bestseller shopping lists'.

Creativity shouldn't be stopped dead on a gatekeeper's doorstep; turned away, discarded. Often unread, unopened and unheard because it's not what 'the market wants or dictates.' Creativity, original thinking and ideas are what create real newness. What we don't know we need until we experience it. What makes the world pulsate, intrigue and inspire imagination. Capture hearts.

Love to you all, Tava x

legal

This memoir is a fictionalised re-creation of actual events in the author's life. As such, creative liberties have been taken, not for literary effect, but out of necessity. The reader should not consider this book a work of fiction, but nor should this memoir be considered entirely a work of fact. Human memory is deeply flawed. It's almost impossible to recall a conversation word-for-word. Minor but crucial details can be forgotten. The events, places, amounts and conversations recorded here have been re-created from memory and/or supplemented. The chronology of some events has been compressed. In almost all cases, the names and identifying characteristics of individuals and places have been changed to maintain anonymity and protect their privacy. Some characters are composites, some entirely fictitious.

Any views expressed are solely those of the author and represent merely the opinions of the author, and should not be taken to be accusations or allegations of any kind.

No one looks back on their life and remembers the nights they got plenty of sleep.

- Unknown.

prologue

Bishopsgate Churchyard - London Winter 2011

I have a little laugh to myself: this is not the type of powder that's usually associated with nocturnal recreational activities. Light feathery flakes of snow fall on the eerily quiet Bishopsgate Churchyard and my majestic Victorian Bathhouse. Her ornate stained-glass onion-dome roof and intricate swirling gingerbread house brickwork glow like a beacon of light in the North Pole, nestled in the stark, striking contrast between towering sleek futuristic skyscrapers. The powdery snow gives the illusion of purity. A Nordic Yuletide picture-perfect snow globe, rather than a setting for a debauched den of iniquity and scandalous all-night party.

Despite the unexpected snowfall (this is usually terrible for business), we've sold out of New Year's Eve tickets, plus the extra 20 per cent we list on the top of our legal venue capacity, to take into account the no-shows and last-minute dropouts. We were named the 'hottest place in London to ring-in-the-New-Year', according to Time Out Magazine. Bad reviews plague nightclubs, but it's the positive ones that damaged us. Blowing open our secret world into the mainstream media and sending our underground pleasure seekers to the next unheard of playground. We were still as busy as last year's NYE party but with a very different type of customer now, and more of the overflow has turned up than usual. It's tight inside. I can see, on the clickers, we are over capacity by fifty-eight people; not operationally dangerous but still illegal if I get caught in a spot check. Which is why we run two sets of clickers: one to show the police and local authorities, and one for us. Inside, the atmosphere is electric: a contagious thrill of anticipation to celebrate the New Year. Nobody seems worried that it's a tight squeeze. Well, for the moment...

20 minutes to countdown. The entry queue is still snaking around the venue. Trickles of customers, wobbling and swaying from pre-drinking, try to score entry with a last-minute ticket on the door. I send them to the pub next door for the countdown, then add them to the free-entry guest list, with a few drink tokens, to come back later in the night when the crowd thins out a little. I love that people come and celebrate with us. It's a weird feeling of awe, guests wanting to spend their precious nights here, especially NYE. I don't want them to have a shit night waiting in the snow to get in. The fact they didn't arrange to buy tickets in advance, which is how most NYE parties operate, can turn around negatively on us in an online review or word-of-mouth, spiralling into "The place is shit. Their queue was too long. Security were dicks and wouldn't let us in." I'd rather keep customers happy. It's better for business in the long run, and it's what gives us an unpretentious reputation. VIP guest list, excellent hospitality, and a few drinks tickets go a long way in clubland.

Back inside, the glitter cannon and metallic gold balloon ceiling drop are straining to explode over party revellers as the clock strikes twelve. I look around the venue and pinch myself.

This is actually mine. It's a good pinch, not a fuck: this is my problem pinch. It switches often. The room shimmers and shines, opulent, magical, and seeped in history. Low-hanging bronze chandeliers with flicker candle light bulbs throw dancing shadows on the thick, red velvet draping. Disco balls project glittery mirrored dots over the pale walls of handmade, fined-detailed macabre skeleton wallpaper; long white taper candles shoved into the spiky tops of pineapples (I secretly think their life purpose is candle holding). The trend for minimalist warehouse nightclubs is booming, and this is the reason why The Bathhouse is so intoxicating. It is the complete opposite: sheer decadence without the pretension of a West End club. Nor the wankers.

17 minutes to countdown. I slink and slide through the hot, clammy crowd, ducking and diving past people's drinks and wild dance moves to find the quickest route to check on the tills, reload the change, make sure the bars are fully stocked. Glasses are making their way back from the dishwasher, ready to go another round. This is one of those nights when we have a license to print money. A delicate but well-oiled ecosystem of everyone doing their jobs properly to keep the flow going, the booze selling, and cash registers zinging.

I poke my head back upstairs to check on security and take a G&T to our guest-list legend, Sissy. I notice that Antonio, our very beautiful, Latin lover Brazilian restaurant manager is now fully relaxed after his shift, and by fully relaxed I mean spangled on MDMA and kissing an equally pretty boy in front of the venue. They look like a glossy magazine ad for Jean Paul Gaultier perfume. He stumbles a little. I discreetly flag security to keep an eye out for him. Mac, our venue manager, is also watching him, so I move on.

13 minutes to countdown. I make my way back down into the beating heart of the club, our DJ, in the towering 12-foot high and 8-foot wide golden birdcage DJ booth: a thing of pure beauty. It rises up in the middle of the dance floor, towering over the sea of heaving, sweaty bodies with its twisted, decorative wrought-iron bars. A large-scale version of what you would see hanging in the window of the 'Cherry Tree Lane' mansion, where Mary Poppins nannies. We triple-check the microphone for the countdown. The DJ is mixing a Franki Valli - Beggin' Remix into the epic acapella Simian Mobile Disco - We Are Your Friends. Everyone is going wild.

Faces spin, laughing, dancing, flashing in front of me as I move quickly through the dance floor. I head down the spiral stairs: each step is ancient, crumbly cream marble and the walls are covered in original ornate 18th-century tiles, handmade and slightly different, with inconsistencies and imperfections, making them perfect to me. Muted reds and midnight blues in dreamy geometric patterns. They are cool to touch as I run my fingers along the walls leading down to my office. I'm surprised there isn't a greasy trail of my fingerprints up and down the tile work. It has become a superstitious habit when moving through the stairwells, always connected by my fingertips. A moment from the madness. The office vibrates god-like Bowie's anthem - Let's Dance. It's hot and stuffy in the basement. No windows or fresh air. CCTV monitors line the walls, creating more unbearable heat into the small room. I rack up a few lines of coke from the large pile, quickly snort one, leave the rest, then head upstairs to oversee the midnight madness.

9 minutes to countdown. Lively from my pick-me-up, I quickly head back to the door to sneak in a cigarette before the count down. There's an odd atmosphere between the guys on security. It feels serious, and their tempers seem a little short tonight. But then the cold really affects them, standing for eight hours in all sorts of weather, often working a double shift. Most of the security team have day jobs, and we tend to feel the burn of their double shift day. Antonio is having an up-close, animated conversation with Mac, the venue manager. Mac is a little off today, as well. Frayed. I clocked he didn't meet my gaze earlier, quickly looking away. New Year's Eves are weird. People are weird. There's heightened tension and expectation with staff, as well as customers. Like it's a magical night meant to change everything and determines the year ahead. For me, it's just another of the regular 365 days in clubland that roll around. NYE lost its sparkle many years ago in Mexico for me.

7 minutes to countdown. Coat-check calls out over the radio that they need more raffle tickets. I nip in to sort it out. Any excuse to talk shit and stand in front of the heater for a few minutes. Not the warmest outfit for this Baltic weather, I'm wearing a skin-tight, high-waisted, knee-length leather pencil skirt. Tucked into it is a ruffled black and gold sheer bullfighter-kind of shirt-blouse thing, with a thick vintage Versace elastic waist belt with two large golden leopards, with emerald jewel eyes, bowing down to each other. Opaque black tights and lace-up pointy, shiny patent stiletto heels, '50's pin-tucked hair, soft curls, and iconic Mac Ruby Woo lips, as per usual. My phone is slipped in between my bra strap and boob, and the five-channel radio with earpiece is clipped to my skirt. I keep a white cropped vintage bolero rabbit fur and black leather gloves with leather oversized bows, where the wrist meets the hand, stashed by the front door to grab for when I head outside.

3 minutes to countdown. Looking out of the frosty coat-check window to security, a quick, jerky movement catches my eye at the entrance. Something's kicking off. I race outside.

It's Antonio, Mac, and... three other guys I don't know? ... For fuck's sake, they're customers! Mac throws a punch and floors one of the guys. Antonio is scrapping on the ground with another. I run over and pull Antonio off him before it gets worse. Mac's dragging him back into a headlock. Spinning around with a huge shock, a dull shove to the middle of my back, knocking the wind out of me...it's a female customer. She's screaming at Mac, trying to climb over me to get him off her boyfriend. I hold her back, and she starts walking backwards up the churchyard, screaming at Nathan, the head of security, "You fucking pussy cunt, you piece of shit cunt!" It's escalating quickly: his face goes from white to grey and his eyes lock on her like a great white shark, fiery and beady, not blinking, not looking away. He runs towards her...wait, what the fuck is he doing!?! He throws his arm back, then smashes her with a closed fist, not holding back as he punches her right in the middle of her face. Everything is in slow motion. The impact makes her face fly to the side. Blood sprays across the snow in the churchyard, and she goes flying through the cold night air. I can't believe this is happening. My security team is turning on our customers. I scramble, slipping on the ice to get over to her. Dragging her out of his way, then crawling to the side of the scrum, I fumble down my top, grab my phone and call the police. Now, this is the LAST thing you ever want to do as a club owner. You try to keep the police as far away as you possibly can. This is totally out of my control. The police are stationed one block around the corner on Liverpool Street. And there are roaming armed response units as well - we're positioned within the City of London Square mile, which has its own independent police force. I make the call directly to the Liverpool Street precinct for help. She's bleeding everywhere and still screaming at Nathan, spitting out blood and bits of broken teeth. She gets back on her feet, wobbling. He's squaring up to her again. My body spiked with pure adrenalin, I wedge myself in between both of them. He's pulling at me to get me out of the way. I refuse to budge. He'll have to start attacking me before he gets to her. I scream an inch from his face... 'BACK THE FUCK OFF!'... He is raging, totally out of control.

5, 4, 3, 2, 1 MIDNIGHT - HAPPY NEW YEAR!!! A dull rhythmic thump in the distance. Thump-thump-thump-thump-thump. In storm City of London police in full riot gear, masks, shields, and submachine guns. Casual. They file methodically into the top of the churchyard and march towards us in an impenetrable formation, sirens whirring, red flashing lights staining the snow, like blood, and the screeching of an ambulance to let us know it's not far behind. They plough through the snow and in a split second, grab everyone in the immediate vicinity and pull this bullshit mess apart. This is my mess, my security, my managers. Panic flashed through my mind. FUCK. The police can't go into the club. We're in full flight of an overcapacity party down there. Double FUCK. The office! What if they want to review the CCTV of the fight right now? With a pile of coke on the bench staring up at them?

Mac, Antonio, Nathan, and the three customers they were fighting are arrested and taken to the police station. Our female customer is taken to the hospital. The police leave as quickly as they arrived. Small mercies; they left without entering the venue, but my short-lived career is unarguably over. That was some seriously bad management all round.

22 minutes past midnight. I walk back down into the club, shell-shocked, my heart still racing as I step over the gold foil confetti debris from the exploded glitter cannon. Empty party popper cases, customers dancing on tables, golden balloons bouncing through the crowd, and bar staff working at a maniacal pace to push out the post-midnight-madness drink orders. It's as though the Armageddon-level shit storm above never happened. They were protected in the bomb-proof party bunker, oblivious to the pandemonium and anarchy outside...

25 minutes past midnight. I lock myself in the office to polish off the two pre-racked-up lines and put my head on the desk to rest. What the fuck am I doing with my life? Break (down) over. Back to running the club. I'm now three staff members short. Well, two apparently on-duty capable members. I place calls to get Nathan's security position filled ASAP, and make a mental note to go and look for one of my precious leopard emerald eyes that pinged out in the fight.

28 minutes past midnight. Back on the floor, tits 'n' teeth out, a fake smile plastered on to deliver the 'night of the year' for our customers and record-breaking bar takings for our accountant. First stop. The bar, to get the staff a round of Jagerbombs. They deserve it.
So do I.

Just a regular hour at work. Well, not even an hour. 48 minutes. I wonder what the next few hours are going to bring...?

NB: My staff were all charged with aggravated assault while the three male customers were charged with drunk and disorderly behaviour. The female customer received 20 stitches, had a broken nose, and needed reconstructive dental work, but didn't press charges for grievous bodily harm against Nathan. Which was really strange. She stopped talking to the police after she'd sobered up the next day. After reviewing the CCTV footage, a few days later, the police were satisfied with how I managed the situation, and they decided to charge the staff as individuals rather than prosecute the venue or take our license to a review hearing. We fired the three staff members involved for gross misconduct. Turns out married, heterosexual Mac had been secretly drinking on the job that night. He was deeply and also secretly in love with our Antonio. He snapped: couldn't stand seeing Antonio kiss random pretty boys while wasted on MDMA. So he lashed out at the pretty stranger and his friends. Gross misconduct. Antonio jumping in, escalating the fight. Gross misconduct. Nathan, our shark security, was apparently sleep-deprived. His girlfriend had left him, and he was hopped up on 'legal' performance-enhancing steroids in preparation for an amateur MMA fight, making him lose his shit on our lady customer. So, so much gross misconduct. It's EastEnders' drama featuring The Bathhouse security and upper management. Oh and I'd love to tell you that I learnt my lesson cutting it fine with the police coming into the office with the coke left out, but I just found a more discreet place to do it in...

QUEEN OF CLUBS

Hello, My Dear Beautiful Reader, my partner in crime for the next 419 pages.

Ok, I think I might have thrown you into the deep end with that opening tale. Usually, I would have split a bottle of wine or three with you before sharing these kinds of stories but here's hoping you're a few cocktails in and I'm your summer read on a white sandy beach or maybe your entertainment on an otherwise shitty, mind-numbing morning commute to work, but most likely a break from a COVID-19 induced Netflix binge. If that's the case, then it's the least I could do to pass the time with you, together.

I've done anything, everything to avoid writing this. Endless excuses, got side-tracked. Moved country, ran away. Can't, I had a baby (said baby is now halfway through her first year of school and had been asking about different religions. Her conclusion – 'I believe we can all live together and still believe in different things'. Ok, Ghandi, I need to pull my finger out and start writing). Taken on yet another creative direction project, so I'm way too busy now. My Mac's 'delete' key has come off after an unplanned encounter with a glass of white wine and a hairdryer, resulting in a bad tech situation. Wasted life, mindless zombie skimming Instagram, busy worm-holing pointless hours spent with nobodies from 20 years ago to get lost in their holiday snaps from Positano, making sure I don't 'heart' anything and leave evidence of my weird stalking k-hole. Hate my life. Hate being so pathetic. Tidy the house: you're not a proper writer, you delusional, dyslexic fuck. Unstacking the dishwasher that could have waited. Back to 'the grid' to check on my frenemy and what she's had for lunch. Stand at the fridge and eat leftover cold sausage, congealed gravy, mash, and peas, using the sausage as the only utensil. Drink a bottle of wine, then self-loathe a bit more.

This is the daily cycle, train of thought that gets between my self-saboteur and the telling of this story. Right: so I'm going to stop drinking wine. Stop trolling social media. (Edit: still doing both.). Stop cry-wanking over how shit my life is now. Stop making excuses and just write the fucking book!

I've avoided thinking back for so many years, I've blocked so much of it out. I'm scared of the truth. I'm scared of the people I've hurt. I'm scared of the bad decisions I made. I'm scared of being honest. I'm scared of digging up the past and rattling cages.

But I've finally run out of excuses.

The time that's passed has made the hurt a little less breathtaking, the memories slightly duller, the stories not so spiky and leaving more space to breathe between the shameful actions, making them (a little) less cringe-worthy. Leaving small, soft glowing shreds of pride, love notes from my former life and the warm feeling of half-forgotten, beautiful, crazy friends. Kaleidoscopic travels to exotic lands, finding my 'Hollywood-fucking-amazing-love,' and a real-life rainbow at the end of my yellow brick road.

Strangely, it has always been my mum saying over the years, "You've got to write a book." She's a white-picket-fence mum: wholesome, unshakable in her love for the family, devoted to her children. Follows life's unwritten rules; a never-faltering moral compass and guiding light of what's right in the world. My dad used to say, "Don't do anything you wouldn't tell your mother." Dad is not so golden. He was a secret pot-smoking Peter-Pan dad, never really wanting to grow up and have the

emotional responsibility of four children. Don't get me wrong: he was a wonderful father, but there came a time when we were older, and it felt like he'd 'finished' and clocked off being a dad. My sense of adventure and my gritty lust for life comes from my mum's mum: Nanny, or BIG, as we call her.
She also ran away to London and lived the bohemian life. Falling for a German man. A deep love affair. Jumping borders and sneaking through passport checkpoints. She is fabulous. Broadminded and has the most profound understanding of human nature. She is someone you want to share a bottle of wine with.

Luckily for the devil on my shoulder, during my 'high' times, I lived over 24 hours away by plane, 12 whole time zones between my family when the Internet, Skype, WhatsApp, Instagram and Facebook chat didn't rule the world and long-distance calls were frustratingly crackly and expensive.
I got away, for the most part, with my bad habits, thrilling adventures, a love affair with East London, and some pretty terrible life choices without anyone interrupting my chaos.

Mum's vision for the book is like a more 'adult' version of Bridget Jones' Diary. Well yeah - kinda, Mum. Maybe closer to a combination of the plot lines of Bridget Jones Diary: the sweet, little bit hopeless, lovable girl-next-door diary-style bit meets Scarface: the drug part, an ode to my insatiable love affair with cocaine, not the machine guns, mafia, say-hello-to-my-little-friend vibe, meets Studio 54: by the age of 33 owning 3 nightclubs meets Factory Girl: a misguided little lady lost in a beating obsession with fashion, drugs, art, sex, culture, music, and finding love.

So, if I'm truthful in my storytelling, this is an unsuitable read for my Mother Dearest, my biggest fan and champion.

She's always been there to pick me up and put the pieces back together. But this apple fell far from the tree.*

There are four O'Halloran children, the first three originals. I'm in the middle of the oldest boy - quiet, smart, focused, with unfaltering determination in business and a dry sense of humour - and my younger sister. Everything is black or white for her: uncompromising, and glamourous in a reality-show-contestant way. And the baby brother born 10 years later. Sarcastic, a BFG, quick-witted, hard-working, a bit of a loner...maybe 'cause we didn't call him an original? The three originals cried when Mum and Dad told us they had a surprise for us. A baby! We thought they were taking us to Disneyland. Gutted.

We were a happy little-big family. We laughed. We danced in the kitchen with wooden spoon microphones to Lou Rawls, Fine Brown Frame. Our parents were in love. Then. It was slightly shambolic: someone always hunting for their missing school sock, crossed legs hopping up and down waiting in line for the toilet, piled on the sofa watching Darling Buds of May or Wizard of Oz 'til the VHS tape wore out. We'd squish in the car for family trips to the snow in winter. Caravanning by the lakes and beaches in the summer, always with Fleetwood Mac blaring from the stereo. Fighting over who was hogging all the space. Or worse still, who'd have to ride in the stupid little seats in the boot. Picnics, bush walks, roller-skating and days spent on the beach made famous by Home and Away.

I'd always be making something crafty with scraps, bits and bobs. Drawing or creating collages. I was obsessed with dioramas and creating little worlds inside a box, miniature settings with crinkly cellophane peephole windows, each with their own atmosphere. Strangely, I do all these things now as

a professional career. I had a passion for fashion at a very early age, as well. One day, I made my own swimsuit from a long rectangle piece of pistachio-and-cream cotton fabric, a cut-off from Mum's patch-work project, and ribbon.
No stitching or elastic. Just held together with tied ribbon straps and a ribbon belt. Very Flintstones-esque-Ibiza-rock-pool-party. It ended in tears, humiliation, and a sewing basket's worth of scraps floating in our neighbour's pool.

Mum prepared for the end of the world with a Y2K-ready food cupboard. Always a touch of the crazy with that one. (This doesn't seem so crazy now, as I send my book to print in isolation amidst the COVID-19 pandemic, and rationing squares of loo roll.) We had two homes growing up: first one burnt down in an electrical fire. The dryer malfunctioned. I was sitting in science class and saw three fire engines screaming up our hill and thought, 'Poor bastard.' The silver lining was that nobody was hurt. We learnt early that 'things' didn't matter and insurance is both a necessary evil and a godsend. The house was rebuilt, more beautiful than the original and sold for a lot more than its former unmodelled self would have. The phoenix rose from the ashes and presented the perfect second O'Halloran house. A beautiful weatherboard beach house with four bedrooms and miles of room for three moody teenagers and baby bro. Both homes were in the now very hipster and expensive suburb of Avalon, tucked away in a sleepy, stunning pocket of Sydney, Australia.

Later, there was some bullying by nasty teen girls and confused dick-head boys, your usual teenage pre-drinking in the park, and gate-crashing a party only to puke in the front yard, but apart from that, it was a lovely upbringing. One of my funniest, perhaps not so typical memories is of a sibling starting life in the entrepreneur world early, digging by hand

a cavern under the house to install a four-bay hydroponics kit, capable of growing up to 200 marijuana plants or 'tomato plants' as the box states. Wiring in the electrics and self-watering system solo. Pretty impressive in anyone's book.
Until Mum came down to the kitchen, in the middle of the night for a glass of water, the whole room was glowing. Lit up from below. Fluorescent lights streaming through the cracks in the floorboards. Game over. Coincidentally there was a police car positioned outside our house for six hours the very next day. Hmm, is there a rat in the family?

I had one spectacular friend. We had our own little bubble: discovering boys, smoking weed, watching Pulp Fiction, painting our nails, and listening to Courtney Love & Hole's - Live Through This - like it was our religion, hatching plans, and always hysterically laughing at our private jokes.
We later lost that connection when I went deeper into clubs, drugs, and parties, and she went deeper into marriage, babies, and people-movers.

A monumental changing point for me was using a stolen ID to get into a Garbage concert at the Hordern Pavilion in Sydney. My Mum found out, and I was grounded to my room for two weeks. I listened to (What's the Story) Morning Glory by Oasis on repeat while reading Twin Peaks; The Laura Palmer Story. That album transformed my taste in music and opened up Brit Pop culture to me. The lyrics painted pictures, dreams, and visions of what that kind of life looked like. A deep wanting in the pit of my stomach. A dragging for a different sort of life. I had no idea what it was, but this album started a subconscious fascination.
This was when I started talking to The Universe.
Today, full circle, twenty years later, standing together,

we found each other. *The Universe has pushed us together, and it started all those years ago. I'm standing in the Hordern Pavilion, Sydney, with my now-husband, to see Liam Gallagher. It's incredible to think we were teenagers sitting in our rooms listening to the same album on repeat. Each on the other side of the world, dreaming the same thing.*
The literal man of my dreams. We are meant to be together. The Universe brought me to him.

This is why I listen to The Universe.

Did you think what's with the weirdo name? Tava (pronounced Tay-va or ironically swap the R for a T in raver).
Mother wanted something different, knowing I was going to be 'special' before I was born (her words). She saw my name all in capitals, shining up in lights (sorry, regular-named siblings). My dad, on the other hand, wanted to call me Michelle, after one of his ex-girlfriends. Dad, always keeping it classy.
Mum found the name Tava looking through the Yellow Pages in the residential listings. She dialled away and spoke to a very friendly man with the last name, Tava. He said in broken English that it was from Estonia, "A very common but good family name and not at all very nice name for a baby girl."
You'll also find my name on all good menu boards in Turkish takeaway establishments: roast vegetables with garlic.
Anytime people say 'Gee, Tava is such a beautiful name,' I have to stop myself saying, 'You wouldn't think that if you knew it was also a dirty kebab!'

I guess I'm just trying to let you know, I'm normal (apart from my unusual name). A girl next door, I didn't come from a wealthy trust-fund family who handed me an unlimited checking account to build night-clubs or the immaculate-conception child of Studio 54 creators Steve Rubell and

Ian Schrage (although this would be an outstanding birth scenario), born into a bloodline of clubland royalty.

So, this is me. In a nutshell. If this were a Netflix series, you'd be caught up, ready to jump into the next episode after a break between seasons. 'Previously on...'

Out of respect for the people who have moved on in their lives, I'll be changing some names, tell-tale details, and condensing a few time-lines. In the essence of full disclosure, although this is a memoir, I was drunk, high, coming down or hungover a lot during the club days, so I'm not swearing on a bible, but I promise unfiltered clarity with the stories of my heart.

So, here goes, friend. This is my story.
Tava x

*NB: I later found out that Mum did, in fact, do two pretty wild things as a teenager (and in my humble opinion, pretty fucking dangerous.). Both times on LSD. She threw a lit firework into an open car window with people sitting inside. Got in a tiny rowboat while tripping out of her head and rowed into the middle of Sydney Harbour. What the fuck, Mum? That's just pure madness. This is why I steer clear of hallucinogenics (but taking them accidentally is another story...).

1

Shoreditch 2005

1:35am. I feel like Maria on top of that beautiful fucking alpine mountain. Euphoric. Free. Spinning around and around like a wind-up toy. I want to make snow angels in the pile of empty cans, sludge, and plastic cups littering the floor. I want to go up to the nearest person and kiss their face so hard that I can feel their heart pumping, pushing blood through their veins and connect to the deepest, darkest part of their soul. Instead, I sit. Totally still. I look down a tunnel at the kaleidoscopic fireworks show, hypnotic shooting stars, an oil slick of dreamscape-coloured patterns in the black velvet sky.

1:36am. I hope nobody notices that I am totally off my head.

1:37am. Fuck. Am I doing anything really weird?

1:40am. The music is so loud I can't hear what song is playing. It sounds like someone is humming on a loop into the speakers. I've started to move through the club in slow motion. Someone is pulling me by my clammy hand. My shoes stick to the thick layer of old beer, cheap lemonade, and sick on the floor. Or are there sticky flytraps on the ground? Through a rabbit hole and up a staircase. Each step is really spongy and springy. I need to take astronaut steps - there's not enough gravity to keep me walking on the ground. Slow, over-exaggerated, and rounded tiptoe steps. At any moment, my tether could break, and I will float off into outer space, never to return. Destined for a life floating around the galaxy. Tunnel vision, everything is so far away, everyone is at the end of my tunnel. Wonder what they're doing down there? Has anyone noticed me moonwalking through the crowd? The Neil Armstrong-style not Michael Jackson-style of moonwalking. MJ style would have been totally normal-ish in a nightclub.

1:49am. The mystery hand in mine tugs me hard through a roadblock of bodies and cold, fresh air smashes into my face and fills my lungs with reality. The tunnel vision slides back to normal. Bright red ribbons swish in front of me, and someone shoves a glass in my hand and pushes it to my mouth. I sip on cold, sobering water. Ah, fuck. It deflates me, and I'm headed back down to earth. Rudely interrupted.

1:53am. Jonny Red is right up in my face, so close he has one big eye. His mouth is moving, but I can't quite work out what he's saying. He's pushing me to have more water. With each sip, I come out of my alternative universe MDMA adventure trip.

2:16am. I'm snapped out of it now. Cyclops Jonny morphs into normal but very stressed-out Jonny. I fully come to, and we're outside the club he works, 666 and Purgatory Bar. He'd got me VIP passes, free drinks, and hooked me up with his drug dealer, which I was enjoying 'til he dragged me outside the club. The entry queue is snaking around the building; people are crowded near the entrance, pushing to get in. I can see his 'Devil' of a boss going mental at the sight of the chaos. Jonny's guest-list girl had gone to the loo and never came back, some overseas generic house DJ was playing, and he needs a door whore. He shoves a clipboard into my hands and barks minimal instructions before running off to soothe the Devil.

The hallucinogenic side of the MDMA has chilled out, but I'm left feeling full of confidence, a lust for life, and utopian love for my fellow man. Right. With thoughts like that racing through my brain, there's no doubt that I'm actually still really, fucking high. I would never have agreed to this if I wasn't so comically wasted. With my synthetic confidence boost and ridiculous zero-fucks given attitude, I step up to my post as unofficial door whore for the night. The practical part of the role is to make sure VIP guests, and presale ticket holders make their way straight into the club through the red velvet rope and down the sad little red carpet. The other part is to make sure the rest of the queue are 'the right type of person' to come into the club. The Devil's standing policy is if you have a pulse and a wallet, you're in. It's a large capacity club and has to be packed full of people with money to spend. Security is beefy, heavy-handed, and can handle anything that lands on its door or kicks off inside the club. The Devil prefers to get the customers in, pay their cover charge, then kick them straight out the back alley fire exits if they are pests.

2:45am. I bounce up and down the crowd, bubble along the queue, passing the time making jokes, unashamedly flirting with everyone, laughing with the customers waiting to come into the club. It's addictive. Like an instant fast track to being the coolest kid at school. Everyone wants to befriend the girl with the clipboard in her hand. I look down. What am I wearing? So high, I'd forgotten. A vivid sky blue, silky satin Laura Lees dress with little puff sleeves, nipped waist, and buttons with the best bit of cleavage showing; matching ribbon belt, and circle skirt with miles of fabric to make it full and lush. Trimmed along the bottom hem are delicate, intricately embroidered neon skulls, roses, poison bottles, lipsticks, and crosses. I love this dress. Vintage Hollywood wave in my hair, red lips, and Vivian Westwood heeled bondage boots. A bit rock, a bit vintage and a little bit slutty. Outfits are my superpower.

3am. My very first door shift finishes. Back into the Purgatory Bar. As I walk through the crowd, one of the guys I let in on the VIP list, called Sonny, smiles and signals for me to come over. He's a tall Nigerian man in a gold silk three-piece suit, a highly decorative ensemble with black fleur-de-lis swirls. He's finished off his look with snakeskin shoes, the pointed tips covered in brass. He puts his hand to his mouth, does a pretend yawn, coughs into his hand and gives me something from his mouth. I close my fist around a tiny ball and thank him for the unidentified gift which I'm hoping isn't a used piece of chewing gum, then head to the toilets to check it out. Sitting on the loo is a welcome escape for my tired legs. Sonny has given me a small, tightly wrapped bullet. I carefully peel the cling film off and give it a dab. Coke. Thanks, Sonny. This is called dealer's tax. He will spend the rest of the evening selling coke to customers in the club, but during the evening, as required, he will keep promoters, security and club staff sweet with his little gift-wrapped party favours. Half a gram here and there keeps him welcome. Until he gives it to the wrong person. Then it's game over for Sonny. Best case scenario would be barred from the club; the worst case would be an undercover cop on the other end of the gift.

3:16am. As I come out of the toilets, I bump into one of my neighbours. A tall Australian guy called Angus with a dry sense of humour, floppy skater-fringe, home-job tattoos and a lust for the Shoreditch nightlife. A small girl hangs on his arm, swaying slightly. He introduces her as Daisy. She has jet-black dyed hair, a cheeky-looking face and mischief flickering in her eyes. She wears a jauntily angled sea captain's hat, fuchsia pink NARS lipstick, black '80's strapless cocktail dress, and amyl nitrate popper burns under her nose to match her pink lips. I like her instantly. We grab a drink with my free-drink tokens and try to talk over the shitty, tinny electro. I slip them Sonny's gift, and they pop into the disabled loos for a quick bump. Daisy has stopped swaying; praise be the sobering magic power of coke after one too many drinks. It's easy to make friends with the 'Shoreditch Currency'. Relationships are forged over free drink tokens and complimentary coke. Funnily enough, these have been some of the strongest lifelong bonds I've made.

3:26am. Daisy suggests we leave and move on to the next venue. She knows somewhere fun... That's if she can remember how to get there. On the way out, I collect my wages. Paid to party. A concept I could get used to.

3:39am. We stumble across the pavement, zig-zagging our way down to Kingsland Road, then onto Hackney Road to The Ye Old Axe. An old English-style pub with an imposing gothic-looking exterior, elaborate traditional mahogany bar, etched bevelled-glass mirrors, plush but dusty draping curtains. By day, it's a strip club. Podium platforms and brass stripper poles dot the venue. On Saturday nights, it transforms into Rock-a-Billy Rebels. An underground club for vintage lovers.

It's hot inside. The windows and glass are all fogged up, and the crackle of vinyl playing makes the energy in the room palpable. It's the fucking coolest place I've ever stepped into. I walk to the bar. It's so packed that with the slightest jolt, you'll be wearing the beer from the squishy plastic pint cups in people's hands. Slick pin-up girls and smooth teddy boys swing to Chuck Berry. It's filled with an equal mix of rock-a-billy devotees and Shoreditch locals who have stumbled onto the club and fallen in love with its contradictory charm. Crazy kids gliding along the dance floor in Fred Perry's and bell bottoms, with the smoothest Northern Soul dance skills. Skinny-hipped boys in tight denim, big hair, skull rings and lust-worthy vintage leather jackets huddle in a corner booth doing bumps of coke and sipping pints of beers. Hanging off them are the female version of The New York Dolls, decked out in short leather skirts and white tulle fairy wings, swinging around the stripper poles and rolling around on the floor.

4:35am. A guy called Leon saunters over in a vintage Burberry mac trench coat. He is nonchalant, cocky, and pretty confident of his station in life. Through one eye (I have to close one eye to concentrate, 'cause I'm drunk now) I stare blankly at him. It's boiling, but his coat stays on. He's a DJ and club promoter. He talks. And talks. Nothing piques my interest 'til he tells me he's a massive Michael Jackson fan. Naturally, I just have to show him my two versions of the Moonwalk. A classic MJ dance routine complete with hee-hees, awwwwwws, and crotch grabs and a re-enactment of the Neil Armstrong moonwalk I completed a few hours ago across the dance floor of 666. He admits he came over to chat me up, but the idea vanished instantly after my manic medley of moonwalks. He's now doubled over laughing and can never unsee my (un)spectacular moves. I tell him a friend made is better than a random laid.

5:05am. We all head out to the dirty kebab shop on the corner of Kingsland Road to grab a pitta to soak up some booze. I tell Leon and the kebab shop guy the origin of my very exotic name and am rewarded with free food for the ridiculous story. Talking shit about Home and Away while they mock my Australian accent, laughing so hard I can't breathe.

5:21am. Daisy gets a call. There's a house party around the corner in a warehouse on Curtain Road. She rounds us up, all the stray kitten party animals, and we stagger across the road.

6:45am. We smoke joints, do lines of coke, and play ping-pong on the roof terrace of Daisy's friend of a friend of a friend's house.

The sky starts to glow a deep tie-dyed pink ombre, and the dawn birds start their morning songs. A motley crew of newly found friends playing a championship of ping-pong to the death. Cocaine concentration is eye-hand coordination's best friend.

7:58am. I wander slowly home into the crisp, fresh air and a rare sunny, stunning London morning. Exhausted beyond belief, I walk next to smug, blissfully happy couples and fresh-faced pals with linked arms heading out for sophisticated breakfast dates and shopping for armfuls of flowers from Columbia Road's flower markets. I realise I made a big mistake last night that I won't make again...

Next time I'll bring sunglasses.

The door of 666 and Purgatory Bar become my home away from home every Saturday night. With the tidal flow of characters and personalities who go up and down Old Street, having the clipboard meant I could talk to everyone. It comes with sass, chat, and free guestlist access to see bands, DJs and club nights, invites to cool after-parties, and dates with pretty boys; blood-brother and sister friendships and mostly the freedom to be the person you want to be.

East London was like nothing I had ever experienced before. Loud, colourful, scary, gritty, overwhelming, thrilling, all-consuming and totally addictive. For the first time in my life, I didn't stand out, but in a good way. This was a pocket of creative, crazy subcultures and communities that made up the mad, eclectic, and electric atmosphere.

Individuality is embraced, expected, and encouraged. Everyone is doing something abstract: painting, creating, in a band, partying like it was their full-time job. Open bars (not to be confused with open bar tabs). Alternative fashion is an obsession, faceless street artists our neighbours, doe-eyed models and muses propped against walls at parties. It was a given that you can do anything, be anything and it will work out. I spend a far bit of time now with a motley crew of Shoreditch locals. A hilarious ginger-haired, lovable rogue-slash-party monster. A charming, charismatic director whom half the female Shoreditch population has rotated through having a crush on. A beautiful exotic songbird, as cool as she is talented, and a cranky, bald-headed northern party promoter, who openly dislikes me with Larry David levels of disdain.

This was a moment in time where everyone is living out their wildest, transcendent dreams and able to make fantasies a reality. Nothing is out of reach.

Well, maybe just normality and a good night's sleep.

Somehow, everyone was still able to have these creative and pretty fucking admirable pursuits while holding down a steady yet low-commitment job to cover the basic necessities, like rent, drugs, not expensive but always fabulous, styled outfits, and fuel their creative side life. Six nights a week is the standard for going out. Half the nights would result in a few precious hours of sleep before heading out to work - if you were lucky. An all-nighter meant straight to work from an after-party, and a decent early night was in bed by 2am. Drugs like cocaine, ecstasy, and MDMA are a daily affair. Drinking and smoking replace eating and sleeping. There are whole periods when I can't recall ever eating, but when I do, late-night drunken bagels are the meal of choice, always from the "good" bagel shops on Brick Lane. Everyone has their preference. Mine was on the left if you're facing them, salt beef with pickles and cheese.

Shoreditch becomes my world. A bubble where my friends became my family, partying becomes my part-time job and drugs and alcohol my lifeline into this clashing, pulsing culture.

Purgatory Bar and 666 are set bang in the middle of Shoreditch, near Hoxton Square. It has been around since the beginning of time and is owned by the 'Devil'. Purgatory Bar and 666 are in a love-hate relationship with a lot of people. Everyone knows them, everyone has been in them, and even though you always seem to end up there, you still fucking hate it and swear never to come back. But you do.

Shoreditch locals are more inclined towards Purgatory Bar, the smaller up-stairs bar above the main nightclub 666. There isn't a cover charge, and the door policy is slightly more selective, it's also marginally nicer... Out-of-towners didn't really know about it, so they go to the main club. 666 is pure hell as the name suggests. It's run down and calling it a spit-and-sawdust club would be rude to spit and sawdust!. There isn't a dress policy for 666. Purgatory Bar has a slightly cooler, mildly quirkier deco vibe. It's still sticky, pretty jank and rundown, but with big windows overlooking Old Street and a more intimate feel.

On any given day of the week, Purgatory Bar was guaranteed to be packed with an electric mix of sweethearts, troublemakers, cool kids, and momentary lovers. Even on a random Tuesday night. If you were from Shoreditch, you could go in alone and know half the people there. It was open until 4am, so you could always get a late drink and someone interesting to spend the rest of the night with, if that's what you were after. This was Shoreditch's old-school version of today's Tinder. We were always granted a hook up at Purgatory Bar, but we also had Myspace. It was used as a "follow-up" tool, rather than the cold-calling tool of the modern-day head fuck that is Tinder. We would go to a party, start talking to an interesting person, go home, and stalk them on Myspace, then voila. You either had a new best friend or could line up a shag for the next day.

The Devil invited me for a chat in his office. During the day, with the lights on, the club is even grimmer. It stinks like an old, damp sponge left on a 1970's shag pile carpet after being used to clean up a pint of beer, layered with fake lemon-scented antiseptic, Stone Age ash-trays, and everything embedded with stale cigarette smoke. Clouds of deadly fruit flies circle in packs. Without the veil of colourful disco lights, the club has mismatched paint; the floor covering is peeling back everywhere, barely held down with electrical duct tape. All the fake leather seating is slashed so that the foam peeks out like hernias and the walls are a bomb site of shitty graffiti and tags. There are even holes punched and kicked into the walls.

On the top floor of 666 and the Purgatory Bar are the offices. The Devil invites me down a long, bare hallway with wooden floors to the draughty office. His cousin is counting the largest piles of £20 notes I have ever seen. Out of the corner of my eye, I can see about ten piles of what looks to be about five thousand pounds per stack. Maths has never been my strong point, but it has to be over 50k just on the desk alone. The walls are lined with CCTV monitors, dusty bottles of limited-edition booze and old club night posters. In the corner is a safe, the size of my bedroom, the door wide open, full, with neatly bundled notes. Packed like a bank vault.

This is the most pleasant conversation I will ever have with The Devil. He is trying so hard to be nice, and I can see it's making him very uncomfortable. The Devil looks like Mr Potato Head. Big round body and little legs with trotter feet shoved into once-cream repulsive-coloured Crocs, worn no matter the occasion, rain, hail or shine. Just with socks added. His false teeth make clacking noises when he talks fast, tripping over his thick Turkish accent. When he feigns enthusiasm or is talking about things he doesn't know about, like particular bands, DJs and club nights, he nods repeatedly and shows his teeth all the way up to his demon gums - I think this is an attempt at a smile - and keeps saying, "Yep cool, yep cool, darlin'." It's a miracle he's survived so long. But he tells me his secret: surrounding himself with "cool" people. People who are connected to new trends and a finger on the pulse of what's going on. All the clichés that people say that when they are trying to explain something non-tangible like "cool". Apparently, he thinks I'm one of those people. I know there were some stellar predecessors, all female and all who I definitely feel are the epitome of cool. I walk out of the office and back down the corridor. And just like that, I'm now the promoter and marketing manager of 666 and the Purgatory Bar. I'm in charge of booking bands, DJs, promoters, club nights. PR, press and increasing traffic through the club doors are my new domain. My objective from the Devil? To bring the club into a more current climate of music, and get away from electro, house, and drum and bass.

Sure. My only experience in any of these fields is "sniffing" out fun places to go and professional levels of partying, drinking and narcotics-taking.

I better work out what the fuck all this actually means and fast. I start tomorrow.

It feels like the first day of school. Out of my depth, genuine imposter syndrome and no idea of what the fuck I'm doing. I have a large L-shaped desk that looks out over Shoreditch. Glancing around the room, I light a cigarette and push up my sleeves. Bookshelves of gifted records from hopeful bands and record labels wanting to book gigs and overflowing bucket after bucket of hopeful DJ mixtapes that never get listened to. Speakers, vinyl turntables, amps, and an army's worth of lost property in towering piles encroach on the office space. Wobbly stacks of NME and Time Out documenting my predecessor's work and inspiration for the future. I flop down on the big, tatty leather lounger in the corner and flick through the magazines. Sure, this is all helpful to know for what happens in the big, wide world, but this is Shoreditch...

Traditionally, you book bands or a DJ through a booking agent. They are expensive, come with food and big drink rider requirements, don't promote the gig, turn up, play, then leave. You have to hope they have enough of a following to get people through the doors. They are usually quite established in their careers, and you need to charge premium door prices to cover costs. To advertise the event, you'll need multiple listings in Time Out and NME, get 5000 colour flyers printed, then do flyer and poster drops to vintage stores, record stores, cafes, and bars.

From what I can tell from my nights out and about in East London, everyone I meet within this small space of under a square mile is either in a band or managing a band, a DJ, in an art collective, starting a record label, a designer, sound engineer, singer, club promoter, up-and-coming film director, performance artist, door-whore extraordinaire, in the experimental fashion scene (which is directly linked to the nightlife culture), a photographer, part of the new wave of bloggers, hand-produced fanzine editors or a drug dealer. So many subcultures and movements waiting for their time in the spotlight. This collection of magnificently talented, passionate, motivated people are out most nights of the week and right on the club's doorstep. What's more, they also have phones full of friends who also want to go out, be on guest lists or cheap lists and invited to underground club nights of the latest band, DJ or party. These people are influencers and decision-makers, who are at the beginning of their careers. Always the first to create trends and cultural movements, they're full of inspiration and the drive to make their passion fucking count.

I can use Myspace to approach and secure talent directly, cutting out the agent. Create digital artwork and exclusively promote the event online so bands and DJs can reach out to their network of fans, followers, and friends. I can introduce collaborations and club takeovers with fashion labels, bloggers, record labels, and artists. Make it aspirational. Online word of mouth. Tap into an underground army of club kids who are looking for a revolution and the next big movement before it even happened. An explosion of art, fashion, experimental performances, live music, and a new style of DJs.

Investing in an army of creatives, not just one big, commercial name talent, to create a nightlife platform like no one else has offered before.

What if I don't follow the traditional rules and formulas clubland has used up 'til now?

2

"First, I'm going to start with undercover officer Sergeant Wilshire and Sergeant Grayman's report of the event, then show you photos and CCTV footage of the individual they are seeking to charge." Time: 22.55pm. Date: November 5th, 2005. IC3: male, 24-25. London accent. Short, stylised facial hair. Piercing in left eyebrow, septum piercing, and lip labret piercing. Combed out Afro-Caribbean hair. Black trench coat.

I feel hot, sour bile rising up the back of my throat. My heart is pounding, threatening to push the contents of my stomach all over the table and the fancy lawyer's manila file. Maybe if I vomit all over it, this will go away.

I know exactly who they are talking about...

48 hours earlier...
I turn the dial to channel three on the two-way radio and checked my earpiece. "Radio check, radio check?" "Loud and clear!" echo the staff, dotted through the venue. Final checks before we open the doors at 10 pm. My look for the night is a '60's-style swing mini dress covered in silver sequins and black Uma Thurman

à-la-Pulp-Fiction wig. Black tights, black and white brogue Mary Jane sky-scraper block heels. The direction I've taken 666 and my club night, Emerge, a psychedelic fusion of experimental music and creative collaborations, has hit the industry right in the face and delivered: diversity, electric pop culture trends, and a home for underground music movements, an exciting explosion of up-and-coming designers, bands, DJs, and performers. Projections of MC Escher's Relativity, his famous optical illusion stairwell print, are cast on the club's bland, blank, canvas-like walls and ceilings. Stark black and endless white staircases rolling into each other and creating hypnotic patterns all over the club. Artist collective Sweatshop has designed large-scale wall art; naked human bodies with stag heads, wrestling and fighting, inside a wooden hunting lodge. The gorgeous handmade wallpaper was created to join together to make 8-meter square images. The entire exterior of the club, from the ground up to the second floor, has A0 paper stapled up it, wrapping around the whole building, printed with images of the interior of the club, giving an inside-out view. Massive 15-foot images of chandeliers and chaise longues in a luxury wooden cabin, naked men with stag heads towering over Old Street. It's striking and stopping everyone who walks past. I'm also collaborating with Styleslut, the fashion and music blogger collective. Their catchcry, "Styleslut is Karen O sniffing coke in the toilets at a John Galliano show while Wiley MCs and Sway cops off with Jamie Winstone. We are talentless pricks with too much time on our hands. Our aim is to take over the music & fashion industry, then destroy it". They have curated the main floor DJ line-up. In the basement, I have booked live performances from epic up-and-comers, Paloma Faith and The Horrors.

As there are loads of acts, performers, and collaborators, I have Leon, my Michael Jackson-loving, new best pal I met at the Old Axe, helping me out with the run sheet and set times for the DJs on the main floor and keeping the Stylesluts maniacs on track with their drink riders, and any guest list issues, but mainly to minimise any diva moments and keep them far away from the Devil and annoying security. Daisy is also helping out with Paloma, her props and her very baffling preshow set up. She is getting ready upstairs in the super-glamorous green room, also known as my office. I noticed Daisy was wearing her signature after-dark look, glazed eyes and wobbly walk. Fingers crossed her level of drunkenness is going to plateau, and she can get Paloma on stage in one piece. It's a maze of secret staircases, entrances, and backdoors from the office to the basement stage.

On the stage behind a screen, Daisy is tasked with cutting open four feather pillows and creating a massive nest for Paloma to slip into, poised under the giant feather cocoon with burlesque ostrich feather fans, curled up in the foetal position under the feathers. Slowly swishing the fans through the air, she sends a cascade of white feathers throughout the basement. It's filled with downy snow; nobody can see as the feathers swirl everywhere. As they start to settle over the crowd and the music swells, Paloma rises in a nude body-suit and prosthetic silicon fake pregnancy belly. She pulls away the masking tape that was sealing her mouth, her beautiful face silenced, spits out a cherry, and begins to sing "Summer Time".* It's gripping and hypnotic... She finishes her act by cutting open her fake belly and letting kilos of pilchard fish spill out over the stage.

The crowd is silent. Stunned. Fishy and feathery. Disgusted and delighted. In awe of this raw, crazy, creative genius.

I now have the glamorous task of getting the debris off the stage. It looks like a massacre on a fisherman's boat, a battle to the death between a flock of seagulls and a few bags of bait. "Maps" by The Yeah Yeah Yeahs is thumping through the basement: electric anticipation before the looming Horrors enter. They silently file on stage. Quiet and refined, each with glossy, jet-black hair, charcoal-rimmed eyes and pale skin. Victoriana Vivian Westwood punk meets Goth cartoon characters styled by Tim Burton for a Ramones video. Big pussy bows, Peter Pan collars, spray-on trousers. Black. Everything black, leather and lace. Satin waistcoats over billowy-sleeved shirts, jewel-encrusted spider brooches, and funeral jewellery adornments, but as soon as they start playing their sound is anything but refined. Uncomfortable. Loud. Cranky. Everyone adores them. Their music is unpolished compared to their death-dandy style.

Back on the main floor, the guys from Bloc Party are DJing and playing "Banquet". Life imitating art? The venue is at capacity, and the dance floor is a throbbing multidimensional game of tug of war.

I pop out to Old Street to check in with the Devil. He surveys the crowd coming in and out of the club from his post on the pavement, while his cousin watches everyone from up in the office on the CCTV monitors, like God in heaven. The numbers through the door and bar takings are excellent, and the Devil huffs and puffs his approval as the crowd comes early. It's a huge challenge that we're always up against in clubland, especially with pre-drinking gaining popularity. I've avoided the "early doors lull" by engaging collaborators and arranging their free list and discount entry to expire by 11pm. This means they round up their fans, friends and crew to get in early, so when we get the walk-by traffic, customers naturally drift in at midnight. The club is packed, and this keeps everyone from moving on to the next venue. Regardless of how incredible your entertainment line-up is, people only want to be at a busy venue. Clubland thrives on the fear of missing out. This is one of the reasons that having the absolute best fucking lifestyle photographers come to the venue is so imperative: everyone looks beautiful and lust-worthy through the view of a nightlife photographer's lens. Dirty, Dirty Dancing, We Know What You Did Last Night, and Billa - key players to get in and capture the crowd, talent, and atmosphere. The photos are edited, posted and shared online, letting everyone know that this is THE place to be. Priceless, viral advertising.

The Devil and his cousins head home around 2am, never saying goodbye, but sneaking off into the night, so you don't know exactly if they're still around or not. Sometimes popping back for the element of surprise to keep everyone on their toes. Now that I officially work at 666 and the Purgatory bar, it's best behaviour for me. Ish. Well, before 2am. Don't get me wrong. I'm never without a double vodka and Red Bull in one hand, but no MDMA moonwalking or pills. Just a line of coke here and there. The Devil is quietly pleased with what I've been doing; so much so, he agreed to sponsor me for a Skilled Migrant Visa.

Leon tracks me down to say bye; he's heading off to DJ at an after-party. I pay him, give him a massive hug, he flicks up the collar of his trademark trench before dashing off into the torrential rain that has just started. Thank fuck it held off till now. Bad weather and nightlife are arch enemies. It's such a great feeling. Fucking really cool performers tonight, no technical or sound equipment problems, all the DJs turned up, happy Devil, solid numbers through the door. Now I can go let my hair down and enjoy a job well done and the rest of my weekend, back in the office Tuesday. I go to pay the last DJs and grab them a few beers: they'll play till the club closes. I haven't touched my nightly tax payment from Sonny earlier, I go and find Daisy. She's lined up some ecstasy pills. We have a group of pretty boys in tow and head out into the rain.

I've moved in with Daisy. My sister has moved back to Australia: her visa ran out, and our ex-flatmate, Jonny Red, went really dark on me and said I have to choose between him and the job with the

Devil. I choose the job. As much as I really liked Jonny, I think he was feeling the strain of the vampire life: the non-stop club life was draining him, and the Devil had mistreated him.

There's no point in getting a cab, we're already soaked, and "home" is five minutes away. Running through the rain, we head down onto our road, Cheshire Street, made famous by the gangsters, the Kray twins as previous publicans of our local pub, The Carpenter's Arms, and also home to one of my favourite vintage shops, the epic Beyond Retro. Casa del Daisy is a corner property in a council estate. It's crude. Daisy gutted all the soft furnishing, ripped up the dusty floral carpet to have exposed wooden floorboards. A great idea at the time, 'til she realised the number of nails that need ripping out and the frosty draft that the tatty carpet blocked. There's a no-bare-feet policy now. In spite of this, she makes it homely with flowers, kooky ornaments foraged from markets, glossy-leafed plants and a host of other things, tinkered with like a nutty inventor and with mixed results for the finished product. Except she has had success rigging up some mismatched speakers, amps, and a record player. She's taken me under her wing, letting me stay on her couch. The house has two other girls: Chelsea, who has been very secretive lately, popping out at all hours and whispering down the phone, and Winnie. She's like a cat. Quiet, calculating, and deeply unnerving.

As we round the corner, our soggy gang of nocturnal creatures is stopped dead in our tracks. Cheshire Street is known for its mistresses of the night. Cars cruise up and down looking for "honeys", but we now have three honeys and their pimp on our front step taking shelter from the torrential rain. He kindly informs us this is now where he and his ladies work when it's raining, and we won't have a problem if we quietly go inside and leave them alone to get on with business. We file past them into the house, like naughty children sent to their room, stunned and momentarily unsure of what to do. The only answer is to double-drop the pills, rack up the coke, and put on the record player. "Africa" by Toto, "Benny and the Jets" by Elton John, our beloved bombshell Blondie and everything by the wondrous Hall and Oates. Our afterparty of guilty pleasures. A black hole of Yacht Rock classics and dancing around the lounge room. Also, the basis of a future (un) professional DJ career for me. On each side of the door, the illegal activities crack on, of very different natures.

The sun is streaming through a crack in the curtains. I wince open one hungover eye to see a very beautiful back and naked body, face down, covered in a mass of long, wavy locks, on the pull-out couch next to me. I'm trapped in a heavy, sleepy arm wrapped around me, unable to escape without waking the beautiful beast at my side. I wiggle and slide down the bed, making my escape, only to pull on my jeans and discover they don't fit. I hop up and down to squeeze into them. It appears that I've grown, like Alice in Wonderland, into a giant overnight. I pull them down and notice they are, in fact, my sleeping companion's. The trend of ultra-skinny boys wearing girl's jeans for a better fit is common practice, but not great for the ego: he wears two sizes smaller in the same Cheap Monday style that I wear. The lounge room is a bomb site. Piles of empty bottles create cityscapes on the table and floor, exploding ash trays, white powder covering every flat surface, like an unexpected winter snowfall. There is a tapping on the front window, followed by another. I distantly remember hearing the doorbell ring while I was half asleep. Those girls just don't stop! I can't believe they've been working all night and are still out there! What the fuck do they want? Pinging little pebbles against the window. The letter flap in the front door opens, then a dull thud on the ground. I pull on a bra and T-shirt and inspect the item from a safe distance, poking it with a coat hanger, worried it might be an entire night's worth of balled-up used condoms or a rock of crack getting dumped, hidden from the cops. Nope. It's a note wrapped around a small stone.

"We know one of you is sleeping with Robbie Williams. Either sell us your story, or we'll tell it, and you won't make a penny...
You have an hour to reply."

I definitely didn't expect that. I run to the window and peep outside. There are six paparazzi and reporters crowded around the shitty little council house step. Sneaky Chelsea has been banging Robbie! HA!

I shake the pretty boy out of the sheets and send him packing: I have to get ready to head into Soho for a drink with Leon, then to see The Kooks. I was given VIP tickets for the show and guest list for the after-party. I'm so hungover and still a bit fucked. I crack a warm cider I found tangled in the sheets and bump the remains of the powder in a wrap that "fell out" of the pretty boy's jeans when I was accidentally trying to get them on. I run under the shower and pull on a '70s style gypsy smock, over-the-knee vintage maroon boots with a wooden stack heel, wide-brim felt hat, and a cross-body, tooled leather bag. Off-duty Stevie Nicks, my dream girl.

I plop down in a cosy pub waiting for Leon, with a Margarita to clear my hangover and ease me into my next hazy phase. I've made a pact and promised myself I won't get too wild tonight. There is a couple next to me who I recognise from the first time I went to The Old Axe. He has big hair like Rod Stewart in The Faces era, but brown, and the biggest bluest eyes ever, framed by razor-sharp cheekbones like a supermodel, and he is so thin. Heroin-chic thin. He is striking and so charismatic. She has fairy wings on again and looks a bit like Joan Jett, He pulls the chair out for her to sit.

I can hear him making nice conversation. He buys her pints. She looks blankly at him. He gets her crisps. She's still not impressed. He asks her what's wrong. Nothing! Sure, I don't know what she's pissed off about or what he's done for her to be so dismissive, but fuck if I had a man that looked like that, treating me like a queen, caring about what flavour crisps I wanted, I would treat him like a fucking king. Packed lunches, cook him meals, restore his soul, blow-jobs, hold his hand always. The works. I ask if I can borrow his lighter. He leans over and lights my cigarette. I want to touch his hands, slide my fingers over his rings and pinch him to see if he's real. She silently fumes, and I secretly catch his eye, and we smile without moving our mouths. Nothing sleazy, it's funny and sweet.

Dear Universe,
Sorry, it's been a while. But I was wondering where is HE?
Lukewarm regards,
Tava

Dear Tava,
Your 20s are for fucking, partying, and finding out who the hell you are. If I give you him now, you won't be able to keep him.
Carry on, The Universe

The after-party has more coke than I've ever seen in my life. In a posh hotel bar in Mayfair with marble toilets and random rock stars wander around everywhere - the least popular members from Oasis, The Killers, Keane, a child of one of the Beatles and a few of The Kooks. And lots and lots of beautiful girls. Cocaine interests me more than rock stars. I work on reducing the coke pile 'til there's a constant trickle of blood running down my nose like an apocalyptic zombie. I just keep going. No work 'til Tuesday.

I blackout.

The back of my head is pounding, and bright lights are shining through my eyelids. I can tell this is going to be a bad, bad hangover and come down. Two heavy coke and booze, all-night sessions back to back. I keep my eyes closed, not quite ready to deal with life behind the eyelids yet. My phone keeps buzzing, vibrating and rattling against my keys in my handbag. Smug that I haven't lost these essential items, which makes a nice change. But I wonder who keeps calling. A dark shadow blocks out the light behind my closed lids. Sheepishly I open them, not sure what I'm going to see. A big head looms over me. Daisy! Thank fuck! Apparently, she came to my rescue after I passed out at the party and brought me to Homerton Hospital. Dehydration, alcohol poisoning, low white blood cell count, exhaustion, a case of bronchitis, finished off with a knock on the back of the head. Not bad, considering I wasn't going to go wild last night. The IV drip is giving me life, and we share cups of jelly to snack on while we recount the past few days' events. Not a terrible way to recover...

'Til I check my phone.

13 missed calls from the Devil, one voicemail and three messages. Fuck. I don't feel so good now.

We jump in a cab, I swap my blood-stained clothes with Daisy and head straight into 666. The fury in the message is enough for me to pull myself together. I walk into the office, and the club managers, two old-looking guys in smart suits, the Devil, and his cousins are sitting around a makeshift board table. All waiting for me.

A hand slides the manila file in front of me. The fiercer-looking of the two men in the suits asks again. "Do you know the man in the photos? The man in question is being accused of attempting to sell narcotics to undercover police. Is he a known acquaintance of yours?" I can't say anything. I don't understand what's going on. Everyone is just staring at me. I'm mute.

I am quickly gathering all the information and calculating what I am going to say, ready to speak, but the mixed feeling of fury and protectiveness is overwhelming and rising up inside of me. Instead of sick, tears start streaming out, burning my eyes and blood pours out of my nose. Wiping it away with the back of my hand making it much, much worse. Spreading the blood around. "Leon isn't a drug dealer! Or the kind of person that 'hooks' you up. He doesn't even take drugs!" This is precisely why I love him so much. My rock of mild sensibility. He is one of the only people I know who will discreetly and politely decline to indulge or he just quietly peels away from a party when the drug-taking start to get messy, like last night. He chain-smokes packets of Marlboro Lights and guzzles litres of vodka cranberry. But never, ever drugs.

The CCTV shows two people in pathetic standard undercover attire: North Face puffer jackets, baggy jeans and chunky hiking boots. You can spot them as cops a mile away. The female has hair scraped off her face, in a moody ponytail. No makeup. Who comes to a club with no makeup?? I can see myself bobbing in and out of the frame, like a shimmering disco ball in my sequin dress. The lawyer freezes it on the moment I hug Leon and hand him the envelope. They are saying that Leon came up to the undercover cops and said, "Let me know if I can get you anything". This is club-host speak for "Let me know if I can HELP you with anything - like directions to the toilet, a place to check your coat, where to smoke, a stamp so you can leave and gain re- entry". It's conscientious hosting. But instead, they have accused him of saying he could sell them drugs. He wouldn't even know where the fuck to get drugs from! They've targeted him for no other reason than being a black male working in a nightclub. It's his word against them, and my protests fall on deaf ears. The bloody nose is not helping.

This is my first experience of police manipulation. And sadly it will get much, much worse as my career progresses into owning my own clubs and I become a Devil. They have used an innocent person as a pawn in a larger operation. They want to get the Devil and to bring down 666 slowly, but their game has begun.

This is a tactical move as they never prosecuted Leon for "selling" drugs. They didn't even question him! They used him as an excuse to make a case that there was drug dealing in operation within the club. They also had a list of other crimes that allegedly happened in and around 666. Assaults, theft, drunk and disorderly behaviour. They are coming for the Devil and hard. This is inconvenient for the Devil, and not for the reason you'd think. He doesn't care about the small misdemeanour crimes: he has these highly paid, well-heeled lawyers on the payroll to make sure none of that escalates. It's because of them he has miraculously managed to operate outside of his liquor license's legal trading hours. If you take into account the past eight years he has been open, these two extra hours, 3am-5am of trading per shift, twice a week, add up to lot of undeclared 20-pound notes. Millions and millions of pounds. No wonder he needs such a huge safe. Now the Devil is being watched closely by the police, he has to say goodbye to these extra illegal trading hours. This is what has infuriated him.

I know I'm on borrowed time with the Devil now…

NB. Leon was hurt. And barred from the club. I was forced to send him a letter on behalf of the Devil that the lawyers dictated to me. Banning him from being within 300 meters of the club. It took a long time to regain his trust.

The pretty boy I politely chucked outside, into the mouths of The Sun and The Express bottom feeders, was a nightlife reporter himself, who was sent down to review my club night. Although he did write a stellar review, I think he enjoyed our hedonistic after-party with the pimps and pros, pills and paparazzi. Maybe more trash bag than traditional rock and roll, but he did write that I was a pioneer of current clubland trends, moving it away from conventional methods, bringing it to the new digital age, and embracing subcultures.

And one to watch out for.

I feel a little bit bad for taxing his coke.

3

Have you wondered how a girl from the sheltered suburbs of squeaky-clean Sydney, Australia, ended up in the modern-day version of Sodom and Gomorrah?

There are two versions of the answer: the practical, logical order of events that led me here and the nonsensical, intangible, and mystical guiding of my heart by the Universe that was directing me towards somewhere unknown, to my someone I needed to meet.

2004 Neutral Bay Sydney
One year before I arrived in Shoreditch - London

Dear Universe,
Something is missing. A nagging piece of me that isn't there. What is it? Who is it? A missing shape and space inside of me. I don't know what this feeling is or what I should be looking for.
Yours in quiet questioning, Tava

Maybe the rational answer will make more sense to some of you. I thought I was in love. In love with your first boyfriend, kind of love. A foolish pseudo-love, made up of bullshit late-night arguments after cheap white wine and too many Stellas, kids pretending to be adults. He wanted to buy a house, in the same safe vanilla suburb with his parents and start ticking life boxes and I wanted to run away and be an actress. Hollywood, New York, somewhere, anywhere I didn't feel alone in my own brain swirling with creativity and ridiculous daydreams. Away from the creative confines of Australia.

Plus, I'd come home with a fancy, new Brazilian and proudly presented this masterpiece, expecting it to be worshipped and devoured. Right? All I got was "Pull your pants up, we need to go." That was not what my deepest heart desired. No, sex does not make a relationship, but it most certainly fuels the passion that keeps the love affair burning bright... I was spinning. Everyone around me taking this kind of "love and life option" but I couldn't. Is this seriously as good as it gets?

My head is thumping in time with my footsteps. Thank God the hangover today is manageable, but the lack of sleep has left me feeling light-headed and scatty. I jump back on the curb, as a speeding car misses me by inches. 25 years old today. Strangely enough, there's a spring in my step. The winter sun is shining (a little too bright, if I was picky), the sky a clear, bright blue with wisps of fluffy, cartoon clouds. I take a deep breath of the super fresh air and smile. Nailed the slutty '50's secretary/librarian look with my preppy, bright red, tight wiggle dress and vintage peep-toe mules, metallic gold soft leather with big round diamante buckles on the strap, with the perfect high heel. Just enough to lift my bum and add a few inches, but not too high to cripple and maim essential limbs.

Topped off with a leopard-print coat hanging off my shoulders, bare arms, and oversized vintage Dior sunglasses. My armour, wrapping me up and holding me together.

As far as weather conditions and outfit choices go, it's a good day to get dumped. I could tell it was coming. Really, it was inevitable: we both knew it, but there seems to be a standoff. Who's going to make the first move? My first move is straight over the road for a flat white, icy cold can of Diet Coke and a filthy chicken schnitzel sandwich. Not my usual healthy food but today I need some fortification, to eat my sins in a sandwich. I need to eat the memories away.

SMASH! Blind-sided by flashes of drunken fucking. No rhythm, clunky disappointing sex on a creaky Ikea Basics range bed with a man that I'd lusted after for months. The tension had built up until it was unbearable. I thought my vagina was going to explode and my head spin off like a wind-up toy. I dashed out of his place in the middle of the night, deleting all my incriminating messages as I whizzed home through the empty streets, the taxi light glowing red, a scarlet woman's chariot home. I called him as I pulled up home, desperate for reassurance that it wasn't a mistake, but no answer. I tiptoe into the cold, silent house and restlessly pass out on the couch.

I showered and got ready for work. My funny little part-time job at a wedding suit and bridal dress rental store, not even a block from my house. It allowed me to go to auditions and acting classes while earning a modest wage. Nothing elaborate but enough to follow my dreams. This did not include buying a house, which somehow I got caught up in agreeing to.

I left my dirty little lie unguarded for 12 minutes while I showered. Just long enough for him to work out my passcode and go through my phone for evidence. Only one missed call to be found. It's enough.

He walks through the door of my little suit shop, and I know. He knows I know and we're both crying. He said, "I get it's your birthday and everything, but I just can't wait one more day to do this. I'm sorry. I don't want to be with you anymore. But you need to tell me if you're seeing anyone else. Who was the missed call to?" My mind races at a thousand miles per hour. Can I escape this relationship with minimal collateral damage? He'd already broken up with me before he asked the question. Yes, I know that's a mere technicality, but I'm taking it. He loses his shit if I put the house telephone ten inches out of place, we haven't slept together in years - apart from obligatory birthday leg-overs. Didn't want me to go to drama school in New York, in case I met someone else. The boy I should have broken up with four years into our seven-year relationship.

"No." My answer is no. "I'm not cheating on you." I choose me. Yes, I made a mistake, and I'm going to have to live with it, probably rot in hell for the lie, but he wanted out as much as I did. I choose to conceal the fact and avoid all the drawn-out drama of the details. Who is he? Where did it happen? And the scrapes of information around the infidelity that will overshadow the actual reason we were breaking up: total, complete, and utter incompatibility.

The best birthday present I could ask for. My freedom.

Needless to say, I didn't have time to eat my sandwich hot off the press. Later, when I tried to eat, it was cold and stuck in my throat. There was no way I could swallow my guilt, let alone my shame-laden sandwich. It was good old karma not letting me get it down. Don't worry: she caught up with me later, many times over.

That evening, with a "gentleman's agreement", I was to be written out of the mortgage. Given a plane ticket to go and move in with my sister in London. Just like that. It was over, and I left the country 24 days later.

I decided, that very day, I was going to search for AMAZING, like Hollywood-fucking-amazing-love. That feeling in the split millisecond when you go too high on a swing, and you're suspended floating in space. Love that lasts for all time. Love that floors me, fucks me, and takes my brain into the place of questioning everything that came before it and that absolute knowing that nothing will come after it. Travelling across the world for it to find me or me to find it. The love of old stories, love songs, fables, Disney movies, myths and legends. Frankie Goes To Hollywood sums it up perfectly for me in "The Power of Love." "I'll protect you from the hooded claw… Keep the vampires from your door…" Fuck yeah! Protection from vampires is the kind of commitment I'm looking for! Do yourself a favour and drink the best part of a bottle of red and put this song on repeat…. then you will know what I mean about finding Hollywood-fucking-amazing-love.

I was going to have to kiss a lot of frogs to get what I wanted. Challenge accepted, Universe! Shall we seal it blood-brothers' style? Or is a palm-spit and shake enough?

Day One – London.

Dragging my jumbo suitcase up each painful stair, one at a time, up seven flights. It was massively overloaded by this very inexperienced traveller, costing £268 in excess baggage allowance. Ouch. Packing felt all too Sophie's Choice for me. I couldn't choose favourites, all my clothes had history, stories of where I dug them out of dusty charity bins and discovered them hidden on discount rails. Gems with their quirky vibes and unique personality. My precious life inside, ready to start this new adventure, pushing at the suitcase's cheap seams and zip. Rainbow sequins; Pucci-print unitards; faux leopard coats; Little House on the Prairie smocks; beaded capes; vintage '70's tea dresses; and too many impractical party shoes threatening to bust out and redecorate the dank industrial stairwell as brightly as a Mardi Gras float. My hand luggage is starting to rip from a more recently added trove - as much alcohol as duty-free legally allows, along with the random items of bulky, heavy clothes that I quickly stuffed to offload some of the weight from my bulging suitcase at the airport.

My sister opens the door to the flat. Somehow it feels even colder and mustier than the stairwell. As we step into the hallway, the carpet is worn down to the floorboards in random patches. The living room is decorated in furniture found on the street for council clear-up or back alley skips. The lounge's arm padding was picked away to reveal the sad, wooden splintery carcass holding it up. Makeshift blinds half-covering the grey, glowing, radioactive sky. My heart is pressing down on my rectum and my breath catching in my throat. My teeth are dry from my fake smile, stuck in an overly wide grinning position. Exhausted and broken, I go to the bathroom to wash the flight grease off and attempt to freshen up my crumbling corpse. We haven't seen each other in almost two years, and bless her, she is so, so excited to see me and show me around town. But I have to sneak away to the bathroom to cry, run the shower, and howl. Except the shower doesn't work. It's like the trickle of piss by a toddler with stage fright. No running hot water, just enough to wet a cloth and wipe down my extremities and stale private pockets. I sit to do the poo that was held off for four days of induced constipation from binding flight food and cabin pressure, only to find that the toilet doesn't flush with the traditional push button. It's a more manual Thai-style flush. I use a big orange bucket filled with water to chase my pathetic, dehydrated excuse of a poo down the ancient Victorian water pipes.

Conjunctivitis set in, hysteria came to play, the vicious jet lag cycle took hold, and I alternately slept and wept for a full 48 hours. My sister went off to my welcome-to-London party at The Egg without me, cheekily debuting one of my frilly party frocks, and came home two days later. Apparently, the premium E's were epic.

A week passed, and I was slowly coming back to the land of the living. My sister had packaged up a thoughtful welcome gift; a pocket-sized A to Z: your bible in London pre-Google Maps, a tube pass, two scarves, and tickets to see a Scissor Sisters concert. Pretty much everything a girl needed to get settled into a shiny new life in London. And I slowly got settled into the London life, albeit, a little dry West London-style, but it was enough to get my toes wet. Everything was so much more socially oriented than Sydney. People met up after work for drinks or meals. Everyone was out dating or hanging out with friends during the week. A far cry from the Sydney attitude where you only go out on Saturday nights. I was free to make my own choices and become independent for the first time as an adult. The relationship I'd just escaped had made me co-dependent, needy, and hopeless at making decisions. I was generally useless at most things.

I stopped seeing the ratty carpet, and the torn couch arms. Began a counter war against the biblical bedbug plague, and started looking out of the grubby windows with excitement at what the world was offering up to me.

Growing up in Australia, travelling to far-flung and exotic locations, other than Bali or Thailand, was pretty much out of the question.

Too many miles away and so, so expensive. When I arrived in London, it seemed I had landed smack bang in the middle of a budget flight boom. Competition between carriers and a strong pound meant that Europe's doors were flung wide open, ready for intrepid travellers like me. Everywhere just a short distance away. My first solo adventure was to Paris on the Eurostar. Once I arrived in Paris, I realised my life would never be the same. This whole big wide fucking beautiful world was out there for me to explore and relish in the art, beauty, and immense, humbling history around me. I skipped through the streets, my neck aching from craning to see the architecture and eating up the stories that appeared around every corner, walking everywhere 'til I was dead on my feet. Eventually, my travels broadened to Rome, Florence, Venice, Berlin, Amsterdam, Morocco, Monte Carlo, and the Italian Rivera over 18 months. I'd caught the infectious travel bug and my growing fascination with all things European.

Next trip, fuckboy ahoy! Over to LA to see Mr Vagina-explosion head-spin-off actor-guy. He is beautiful. In a classic actor, black and white headshot way. We met while I was casting a play for Rubbernecks Productions, a theatre production company I had set up in Sydney once I got sick and tired of waiting for decent female parts to come up that weren't just for model-turned-actor types (cue tumbleweeds. Apparently, I'd still be waiting if I'd stuck with this line of work.). We spent the next 24 days in Australia. Talking 'til the sun came up: that couple in the corner of the bar intertwined, sharing breath and whispering secrets. It was thrilling. Turns out the pressure and expectation of an affair/cheating scenario were quite intimidating during our first sexual interlude. When we met, he was planning to move to LA to chase movie dreams around the same time I was leaving for London. Perhaps if we weren't both leaving to go our separate ways, we wouldn't have jumped in so deeply, but we kept in touch and arranged to meet in LA for Christmas. We talked about a road trip to Mexico.

Flights booked to LA, but a whisper in my ear told me that something was changing. I could feel that ever-so-slight distance in his voice, the long delay in responding to texts, distraction on the phone. He was hard to pin down and talk to. I was in my emotional spin, reeling from the move to London and the overwhelm of a new city and new life. I clung to those last whirlwind 24 days in Sydney and the idea of finding my Hollywood-fucking-amazing... could it be him?

Dear Tava,
Come on you fool. This is Hollywood-fucking-amazing-love you're asking for. Do you think I'm going to give it to you just like that? The first guy off the rank? No lessons learnt? No personal growth? Did you even have an orgasm?
No? Grow the fuck up!
- (Not impressed) The Universe

He admitted that he didn't find me as appealing as he once did. He hated hearing me crying, needy and emotional down the phone. He fell for the confident, effervescent actress who was cheating on her boyfriend. Forbidden fruit, huh? Okay buddy, cheers for that. With non-refundable, non-exchangeable flights booked, my knight-in-shining-armour sister pays way over the fair price for a ticket to LA, and we plan our own road trip to Mexico for New Year's Eve! A lovely silver lining to the temporarily bruised heart/ego bullshit.

I had two glorious days to myself before Karla's flight landed. I spent my time vintage shopping. It was heaven on earth: LA vintage is exceptional. I met up with the Actor on Christmas Day; he didn't want me spending it alone. How kind. He arranged to collect me at midday for a nice lunch and arrived four hours late. Fucking annoying sitting and waiting for four hours in perfect hair, full makeup, starving, resting bitch face, and an uncomfortable yet killer "look what you're missing out on fucker" outfit. Turns out his LA girlfriend had a small child who he didn't want to leave on Christmas Day. Plus, there was the fact that she didn't know about me. Well, he neglected to tell me about that little detail back in Sydney. Usually, I would have fucked him off for being so late and being an asshole, but I was starving. There was no room service in my divey hotel, no spare cash for cabs and without a car to get around in LA, you're stranded. We went bowling and had a Reuben sandwich at the Jewish deli, which was the only place open. As far as spending a holiday with a fuckwit goes, it was okay, I guess. Whatever spark there was is now replaced with gritted-teeth tolerance and 'what the hell did I ever see in you' vibes. From both parties. I was keen to head back to my hotel and enjoy the rest of the evening with trashy TV and my new purchase. Having spent yesterday skipping down the streets of LA, I also popped into a sex shop to get a Rabbit vibrator.

With so much hype going around after Sex in the City, I finally had to try one. Back at my no-star Hollywood hotel, the world stopped. Tension was building in my body, my heart beating in my brain. Tight breathing. The dramatic snap of release and the overwhelming feeling of the best E ever! I have my very first ever orgasm. My mind was blown, floored. How could I have not had one before? I'm 25! After that moment, I was a much more chilled-out lady, loving the fact I could be in control of my own satisfaction. So liberating. Maybe this is why I love LA so much. Good vibes... Pun intended! My sister arrived in LA, and we travelled down through Mexico for a hellraiser chaotic week, and I jumped on a flight back to London, with her to follow on a later flight the next day.

Back home, that shitty flat in Fulham and my family of bedbugs never looked so good. I turned the key to go in and sleep for a million years, only the key wouldn't turn. It seemed jammed. I give it a jiggle, but nothing happens. I knocked on the door. No answer. Looked through the post slot and see all of our stuff was bundled up in bin bags, striped laundry bags, and our sad bits of bedroom furniture piled up in the hallway. Even the bedbug bed was dismantled, ready to go somewhere.

Those flatmate fuckers of ours had changed the locks.

As soon as I realised we were being hustled out of our own flat, I dashed down to the Internet cafe and booked a few ready-to-move-in places to view straight away. Next, I called the landlord to find out what the fucking hell was happening. He told us that we have been evicted from our room as we "Posed a threat to the other housemates' living conditions, stole personal items from them, and took illegal substances on the premises and acted in an unsafe manner."

My sister had known these guys for over a year before they'd all moved into the flat together. Everyone was either from Australia or New Zealand, and it had been a party flat until a new guy moved in.

Yeah, we were a bit loud, smoked joints, had the occasional parties – which, incidentally, our shitty flatmates would also be at with their shitty friends. We were a bit messy, but we NEVER stole anything more than bread and cheese (midnight-munchie snack). Maybe we were really annoying at times, but that's not a crime. The landlord also said he was keeping our deposit since we'd broken the contract and he wouldn't be able to fill the room quickly as he said we hadn't looked after the flat. Bullshit. It was already a burn-it-down shithole before we arrived and there wasn't even a signed lease!

The landlord said we could have access for 15 minutes, the next day, to move out our things.

I crashed in the rooms above the pub next door, exhausted and jet-lagged. The following afternoon, I arrive back at the flat, and a random dude lets me in to pack up. Everyone is at work, the place is empty. He said he'd be back to lock up. The flat had been gutted, all the old tatty furniture was taken away, the gross blinds gone, brand new carpet, fresh paint and a lot of commercial-grade bleach spread around every nook and cranny. It actually looked a million times better.

Oh, and surprise, surprise. Someone has already moved into our room. Stupid backpacks and stupid hiking boots neatly lined up along the wall ...it's our cock flatmate-extraordinaire Dick's sister and her boyfriend. They arrived a few weeks before we went away and crashed on the couch. Everything instantly became clear. Those sneaky bastards had planned all this while we were away. It pushed me over the EDGE. We'd been royally fucked over.

On the one hand, we wanted to leave anyway because the place was a complete dump and I hated boring West London, but telling the landlord a load of bollocks to get us chucked out and not only lose a deposit of £500 (when I only earn £200 a week temping), but also turfing us out onto the street with nowhere to go, is seriously crossing the line. I feel like I'm seven again, my blood boiling when my sister is being bullied on her first day of school by some little cunts for having a mole on her forehead. I see RED. Blood pumping in my ears and I make an exit plan before the guy comes back to lock up.

I get a knife, ping off the skirting boarded underneath the kitchen benches and rolled eight overripe oranges into the under cabinet void where they will slowly rot and stink out the flat long before those wankers will work out where the horrible smell is coming from. I run into the bathroom to clean the sink and soap-scum covered taps with their toothbrushes, not forgetting to give the toilet a good clean with them, as well, getting right under that lip bit that never gets properly washed. I flush the toilet, rinsing the toothbrushes in the loo water. They got the non-flushing loo fixed while we were away. Mega cunts. They were really fancying up the place now. I pull back the lino sheet flooring that already has a mould problem under it and gave it a booster shot of a litre's worth of natural yoghurt, a thin layer all over the damp concrete, then carefully put back down the lino sheet flooring.

Lastly, I grab the industrial-grade bedbug spray that the house shares, tip half of it into a container to take with us (in case the little fuckers follow our hot trail) and carefully decant the steaming piss I just did in a Chinese takeaway container straight into the bedbug spray, ready for our ex-flatmates to spray over their mattress and bedding. Just for good luck and my own personal satisfaction, I gave their beds and pillows little spritz of eau de urine de Madam T before putting it back in the laundry.

Just as I finish with the final touches of my parting gifts, the door opens, and the dude strolls in. Sweating and red-faced from running around like a demon on a 12-minute speed terror, I pick out our clothes and leave all the other shit there for them to sort out. Hopefully, a blood-hungry bedbug family included.

Laters, losers.

My sister's flight lands, and we get a cab straight to our new flat. It pulls up out the front, and she is fuming. She agreed to let me sort our new place out without her seeing it. Being a sheltered girl from Australia, I wasn't familiar with the council housing projects in the UK. Packing in whole extended families, grandparents, cousins and their dogs, piled into these tiny two-bedroom flats. Everyone was spilling out onto the common areas. Washing strung off any spare hook, zigzagging cut-throat clotheslines down the walkways. Garbage bags of rubbish piled up outside doorways, clogged garbage chutes packed to the brim and old piss-stained mattresses dragged outside and propped up in the hallways, begging to be set on fire by bored prepubescent loiterers. The sad little plastic playground in the centre, once the jewel of the block, was burnt down, the slide and seats melted all over the asphalt, leaving just a twisted metal skeleton behind. Rats outnumbered people, and the pigeons outnumbered the rats.

I didn't see any of this. Or more accurately, I didn't give a fuck. 30 seconds to Brick Lane, an eclectic, random hybrid of shops, one hundred and one curry houses, pocket-sized bars, vintage stores, 24-hour off-licenses, markets and the best bagels in the world – a six-minute walk to my soon-to-be Mecca: Shoreditch. I don't think my sister understood the challenge of getting two available bedrooms in the same flat in East London with our measly budget that didn't have plague-era black mould growing up the walls or Quasimodo living in the basement.

Oh, and did I mention we had to move in today?

Our new flatmates seemed really friendly. One is called Jonny Red, from Berlin. Lanky and almost 6'2", with long shoulder-length dyed bright cherry red hair. He works in club promotions and PR. Our other new flatmate is Sammy, originally from Chile. She is petite with a bleach blonde pixie cut, only wears black, kinda like a goth elf. She works as a refugee housing adviser. They both seemed sweet and super bubbly. This was a far cry from our old ass-hole flatmates.

Jonny Red was my gateway into Shoreditch. Into clubland. That one door-whore shift that I covered at 666 changed my whole life...

4

Sucking in the last few precious moments of the breeze on my face. Sanity before I step back into World War 666 and eight hours of solid sniper attack. Me versus the Devil. Thank fuck it's Friday. Whizzing through the back streets of Shoreditch on my gorgeous vintage Dutch bike, I take in as much air as my lungs can hold. I love this bike and the freedom that comes with it. Customised with chopper handlebars and a big wicker basket on the front, it's a thing of architectural elegance and envy. Someone snaps, 'Watch out!' as I ride by. A wild minx, riding with carefree abandon all over the road like a rash in a flowing 70's leopard print dress which flaps in the wind around my waist and my beloved but very tired second-hand Terry de Havilland Margaux snake wedges. Hair whipped into a frizzy messy bird's nest. A cover of Kate Bush's 'Hounds of Love' by Future-heads blasting in my headphones. The only way to travel.

The mighty social artist Shepard Fairey aka OBEY is doing an installation in the Purgatory Bar. I stop by to say hello on the way up to the towering office of evil. He's having a sandwich with his mum - cute - and he gives me four beautiful off-cut pieces from his installation, which the Devil confiscates off me the moment I go upstairs.

'Hi, I'm Kitty. It's so great to meet you, wee love! I'm looking forward to working together'. She is trembling ever so slightly. This was not what I expected when I stepped into the war zone. Sitting at a newly created desk in my office, wide-eyed, pale skin, Irish. Annoyingly pretty, with a halo of loose strawberry blonde curls and a deep fringe sitting above her long, full lashes, and doe eyes. The faintest freckles on her nose. Understated, natural beauty, except for the perfect cat eye liner and big gold hoop earrings. Wearing a baggy oversized white argyle cable knit jumper, skinny black jeans, and plimsoles. There's a banging body under the vintage grandpa jumper. Double fucking annoying.

'I'm the new assistant'. Things are looking up.
The Devil openly hates me now, venomously trying to trip me up at every turn. He would get rid of me in a heartbeat if we weren't riding such a massive wave of success. Apparently, this is his peace offering to make my life easier. A truce. He can't deny that I'm good at my job, albeit a bit of a fuck-up, but that comes with the job role, partying. But with guests and performers such as Adele, Lily Allen, Peaches Geldof, Wendy James from Transvision Vamp, Jack Penate, Alex Claire, Laura Marling, Paloma Faith, The Rakes, The Horrors, Metronomy, The Mystery Jets, The Maccabees, Kate Nash and Ellie Golding visiting or playing at the club, thanks to the promoters and the parties I am booking. Also a ton of amazing bands who have yet to create a commercial stir. But are equally talented and loved as those on the list mentioned above. It's all about timing and who you know in this industry.
Sadly, things aren't always solely based on talent. The venue is busy, back to being beloved by locals. Our parties and events are gaining loads of press coverage, but so am I. The Devil is getting pissed off that the articles are mentioning me and not him. I've been asked into the studio for an interview and photoshoot. An article called 'Queens of The Night'. He said no. 'You can't have

the morning off work', but he could do an interview and shoot with them if they wanted? They didn't, and that didn't help his case of deathly disdain for me, even though he seemed to miss the fact it was a feature of females in the nightclub scene.

He's also said I can't DJ at any other venues or at 666 or Purgatory Bar anymore, something I do regularly now. 'Sure'. I bite my tongue but all I think is 'How does get fucked, you controlling bastard,' sound? A while back, I had a DJing lesson from a friend at Gary's Bar, an illegal after-party in a warehouse above a napkin and loo roll suppliers. I picked the basics up pretty quickly, and my head exploded with a crazy collection of amazing set ideas. I'd been practising after work in Purgatory Bar 'til I got the hang of it. Nothing too technical. Tits and Teeth DJing, minimal skills but maximum song choices. I loved doing it.

The dance floor is throbbing, banging out 'No One Knows' by Queens of the Stone Age getting ready to mix it into 'Spread Your Love Like a Fever' by Black Rebel Motor Cycle Club. I'm DJing at Hoxton Bar and Kitchen out in the back room, which is packed with over 200 sweaty bodies. A face pops right up into the DJ booth. A spotlight makes it hard to see who it is until they're an inch away from my face. 'HIIIIIIYA WEEEE LOOOOVE!!' Fuck, it's Kitty. I tell her she can't tell the Devil I'm DJing here. I can't be dealing with more demonic drama. "Don't worry, I fucking HATE the Devil, too. I just really needed a job!"

"Do you want a wee line and a fag?" Now, it's me and Kitty versus the Devil.
I teach her everything I know. Kitty has a passion for electro and is full of ideas for club nights and promoters. She really wants to learn; she soaks up all my little lessons and earnestly writes down all my advice in a book. Once we get past that I was a mega prick when she first arrived! There's a really cool wave of electro talent

bobbing round, which she loves. Fake Blood and Duke Dumont. Even though it's not my personal taste in music, it's popular, and I want the club to always be bang on what's happening, so it's great to have her join the office. We programme a 'Fuck Glastonbury Party'. Kitty books the music and we cover the main floor of the club in real grass, turning it into a mini indoor field, fit for an anti-festival, with the rolled-out turf and one-man pop-up tents suspended from the ceiling. Projections of footage from the wild festivals of the 70's cover the walls. It's amazing. The floor is as muddy and as fucked as a wet Glastonbury by the end of the weekend, but as far as stunts go, people loved it: the photographs from the event get huge social traction.

Kitty and I bring out the very best and the very worst in each other. Such an unlikely pair, but with one main shared passion: partying. We're always chasing the never-ending good times. She is the most hilarious person, kooky as fuck, kind with a heart of shining gold, but equally super fucked-up around narcotics and booze. Like me. Her trademark move is losing bags, keys, phones... She's regularly replacing, sims, cash cards and random shoes.
Frustrating as fuck, yet endearing at the same time. She brings ridiculous fun and unexpected chaos to most days in the office. And the rest of my life. Kitty transforms a bad idea into something which sounds really wholesome by putting the word 'wee' in front of it. "Shall we have a wee pigs in blankets (her term for bacon sandwiches)? Shall we have a wee line and a wee beer? Shall we buy a few wee grams of coke?" By putting 'wee' in front of anything, it lessens the impact of the sentence's back end. We would finish up the work day and grab a nice, quiet, wee beer that magically turns in to a wee all-night MDMAmazing disco party and finishes with Kitty and I strolling into the office the next day, not with a wink of sleep between us. There's a tiny broom cupboard office used for storing flyers and old tat, but we found a mattress tucked away in it, so we could take shift nap breaks during our lunch.

Kitty would always go first. I'd guard the door from the Devil, then go wake her up to swap, but she would never properly wake up. Dribbling and muttering, "I'll be up in a wee minute". No nap for me. One night at home after work, drinking wine, and Kitty is doing my hair extensions (she was a hairdresser in a past life), we decide that with a half-head of extensions in - left-side nipple length, thick and beautiful; right-side - shoulder length, wispy and hideous - that we should take a wee break and go to Fabric. As in the 5000-capacity nightclub Fabric. Extension session break turned into an all-night party that turned into no sleep, then work, then the next evening's activity of speed bombs at a Prince concert, still with half a head of extensions in. Then an after-party back at my place, when the sun was coming up, we decided that more drugs was the only sensible solution as we wanted to get a dingy and go up Regents Canal, so, of course, we needed more pills. We only had one problem, lack of cash. We jumped in an illegal minicab, negotiated a fixed-rate for a return trip and headed into Shoreditch to an after-party that was known for drug dealing. I knew the security and the promoter, so while Kitty waited in the cab with the engine running, I walk into the club, quickly finding a dealer, grabbed 5 Es, tucked them into my bra, said I would just get some cash and ducked through the crowd, run out the door, gave the security a high 5 and jump into the waiting cab, yelling at them to GO!

The Devil is desperately trying to get around the fact he can no longer sell alcohol between 3 and 5am. He tries pre-selling drinks vouchers and turning the music off and lights on – never a great idea in a nightclub at 2:50am and announcing to the customers they need to go to the bar and bulk buy their drinks to last them for the next two hours. Our suggestion was selling balloons filled with nitrous oxide. Whipped cream bulbs, affectionately known as Nanging, Whip-Its or Bulbs, depending on where you are in the world. These little bullets are the same as the delightful happy gas you get at the dentist. Inhaling nitrous oxide gives you a rapid rush of euphoria, a feeling of floating, a burst of excitement for a short period of time. It's not totally illegal. Yet. Once we get them in the office, lots of testing obviously had to be done.

Kitty whispers "Shall we do a wee balloon?" CRACK. The bulb twists in the canister. FRRRRRRAPP. The gas fills the chamber, and it's released into the balloon. Followed by silence as we suck the gas out of the balloon. BWAHAHA (hysterical laughter). STOMP, STOMP, STOMP. Two seconds later, the Devil runs down the hallway and busts through the door and tries to catch us using all his precious bulbs. This incentive didn't make him the thousands he was used to making per night, but it did mean an enjoyable work perk for us. Well, until he took them out of the office and into his mega safe.

"The Devil is trying to get rid of you." She's shaking. Kitty can't conceal it any longer. Our friendship is so close and I'm helping her learn the ropes about how clubland works. But she was put in the office to eventually replace me. Kitty was to find out all of my contacts, learn how to do the job so the Devil could fire me and take over my role with Kitty as his support. Fuck. I'm squeezed into my black 1940's sweetheart bust cocktail dress with the satin skirt. It's an elegant tulip-style silky satin which falls at a modest knee-length, with fishnet stockings and black lace-up high heels, trimmed with fur around the ankle. It's tight, and I can't breathe at the best of times in it. The corset boning pinches my ribs with each breath. I can't take it all in now, although this isn't a surprise. Like Kitty said all that time ago, she just needed a job. I know she fucking hates the Devil too, maybe more than me now. I can't blame her: she didn't know me then, so it wasn't like she took the job in malice. It's the same as when Johnny Red tried to warn me off working for the Devil. We have our Christmas party in the Purgatory Bar starting in two minutes, and I'm due out on a flight to Australia in eight hours. Kitty slips me a wrap of coke to share. I pop it in with my cigarettes for safekeeping until I have a chance to have some. The Purgatory Bar is decorated in branches of blue spruce, trimming all the door frames and windows. 14-foot fresh Christmas trees wrapped in twinkly lights are dotted around the venue. The smell of fresh pine and mulled wine is heavenly and huge chandeliers of mistletoe hang from the ceiling. It would be a truly magical winter wonderland if it weren't such a shithole.

The Devil is in charge of mulled wine. His glasses are fogging up, he's muttering and sweating like the Christmas Grinch...he doesn't look me in the eye anymore, so I openly laugh in his face. I've booked an incredible band called Florence and The Machine: the singer looks like a Celtic princess out of a medieval folk story. Shocks of wavy auburn hair and a long, flowing, bohemian dress - she's rumoured to be the next big sweetheart of the commercial music charts. The smoking ban is now in full effect. Annoying and inconvenient, just as she finishes a haunting soul-shaking cover of Beirut's 'Postcards From Italy,' I pop outside for a quick fag and a bump of coke. I'm with a guy called Beans on Toast. A political singer-songwriter. We head out into the freezing night together. He looks like a real-life version of Beetlejuice. Baggy clothes, scruffy, long hair, dark circles under his eyes, and beanie pulled down to his brows. An unlikely pair walking down the road together. I forget to grab my coat - this smoking-outside thing is bullshit. Oh well, I'll just be quick.
I need to get back to the party to pay all the acts. We stand on the corner of Hoxton Square, talking and smoking. Nothing memorable, just a cool chat.
A car drives past. Then past again. I don't notice it.

"I am arresting you for possession of a class A drug. You do not have to say anything, but it may harm your defence if you do not respond when questioned, which you may later rely on in court. Anything you do say may be given in evidence. Do you understand?"

The handcuffs snap on my wrists, clamping my arms in front of me and making my cleavage even more pronounced as I'm led into the back seat of the police car. Beans on Toast is trying to talk them into letting me go. That I've got to catch a plane to see my family in a few hours.

I didn't notice the car driving past till the third lap. It pulled up right in front of us, let its siren off for one whoop and turns on its flashing police lights and high beams. A voice booms over the speaker, instructing us not to move.

The police ask to see Beans on Toast's ID, then proceed to frisk him down and ask if he is carrying any drugs. He says no. A deep voice that isn't mine rises from inside me and says, WAY too loudly, "I am!" And with a knee-jerk reaction, my arm stretches out, handing my ten-pack of Marlboro Lights to the police. "I have cocaine". All three just stare at me, the two police officers and Beans on Toast, with massive wide eyes screaming, "WHAT THE FUCK ARE YOU DOING!!!???"

The air is punched out of my lungs. In the back of the police car, streetlamps crawl by in slow motion. "I'm really, really, sorry. Can you please just let me off with a warning? I was always told that if you admitted you were carrying a small personal amount, then you'll be let off with a warning?" Straining for breath, sobbing so hard. "I just thought that if I were honest, you would let me go! You were going to search me after you finished with Beans on Toast!" We're stopped at the lights, and the policeman at the wheel turns around to talk to me. "Yeah, that normally is the case, but didn't you see us drive past twice? We'd been called out by the department that monitors the city's CCTV to investigate a suspicious-looking male and search him for drugs. You weren't even mentioned and wouldn't have been searched as we didn't have a female police officer present to physically search you." FUCK. I did not judge this situation well at all. He continues. "Now that the CCTV has logged the request for an investigation, we have responded to the request. Which is all captured on the CCTV, so there's no opportunity for leniency or a warning. We had to arrest you". He sounds genuinely gutted for me.

Holy fuck! I'm flying out to Australia to see my family at 6am. Now I'm howling. Shit. The Devil. Now I'm snot-sobbing. This is the final nail in the coffin that he needs to fire me. My Christmas party: I just walked out with a packet of cigarettes, the coke and my mobile. I needed to collect my pay to take on holiday. And I have no keys to get into the club and get my wages if I don't make it back before the managers lock up at 5am. The police station is empty except for a poor little junkie in the corner, shaking and shivering, long overdue for his fix.

The processing begins. I'm offered a lawyer and a phone call. I turn down both, I don't wait to waste time waiting for a court-appointed lawyer. I have a flight to catch and who am I going to call that would actually be able to help me right now? It's a harrowing feeling of utter loneliness. This is the exact moment when you want to pick up the phone, be rescued and told everything will be okay by your mum and dad. 'Please put your clothes and shoes in this bag and put on the paper jumpsuit".

"I can't wear this!" I protest.
"I'm sorry, but you have to." The officer doesn't understand, so I elaborate. "I don't have underwear on."
"Well you have to. We can't put you in a cell in your clothes."
"Seriously I can't. I don't have on a bra under this corset." He shifts uncomfortably. "Ummmmmm eeerrrrrr...okay then. We don't have a female officer, so we can't conduct a full search until one arrives. Please take out your shoelaces."
"Officer, these are little satin ribbons: decorative bows, not real

shoelaces. See?"

"Please take them out."
I hand over two little ribbons. I certainly won't be hanging myself with the ten inches of decorative ribbon that would barely have wrapped around a small ring box. I'm shuffled from room to room until we finally get to a long room for processing. All my details are taken down, retina scan, mouth swab, drug test, alcohol test, and fingerprinting. I face the camera for my mugshot, and hold a board with my name on it. I instantly smile for the camera and I'm sternly told not to. Old habits die hard. Just like in the movies. If I didn't have the gut-wrenching feeling of pending doom, that my life was going to be royally fucked, I would have enjoyed this bizarre routine. Thank goodness my alcohol level is .03 or they would have had to wait 'til my levels came down to interview me. I have a ticking clock and a non-changeable or refundable plane to catch. No unnecessary delays. To be fair, if I was going to be drink and drug tested, this is the ideal moment. Two small glasses of mulled wine and zero coke in my system. Now that's a fucking miracle and rare on most days of the week. It's also almost unbelievably ironic that I've been arrested for possession and not even touched a speck of it.

The arresting police officers say bye as their shift finishes and wish me luck making my flight. Now we're in a little interview room with a glass wall, 1970's laminate table, old chairs. I make a joke that they could step up to the 21st century and swap the ancient tape recorder for a nice mp3 player, which could give them a more modern feel. His stony face tries not to move, but I catch a tiny twitch of a little smirk. In uncomfortable situations, when I'm faced with direct questions, I always cry. It's not because I'm sad. It's a weird trigger, like when the principal calls you in, or you have to talk to the doctor about something personal. So they question me, and I cry. They give me a break to compose myself. They ask again.

I cry. We go round and round. They keep pressing me about where I got the coke from. Where did I buy it? Who did I get it from? How much did I pay for it? Where do I work? I can't remember the other questions because I didn't have to lie about those. These were my danger questions. I needed to avoid telling the truth. "I walked into Hoxton Bar and Grill and bought it from a guy, skinny, tall, white, English. I never met him before." They look surprised. "I paid £40. And I work in marketing. Freelance."

I'm scuttled back to the holding cell. Turns out those little ribbons are more than just decorative ties: they keep my shoes on. The door has to stay open, and when I need to go to the loo, the police officer has to stand at the door. I'm forced to leave the door open, but he will turn his back. It's a vile metal toilet, covered in runny shit, piss, and vomit, which also surrounds the 50cm of floor around it. I scrunch my toes to keep my shoes on and try not to slip in the forced detox décor.

I squat over the top, desperately trying not to let out a sneaky fart with the policeman a meter from my bare bum hovering in the air. I might be a degenerate, but I'm not an animal.

Back sitting alone in a bright white cell. The crying has given me a migraine, not being allowed to smoke, and the flickering neon light is making it worse. I reflect on the bizarre interactions with the police over the past three months. The set-up with Leon and now this. Both incidents are fucked, but on the other hand, there was a totally different experience with being on the other side of the law...

6 Weeks Earlier

Walking home after the club night with a pretty boy I had been casually fucking - there's no point explaining which pretty boy this is, I won't lie. There were many, all with their different personalities and stories, but they all have one thing that makes them the same in this story. They weren't 'him'. Always knowing with each new stranger that this isn't how Hollywood-fucking-amazing-love begins. In a bar, you both pretend the other is more interesting than they are, all the while knowing it's never going anywhere. Half-heartedly looking for the one, but really it's more like temporarily filling an emotional black hole with a penis (sometimes a vagina). Physically connecting with another living being, a defibrillator to your heart. Keeping you going till the Universe, fate, God, Cupid, luck whatever you wish too, believes you're ready for the One.

The pretty boy and I turn onto a side street off Brick Lane, and four Bangladeshi boys in hoodies with bandanas tied around their mouths swing round out of the shadows and surround us. "Your bag! Now!" I throw my bag to them, ready to keep walking: they have what they want now. As I push past, I feel hands grab my shoulders, and I'm thrown to the ground. The wind is knocked out of me, and the pretty boy is just standing there. "Help me!" I scream at him. Why doesn't he move? Then I see. There's a knife at his throat. One of the boys jumps on top of me and flicks something. A police truncheon presses across my neck. I'm struggling, pushing them away. One of them grabs my head, lifting it up with a fistful of my hair and slams it into the road. Two others are pulling at my clothes.

Dear Tava,
It's about family values for these boys. And open your legs. Be strong and fight back.
Love you, The Universe

I scream at him, "I KNOW YOUR MOTHER! We live on the same block! I know your family!" He looks deep into my eyes, confusion.

I keep my legs spread, as wide as I can. They pull and rip at my jeans but can't get them down when I do this with my legs. Headlights fill the dark street with light. They run.

I never wear jeans out at night. Ever. That day, I'd returned from Amsterdam. I'd been to a flea market and bought an epic pair of flat suede over-the-knee boots with vintage Harley Davidson patches sewn onto them. They looked really cool over skinny jeans, and I wanted to wear the boots out. Thank fuck, they saved me. I never actually met the boys' family or knew that opening your legs in that sort of situation - the exact opposite of what you would imagine you would do if you were being sexually attacked - could save you, along with my guiding light – The Universe.

The police and detectives were very helpful, and they caught the attackers on CCTV a few weeks later and found my driver's license in a car during a stop and search. They charged them with attempted sexual assault, assault with a deadly weapon, and theft. Although, I never did get those amazing fucking boots back from the evidence department.

How did I get here? Not just the police cell; I mean so deep into this odd life. What about acting? What about the life of that fresh-faced girl from a loving family? How did that just disappear? Who had I become? What is this self-destructive burning that glows so bright inside me? My body is much thinner, but not on purpose, and my face has a 'coke-bloat' puffiness. There's a permanent deep, rattly cough that takes my breath away, never shifting. I always have the flu and small sores and rashes on my wrists and ankles and inside my nose. Impromptu nose bleeds. Deep black crescent moons under my eyes. I cover all these crumbling signs of wear and tear with makeup, distracting outfits, and elaborate hairstyles. Smoke and mirrors. Nobody sees the real me. Not the way a mother looks at her child or a 'significant other' sees the innermost depths of their lover. I get away with this destructive behaviour because I am far, far away from real, deep love. And even though I'm sitting in a police cell with my life about to fall apart, I know I'm not finished with this dissatisfaction itch in the pit of my stomach. There is something still pushing me. The seeking and searching.

I'm being released on police bail and have to come back to be charged when the test results of the 'illegal substance' are returned. As a gesture of good faith, down to my cooperation, the police allowed me to leave the country into the care of my family in Australia. I have 40 minutes before the managers of the club leave for the night. I ask for a lift back to the club. It's 4am in December and fucking freezing outside. "No, sorry. It's against police policy to give lifts to criminals." This is a dangerous area. I have no money for a cab, so I start walking, trotting back to the club. The police car follows me all the way there. Driving five metres behind me at five miles per hour to make sure I get there safe. Seriously, I couldn't have just hitched a ride? I make it to the club, run up to my office, grab my wages, go to my desk, collect my handbag and coat and run home, empty my dirty-washing bin and chuck the clothes covering the floor into a suitcase. Then back out onto the road and jump in a black cab all the way to Heathrow. The plane is boarding in 60 minutes, and it's a 45-minute drive to get there. With bare minutes to spare, I make it to the check-in desk. My flight is overbooked, and I'm offered a flight six hours later with the option of a business class seat or £250. I take the cash, sit, and stare at the wall for 6 hours.

My mother... The look of distraught sadness when she sees me tells me everything I secretly know: I'm a fucking mess.

I try AA, but can't get behind the concept of God being the vehicle for my sobriety. Clean living and time with my family rebuilds and restores me. I have more time with them than the two-week holiday I initially planned. The Devil found my bail papers on my desk. Just what he needs to fire me. This promptly sends my life to the next chapter. With my bail papers in his hands, it was as if the Universe has given him written notice to release me from his grip.

The cold water surrounds my body, floating in the salty sea off Palm Beach, Sydney. Out the front of my parent's little boathouse. Staring at the sky. I'm free and fucking terrified.

Dear Tava,
Go and do your own club now. You're ready, I believe in you,
The Universe

NB: The coke came back as 79 per cent pure. Not bad at all. The police dropped all charges and offered to go tell the Devil he couldn't legally fire me as they dropped the charges. They kindly wrote me a letter of recommendation to the Home Office to assist with my next visa… Little did they know it was yet another one of my illegal life chess moves.

Beans on Toast apparently wrote a song about the arrest. With my name changed to Melanie and cocaine to ecstasy pills.

5

"I, Tava, take you to be my lawfully wedded husband, to have and to hold from this day forward, for better, for worse, for richer, for poorer, in sickness and health, until death do us part."

My hand shakes as the ring slides past the fleshy bit of my finger. A £10 band from Old Spitalfields Antique Market. The sun streams through the window. If I believed in God, this would have been sending mixed messages. The light through the stained glass window of Islington Town Hall shines on us like a biblical blessing of consent.

Tears pool in my eyes. Quietly, without my body moving, they slowly make their way down my face. Tears of a bride marrying the love of her life? Tears of a girl who got her boy, her deepest heart's desire and the beginning of Hollywood-fucking-amazing? No. Tears of deathly, soul-gripping terror that I have royally fucked with the Universe and her plans for me. My groom goes back to work straight from the ceremony. A wonderful, kind friend doing me a seriously huge 'life' favour, Daisy, my witness at the visa 'green card style' wedding, pulls out a bottle of pink Veuve Clicquot. We sit on the steps of the town hall and drink it right from the bottle, in the sun. I have on my 'Marilyn' dress. You know the one, from the famous air-vent scene in The Seven Year Itch. Satin halter neck and a full pleated skirt. Unlike the iconic bombshell's snow-white original version, mine is emerald green. With sky-high 70's strappy gold stilettos and a fresh bunch of Hackney's most exquisite front garden roses. In the dead of night, Daisy and I had hit the streets on our bikes, armed with kitchen scissors, and filled our baskets with heady roses in full bloom. An armful of flowers ranging from pastel peach to deep dusty pinks. My hair is chopped into a loose bob, framed with a heavy fringe.

Daisy and I drink our way around Shoreditch, still without my groom. I make my way round to the current pretty boy's house to smoke joints, eat his leftover pizza, and watch The Simpsons. Not quite how I imagined my dream wedding day, though, to her credit, Daisy did an epic job as my maid of (dis) honour. What a monster of a walk of shame the next morning, in my Marilyn dress. Ironic, now I think about it. That particular pretty boy, the one I slept with on my wedding night, when freshly married to another person, would be the very last pretty boy I would ever sleep with in my life.

There's a constant knot in the centre of my stomach. The fear that I've tempted fate and forever messed with my chance of finding Hollywood-fucking-amazing-love. I've disrespected the holy sanctity of marriage in the name of getting a spouse visa, something I never would've considered doing if the situation wasn't called for. But it was a necessary evil, the next step in my plan: opening the most incredible nightclub that London has ever seen.

I jump off my bike outside Liverpool Street Station and study the print-off of the property listing, which has a small map. A labyrinth of Victorian, Oliver Twist-esque streets lands me in a graveyard. How odd to find it here in the middle of the city. Where the Wild Roses Grow starts playing on my iPod shuffle. This could eerily be the set for a Nick Cave music video (Red Right Hand would be slightly more fitting). A cobbled lane runs down the side of the majestic, towering church, dotted in stained glass windows and terrifying gargoyles. Hugging the path are beds of scarlet tulips in full bloom, each flower's head the size of a grapefruit. Wrought iron arches stretch up and over the path like permanent metal rainbows leading me to my destiny. I walk my bike. I turn the map around and around in pre-Google Maps frustration. The path opens up to a clearing where I see a tiny gingerbread house sitting there in front of me. It would have been more at home in the Black Forest of Germany, not set in the shadows of a futuristic skyscraper and the London city skyline.

It's fucking beautiful.

Like so beautiful, it's almost comically fairy tale. Like I should be following a trail of boiled sweets and lollies to the door. There must be a mix-up with the real estate property listing, which boasts an 80-seater restaurant or 150 capacity standing venue with full cocktail bar and lounge area, commercial kitchen, and 6am liquor licence. Well, from the outside, this tiny gingerbread house looks just about big enough for an intimate tea party for two. The interior photography on the property listing shows it looking like a poor man's Planet Hollywood. A tired pizza parlour that may have once have been charming. The address has to be wrong. There's a pub next door - that must be it.

But I take a tourist time-out to breathe in this little thing of utter beauty. The building is a mixture of burnt orange and sandy caramel handmade terracotta tiles with ornate patterns set into the rectangular building, no bigger than five meters by three meters, with arched windows set all the way around it. Each window has deep sills and high, elaborate moulding and flourishes. Pale, periwinkle-blue glossy tiles cover the front of the venue. Catching the light, a wrought iron stack with a stained glass onion dome sits like a crown on top of the small building. It looks like a single turret from the Red Squares, Saint Basil Cathedral. Topped off with a lightning rod steeple, a crescent moon and star on the tip of the rod, reaching up towards the heavens.

A minute passes and I circle back around from my little walk of wonder around the building. The agent is standing in the doorway as if he appeared out of thin air.

Despite my initial scepticism, I'm in the right place. I follow him into the gingerbread house and through the cool, dark entrance. My eyes need a moment to adjust to the light. A grand spiral staircase twists in front of me. Creamy, crumbly marble covers each step. As we descend, I note the walls are covered in handcrafted glazed tiles, a tessellated jigsaw pattern of interlocking designs weave together to create a gorgeous mosaic on the walls. Rich maroon and midnight blue, inky uneven hues, soft corals and creams. I look up into the
onion dome crown and gaze into the belly of the blue sky. One hand on the cold, smooth brass railing and the other is stretched out with fingertips grazing the tiles as I wind down the stairs, trying to read the building's stories from her walls.

At the bottom of the stairs is a marble landing with a room shooting off to either side. To the left are a sunken bar and lounge area, to the right a large dining room. Both have low ceilings, no windows. Mismatched, ageing restaurant furniture, booths, and decor straight out of a man-cave, circa the mid-1990s, are blandly strewn around the room. There's a flashing jukebox in a corner, light-up Heineken signs, and large fish tanks with dinky deep-sea divers, treasure chests, and a smattering of sad-looking tropical fish. Dusty plastic palm trees and hundreds of photos are tacked up on the walls, pictures of the current owner with celebrities he's met on his travels over the past 30 years. He seems to be in a band, or maybe in the entertainment industry. I notice with mild respect as I go through the photos that as he ages, his hair thinned, but in the most recent ones, he seems to have replaced his thinning hair with a full head of rock-and-roll locks. Microbead hair extensions – it takes an expert to spot them. Past the tat and questionable photo montage is a stunning Grade 2 listed building with hand tiled archways and columns. The intricate alcove and features are begging to be stripped back, polished to its former splendour. It's utterly incredible, mesmerising and totally breath-taking. If the venue were a person, it would be Grace Jones.

An original Turkish bathhouse, built in 1885, with various utility rooms offering spas, baths, shampooing, steam, and relaxing rooms. If these walls could only talk…The baths managed to survive the Blitz bombing while all the buildings surrounding it were flattened during the war. What ultimately finished its steamy existence was modern bathing amenities being fitted into homes. The Turkish baths closed in 1954. It was then used for storage vaults until Hero and his hair extensions took it over and turned it into a pizzeria-come-shrine to C-grade celebrity culture.

The agent rattles through the features and details of the space. 'Hero' wants a quick sale as he has another project that needs his attention. He's looking for a premium, a goodwill payment for the existing business, of £40,000 for the venue. The new tenants will need to be approved by the landlord. The holding deposit for the property is £30,000, the rent is £90,000 plus VAT per year, the strata levy of £33,000, and business rates are in excess of £20,000 per year.

I have to scrape my jaw off the beautiful marble floor.

"The current legal capacity is 110 people, but with the multiple fire exits and floor space, that can easily be increased to 200 plus."

Okay, that's better. In a boutique nightclub/bar model formula, a venue needs a bare minimum capacity of 200 people. During the six hours of an evening shift, the site needs to be operating at capacity for a solid four hours. The turnover needs to hit a total of 350 guests per night to achieve a nightly target average of £12k. That's £35-ish spent per customer. It doesn't sound like much per person - I can't seem to leave the house on a night of drinking without spending £100. But some people will pop in for one drink and spend £6 and some guests, my very favourite kind, will spend their hard-earned money drinking their way through the cocktail list.

With this venue's remote location and non-existent foot traffic, it's unheard of to even consider it as a nightclub. On paper, I would never have come to see it, but something about the venue intrigued me. Bars and nightclubs rely on a prime location and organic customer footfall to fill their venues. If someone is walking through a graveyard in the middle of the night, do you really want them to pop into your club for a nightcap?

The only way it would work is as a club that isn't just someplace on the high street, which serves drinks and plays music. It needs to be a fucking cultural revolution. An institution for misfits, decision-makers, trend-breakers. A true destination venue that our people will seek out. But regardless of my heart-stopping lust at first sight for this fairy tale venue, the sums are miles off, way beyond the amount that I crudely calculated as my starting point for a site. I'd seen over a dozen other properties that now seem like ugly wicked stepsister venues. Traditional pubs, bars, strip clubs, warehouse conversions. All of them with much lower price points, higher capacity, and better locations, but none that inspire that immediate gut instinct that this was a place of immense power to shape and redefine the nightclub industry.

My head is spinning with a million ideas of how I can make this work, financially. I will make this venue mine.

I jump on my bike, blow a kiss to my beloved venue-to-be and ride home to get ready for my birthday party at Shoreditch House. I've booked a private room to hold fifty of my closest friends. My sister has stopped over in London to celebrate with me tonight, then we'll fly out to Rome tomorrow to meet my family, then to a luxury six-bedroom villa nestled in a vineyard right in the heart of dreamy Tuscany. Thank you, successful older brother. But I can't stop thinking about the venue. I just want to get deep into raising funds for my venue of dreams.

The room is packed with a totally random-looking crew of beautiful, cool fucking people. I can't believe I've made such dear, deep connections in such a short time in London. My colourful crew of characters; nut jobs, corporates, DJs, fashion darlings, film directors, and lots and lots of pretty boys who have been collected and placed on a shelf along the way.

My birthday party look is a sheer black mini dress with puff sleeves, and big, colourful polka dots embroidered randomly over the dress, finished off with a big silk bow belt tied around my waist. My hair is up in a swishy high ponytail, and lots of gold chains and ghetto gold hoops with Virgo written across. Bright red matte lips, cat-eye flicks, stupidly high black Vivian Westwood dominatrix heels. I look like a neatly wrapped present.

I chat to Chaz, long-haired, in a leather waistcoat highly inspired by Russell Brand. He's a DJ slash comedian slash lothario slash club promoter. I met him through his ex-girlfriend who I recorded a six-part pilot radio show at the BBC with. I fucking loved doing the show, but she booted me out to follow her solo career. Anyway, Chaz has booked me a few times to DJ at his club night. He reintroduces me to Rich Pack and reminds me I've done the DJ warm-up slot for him a few times at The Macbeth on Hoxton Street.

We don't need an introduction. We know each other. The past six months, I've been bumping into him at parties, on street corners of Shoreditch, with friends of friends, at club nights. Always with a different pretty girl on his arm. Randomly one night when he was stumped for a reply to a filthy sextext sent to him by a girl in LA, someone he'd met on his last trip over there, I sent a response on his behalf. It was impressive in its steaminess level. He's funny, charismatic, and fucking hot. I always walk away with a massive smile on my face after I see him. I introduce him to my sister, and I comment that I think he's really cool and cute. She's shocked. "What the fuck?! You mean the skinny, praying mantis in the too-tight leather jacket with the big bug eyes and David Bowie Labyrinth hair!?!"
Yes.
Clearly, we have VERY different taste in men.

Remember back to that man I wanted to reach over and pinch to see if he was real? The one I sat next to who was out with his, fairy-wing wearing girlfriend at the Soho pub all that time ago, right before the Kooks concert? Well, bug-eyed-Bowie Rich Pack is HIM. Apparently, he and his Fairy broke up shortly after the pub interlude. Now he laughs when I say every time I see him, it's with a different girl, with a South London smile and laughing eyes, never denying all the rumours I hear about him. He's a player. Standing here in the Shoreditch House facing each other, I can tell at this very moment there's something different. He's also searching. I can see a deep sincerity in his eyes, offering up something that wasn't there before.

I just stand, staring at him. I see him through a total stranger's eyes like I've never really seen him before, but my heart knows every inch of his soul.

Dear Tava,
He isn't one of your pretty boys.
You're both ready for Hollywood-Fucking-Amazing-Love.
As promised, I delivered.
Love you, The Universe.
PS: DON'T FUCK HIM YET!

I can't breathe, my heart is swelling up, taking over all the designated space for my blood, organs and bones, threatening to explode my skin and blast my body in little bits all over Shoreditch House. I squeak out a weird "Bye!" and walk away from him, focusing on every step to make sure I don't trip, slip or generally fuck up. Next morning, he sends a funny, sweet birthday text.

Each night when I close my eyes to go to sleep in the Tuscan hills, a mantra runs through my mind. Get him. He is yours. Make him yours. You belong together. He's the one. It runs through my heart, mind, my body and crutch on repeat. The mantra doesn't stop; it drums through me, a constant loop. When I shut my eyes lying by the villa pool. At night, sleeping in the sweetest little girl's room, perfect for a little villa guest, decorated in pale pink taffeta frills, bows, feather fans, and a Baroque oak miniature child's four-poster bed. Tucked up in the pink meringue bed, I wake up in the middle of the night with my heart thumping as though I'm in mid-flight, running from my demons. Get him. He's yours. Rhythmic, hypnotic, powerful. I know what I have to do. The Universe isn't fucking around this time. He is literally the man of my dreams.

Back in London, a week later, and hot on the trail of my fairy tale venue, my family has astonishingly lent me £10,000 to get things off the ground. They are proud of how I've cleaned myself up. They can see my real dedication to the idea, and I think (hope) they genuinely believe I'm really good at what I do. They saw how much I loved my job with the Devil and put their trust in me by lending that money. But they make it clear it's a loan, not a gift.

I now have a plan. A business plan.

My Dear Beautiful Reader,

I just need to take a second to run something by you: a slight bit of story admin. There is a fork in the road, and I need to make a decision on how to progress. From this point onwards, I had a business partner. This person is still in the industry today, and I don't want to bring any unwanted attention to their projects or make things messy for them. We are still friends, and in no way is this a shun to them, but this is a story about a period of my life in clubland, not a 'how-to' manual, or an essay on my business (actually how NOT to do business would be more accurate). I take sole responsibility for any negative backlash, repercussions, and am the only party to blame for what happens next by sharing this.

I'll just try to keep to my side of the story.
T x

So I have £10,000; my business partner has £15,000. We need to raise more funds. WAY, way, way more capital, if this is going to happen. On top of the £21,3000 for rent, first-year business rates, and the ridiculous premium request from "Hero hair extensions", the current venue occupier. But these are all figures we can get down with some tactical negotiating.

The thing is, this doesn't include the on-going weekly costs of staff, booze, security, utilities, and tax that start piling up the moment the doors open. Not to mention the additional start-up expenses to have the venue ready to open...

- Building works: £10,000. We need a new small bar off the dance floor in the main restaurant area, to strip the existing decoration and remove rubbish, repair and make the building ready for painting and decorating.
- décor: £10,000. Ornaments. Tables, chairs, café set up, and amazing flourishes which will make the venue incredible.
- Bar set-up costs: £10,000. Two glass washers, glassware, back-bar liquor and cocktail ingredients; everything necessary for a bar from bottle openers to ice buckets to mop heads. Initial stocking of the bar with alcohol for the opening week.
- Legal fees for the lease and contracts: £15,000.
- Licenses and insurance: £12,000.

Included and all the very basic just-hanging-in-there condition CCTV cameras and monitors, kitchen set-up, industrial pizza oven and equipment, air conditioning units, one large ice machine, two till systems plus amps and speakers. These amount to huge savings, something we desperately need wherever we can get it.

That all adds up to £263,000, and it looks like we can open and make everything happen with £90,000, then pay things, like the lawyers, on a 90-day payment plan and utilities as they arise. We just need to arrange generous payment accounts with alcohol and food suppliers. We can deal with the rest of the bills from the weekly takings. It's critical we do as much negotiating as possible to get costs down.

The venue needs to be successful and financially stable from the first week it opens if this is going to work. It's a considerable risk. We're gambling big to invest so much. There's no margin for error, no contingency fund or room for it to be a slow and steady burner.

Basically, working our way up to incredible isn't an option.

Now, this might seem like an enormous start-up cost and commitment. Writing it all now, I'm screaming at my younger self, "STOOOOP!" But when did hindsight ever make for an exciting story?

The concept is to create a day-to-night venue. Upstairs on the street level, the tiny gingerbread parlour will be a café. Coffee and pastries in the morning, takeaway pizzas and cold drinks for the offices surrounding the venue at lunch. At 6pm, down in the basement levels, the cocktail bar, lounge, and restaurant will open as a cabaret, burlesque and entertainment dining space, which we will turn into a late-night club after midnight. With DJs, walk-around entertainment, all-night dancing and romancing till the sun comes up, thanks to our rare 5am licence.

With the concept developed well beyond the traditional nightclub to multi-use entertainment and leisure venue, generating revenue streams from the café, restaurant, bar, nightclub, and private events, our accountant forecasts the gross profits at 800K. That was with conservative projections. It was unofficially said that a one million pound gross profit was achievable in the first year with the unmeasured cash incomes of door/entry cover charges and coat check, the great secret earners of clubland. So although the expenditure and start-up costs are more significant than we first calculated, the venue's potential opportunities are exceptional.

We produce a thoroughly researched 40-page business plan, including Introduction and Concept; Key Success Factors; Business Goals; Research and Analysis; Key Competitors; Prices and Charges; Management Plan; Licenses and Regulations; Example Rota; Start-up Costs; Monthly Running Cost, Profit and Loss Forecast; and Appendix. Phew. It's amazing what you can do when you sober up a bit. Although I dig at the Devil, I learnt so much from him and for some unknown reason, the nightlife industry seems to come naturally to me. Abstract thinking of how can we get around the hurdles – which is a daily question when you're dealing the police, council, and licensing, how to get more people in the venue to make more money... These are the daily challenges in clubland. Both these trains of thought and finding the answers to them are natural to me. To this day, I can go into a venue and in 15 minutes find out what's wrong with it, and what needs to be done to sort it out.

As we got all our research done, ready to start raising funds, the worst possible headline hits the news. The bottom falls out of the market, kicking off the Global Financial Crisis. We're instantly told that high street banks won't lend to vulnerable sectors, which includes the 'night-time economy industries'. The only way they'll remotely consider giving out a loan is with matched funding. We will need to come up with pound for pound in what we want to borrow. FUCK.

Back to the drawing board. We research other lenders and a few high street banks that are offering better deals than match funding. We're booked in to pitch at a local small business start-up investment board (Angel Investors before they got the fancy buzz title).

There are two defined stories and concepts of the venue that unfold. What is presented to the banks and lenders, and what is actually going to happen. The bones and financial structure are the same, but the atmosphere, entertainment, look, feel, and branding will be polar opposites.

Mission Statement 1 | The bank's venue version
We are committed to providing our customers with a unique experience, one where they can escape and enjoy a social evening with friends, both old and new. We aim to build a loyal, frequent customer base and see consistent financial growth, month to month.

Mission Statement 2 | My personal venue vision
To create a fucking cool space in the most electric, eccentric, beautiful venue fit for daydreamers and trailblazers, with queues around the block and money ringing through the cash register. To have a cultural, positive impact on the creative nightlife scene.

Two mission statements mean two sets of mood boards and concepts to match.

Board One | For the bank - Photographs of the venue's exterior and interiors. Hand-drawn sketches for my conceptual plans. The building layout and floor plans, fabric swatches of luxurious velvet, gold, braided trims and tassels. Opulent branding. Collages of beautiful cabaret dining rooms, vintage shots of the Rainbow Rooms NYC, Victorian table settings with elaborate cut-crystal glassware. Polite and sensible drinking scenarios, cocktails and high teas.

Board Two | The Reality – Decor and trimming as above but with an added darker, exploratory side of Victoriana - anatomy, erotica, and macabre skeletons and skulls intertwined with bold, rich botanicals. A secret supper club with salty burlesque dancers transforms into a hedonistic nightclub, pulsing with the ghosts of icons past. Studio 54 fashion; NYC club kids, circa 1990, collides with Andy Warhol's

The Factory. A wild, colourful, eclectic private club at the bottom of a churchyard and down a gingerbread house stairwell is a world where everyone shines the truest version of themselves.

First up are the angel investors. It's like a Dragon's Den pitch, asking for £50,000. We've used our initial £25,000 as proof of funding for the angel investors; they only require half the amount of the total amount you wish to borrow. We pitch them an inspiring concept with solid research and industry knowledge. Once the angel's funds are approved and secured and released into our account, the next step in the plan is to use it as our "cleared funds" for match funding to go to the high street banks for the remaining £75,000. Now, this is technically illegal. But I see it more of a stretch of good faith and - granted - not really great business logic. If the lenders knew we were doing it, the loans would have been instantly rejected. But there's no getting around it: we will massively over-borrow.

It's a domino effect of fundraising that is incredibly flawed, and each level is dependent on getting the funding before it. Even if we pull off the funding house of cards, we are still short and getting pressure to put a deposit down on the venue from the agent. The current owner and his hair extensions want to do a deal. We head over to his other Knightsbridge restaurant to meet him. We walked out of the meeting 25 minutes later with the premium payment of £40,000 for 'goodwill' totally dropped. And a high interest, short-term loan of £20,000 from him if we make an offer and take over the venue. We should have heard the clanging alarm bells and run from the deal. Why was this guy willing to drop 40K and lend us money just to get the deal done? We didn't even question it. Ignored the signs and pushed on to build the venue. Trying to negotiate with the landlord for the venue terms now begins. The lease terms are archaic and financially steep. They dropped the holding deposit to £20,000. Hmm... Funny isn't it? That's the exact same amount the current tenant Hero and his hair extensions lent us....

We now have a larger pot of money, and the initial start-up layout expenses have dropped. I sit by the phone and wait for the news on the funding. The first round of fundraising from the angels' pitch… LOAN APPROVED. A heavy sigh of relief and quickly move the money over to the business bank account. Next step is submitting a bank statement as 'proof of funds' to the high street bank… LOAN APPROVED. Finally, we send the bank statement with the collected funds over to the landlord for proof of our financial position… LEASE APPROVED. Of course, this is real life and not a Hollywood movie, so no spinning newspapers or an uplifting 'go get 'em' Dolly Parton mega-mix sound-track playing behind a montage of the loans being approved, shaking hands with the big-cheese banker and cool indie angel investors, hair extensions handing over the venue keys with a smile, and cut to a pumping busy Saturday night in the successful club with me counting all the piles of cash money. None of it was as straightforward or as easy as that. Think nine months of a rollercoaster ride backwards and forwards, meetings; bitter negotiations then renegotiation; metaphorical arse-tearing, cock-sucking and deep-throating; locking in interest rates, balls-in-a-vice terms, scrapping around to try and supply supporting documents that we just didn't have; jumping through never-ending hoops like prize show dogs. Expensive contracts, draft after draft after draft from the multiple lawyers involved in the deals. It's taking so long I've forgotten what I'm fighting for.

Is anyone even going to come to this fucking club, let alone care about if I ever manage to get the fucking thing opened?

But luckily, my mind, body, and heart had been kept busy in other exciting life departments.

6

None of the things I say here will even get close to capturing what happened that very first night. Put simply; electric chemistry and a profound connection that I've never felt before. Crackling and hypnotic. It was like falling into a deep trance. If he asked me to spend the rest of my living days by his side, I would have said 'yes' a thousand times over. On the very first night.

Our first date was easy to arrange, strangely enough. After I got back from Italy, I 'casually' texted him – 'casually' meaning I wrote it and rewrote it no less than 3000 times, sent it to multiple friends to check tone, wording, kiss or no kiss, and determine whether or not the blood of the virgin Moon was rising in Mercury before sending the loaded gun enquiring 'why we never hang out more.' He asked if I wanted to go see a band on Wednesday night and I asked if it was a date? He said 'Yes, this is a date'. It was a straightforward, simple exchange. The band we'd planned to go see was cancelled, so he suggested a bar he thought I might like. He hasn't been there before I know he's a 'spit and sawdust, New York dive bar' pint kind of drinker. He didn't realise it, but it was my all-time favourite place in the whole wide world. Lounge Lover, In the back of Shoreditch.

The very best, most beautiful fucking mental cocktail bar. Part antique auction house, part Miss Havisham cocktail parlour: part eccentric-exotic but full of exceptional-taste-hoarder bar.

I dress low-key. Well, low-key for me. A high-waisted denim pencil skirt and sheer white top with a lipstick kiss print all over it, with a bow tied at the side of the neckline. I have my soft leather jacket on and with a leopard print scarf, vintage bucket bag, red tights, and sky-high chunky leopard heels. I wear my hair out just natural and MAC Dangerous matte lipstick.
A bit fancy and a bit fun. He has on skin-tight girl's jeans - so tight the crotch looks ready to reveal its secrets at any point in the night - a fitted black T-shirt with the hem cut off the bottom, so it sits just above his vintage white belt and shows off his heroin-chic hollowed out waist and hip bones. And his bum crack when he bends over. Purposely off-white shoes and a vintage leather jacket with the perfect amount of worn-in patina. His trademark 70's hair, short fringe, spiky halo through the crown, the back shoulder-length and straight. It shouldn't work, but it does. His hair is genuinely spectacular. His fingers are full of chunky silver rings, skulls, panther's heads and bands studded with cloudy semiprecious stones. Strong, masculine hands. I want to hold them. His thin wrists are layered up with silver bracelets and fob chains. Creeping down and around his arm are intricate tattoos of flowers and leaves. Around his neck is a delicate chain with a silver feather charm. Trinkets and jewels collected from his travels to LA and signature pieces I recognise from the Great Frog and Crazy Pig jewellers in London. He is so well turned out. Confidence and what could be taken for arrogance fill a simple outfit of jeans and a T-shirt. On anyone else, this would look plain, but his energy lifts it to a level of haute couture and intrigue straight out of the pages of a glossy editorial spread. He's like a peacock, filling the room with unconventional beauty, pride, and warmth.

He's brought me a mixed tape. A CD. Fuck. Me. Now.

We're sitting in a ridiculously eccentric, private corner alcove in mid-century Eames-style chairs with a family of taxidermy goat heads in diamond tiaras and bejewelled dangling clip-on earrings fit for the Queen Mother perched above our heads. Facing each other with a fucking annoying but beautifully elegant etched glass coffee table between us. We're leaning in so hard towards each other, like weeping willow stretching towards a stream. There aren't enough moments in the evening to say all the things we need to say to each other. Stories come so easily. I'm surprised by the depths of the topics we cover. We start with light and frothy 'Oh, you know Billy Blogs and Archie Rose?' to our shared passion for LA, vintage, music, cocaine and the club scene. He'd been a DJ for over 16 years and has a club night at the infamous 12 Bar Club in Soho. During the day in his 'real-life', he's a designer. Then we transition to the deeper end, his struggle with losing his mother to cancer, his interest into something 'more' with Kabbalah, our share conspiracy theories around 9/11 attacks. To narrowly escaping death at the hands of a junkie who wanted his wallet and stabbing him three times in the back to get it. It's so different from the conversations I usually have in Shoreditch.

He fidgets slightly but holds intense eye contact. He's so easy in his way of being, but there's a glimpse of something that I don't think people often see through his veil of smiles, confidence, and never-ending humour.

Has it been saved just for me?

We bar-hop and drink our way down Brick Lane, happily in a bubble of two people who know something special is happening. Randomly, I get called a prostitute. Not once, but twice. At different times during the night. By two actual prostitutes. And here I'd thought I looked demure for once. We laugh so hard at everything and at nothing, walking hand in hand. We kiss at the top of Brick Lane. (Although he will argue it was the bottom of Brick Lane.)

There are certain things to be guided by when choosing a soul mate. For me, there's a non-negotiable list. Humour, a well-aligned moral compass, mind-numbing attraction, matched sexual appetite and taste, a deep blood-brother friendship, and the right timing to allow you to form a connection when the stars are aligned. Every moment of that date started checking off the boxes and rewrote desired traits in a mate that I didn't know even existed or were essential to me.

But I also had a highly superficial secondary checklist. The whole thing could all fall away quite quickly if the little things revealed behind closed doors don't make the cut. It could make this dreamboat candidate for Hollywood-Fucking-Amazing-Love into just another special, yet pretty boy. You learn a lot when you enter someone's home. You learn even more once you see them without clothes on.

He lived in the penthouse of a converted warehouse on Brick Lane overlooking Shoreditch. It was decorated à la boy, but clean and tidy, cool artwork, houseplants, Technics decks, and filled with endless rows of records. Excellent start. Nice sheets and bedding. His shoes were Alexander McQueen, his feet were nice, and his cock was excellent (don't worry Universe, I quickly looked but didn't touch.). He had a tattoo running from his butt cheek and down to his thigh, a vintage Smith and Wesson with his initials inscribed into the gun's handle. We lay side by side, his arms wrapped around my back. I'm wearing one of his friend's band's T-shirts, The Quireboys. It's too tight. They were once managed by Sharon Osbourne, and supported ACDC and Guns n' Roses. My legs are still in my thick red tights because I didn't shave my legs or get the well-overdue wax to deal with the Victorian-style topiary of my vagina. I kept it as an anti-fucking device. What can I say? I can lack self-control in the pants department. But I feel a pleasantly hard cock pressing against my back. I'm trying to sketch it up with my virtual mind mapping tool its width and length. I could easily just roll around. I can feel the energy pulsating between us.

There's a funny thing that happens when you fuck someone straight away. That elusive, intangible magic disappears. You're theirs. They own a tiny part of you, and the anticipation evaporates, losing its shine. It's inevitable. They don't mean to do this, and I don't think they realise it, but the simple theory of having something you can't is a core human driver, at least in my experience. He's going to have to wait four weeks before we fuck. He doesn't know it yet, but we are going to date. The old-fashioned game of getting to know you before he sees my insides. This is the reverse of any other pretty boy. The sex bit isn't the intimate part. It's the side of your personality that is carefully hidden from the rest of the world.

I pretend to sleep. I close my eyes, but I can't sleep knowing that I have met the man of my fucking dreams.

How can I not fuck this up?... I want to live in his blood.

This isn't being overdramatic. It's not morbid, and I'm certainly not turning into a Tim Burtonesque emo-goth, but I physically and emotionally can't get close enough to him. Carefully slicing a tiny bit of his skin and slipping into his bloodstream seems to be the only sensible solution.

Okay, I can hear you thinking. Well, that's not a great start to not fucking it up...

Not only did he tick all the boxes, but he also created whole new infatuating categories that I didn't know my heart, body, mind or vagina were now demanding from my Hollywood-fucking-amazing-love. Humble. Confident. Engaging. Hypnotic.

Next morning, sunshine streams brightly through the window and thin curtains. The air is so still, with a crisp twinge to it, but I'm cosy in a cloud of feathery Egyptian cotton duvet.

I lie on top of him, and we kiss. His pointy hips dig into me. When you kiss someone who has had a million other lovers before you, you can feel the impression of these people; the marks and fingerprints they've left behind. I can feel that with him and sure he can feel it in me. His kiss is conservative, not yet invested. Slowly, the ghosts start to disappear, making way for a new normal, a new way you both kiss. Together. The same goes for fucking. When you have had so many partners, they leave their ways of doing it with you. Over time, it builds up more layers than an onion, becoming an almost watered-down personal style and preference for nameless, faceless fucking. You never know when you'll find the person you can fully be open with. The intimate moments are really private and personal in a bed, but fucking is almost like a business transaction. An exchange of needs, expression of power, the craving for the void to be filled, and the loneliness put to an end. It can be profoundly impersonal. But kissing deeply, with your arms wrapped around each other, is like unlocking the layers of lovers and fuckers who held your new beautiful person, so many times before you. This happens slowly, once the Universe allows you the luxury of time to explore it.

I have an actual pash rash.

We go for coffee and share a gigantic orange and poppy seed muffin. What was I thinking? Evil little seeds in my teeth! He offers to help me with the design hurdles I have at the venue. Starbucks had never tasted so good. The walk through the crusty back streets of Whitechapel to Bishopsgate, a seriously un-glamorous part of London, feels heavenly. I'm skipping a foot from the pavement. Holding his hand, staring into his sunglasses when he talks. Laughing so hard at his jokes. I can feel myself being creepy. The reflection in his mirrored aviators confirms this. I dial it back by the time we arrive at my gingerbread fairy-tale venue. I was given access to measure a few things up and had picked the keys up the day before.

He is blown away. Struck by its beauty as much as I am. His excitement completely matches my own. We sit in the marble stairwell and do rubbings of the walls with sticks of graphite and charcoal. Like how you rub bark or leaves as kids. We rub the beautiful tiles, talking easily, transferring the history and beauty onto paper. I have an idea to create a tessellated wallpaper using the tiles and design it to a repetitive pattern to incorporate my beloved Victoriana skeletons. A designer made a first attempt at the logo and branding, but it needs more work, so he takes my ideas, drawings, mood boards and mock-ups to work them up for me.

We part ways.

What the fuck has happened? I'm nowhere near prepared to deal with how much my heart aches as we walk away. I feel overwhelming emotion. Panic. What if this is goodbye and we are never together again?

I can't imagine having to live without him now.

Was he always here, ready to meet me and it's just as simple as timing? Was it decided and mapped out in the stars that we were meant to be from birth, travelling on our own individual journeys through the galaxy on course straight for each other? Did I call him to me? Somehow manifested my Hollywood-Fucking-Amazing-Love. Has the Universe delivered on her promise?

How can two people be actually made for each other? Actually, hold that thought. We haven't fucked yet, and fucking could definitely spoil it. What if he can't keep it up or comes too quickly or he's into some weird arse fuckery? Or my mapping was wrong, and he has a small penis? Or am I being totally delusional? How can you fall head over heels in love in a split second?

All of these options are possible.
And only time will give us the answer.

Three weeks later, my parents are visiting me. They're staying in my room, so I'm camped on the airbed upstairs in the lounge room. Rich and I slept together for the first time the day before. No problems in the penis performance department. As expected, lots of ghostly past fingerprints, but a good solid sex base to build on. Mum and Dad have stopped by London after Italy, so we all went out for a nice lunch. He charms and delights. He leaves us to go get more of his arm tattooed by a visiting artist from LA before heading out to DJ until late. I wasn't expecting to see him for a few days.

I drift in and out of sleep, trying to block out the street lamp shining through the front room, which doesn't have any blinds. My phone pings. 'I'm outside x'. I peep out the window and spy a slightly swaying, drunk but devastatingly beautiful man at my door.

He's come around to ask me if I would be his girlfriend. I feel like a stupid giddy teenager.

Freshly brewed coffee drifts in from the kitchen where my parents are planning their upcoming trip to Ireland. The dead weight of an arm wrapped in cling film tucked tightly around me. The sheets have ink and blood smears from the huge tattoo. Naked apart from a pair of small, tight, black boy leg underpants, he flops off the airbed with all the elegance of a one-legged flamingo. He heads to the bathroom. In his pants. I remind him my parents are here. He heads back in the room, looks in the mirror, fixes his hair, looks pleased with the results and then walks straight out again to see them. *Still only in his pants. But with exceptional bed hair, bloodshot eyes and a smile.

I think he's still drunk.

The very next day, another unexpected text popped into my inbox.

'I think I'm falling in love with you x.'

He leaves for a month-long trip to DJ in LA and NYC which firmly lodges a tight knot in the pit of my stomach and a heart-shaped lump in my throat.

*This story isn't stolen from Notting Hill. Just ask my mum.

7

My eyes scan each table, flicking over the objects. Quickly moving through the rows and rows of distracting tat. Boot sales are an obsession. The smell of damp grass, cheap, fatty burgers sizzling on the grill, and the thrill of finding strange bric-a-brac that you never know you needed until the very moment you set eyes on it. Objets d'art pennies. Each table is a new possible trove of treasure, tiny brass animals, elaborate candle holders, intricate picture frames, stacks of well-worn leatherbound anatomy journals, and birdcages. Oddities. Curios. And if anything wasn't already my most-loved shade of metallic bronze, brass, copper or gold, it soon would be, with a veil of metallic-à-la-fabulous from a can, my new best friend. Everything looks better sprayed with warm metallic tones.

Heading back to the car, I'm thrilled, dizzy with my haul. A mystery item catches my beady eye. Leaning against a transit van are pretty, curly wrought iron panels, broken up into pieces, over seven foot high. A huge outdoor pergola, rusty, white paint peeling, with a domed roof cage. I have found my DJ booth. A human-sized birdcage. To be sprayed golden, of course!

Loading up the boot with cardboard boxes of cut-glass vases, dressing table vanity sets, shallow bowls and little lollie dishes, vintage cocktail sets, absinthe fountains, decanters, and elegantly bevelled bottles that once held unidentified liquids, tonics and toxins for the back bar. My mind is mapping out the possibilities for my newfound treasures and how to use them. The back bar should be practical but fucking dazzling. Bartenders need to be able to grab booze bottles quickly, but the customers on the other side of the bar have to be captivated as they stand there, waiting for their poison of choice.

One of the most significant expenses are the two pieces of custom moulded brass tops for the dance floor bar and the cocktail bar. I already know it's going to be such a pain in the arse to upkeep, but its lux beauty is worth the agony. I've negotiated with the Asahi beer company to have brass beer pumps custom made and fitted for us; a golden eagle about to take flight with spread wings perched in front of the taps. Bold, masculine, but beautiful.

Although the building's heritage is Victorian, I layered up my decor vision with all the luxury of old London back street opium dens and forgotten Catholic crypts. I've had an obsession with religious iconography since I was a little girl, mainly Catholicism (driven by the visual aesthetic, not biblical devotion), so the building's interior has the feeling of Dolce and Gabbana meets Baz Luhrmann's Romeo + Juliet. At the end of each of the bars is a shrine display. I have five-foot-tall resin statues of Jesus and the Virgin Mary. Catholic saint pillar candles and flickering cross candles, bowls of blood-red roses with heads so juicy they're on the brink of cascading into a stream of petals with the slightest gust of wind. At the feet of Jesus are cut glass bowls and old-fashioned Victorian weighing scales, brimming with fresh fruit. Oranges, lemons, and limes to be sliced up, sacrifices to garnish guests' drinks. They're intermingled with piles of exotic displays of dragon fruit, figs, persimmons, and lush strawberries that later will be devoured by customers. Like an offering to the gods of hedonism. Nag champa snakes through the air.

You'd think that any God-fearing religious man would burst into flames upon entering the venue, but later down the line I befriended the priest of our courtyard's parish, sharing a sherry or three with him in his office and hosting fifteen of the highest-ranking visiting priests in England for a three-course lunch (with wine, of course) in our restaurant. Which they all loved, by the way. But then again, they never knew about the sex and drugs that went along with the blasphemous decor.

There are four private VIP booths which run along the far side of the venue, decked with old velvet theatre curtains for privacy. The interior of the booths is fitted with black leather banquet seating and antique brass Flemish chandeliers that hang so low over the table that they'll graze your head if you're careless. They looked so good it was worth the occasional drunk customers bumping their heads. I even found little light bulbs that look like candles, with flames that flicker and dance exactly like the real thing.

Small tables are dotted around with floor-length tablecloths set with carved high-back wooden chairs. On each table is the holy trio: tiny cut-glass vase with a full bloom rose, cut short to a buttonhole length; a brass candlestick with taper candle burning bright; and a chic brass animal. A horse, cat, deer, cock or pheasant. Each setting is individual and highly coveted. They will have to be replaced weekly. The temptation to not to slip the little oddities into pockets is too much for most people. I totally get this, to a degree. Trinkets and tiny treasures to remember an incredible night. Sure. But you'd be astonished at what some fuckers will take...

The food menu is placed into leatherbound Victorian anatomy journals which feature graphic illustrations and dated scientific theories. The printed card menus are held in with old-fashioned photo album corners. The tables are finished off with cocktail menus printed on thick cream paper which is folded in three. A piece of dried lavender is placed in the middle, secured with blood-red sealing wax and our own bespoke seal.

There is not one penny to spare in the budget and corners have to be cut and then cut again, then whittled down some more. Everything is haggled for, price-checked: we're forced to consider alternative ways to achieve the look. A small ring of friends help with the labour, painting, and decorating, but the effect is lush, luxurious, and astonishingly we achieve it on a shoestring budget.

The ambient beauty of this club is controlled by dimmer switches and excessive candlelight. This hides a multitude of sins.

We paint, scrub, remove years of rubbish and build-up. Neglect found in every corner, crack, and crevice. Rub back paint, and the panel of plasterboard comes off. Fix up a loose tile and three more clatter to the ground. Change a light bulb, and it trips the lights of a totally different circuit. The venue is patched up and made 'good'. We don't have the funds to fully restore her. Just make things pretty and paper over the cracks. Literally.

Dark, richly red velvet hides anything offensive to the eye. Exposed cables? No problem, let me drape a little bit of velvet over them. Horrible ceiling with halogen spots lights? The modern eyesores that jar through the grace and elegance of the old building... Sorted! A bellowing canopy of velvet creates a false ceiling – which will smoulder, smoke and will threaten to combust into flames many times during our reign. Need to create a VIP area in a flash? Drape some red velvet and light candles. Everything looks better in red velvet.

The venue is already so gorgeous. Down to its bones, it radiates pure beauty and class but with the additional new flourishes and attention to detail with the deco, helped by low lights; warm, muted tones, shiny metals, flickering candlelight, and dripping with velvet everywhere. The effect is truly transcendent.

The idea for the bespoke tile-rubbing wallpaper had to be rethought after the quote came back over six thousand pounds to print just enough rolls for the large dining room-cum-club space. I loved the idea of mirroring the walls with the tile rubbing wallpaper, so I wasn't about to let go of the option that easily. The design that Rich did was so beautiful. It had meaning, for me and for the venue. I went to Kwik Kopy and got three sheets printed in A0 black and white then I mixed up some wallpaper paste and started 'wallpapering' it up. It seemed to go up okay, so I left it to dry overnight, expecting it to pucker and shrink, like your fingertips after you've sat in the bath too long. I messed around, covering entire walls in A0 paper in the trial run of simply staple-gunning it up. It looked amazing. The thousands and thousands of pounds that I was told would be the only way to get my tessellated design on the wall was achieved with two hundred sheets of A0 paper. It dried in a perfectly imperfect way, giving the effect that it had been there as long as the original tiles. It's truly magnificent: my most creative genius idea to date. My inbox over the years is flooded with endless requests asking where to buy the wallpaper. It was only made sweeter by the fact I created it together with Rich.

Blowing up images on A0 and plastering them onto the walls gave me an idea for the bathrooms. They were ugly but functional. I snipped and glued black and white Victorian erotica. Beautiful breasts, hairy muffs, poised on chaise lounges, all of which spoke of decadent nights and lust. I sneak Betty Paige in, despite the fact she shows up a bit later in the erotic scene. She is one femme-fatale I have a hot spot for. At first glance, it looks like a mish-mashed grid of shapes and bodies, but when your eyes adjust, all the little lusty images start coming to life. The paper goes up the walls and over the low-hanging ceiling. It's imposing and in no way subtle but it is fucking cool and will go on to be the most photographed nightclub loos before the narcissistic, poorly-lit bathroom selfie rears its head. It takes an army of hands to get this paper up and also a few layers of marine varnish to protect it. Nightclub toilets get wet and wild.

Three Days to the Launch Party

The only advertising for the opening is a Facebook event page. Minimal text, no photos of the venue, just the logo and the promise of what's in store. These are the golden days when Facebook was algorithm free. If people click 'Attending' on the event's page, you had a pretty accurate idea of numbers. Over 500 people confirmed so far, and that doesn't include loads of chatter in the club scene. But you never know. If it doesn't open with a smashing launch party, it will be a slow burner, which means it will never really take off. London is fickle as fuck. This needs to be the hottest, most desirable underground party to get the right people there from the beginning and trickle down into mainstream channels. The weather will always be the ever-present mistress of club life, deciding on who can be bothered to get out of bed if it's windy, raining or God forbid, snowing. But what happens if there's a last-minute launch party with a must-see VIP or we miss the target with the 'minimal' underground marketing?

Trolling has started on the Facebook page. We don't want a sex club opening here. I'm going to get you closed down before you even open…

What the fuck?!?

Representatives from the licensing department of the City of London Council arrive with reports of an 'after-hours club with full nudity' preparing to open. I'm quick to point out we actually do have a full entertainment license, and because it is so old, the grey areas mean we could do full nudity if we wanted to. Secondly, we're doing burlesque. Nipples and crotches are traditionally covered, so there's nothing for them to worry about. Oh, and finally, we're an over-18 venue. We're informed that he's pushing for burlesque to be reclassified and moved into adult entertainment. From his department's perspective, we don't have the proper licenses, and we open at our own risk. He hands me a letter filled with hot air jargon. I call our lawyer. He laughs.

So I file it under G.
As in 'Go Fuck Yourself'.

Three hours later. The next knock on the door. A visit from the licensing police and local sergeant. They have also received reports of an illegally operating strip club in the venue. This is despite having lodged all of our licenses, our CCTV camera layout, specs, operational policies and procedures with the City of London Authorities. The brain isn't talking to the hands. I hit redial and pass the phone over to the sergeant. Just like that, they're gone.
I wish I had a lawyer in my pocket to pull out every time life throws a curveball.
They leave a false first impression.
The police are never that easy to get rid of in the future.

But what I want to know is who is stirring shit before we've even opened our doors.

Rich returns after a month in LA and is DJing tonight at 666. The Devil has banned me from the club. Daisy pops over to have dinner and wine after a massive 15-hour stretch of venue DIY with Mum, who had come back over to help with the opening. We drink and chat shit. Mum heads to bed, jet-lagged, and Daisy pops over to the off-license for more wine: two-for- a-fiver special. Two bottles of the nastiest, cheapest white wine the world has to offer for just £5. We've already had four. Daisy has a brilliant idea for us to dress up in disguises and sneak into 666 to say 'welcome home' to Rich, while he DJs. We're utterly hammered, white wine-wasted. Wobbly and slurry. I put on an Uma Thurman Pulp Fiction style wig, which incidentally looks remarkably similar to my current hair. Shows how wasted we are to think this is some kind of excellent disguise. I top it off with a polka dot scarf, a big bow tied at the top like Minnie Mouse. I swap clothes with Daisy and put on her 'boyfriend' jeans, a button-down collar black shirt and lesbian-chic Doc Martins, thinking that a 'non-frilly' outfit will add a perfection layer of deception to my anti-Tava disguise. This is so far from an awesome idea. (STOP NOW!)

We get into the club. This in itself is astonishing, as I'm almost walking in circles: I'm swaying, so drunk. My photo is right in the middle of the Wall of Shame of banned customers. In the club, with one eye closed to focus, my blurry double vision spies Rich behind the decks, unpacking his records and talking with a very tall, very blonde, and beautiful girl. The white wine flicks a switch. Zero to crazy in three seconds. I storm through the crowded dance floor. I can hear myself muttering drunkenly, but I can't stop. I wave my arms like a mad man. My wig slips from the weight of the comically large bow and clings sadly askew to my head, but I ignore it and keep pushing through the heaving dance floor, yelling at him over the decks, past the blonde girl who is wedged between him and me. Screaming myself hoarse. 'You've disrespected me/you're an unfaithful fuck-wit/you aren't who you say you are/player/dick...' You name it, I slurred it. But that wasn't enough. He told me to leave. Kinda laughing, kinda fuming but still polite. I won't have it. I grab my wig and throw it in his face. With my own hair plastered down like I've been wearing a sweaty condom all night, a semi-circle of car crash viewers breaks apart. Instantly, my feet are dangling off the ground, and I'm fireman-lifted up by two gorilla-sized bouncers. The Devil's henchmen cousin removes me from the club, kicking and screaming. The last thing I see is the look on Rich's face. Devastation mixed with disgust.

Two Days to the Launch Party

I wake up in the morning with no clear recollection of the previous night. *'The Fear' is next level. Piecing it together with only scraps of shameful information. I realise the wig is missing. Oh shit. The deadly doom increases with blinding flashes of my abysmal behaviour and a jackhammer hangover in my brain. But that doesn't compare to the hole I've managed to blast through my heart.

He won't return my calls.

I'm such a fucking idiot. Daring him to leave me, pushing him away with drunken, insecure B-grade slapstick comedy fuck-ups. Trying to prove it's not real and he's just like every other man who's crossed my path before.

And I can't even rest in my self-induced cocoon of shame and severe dehydration.

I have other significant problems.

I'm out of cash. My credit cards are maxed out, my bank account is overdrawn, and I've cashed in all my IOUs from friends. I'm so, so broke. Like, don't have any money to buy the pack of Marlboro Lights I need to stop my head-pounding nicotine withdrawals, let alone the booze order to stock the bar. So many alcohol reps have been beyond generous with free booze in the hopes that we'll stock their brand in our venue, but it falls short of the 30 cases of beer, 10 cases each of vodka, gin, whisky and mixers we need to operate. It's more like a selection of fancy cocktails liquor and exotically spiced rums. I wait to the very last moment to place my booze order and write a cheque that I know is going to bounce as soon as it's cashed. I calculate that if I place the order this afternoon, the cheque won't be banked until tomorrow and will need a day or two to clear depending on who they bank with. Putting the weekend between the issuing of the cheque and when the money will be drawn... Fingers crossed I make enough money to cover the cheque over the weekend. I borrow £800 off my Mum's credit card (she still refused to buy me cigarettes) for a change float and an extra £200, so I can do the food catering for the party.

Can you die from someone not calling?

One Day to the Launch Party

He still won't return my calls.

In the Dead of Night Before Launch Day

Shaking from exhaustion, on top of the world's worst hangover, I am so far from being able to sleep. Tossing and turning, my heart is hammering hard and fast against my rib cage. The blood rushing through my body feeds my brain, which is busying over lists of everything that needs to be done to get the place open in T-minus 18 hours. A clock counting backwards to the moment we open our doors, chaotic thoughts, worries, and delusions race through my mind. I'm sleep-deprived but also time-poor and drifting off to sleep is not going to happen. That would make this 'time wasted'. I can sleep once the venue is open. I give up trying to sleep and get up at 2 am, jump in a cab to the 24-Hour Tesco in Dalston and shop for all the ingredients on my list for the canapés. I cook until the sun comes up.

AM Launch Day

He calls. He's cold and distant, but at least he's touching base. He's DJing at the opening tonight and checking in to see how I'm doing. I can't even start with the shitstorm of emotions I feel. But thank fuck he called. At least he hasn't permanently ghosted me. It was on the cards, but I can tell from his tone I'm not in the clear yet.

The charcoal paint is still wet, the gold trims and skirting are still being painted as I race into the venue. Builders are finishing up the snagging. Sawdust reduces visibility by 40 per cent, and a fine layer of dust covers every surface, including the soft furniture and damp paint. The plumbing in the dance floor bar isn't connected yet. It's trial and error, causing the bar to flood and run out into the main club area. 1500 glasses are still in boxes wrapped in individual tissue, and the booze is sitting on a pallet on the dance floor. Fuck.

Can you have a heart attack at 29?

PM Launch Day

My phone won't stop ringing with guest list requests. Old friends and former colleagues all come out of the clubland cracks. The guest list girl (who is also my 'radio-show partner' and hadn't told me I was kicked off the radio show yet) is having a total hissy fit melt-down over the fact her ex is also on the guest list. Her ex is Chas, the Russell Brand lookalike. He leaves long, rambling voicemails and texts which are getting more and more annoyed. I don't want to be dealing with the drama and tell them both to fuck

off and get Daisy to do the list for me. Suppliers want directions for last-minute delivery. I'm losing my shit.
Thank God, my Mum is here. For the last month, she's been mainlining me Pret sandwiches and forcing water down my throat whenever I stop for a moment to think. She's been an invaluable source of help and support. There's no reception in the basement, so every time I have to take a call, I make the dash up to daylight. Every second counts. A number I haven't saved in my contacts keeps ringing me. I'm running out of time to get everything done, but I dash up to take the call the fifth time it dials me back. Little did I know that this call from Addie Chan, a nightlife reporter, will change everything.

The doors open in 30 minutes. I'm covered in paint, dirt, days and days of dry shampoo which has turned to clag from sweat and grime. I have the taste of metal in my mouth from sleep deprivation, I haven't slept in over 24 hours. Someone put the canapés in the freezer, not the walk-in fridge, and they are frozen solid. It's always the small things that tip me over the edge. Fuck. FUCK. FUUUUUUUCK.

The Launch

The venue is already over capacity. The queue snakes down the churchyard five-people deep. There's easily over 350 people inside and another 250 waiting to get in. Beautiful people. Faces from my past. Strangers. Heart-achingly cool club kids. Shoreditch Mafia. It's a kooky mix of East London's most exceptional, pleasure-seekers and fashion darlings mingling with the opposite no-fucks-given about any 'scene' friends. The combination of people shouldn't work, but magically it does. And it's fucking amazing. Faces like Moloko songstress icon Rosin Murphy to beautiful boy model-turned-actor Tom Payne. Paparazzi wait in the churchyard.

A string quartet is booked, to play on the roof of the gingerbread house. Fill the churchyard with chamber music, as guests make their way down the past the church. The pathway is lined with hurricane lamps burning frankincense candles and scattered with a sea of blood-red rose petals. The musicians flat-out refuse to get on the roof. Instead, they play in the cocktail bar as people arrive. It's not as impressive as the roof, but the chamber music is haunting and melodic nonetheless. We've designed a progressive cocktail list: every hour a new cocktail and a paired amuse-bouche canapé. Waitresses dressed in silver-sequin mini dresses with white crisp cotton aprons, the top bib designed as a heart and trimmed with gathered lace, flit around the room. Their hair and makeup are professionally done in a runway style of slicked-back vintage curls; the makeup is stark and modern. It's a clash of eras, and it's exactly what this venue is. A crazy hybrid mix of style, periods, and tastes.

A collection of DJs are booked to play through the night. Paloma Faith does the first set, complete with a red stiletto for headphones; then the fabulous Bishi, Fashion Week darling, Nathan Gregory Wilson, and Rich Pack to take over from Midnight. Rich is the most incredible DJ, but he'd stopped playing gigs and moved into producing music. I begged him to come and DJ the launch party. He begrudgingly agreed and thank fuck he didn't continue the 'white-wine freezeout' on me. His music sets the tone of what makes the atmosphere the palpable beast it is and to go on to reach cult status.

24 hours after the Launch Party

Finally catching up on some elusive sleep. I didn't have the keys to the safe in the office, so there's an American Apparel tote bag busting at the steams with 14k in cash. Grubby crinkled club notes from the launch party takings, even though there was a free bar for four hours. Thank fuck I can cover that bouncy cheque I wrote for the booze order. The idea of a progressive cocktails list was quickly thrown out the window. It became a mad free-for-all at the bar. Drinks were pumped out as fast as the staff could make them. Electric atmosphere. Exceptional music. Beautiful faces. It wasn't how I imagined I would handle the opening. I envisaged gliding down the marble staircase to the sound of enthusiastic cheers and clapping, wearing a flowing floor-length pleated silk gold dress and cape, like if Gucci did a Cleopatra collection. Day dreaming that a small speech and cutting a ribbon would've been a nice touch. Reality is vastly different, of course. It was more running around collecting glasses, no time to talk to anyone, and kinda too embarrassed to. I felt like a hot steaming mess not able to shower properly but sparing a second to chuck a few leftover orchids in my hair and another layer of dry shampoo in attempts to look more presentable amidst the opening madness. The only people I could face were Mum, who was working coat check, and Daisy, who was drowning in the sea of revellers on the door trying to enter the building. Half the night was spent lugging bin bags of ice borrowed from the pub next door after we ran out, unblocking the ladies' toilets, mopping up sick in the pretty VIP booths and firefighting first-night teething issues left, right and centre. Now, that's not to say it wasn't a roaring success. It was. It just means I've been smacked in the face with the title of Nightclub Owner and this divine pleasure-seekers' playground I've created wasn't made by me for me to play in.

I open my laptop, expecting to find an email from the council raining more post-apocalyptic terror on us for our business plan of nipple tassels and vintage striptease.... But it's filled with pages and pages of unread emails. Over 500. All notifications of email/newsletter subscription sign-ups. And press requests for interviews. Thanks to the glowing teaser article by Addie Chan, and a wild-fire of clubland word of mouth.

The consensus: this is something very, very different and very, very fucking cool.

The Bathhouse is born.

*The Fear according to Urban Dictionary: 'The Fear' is the sense that you have done yourself lasting damage after a night of drinking. Its symptoms are:
- A feeling that you are going to die soon (and not just due to other hangover symptoms);
- A sense that people or organisations are out to get you;
- The angst that you may have offended, inappropriately acted or physically attacked someone the night before;
- Foreboding about the next time you meet the people or return to the bar where you degraded yourself the previous night.

The Fear is often accompanied by 'The Remorse,' when you are genuinely ashamed and sorry for the way you behaved, as well as simply frightened for the sake of your own wellbeing.

8

The air up here is hot and surprisingly thick. My teeth are as dry as a box of chalk from the line I just did, a few moments before I'm grabbed and thrown up into the spotlight. I wonder if I look wired? I can't see anything apart from a huge black fuzzy spot - my eyes are trying to adjust to the light. I'm trying to close my mouth discreetly, but my lips won't close around my dry sandy teeth without the tell-tale sign of cocaine 'dry mouth'. Then I run a quick mental check without looking down. Lace tights, gold strappy stilettos. Black and white harlequin-print sequin 70's dress. Good hair. A half-up, medium-sized beehive with the waves past my shoulders, freshly reapplied lipstick, and nose checked for powder in the mirror - twice.

Happpppppybirttthhhhhhhdaytoooooyoooooou! 300-odd of the most fabulous people in London belt out the 'Happy Birthday' song. Most of them are total strangers. 30-years old today. Standing on a grand piano in my very own, actual real-life nightclub, freshly-crowned Night Club of the Year. Hollywood-fucking-amazing-love firmly in motion. I close my eyes and blow out 30 candles on the biggest, most beautiful chocolate cake, decorated with fondant flowers, gold leaf, and piled high with gorgeous truffles.

I don't make a birthday wish because I'm living out my wildest dreams and darkest wishes at this very moment. Everything I could have hoped for, everything I asked the Universe for.

I'm waiting for someone to smash the pretty cake into my face and scream "Wake up, bitch! It's all a fucking dream, and none of this is for you!" Of course, I'm stark naked and everyone is pointing and laughing in my face.

Except, amazingly, that doesn't happen.

We end the night with a lock-in with a handful of friends. The CCTV cameras are switched off. Daisy is asleep under a table with her feet poking out from under the tablecloth, like the Wicked Witch of the East. We drink bottles of Dom Perignon straight from the bottle. I fuck around showing-off my soon-to-be in-famous party trick. Slicing off the top of a Champagne bottle with a knife, sending the cork flying and spraying bubbly across the room and everyone within 10 feet. I'd seen it done on Youtube with a large ceremonial sabre, but figured out that a chef's knife worked just as well. Much to our delight, it worked a charm! Until the next bottle shattered mid-blow and exploded into my stomach, slicing through the fleshy part of my thumb and palm. Instead of a spray of bubbly, this was a 10-foot spray of blood. All the excitement happens after-hours when you own a night club. You can actually enjoy letting your hair down without everyone watching you and not get thrown out for doing whatever you want!

The Bathhouse is on a runaway train of success. A balance between making money and staying true to the creative vision. Working with cutting-edge promoters and filling the club every night is an algorithm that I perfect daily and fiercely protect: a series of precise and highly calculated decisions that make it the most magical place to be. The atmosphere on any given night is electric, dynamic, and ever-changing. We are working with the kings and queens of the underworld to bring a chameleonesque range of performers, guests, VIPs, and customers. We all know that this is something special. A bubble. An institution. An exclusive but all-inclusive cultural movement that we never want to end. This majestic historically-listed building survived the Blitz bombing of London, but it's a miracle it survives a busy weekend, with the thousand-odd pleasure seekers that pass through the doors of our psychedelic dreamland.

The Bathhouse has a Jekyll and Hyde split-personality. Elegant candlelight, crisp white linen, fine dining and heady cocktails in the early evening, enjoyed with a side of salty burlesque dancers and avant-garde cabaret that transforms into a sexually elastic, eccentric, fashion-forward hedonistic late-night club open 'til the sun comes up. Our staff consists of tattooed rock-a-billy pin-up girls and slick-styled teddy boys. With a deep-running passion for spirits and the addictive high-octane life behind the bar, some of the hardcore ones love the place as much as I do. A sweet little Welsh guy called William becomes my right-hand man, all tweed, bow ties, thick-rimmed glasses and slick hair. I warm instantly to the handsome geek-chic classically trained ballet dancer in his first interview. He starts as a bartender and waiter and works his way to the role of assistant manager. He is the master of red velvet. He works his tiny little dancer's arse off, especially during the early cocktail bar hours and cabaret shows. He loves his job and thrives, as long as we don't push him too hard, but of course, I do. He slogs out long hours. I also regularly work 80-hour weeks for this first year. It's draining but a necessary evil. Thankfully, there are 'synthetic support tools' to aid with sleep and energy. Monday to Friday 'office-ish hours' are based in the dingy little office; tasks like marketing and promoting, ordering, rotas, and entertainment programming. The night shift duties loosely involve ensuring the venue is picture-perfect upon opening. Running smoothly, troubleshooting and problem-solving during the shift, and cashing-up and closing down the venue. Which I also manage. But we're now in a position where we have a stable stream of revenue. We've taken on a nightclub manager - Mac - a big Canadian guy with a bundle of nightclub and promotion experience, and the beautiful, Brazilian-smooth and full-of-sass Antonio as our restaurant manager.

Working with promoters is an integral part of operating a nightclub. The Bathhouse is open during the day for coffee, snacks, and light meals, then reopens from 6pm until 10pm for drinks in the cocktail bar and dining room. After 10, the restaurant is stripped down to accommodate our nightclub guests. There will be a cover charge on the door to get in, usually something like £5 before midnight and £10 after. We always like to get the majority of customers in before midnight. That way, we have the perfect formula to hit our 'through-the-door' targets, which equal the bar's spending targets.

Put simply, promoters care about the door charge, and we care about the bar takings. There are varying arrangements between venues and promoters. From as basic as promoters taking the cover charge/door takings, providing and paying for DJs, entertainment, and door staff. And we keep the bar takings and cover all venue outgoings; i.e. bar staff, security, booze and the costs of operating the venue. The thing is that each party often want a piece of the other's takings. This is where it can get stressful, complicated, and moody. When that happens, expectations are raised. In a perfect world, promoters would bring us a well-promoted club night, with a professional, enthusiastic promotion team, a well-curated line-up of performers and DJs. Their guests would arrive before 11:30, relatively sober and not on any recreational drugs, apart from a bit of coke. Purchase an average of 5 drinks, look amazing in the club photography, enjoy the club night, then leave without any issues. That's the dream. I can dream, right?

Cocaine is the best friend of bar takings. It keeps customers pounding through drinks, but it also keeps them steady and on a relativity sober level when consumed together. You don't get 'all weird or aggressive' on it, and it keeps the vibe in the room amazing.

Promoters can be temperamental but venue owners can be pig-headed, believing it's the club that's the main attraction, while promoters believe it's their party that draws the crowds. In truth, if we're each doing our job correctly, we both need each other. The same way a fashion designer has an incredible couture outfit but needs to work with a supermodel to properly showcase their genius creation. Together, they create fashion. My job is to provide this press-worthy venue, yes, but it needs to operate like clockwork. The bars need to be fully stocked with a good range of booze; friendly, cool, speedy bar staff; discreet but thorough barbacks to make sure the place is kept in good order. No spills left on the ground longer than a few minutes, no broken glass, trip-hazard bottles. The glassware is collected, washed, dried and back behind the bar ready to go again and again. The beer needs to be cold and the service hot. The loos need to be tidy and maintained with just the right amount of toilet paper. Not enough and there's a riot on your hands. Too much, then the place will be flooded by 1am with blocked toilets. Security needs to be friendly, communicative, ego-free, thorough, firm but professional, and culturally switched on. All of the venue decoration, fixtures, fittings, and paint needs to be maintained with weekly upkeep. The sound system and DJ equipment need to be to industry standard, serviced, and balanced often. DJs LOVE to fuck around with this. We have to have exit policies in place and ensure patrons leave the venue quietly and safely. Fire alarm systems, noise pollution reduction strategies, drug-safety awareness. Responsible service of alcohol. So basically appear loose, wild and a place to let your hair down. But behind the scenes, we're crossing T's dotting I's and maintaining a solid structure of red tape to keep everyone alive.

… and it has to have the reputation of the most desirable venue to host your parties. Functional but fucking fabulous.

I have high expectations of The Bathhouse promoters. I expect them to hold up their end of the deal. We meet weekly to discuss club nights, any incidents, the breakdown of figures – how many customers through the door, spending per head, and bar takings versus expectations.

The promoters we're collaborating with are a varied crowd, diverse in music policy, unique in the flavour they bring, but always with a cool, cutting-edge approach. These were the major talked-about parties that you wouldn't want to miss. The high-contrast club photography edited with a fine-toothed comb, which we put out onto social media, is a world that everyone desperately wants to be a part of. And anyone could be. Get your name on the guest list and turn up next week. Dress the part or don't. Just don't be a dick when you get to the door.

A curated selection of whimsical and cutting-edge promoters that now call The Bathhouse 'home'. They are strikingly different to ensure there is a diverse entertainment offering and wide net to capture the heart of London's culturally demanding tastes and engage her hedonistic pleasure seekers.

Caligula

Caligula is the brainchild of underground club godfather Jim Warboy and a celebrity fashion stylist called Leo Belicha. Warboy is the man driving club nights and music movements that pave the way for the rest of the scene. I'd been to a few of his parties during the new rave trend. Not really my vibe at the time, but Warboy and I were both mentioned in an article by one of my old pretty boys, stating we were at the forefront of the next clubland movement, using digital platforms. This was at the time when social media first came into play. We both grab the opportunity to jump in to connect with talent and party scenes directly. Leo is the walking parody of a fashion daaarrrrrling. He is Brazilian, and completely bald but always with a jauntily placed statement hat or mask. He's often wearing a floor-length cape, which he uses to pose in a Dracula stance when being photographed (the cape, pulled across the bottom half of his face), designer shorts, knee socks and very fancy shoes. He is always styling the newest rising stars and is so well connected with all the iconic fashion darlings and dresses pop royalty, Rihanna. He calls everyone 'biiiitch'. Leo is a Fashion-Week staple with an equal amount of arrogant piggishness and charming charisma. Warboy is serious and not into the fluffy, fussy fashion side of Caligula (although he has been known to change into a pair of black mid-heel pumps after his DJ set). He cares about creating and curating scenes and subcultures. Music is the core driver of everything he does. He's a total perfectionist and utter control freak, in a professional way, whereas Leo cares about VIP treatment and diva dollies. Somehow the two visions uncomfortably collide and create the hottest club night in town - Caligula.

Caligula has electric energy and is highly charged with sexuality. It's a scene lead by fashion and electro music. The mix of Leo's VIP little black book and Warboy's exacting music policy and performer connections make it an instant success. The crowd is the new incarnation of abstract '90s New York club kid scenes, mashed up with the glittery glamour of Studio 54 boys dressed as girls, girls dressed as boys, trans, non-binary, non-conforming crowd. Drag queens, daddy's-trust-fund student fashionistas, costume designers, models, muses, and actors. It pulsates creativity and individuality at the same time as equal amounts of sex and lust. A place where everyone is allowed to be exactly who they want to be, even if it's only for one night a week. A beautiful addition to the scene is host Andre J; a transcendent soul, more beautiful than anyone in the room, inside and out. Andre's soul shines. Straight out of New York and the first male to be on the cover of French Vogue, with Carolyn Murphy, dressed in the tightest mini dress, killer pins towering in stilettos, a full-face beard, long shining weave and an equally radiant grin. Always right at the heart of the party. In my opinion, the ultimate host and the ultimate human.

Each week, there is an unofficial whisper: murmurs of a special guest or performer. Nothing is ever officially announced. You just have to be there to catch it. This is the magic of Caligula. Some of the guests and performers, so far, include Bjork, Boy George, Princess Julia, Lovely John Jo, the 11th Dr Who - Matt Smith, Jodie Harsh, Massive Attack, Ana Matronic from Scissorsisters and soon-to-be activist Munroe Bergdorf. You never know who will pop up in the DJ booth, singing at the baby grand piano or topless on the dance floor. Caligula crosses boundaries, has no gender, no aggression and lots of drugs.

Boom Boom Club

Riots rhythms and gin-soaked cabaret. Trail-blazing, hell-raising, the new wave of burlesque... the Boom Boom Club! A richly decadent, layered, dark yet hilarious cabaret show. Later in the evening, delinquent beats and wildcat howls from the Boom Boom Club DJs - from '50s swing and rock n' roll to girl groups, surf, sleaze and exotica. A hedonistic feast for the senses, from the exquisite to the extraordinary, from the lyrical to the downright despicable. It's perhaps the most daring and innovative rock n' roll cabaret in town.

The format of the night is a decadent supper-club stroke cabaret-style show followed by DJs and dancing 'til dawn. Produced by Dave Harris, a slick vintage-suited and booted professional promoter and his creative partner, who is ready to spit his dummy out of the DJ box at any moment. Curated weekly performances by Vicky Butterfly, the most amazing burlesque performer in London. She's like the living incarnation of a Venetian music box porcelain ballerina, a priceless family heirloom. With poise, style, and grace. She makes her own costumes which are so exquisitely crafted they look fit for the V&A Museum. Ms Butterfly's stage is custom-built, a miniature Theatre Papillion, with gilded staging and red velvet curtains, like it was made to fit perfectly into The Bathhouse. Dusty Limits is the compère and host. His acid tongue, vast vocal range and quick wit make the experience a mix of pleasure and pain. You never have any idea of what he is going to do or say next. Nothing is sacred, and nobody is off-limits. The last resident performer is Kitty Bang Bang, who is both dangerous and sexually charged. She is a fast-paced, energetic, loud and hypnotic entertainer. Totally captivating, whether she is lighting herself on fire en-pointe to 'Welcome to the Jungle' or pouring gallons of milk down her feline-like, curvy body, popping out of a bejewelled trash can. Pure rock and roll anarchy.

Boom Boom club feels like an intimate backstage preview. Each week, a feisty new line-up. From the classical piano player and beauty Chrys Columbine, performing her act 'Naked Nocturne', a flawless performance of Chopin's 'Nocturne' on the grand piano. While disrobing, she never misses a note, finishing in nipple tassels and a demure smile. To the hilariously dry stand-up comedian and magician, Piff the Magic Dragon. Dressed in a full-body dragon costume, he's all self-deprecating humour and deadpan delivery. He is assisted by the scene-stealing Mr Piffles, a tiny teenie rescued

Chihuahua in a matching miniature dragon costume, now with their own headline residency and calling Las Vegas home.

But don't be fooled by the words 'cabaret' or 'burlesque'. These words are twee and tired. Boom Boom Club is none of this. This is a new movement, but cabaret and burlesque the closest notions to hook the concept on. It is visually decadent, the performers outrageous, all singing, all dancing, striptease and comedy at it most raucous and raw.

The customers are top-to-toe immaculately turned out in vintage three-piece suits, spats and highly shined shoes. Flat caps and perfectly Brylcreemed hair. The ladies are the most exquisite that vintage has to offer. From swing skirts and frothy petticoats to duchess satin second-skin wiggle dresses and seamed stockings. Victory rolls and French twists. Highly bejewelled hairpins, fascinators; never a hair out of place. The guests ooze glamour, class, and style. This is a dedicated crowd who returns each week. They swing-dance, Lindy hop and jive. They love dry martinis, red wine, small-batch gin, whisky on the rocks, and champagne. They don't drink as much in volume as a traditional club night, but they drink better-quality liquor from the back bar and steadily sip on drinks throughout the evening.

The DJs play electro-swing, psych, rock-a-billy-blues, soul, and vintage rock and roll. The dance floor is a colourful patchwork of twists and twirling skirts, sequins, and diamantes. It's a kaleidoscope of highly skilled dancers.

Intriguing guests so far have been Amy Winehouse and showgirl Immodesty Blaze.

Boom Boom Club is the darling that the press can't stop talking about.

Love to Love

This is, by far, the most commercial, pop culture club night but it still retains that all essential cool factor. It's high-street fashion meets celebrity pages and gossip columns. Paparazzi hover in the churchyard and doorstop the customers. Love to Love is the party place for actors and models who are on the precipice of cracking the big time. It's fun: shiny with just the right amount of cheese. Playful enough to attract crowds by the clubful but unpretentious enough not to alienate anyone.

This club night is a collaboration between the princess of pop Sophie Ellis Bextor and her husband, Richard Jones from The Feeling, joined with the TV producer Lucie Veitch and lifestyle aficionado Anna Barnett. Together, they produce this fun and super popular night. They are on the cusp of the Instagram avalanche.

It's tongue in cheek, and the DJs are often more style over substance, but the crowds don't care. Playing Lady Gaga, Rihanna and tracks from Footloose and Dirty Dancing, it's a hot mess of music. They put care into planning themed events and relish in dress-up parties. Highlights so far are Sophie Ellis Bextor dressed as 'Carrie', performing the 'Monster Mash'. For the Christmas event, Tony Mortimer of East 17 was booked to play Stay with a full backing band.

The customers are on the younger end of The Bathhouse spectrum, usually around 18-25. They show up wearing the latest trends straight from the street-style sections of Grazia and faces from the pages of Stylist magazine. Pretty boys and beautiful girls who drink vodka cranberry or vodka lemonade and house white wine. And they drink lots. It's messy and a little wild, but the party clears out around 2 am, which is an indication that the majority don't seem to use drugs. The regulars include Alexa Chung, Caroline Flack,

Nick Grimshaw, Henry Holland, Ruth Lorenzo, Pixie Geldof, and Jameela Jamil.

The Night With No Name

Seriously, we didn't name it until Daisy joined us and christened it Golden Birdcage. Even then nobody used the name. It was used as a listing for magazine and press, and finally, we agreed it was time to start advertising beyond just word of mouth and Facebook. It has always just been 'Bathhouse on Saturday night'.

This is my Bathhouse. The night which, in my eyes, was the most authentic version of the venue. It pivoted around the music. A vast melting pot of genres, eras, music styles and artists. No hook, no gimmick or theme. It was just fucking amazing music, in a fucking great venue with fucking awesome customers.

It grows into a solid and intense burning club night that was always at venue capacity by midnight, with a decent-sized queue to get in and a hotch-potch' of guests. The average guest list ran around 220 people, and the VIP booths booked up well in advance. It always sees the most substantial bar takings and has the most amazing customers. And it is mine. Along with the door takings (which, as always, is the icing on the very delicious clubland cake).

Maybe because it was on Saturdays, which naturally are the biggest night for people to go out, but at the same time, none of it was an accident. The Bathhouse wasn't a place you'd just happen to stumble by. It was hidden, tucked away behind the church and graveyard. It was a place people found out about through friends of friends. The Bathhouse had zero aggro but still had the right amount of energy for things on the dance floor to kick off at any moment. I think we're responsible for bundles of hook-ups during the pre-Tinder days! From week one, it's in full swing to the day we close our doors and hand over the keys.

Rich and I would always arrive at The Bathhouse together: two perfectly polished love-birds ready to take on the night. We both peel off at the bottom of the marble staircase, parting ways. He will DJ and I run the club. We barely speak more than a few words during the evening. But as I moved around the venue in and out of tasks, conversations, his music seeps through me: it feels like a beautiful love letter. These songs are just for me. His subtle choices, his different sets and mind-blowing skills. It evolves with the night. Shifts and shapes the dancefloor. I hear the opening notes dropping of the new mash-up track he'd been working on in the home studio into the mix. I notice everything. I know the exact bar he mixes x into y. These are our songs. The soundtrack to our life together.

This is our time and I fucking love it.

On Saturdays at The Bathhouse, you'll see dirty rock boys and glam indie girls, Mods, Northern Soul kids, east London natives, and clans of people who didn't give a flying fuck about fads or the latest trends. They were there because they just loved the music and atmosphere. From T. Rex to Fleetwood Mac to the Kinks. During the first few hours, they drink old-fashioned blackberry brambles and Doris Gay martinis, my most-loved cocktail after the classic margarita. The drinks were served by William during the civilised candlelit cocktail hour before the madness and mayhem of the club night crept in. Then it's cans of ice-cold Red Stripe, Prosecco drunk straight from the bottle, endless shots of Patron tequila and rows and rows of Jägerbombs. And a small amount of coke; enough to keep the party going but not so much as to make it weird. It was always done behind closed doors in the bathrooms, but you can still hear the deep sniff with the simultaneous loo flush or 'cough'.

Officially, we have a zero-tolerance drug policy. If anyone is found brazenly doing them out in the open, they'll be instantly removed from the venue. We also have toilet attendants stationed in the bathroom to minimise public usage, but it's a part of the nightclub culture. People don't go crazy on cocaine, plus they still drink. MDMA is also okay in small doses. It's when other less sociable drugs start trending that it gets tricky. The rise of ketamine and GHB had to be stamped out quickly. It crept into the Caligula crowd over a few weeks, with hallucinating customers flopping around like jellyfish and crawling like sloths down the stairs, but we address it. It's gross and doesn't fit The Bathhouse scene. I am not a fan of hallucinogenic drugs. In my club or in my body. *

The VIP booths were booked mostly for birthday celebrations. They come with a drink and entry package, so guests receive a shared cocktail in a bespoke miniature cast-iron bathtub, kindly created by Bombay Sapphire especially for us. The drinks are as mixed and random as the beautiful crowd.

The celebrity guests are as pretty much of a mishmash as the other key elements of the club. Prince Harry popped by for a late dinner and drinks, with full security detail with firearms in tow, buying a round of tequila for the staff on the way out. Bill Murray and David Schwimmer. (My gut feeling is a fancy concierge is handing out our details for where's good to go for drinks.) Ke$ha had the release of her debut album, 'Animal', here. Keira Knightly poked her head in to check out the architecture of the building. Vivian Westwood, who said the venue was stunning but would definitely be better without any music (I tend to agree the moment before the doors are open to the public: the venue is haunting, mesmerising in its beauty. But also the anticipation of what the night will be). Pretty poppet Little Boots and nice as pie Duffy. Always mischievous Noel Fielding dicking around in the DJ booth. Plus loads more that slip in and out unnoticed like the tide.

*I was visiting Rich at one of his DJ gigs at Camden Bar Fly. The promoter never paid the going rate, but he balanced his payment with your drug of choice. Rich's drug of choice was cocaine, the same as mine, but the promoter's personal taste was placed in the ketamine camp. As the night goes on, I swing by to see the rogue promoter, and he holds up two bags. One of ketamine and one is cocaine: I can visually tell the difference. The ketamine is more powdery and pure white, and the coke is a slightly thicker grain; the powder is slightly off-white. I grab the bag and head into the loos. We repeat this little game as the night goes on, bouncing around having a great time and drinking loads of beers. I stop by on the way out, to grab a line, while Rich packs up his records. I'm feeling pretty drunk and high now. I have to close one eye to focus on the two bags of powder, grab the coke, go to the toilet and rack up a big fat line for the road. High-five Rich on the way out and clap the gear into his hand and wait for him at the bar, with his pal Jason. I rest my elbow on the bar, and the wooden floor starts dipping and falling away from under me. The floor's turned to spongy jelly, there's an earthquake splitting the ground apart. I grab Jason's arm and move my mouth in weird slow motions. I can't hear my voice. "STOOOPPPPP RICH!!! IT'S KETAMMMIINNNEEEEEE!!" I slip into a massive K-hole of bright green rolling grass hills that move like a conveyor belt on a wonky sushi train. Enormous Super Mario mushrooms bob around the room, and the red and white polka-dot caps repeatedly turn inside out. Spinning around and around. A time warp has sucked me in, and Rich has been gone for three hours. He's left me here alone. I can't get out...

That'll teach me for taking liberties with someone else's 'coke'. Rich was gone for less than two minutes. Jason made it to the toilet, banging on the door as Rich's nose was about to hit the powder. That is one kooky drug. I like my mind, where I can see it, firmly placed in the reality of my skull.

9

With the most earnest of promises, I crossed my heart, hope-to-die and stick a needle in my eye that I will NOT drink two-for-a-fiver white wine again. Keeping this promise I made to Rich a few months ago, after I went fucking bonkers throwing the wig at him at 666, is made a little easier as I can now pinch a pretty posh bottle of Sancerre from the fridge at work. But still, a promise is a promise. And with it, that is how we move forward with my Hollywood-fucking-amazing-love story in the days after white-wine-wig-gate. (To this very day, he still shudders when we talk about it, and apparently, it was touch and go whether he was going to continue seeing me. Fickle fuck.)

And remember the beautiful blonde behind the DJ booth? Don't worry, I haven't forgotten to fill you in about her. She's a go-go dancer from Ibiza. Yep, I had no idea that's a real job, either. She's the girlfriend of one of Rich's friends. They were just chatting in the DJ booth. As simple as that. Nothing happened, nothing was going to happen. They were just talking. But the thing is, I had wound myself up into a frenzy while he was away in America. Fucking social media. He'd been posting pics and getting tagged in photos with LA babes. All just friends, but why the fuck was every last one of them so beautiful? Long-haired boho beauties who oozed a whimsical, carefree vibe, like they could just fall onto his cock, and it would all just be a sweet misunderstanding on my part. I spiralled into crazed jealousy for a little while. He has so many past fucks, baggage and ex-girlfriends, it is genuinely unnerving. Every party, club night, or art show we go to, seemingly every other girl we bump into on the street corners, some waitress at The Bathhouse opening party, he had fucked them all. My stomach feels heavy, like it's filled with cement. Shoreditch is a landmine populated with the ghosts of Rich Pack's past fucks. And while my insides are cut up, like I've eaten a plateful of broken glass and barbed wire, he didn't care about my past, all the pretty boys. He never asks questions or breaks a sweat like I do. I had to trust him if this was going to work.

Monogamy and total, utter truthfulness, we ploughed forward together head-first into deep, sweet, blinding and furious love. The crazy wall of protection I hide behind slowly dissipates and transforms into an unwavering trust.

As we head to the hotel room, I patronisingly remind Rich, "The beach won't look like the travel brochure. So don't get your hopes up." This is because I'm a beach expert, you see: in Australia, everyone claims we have the world's best beaches. Now, I know this is utter bullshit spun by the Australian tourism board to make sure no one ever leaves. Right in front of my eyes is a pristine sandy beach, postcard-perfection. With palm trees that reach lazily towards the sand, their fronds gently swaying back and forth in the breeze and casting their cool shadows on the warm sand along the shores of the sparkling diamond sea. The Australian tourism board has clearly never been to the Caribbean. Paradise exists And I am never going home. Ever.

Our first trip together. Seven days on the beachfront in Tobago. Salty skin, rum-heavy cocktails garnished with the little umbrella and afternoon sex naps with nowhere to be. It's the first time I've ever been able to upgrade to a beachfront room.

I feel like a proper adult.

We cycled down the unpaved roads to a nearby heritage park called Pigeon Point. Beautiful palm trees, tropical gardens, and endless sandy beaches, completely deserted apart from us. We decide to take up the reception's suggestion to go on a glass-bottom boat trip. So we sat at the beach bar, drinking beers, trying not to burn while we wait for our boat tour. I keep thinking about The Bathhouse and what's happening. Has it burnt down yet? A customer overdosed, or maybe it's been raided by the police? It's starting to get annoying for us both.

I need to let it go and forget about work.

The boat trip is stunning. A glass-bottom boat with a brightly coloured painting of Bob Marley in primary colours down the side. The glittering water shimmers in every shade of topaz blue to emerald green. Flowery blooms of coral and glistening tropical fish dance under the glass panel. The wind whips away my worries, the never-ending sea, salt air and the curved horizon shimmering in the distance. It's all pretty fucking spectacular. I'm tucked in the crook of Rich's arm. We cruise in the dinky rocking little boat for miles, just us two and the driver. He doesn't really speak English, but none of us is in the mood to chat.

He cuts the engine and points to the water. It's clear and looks shallow, but we are miles out to sea? I have no idea what he means. Get out in the middle of the fucking ocean? Miles from the shore? What the fuck?

We slip into the water. Is he leaving us here? Robbing us of our thongs and a few loose coins? It's surprisingly warm and shallow. He hands us a laminated A4 sheet.

The Nylon Pool. According to legend, this area of the sea is magical. For women 'of a certain age', it's said to reverse ageing by 10 years.

For men, the water is reported to promote 'male enhancement'. For young couples, the story says if they kiss in the waters of the Nylon Pool, their love will last a lifetime.

Rich holds both my hands. We take a deep breath and kiss underwater. The fact he takes the lead for such a sweet romantic gesture sends my heart soaring on butterfly wings. He is mostly jokes and bravado, so the unguarded sweetness catches me by surprise and makes my stomach do a pike flip.

This underwater kiss sealed the deal.

On the lazy ride back to the resort, there are lots of roadside stalls selling shells and handmade souvenirs for tourists. We're not in the market for trinkets, but something piques our interest. A hoarse whisper as we ride by "…Cocaine, Charlie, hashish, weed. Cocaine, Charlie, hashish, weed. Cocaine, Charlie, hashish, weed…"

We keep to the road and head back to the bar for some sundown cocktails by the pool. I love over-dressing for dinner on holidays, in my vintage '50s tropical-print strapless dress with a full swing skirt, matching bolero crop jacket, hair piled into a messy side bun through which I've woven fresh magenta bougainvillaeas and with Vivienne Westwood Melissa pale pink slingbacks with big black hearts on the toes. Ready for our dinner date on the beach. It's totally deserted and lit with tiki torches and citronella-oil burners. The sky is pitch black and dazzling stars twinkle next to the perfectly round cheese moon. Far from the glowing radioactive night skies of London. We eat lobster and whole fish and drink frosty pints of Caribbean beer with tequila chasers. It's twee-level romantic, straight out of a scene from one of Elvis' Hawaiian movies, when he courts his love interest. But in the Caribbean. You know what I mean. It's clichéd but epic cute.

Back at the resort, it's Margaritas in the cigar lounge then nightcaps in the piano bar. Endless hours of those drunk, intoxicating getting-to-know-you talks. I need to know every single thing about him. What was he like as a kid? Did he sleep walk? Who was his favourite teacher at school? What was his best Christmas present? A million questions and answers that go deep into the night. I can't get enough precious background information.

I need to live in his blood.

We wander along the beach and slip into the sea for a skinny dip, lured to the water by the idea of moonlit sex, but I chicken out halfway through. I'm too creeped by the black water, thoughts of hungry hermit crabs or a deep-sea monster coming up to nip me on the clit! Soaking wet, shoes off, we walk back to the room. I keep one eye closed to stay focused on the path and a very wobbly Rich Pack.

Ahhhhhh... The sweet relief of the freezing air conditioning and the comforting background noise of lapping waves mixed with the sound of The Simpsons playing on the laptop. Balancing perfectly still, with one foot on the ground to stop the room spinning, I ripped off my dress. It's so claustrophobic. I'm wet and sandy, stripped down to my knickers, taking in deep breaths, desperately trying to sober up. I need to be sick, need the bathroom to wash my face. That will help. The tiles are moving under my feet. I put one foot in front of the other. Breathe. Blurgh. Breathe. The deep breath doesn't help. Instead, projectile vomit blasts across the room like a semi-automatic machine gun. All kinds of drinks sprayed all over the pristine bedroom. Over the entire hotel room. Rich jumps up to help, right as I slip in the lumpy red seafood-sick and fly straight up into the air. My tanned feet flip on over my head, above me as I fall, and feel my massive white DD boobs flop and slap me in the face. I land splat flat on my back in my pile of sick in a reverse belly flop. A back flop. Scrambling like a turtle stuck on its shell, I can't get up. Rich grabs my arm, pulling me up as I spew again, all over him. It gets caught in his bracelets and wrist. I'm ice-skating in my own sick. He slides me to the bathroom where I spend the next few hours, ears deep in the rim of the toilet. I have a red mark across my boobs from the pressure of my drunk body leaning against the toilet.

I wake up to the gorgeous sound of birds singing and waves lapping the shore. I open my eyes to the sight of a beautiful new day and how lov- ... Oh fuuuuuuuucccccck!... It all comes flooding back: the sick, the flopping tits... doom. I've never even farted in front of him. This is bad. I roll around to start my big apology and ready to launch into the world's best making up ... and the only thing that could make it all better happened. "Don't come close," he mutters. "I've pissed the bed."

Since I'd hogged the toilet all night, he went to sleep with a bladder full of cocktails, beers, and tequila. This was after he did a Pulp Fiction Mr Wolf drunk-style midnight clean up and mopped the sick up with the weird top blanket hotels have that no one ever uses. He dumped it outside, and now it's black, teeming with a biblical plague of ants, blowflies and unidentified tropical insects.

Argh, I don't feel much like a smug adult right about now, looking out of my beachfront room, past the nest of sick and flies, but the lure of the hair of the dog, a medicinal swim in the ocean, and a soul-reviving bike ride quickly fix that.

A few breakfast beers later and we can't help but wonder what the coke would be like so close to the motherland. It's just a hop, skip and a drive through the jungle and a small jump across the water to Columbia. We're off to see a man about a conch shell...

Yep, we did. You can take the cokeheads out of East London but...... Really really really fucking stupid idea, huh?

We ride back past the stall selling shells and tropical trinkets. The same guy is there. "Cocaine, weed, hash..." I pretend to look at the shells and wind chimes while Rich starts casually chatting shit with him. He quickly offers to sort out some cocaine. He tells us it's 50 USD and we need to buy a big conch shell and to come back in 30 minutes. We ride away. I don't have a good feeling about this. Is it a setup? We circle back, and the guy hands Rich a plastic bag with a large spiky conch shell, takes the money, and whispers "Quick! Go, go, GO!" We peddle as fast as our little cocaine-loving legs will go, right as a tropical thunderstorm rolls in. We ride and ride through the pelting hot rain. My lungs are burning. Legs are jelly, speeding round the corner, past the resort gates, and straight up to our room. Expecting an ambush of police or a blackmail drug set-up. I've watched too many movies and episodes of 'Banged Up Abroad'. I don't know why he told us to "Go! Go!" Maybe because of the storm coming, not police dogs...

The coke is twisted tightly into the spiralled centre of the conch. We sit on the balcony doing lines, smoking Marlboro Lights, and drinking beers, watching the storm roll through, ripping the sea apart and lighting up the sky with cracking electric bolts.

In the morning, the light creeps through the blinds, and we hide like vampires all day, watching 'True Blood' in our bed that still smells a bit of day-old sick as the Caribbean paradise, in all its glory, makes its way through the day outside. We order room service, rum punches and a couple of rounds of club sandwiches.

What fucking savages we are. I know, I know. We don't deserve to be in paradise. But it was a fucking great first trip together.

The venue didn't burn down, the police didn't raid us, and The Bathhouse world keeps on spinning. Our club nights build, we increase our staff, place ever-growing booze orders and more customers come each week. In droves.

We've recently been crowned with a load of lovely accolades including 'Club of the Year' - 'Number 1 Thing To Do Now!' - 'Hottest Venue' - 'Top 50 Things To Do In London'.

They say all publicity is good publicity. Well, kinda. It would be great if I had a venue where I could extend legal capacity, floor space and add amenities, like extra toilets and bar service areas when I need them, but sadly that's not the case. We have a scrapbook bursting with complimentary press articles and kind reviews that send customers to us in droves. Queues of people trying to get in, snaking down the churchyard. Overwhelmed security who work placating customers who aren't going to enter the venue for at least another few hours; promoters freaking out as they see pound signs standing in the churchyard, slipping out of their grasp the longer they wait outside. An overly full venue means customers can't get to the bar or the toilets, can't move about without a ball ache, can't dance and will leave due to pure frustration, leave a shit review and never return. That's on top of then telling everyone how shit it is. Our neighbours have installed additional CCTV pointing straight at our venue and hired security, so our customers don't go near their building. We are in a vicious circle of success, biting us in the arse. Things need to be ironed out. It's time for some reconfiguration. We now open earlier, drop the entry price, and add a happy hour between 9-10 pm to get customers in earlier, enticing them with a discount after 2am, for when the early bird crowds head off.

We get tougher with promoters, but we can't seem to get it working smoothly. The new staff aren't the same. They don't have the passion or desire to live and breathe Bathhouse. Slowly, I find I don't recognise the faces behind the bar, and I question Mac. "Oh, that's such and such." He adds a little bit of background as to why they're so great. The customers are coming from further afield, like Essex and Lewisham, now. Our initial East London trendsetting, hypnotic, exotic, fashion-forward crowd have started migrating on to the next exciting new pasture. It's a curse of the industry, but we're grateful that they helped establish Bathhouse as an aspirational cultural movement. I still have my solid, beautiful Saturday night crowd.

Holidays, celebrations, and landmark events are a big deal in clubland. Customers are up for any excuse to indulge in festive cocktails and dance the night away, all in the name of marking a holiday. Promoters also put effort into themes, special guest DJs, entertainment, and promotion. You can also rely on excellent bar takings if the preparation is in place.

It's also a way for me to mark time. Often, weekends blend into the weekdays, as most day and night routines are similar, but distinctive events and holidays punctuate the passage of time in my memory. This is always how I think, in terms of how things happen at work. I do the same thing with my personal life and my love affair with Rich. Holiday, seasons, times of year, what we were wearing. Maybe time is a haze for me, swinging between drunk and high, or as I like to call it, elegantly wasted. Fun drunk or necessary stimulation and self-medication. It's a foggy high that slides into a series of comedowns and hangovers. None of it is excellent for my short-term recall, but my long-term memory can hitch a ride back on the holidays for prompts.

Halloween

Our VIP booths are fully booked, and the guest list is apparently looking nice and long. I can see the promoters spreading the word about the parties on social media, which pleases me. A box pallet of pumpkins has been delivered, ready to be hand-carved by one of our kooky, cool-as-fuck kitchen staff, Maggie. He whittles carvings of witches on brooms, craggy ghouls, even the double-C Chanel logo into the festive vegs. We collected ten bin bags full of crunchy golden autumn leaves from Victoria Park (careful to avoid the camouflaged dog shit and syringes) to spread all over the floor of the club and smear blood-red handprints on the mirrors. Miles and miles of spider webbing deck every corner of the club and we add red gel lenses over the lighting as a finishing touch. Theme décor always looks impressive when it's simple but high volume. The leaves are a bastard to clean up, but they add eerie drama as you walk down the staircase covered in leaves and hurricane lamps. The venue looks like a haunted Victorian chamber.

The place is packed, and everyone loves it. The bars are running smoothly, the venue is at capacity at 10.30pm, and our customers arrive early in the evening, dressed to the nines as Love to Love are hosting the party 'Dead Icons and their Lovers'. We are down a barback, so I nip out and start pushing glassware through the dishwater. It's hot, and I'm sweating, but each glass back to the bar is worth a potential £5. It's worth the sweat. There are two fire doors between the washroom and the dance floor, so I can hear pockets of club noise every time the doors open with the staff's comings and goings. I like keeping my hands busy, especially if I've had a few lines. I just switch off and push through, giving into the zen of the repetitive task. Apart from the wet feet. I zone out for a bit. Silence. That's weird. Both doors must be closed. Then I hear angry jeering. Fuck. I run out into the main part of the club, still wearing my white plastic apron and Marigold washing-up gloves. It's pitch black. The emergency lighting kicks in, but it's dim with barely enough light for me to make my way to the DJ booth. It doesn't matter. I know every inch of this club, so I can dart around in the dark. Some cunt is tangled in a load of cords, sprawled out on the floor. His once-full pint has spilt onto the power board connecting all the DJ equipment. Security had already given him a warning to stop fucking around. All the electrics are linked, and if there's a power surge or a fuse blows, it switches to emergency mode. That means flashing red lights and a siren kick in, ready to prompt clubgoers to evacuate the venue.

Right. Next stop, the electrical power-board cupboard. It's behind a concertina door. To get to it requires moving tables, chairs, and customers out of the way. Security helps me clear the space, and I scan through the board. The semi-circle of eyes burn into my back, watching me. Fuck. One of the fuses has blown, and it's smouldering. I take it out and hope I can replace the wire by hand, but the whole unit is singed and partially melted. Everyone is jeering and chanting. I'm sweating, trying to replace the wire. I slam it back in, flick the switch and pray for the lights to come back on. Instead, it cracks and sparks fly out with a puff of smoke. Ah, fuck. This is not a patch job. Victorian electrics. This is a job for an electrician. It's 1am on Sunday morning. I dial my regular guy but just to go through the motions. I don't even know why I bother, because I know he won't answer at this hour. But I can always hope he's drinking in the area, which he often does. There's no other choice, I have to clear out the club. The customers begrudgingly trail out, and we have to evacuate them out of the churchyard and away from the neighbours' new security patrol. Then it's back down to face the promoters. To be fair to the Love to Love girls, they are okay-ish about it. They're a bit drunk and have taken in loads of door money. But the inevitable backlash will come over the weekend, once customers start complaining about the paid entry and having to leave the party early. It will cost me a load of drink vouchers and a free admission next week, so I can reimburse the promoters. But poor fucking me. The lost bar-take will be over 10k. Who's going to compensate me that? Certainly not that little cunt in the DJ booth who scurried out before I could slap his stupid little rat face.

As predicted, a firm but fair email from the promoters requesting reimbursement and drink vouchers as compensation for the power shortage. This tasty little Monday morning came with a cherry on top. A summons to the City Police Station in Bishopsgate by the licensing department Chief Inspector.

Sitting stiff and straight, like a visitor to the principal's office.

I'm wearing my most sensible outfit. Puff-shoulder tuxedo jacket and matching pencil skirt. No tits on show today, although maybe that would have helped? Waiting in his fishbowl meeting room in the middle of the station, I stare at the sizeable three-ringed binder sitting proudly in the middle of the table. Apparently, it's a dossier (I had to look up the word dossier as soon as I left the station. It's a factual collection of evidence). In it is a statement of evidence collected by Dash Towers Security and Management, our arsey neighbours, a 55-storey sleek office block. Presented by their legal team with an affidavit stating the information is true.

It is beautifully presented, complete with colour dividers, good quality plastic sleeves, a table of contents, image library, appendix, tabs with typed labels and even a reference section. And packed full, right to the very top of the curved-arch bit. My gut feeling and that overstuffed folder of evidence tell me I'm in deep shit. I skip the little icebreaker joke about their impeccable presentation and stationary choices I would've made in other circumstances.

'Evidence' of Bathhouse customers having sex in the churchyard, side streets and the forecourt of Dash Towers. Heterosexual sex, homosexual sex, and a mixed-group orgy, documented with enough pictures to make your eyes water. Illicit drug use, drug selling and purchasing. Urination. Defecation. Loitering. Littering. Drunk and disorderly behaviour. Submitted in a logbook, supported with photographs, witness statements, and CCTV footage logged, dated and saved on USBs.

I need wine. Now. Mainlined right into my veins to get through this meeting. I should have brought my lawyer. We go through every single piece of evidence. I explain, make excuses. My words are met with deadpan, stony eyes that don't seem to blink. It looks much worse than it really is. I agree we could do with implementing a few changes to minimise the strain on the surrounding community. Also, thank you for bringing this to our attention so very thoroughly. Teeth gritted, and fingers crossed behind my back. I politely question whether this is a breach of privacy, as some of the photographs are on private property? And, ever so diplomatically, inquire whether it's been established that all of these people had, in fact, been in our venue? There are multiple late-night bars in the area. Even before we moved to the churchyard, it was a known meeting place for nocturnal 'hook-ups'. But I have to play the game and make constructive, tangible changes to policies and procedures. Going through the evidence systematically but never apologising or getting angry. Ready to offer solutions to the issues but also never overcommitting to anything unrealistic, because we have to live with the changes I propose. The suggestions go on the licence as 'recommendations', and if we get caught not following them, our licence will go to a review tribunal – which I promise you, never ends well. You may get taken to a review for one small thing, but it opens up other recommendations to be made when the review is in session. For example, you could have your opening hours reduced even if you are summoned to an investigation for not managing your waste removal properly. It's a dangerous game.

I propose:

- Adding two roaming security members in high-vis vests to the team

- Introducing a policy of no bottles or glassware outside the venue

- Creating a smoking area/pen to contain smokers. With area attendant. (This will be impossible but effective if it works. I can see the satisfaction on their faces when I bring this up.)

- No more than 15 people smoking at a time.

- Not allowing lingering around or near Dash Towers

- Having security to escort customers to Liverpool Street Station or Broadgate Street, to avoid loitering.

- Increasing CCTV cameras to cover more of the outside of the venue and perimeters.

All do-able but annoying. And an added expense I could do without but, to be fair, the meeting went better than I imagined, considering the mega book of tattle-tale dossier. But this means impending police visits over the next few weeks to months, which is never pleasant. We'd stayed neatly pretty under their radar until now.

I still need that wine. And a line.

I go straight from the police meeting to see Rich at the Scolt's Head pub in De Beauvoir Town and have a very stiff drink. He's having a beer with one of our drug dealers. Rich has the touch: effortlessly and easily makes friends with everyone. We have a few dealers, but this one is our preferred Number One dealer. He is connected to one of the biggest crime families in London. He's got the best quality coke and a fair price, but he operates during social hours; i.e. he finishes work at 11pm, which can be a problem. This is why we currently have three other dealers. Number Two has good gear and comes after 11pm, but won't drop off near the club due to the high number of police, but is a reliable backup if we are home or if Number One is out-of-hours. Number Three is the one who comes out after 5am. The gear's nowhere near as good and way more expensive, but hey, we're not fussy at 5am, wanting to keep the party going. 'The party' is usually just Rich and me playing our favourite songs on Youtube in his studio, drinking cans of Red Stripe (these are my favourite kinda parties). Then there's the last resort, Number Four, for when hell has frozen over. Shit gear but worse than the shit gear is the fact he wants to come in and hang out. We learn this the hard way. Number Four is only for when we're absolutely desperate or having a house party.

Rich is chatting to Number One. He's more London than London is, with good manners and follows a set of unspoken rules. He comes to my club but would never sell gear there, which would be disrespectful to Rich and me. He buys lots of bottles of Veuve, entertains, but is generally pretty low-key. They're sitting at the bar with a few young boys in posh tracksuits with ankle tags over the top. I've never met them before. They'd been arrested for repeated smash 'n' grab scooter robberies of a load of fancy jewellers in West London. They're all underage so, instead of jail time, got off with community hours, house arrest, and a fancy ankle bracelet. So weird. This has been a weird end, to a bizarre week.

And with more than I bargained for in the wine and line department.

I spent the best part of the day with the police and the best part of the evening with a drug dealer. Talk about the clichéd life of a night club owner... We ended up back at Number One's flat and ploughing through all his personal coke stash. And then all the way into his 'seconds lot'; a big black ball of coke kept in a sandwich zip lock bag. It's not suitable for sale on the street, and if you asked me if I wanted some when I was sober, that would have been a hard "fuck, no" but after a session of 10 grams between 4 people (1.5 grams is a nice amount for me on a normal night.) and all of the wine in the world, I didn't turn the black tar gear down. We ploughed through the black sticky bag and well into the next day. It burnt the back of my nose, made me dry-retch from the petrol fumes as I inhaled it though the rolled-up note and it tasted like licking the floor of a gas station. It had been tainted by petrol when it was shipped into the country inside the mechanics of a car. Fucking grim. My nose bleeds for 2 days after this session. The irony is that I drink green smoothies, use preservative-free face creams, take vitamin supplements, buy organic vegetables and hormone-free meat. And then put shit up my nose. I am a walking cliché, a contradiction in every sense…

10

Christmas
The Brief
50K Budget | 40 VIP guests
Festive Celebration in 'The Bathhouse Style.'

Guests arrive at the secret pick-up location and board the vintage horse-drawn carriages with soft cashmere blankets and vintage fur wraps for an open-top carriage a ride around the streets of Bishopsgate. Then it's back down the churchyard to arrive at the venue: a winter wonderland complete with incredibly realistic artificial snow blanketing the ground, piled up in drifts and gently falling from the snow-capped venue. The walkway leading into the 'Welcome Space' is dotted with wrought-iron fire pits. With chestnuts roasting, spiced hot rum and mulled wine in copper mugs for guests to sip and enjoy while listening to the Victorian carollers with ye olde cover versions of Wham's 'Last Christmas' and Mariah Carey's 'All I Want for Christmas is You'. Then it's on to the pre-dinner entertainment: a miniature ice rink on the terrace set inside the stunning Spiegeltent with company-branded ice skates. A Santa's Grotto with hidden sensory discoveries and a professional photographer, personalised gifts of faux-fur hand muffs and silk cravats, each with hand-embroidered company initials in the corner. Guests then enter the beautiful, iconic stairwell of The Bathhouse and into the drinks reception with Dom Perignon and Caviar blinis, with all 50 guests taken into the dining room for a three-course festive degustation experience accompanied with the finest wines and rounded off with artisan cheese and aged port. Roaming performers with a Victorian twist delight dinner guests: sleight of hand magic, masked opera singers, and harlequin contortionists. The event proceeds into the drinking and dancing portion of the evening with an open bar, which includes a full cocktail list, champagne, and access to vintage top-shelf liquors. A DJ set by Jarvis Cocker.

Reality
20K | 300 Staff and Clients | Bosses wife's idea of a 'nice' party

Substantial canapés, one cocktail on arrival, three tokens per person to exchange at the bar for a local beer, house wine or soft drinks. Can-can dancers and a branded gift bag with company pen, mug, and water bottle.

Surrounding our eerily quiet, Victorian time-warped Churchyard, we are wrapped around in big corporate giants. Banks, insurance companies and Fortune 500s.

The party brief is given to junior white-collar recruits or a fresh-faced perky PA to go and find out where the 'cool' new venues are for a super spectacular all-singing, all-dancing, no-expenses-spared event. A night to remember. But more importantly, a night to show off how much taste you have, how deep your pockets are, and how you take care of 'your people'. I quickly realise that this is the formula. I'm asked to curate a 'Bathhouse Style' event. Luxe, extravagant, with just enough quirk to show the city boys they know what's 'cool'. We plan, source, and create this dreamy experiential event proposal for the client. They return it to us with the budget slashed, the number of people increased, and all the lovely stuff and guts of the event chopped out.

Now, this sounds like I'm whinging. I'm not. The creative side of my soul weeps a little, as I adore curating totally immersive experiences, but the level of production that goes into such an extravagant event is untold. The profit margins are minimal as I have to bring in so many outside suppliers that I can only really add ten per cent to the top of their bill. The mark up on luxury liquor isn't as high, as I have 'pouring deals' in place with my regular booze brands. I bulk buy house spirits, house wine, and pallets of beer, which means we get our regular stock at really, really reasonable prices and allows a maximum profit. These are churn-and-burn stock-standard corporate Christmas parties. Boring is easy and easy means significant profit margins. Sixty per cent, in fact. Corporate Christmas parties only want mid-week lunches and evenings before our club nights start. All they want is to put the Bathhouse name on their invitations for kudos and a beautiful venue to host their basic party. Easy. So our weekend club nights stay as they are and I get to eat the sickly sweet corporate cake. I was going to say 'suckle on the fat cat's teat', but that made me feel physically sick. From the second week of November 'til the last working Friday before Christmas, we jam-pack them in day and night. If I hear Michael bloody Bublé one more fucking time, I'm going to cut my own ears off. But for the money we've taken the past six weeks, we could buy a three-bedroom terrace in E1 outright. Instead, we use it to finally pay off the 'start-up cost' and a big chunk of built-up debt. So I'll let Bublé crawl into my bleeding earholes, set up a tiny Christmas grotto, and sing 'Holly Jolly Christmas' all year round if I can take that kinda cash.

The lease is up in the little terrace I share in Hackney. Backing onto the charming Dalston train line, it looks quite pretty at a glance. Someone had tried to cheaply tart it up with a feature wall of Laura Ashley 'Toile' wallpaper, stripped back the floors without filling

the gaps or properly sanding, added an Ikea chandelier here and there. On the surface, it looked amazing compared to the other flat-share dumps in Hackney, but my bedroom walls turn into a live waterfall feature when it rains, and I have to share the space with fleas, damp, and mould. Paper-thin walls make for pretty tiring living arrangements. The one saving grace that makes it a delightful place to live is my darling E-doggy. A dear, sweet, utterly divine creature. She likes hats with fascinator veils, swishy floral vintage tea dresses, heavy brogues, and big Karen Walker sunglasses. She has a deep connection to the feline species and calls everyone 'Babez' (in her kiwi accent). Her heart is big, beautiful, and utterly pure. She's in love with the idea of love. She sleeps in a satin eye mask, earplugs, and looks like Audrey Hepburn in Breakfast at Tiffany's when she opens the door to Paul/Fred. A daydreamer, hilariously funny, and an eternal optimist, E-doggy is also partial to ketamine and hallucinogenic drugs. I adore her. Everyone could do with an E-doggy in their life. E-doggy has T'ed up to move in with some pals and so have I... well, one pal.

Coincidence maybe, but I see it as a divine sign from the Universe. The lease on Rich Pack's bachelor pad is also up at the same time. And I have found the PERFECT place for us to call home. Shoreditch is too crazy now. I'm tired of Dalston, but there is a teeny tiny pocket behind Kingsland Road called De Beauvoir Town. Rows of terraces around a big green square filled with mature rose bushes. One side is a large housing estate, and the other is Regent's Canal. Quiet. Quaint. And somehow missing all the action of its boisterous neighbouring suburbs, although parts of this area have a huge gang problem and street youth culture around the estate. It will never be far from your mind when you're walking down a quiet street after dark, but that's the London life. Or any major cities with a rapid pulse, for that matter. The street lined with cherry blossom trees and bay-windowed terraces. The moment the listing goes up, I stake out the agent and get a viewing straightaway.

It's a three-bedroom Edwardian terrace flat with a glass conservatory and back garden with a pear tree. A real-life fruit-producing pear tree! There's a fancy kitchen with a double oven, polished floorboards throughout and sisal carpet in the bedrooms. Our bedroom is at the far end of a long corridor. Quiet, calm, complete with every 24-hour clubland residents dream - blackout blinds! It has enormous doors opening out onto the garden and a marble fireplace in the corner. Off the corridor is a bathroom with a big, deep bath. We get another room each. Rich has a bedroom to convert into his music studio and house his enormous record collection, and I get my very own dressing room. All my pretty, frilly things in one glorious space. Vintage dressing table, Venetian mirror, racks and rails. Soft sheepskin rugs on the floor. The living room is bright and airy with bay windows. Deposit down without anyone else getting a chance to view the dream abode. We. Are. Moving. In. Together!

Or we were meant to be… Except for a family-sized bag of cheese Doritos that sent the co-habitation well off course. Walking back from the off-license with a post-moving snack, a bag containing a six-pack of Red Stripe beers in one hand and another bag with a tasty pack of Doritos in the other. Rich is annoying me. Like fucking me off. He's been snappy and a bit cruel. All day. Moving in the rain isn't fun. It's cold and wet. We squabble and peck at each other, and he keeps digging, saying this thing he thinks is funny, and I just think it is mean. 'Moody cow'. For the first five times, I just say, "Stop saying that!" With each 'Moody cow', my annoyance rises. So he repeats it. And the plastic bag in my right hand goes swinging.

Powerful and steady, the arc is on course. It smashes him right in the face. He's shocked. I'm shocked. For that split second before pain registers, he thinks I've bag-slammed him in the face with a bag full of beers. I had to look down and check. I may as well have hit him with the cans. He's livid. I'm livid. I did tell him not to say it again. He storms back to his bachelor pad, and I drink and eat the offending weapon in our new home. Alone. Just me and the boxes.

I gave him fair warning not to say it.

He comes 'home' 24 hours later. It seems I missed a trick here, 'cause he came back to a totally unpacked, set up house. Not the cutesy moving in romantic comedy montage I was hoping for but a reminder that not all is smooth sailing in the Hollywood-Fucking-Amazing-Love game. Honestly. He should feel pleased it wasn't the bag of Red Stripes. 'Cause for a split second there, I thought it was.

He apologises. Overwhelmed and tired. He's never officially lived with a girlfriend before. Moved into their flat-shares, yes, but this is the first 'official' signed, sealed, locked into a lease. It's a big step, and the weight of the commitment caused a last-minute kick off.

The Hollywood-Fucking-Amazing-Love home is decorated with ornately twisted, immensely uncomfortable but beautiful Gothic Jacobean furniture. House of Hackney soft furnishing, my collection of antique chandeliers wired in and oddities collected during Bathhouse decorating hauls that were so special I couldn't help but keep them for myself. We invest in a stupidly expensive but deeply soul-soothing, life-affirming lounge suite. It takes up half the floor space, as deep as it is wide and converts to a king-sized bed. The bedroom is kept simple. An enormous mahogany and rattan Louis XV bed and over-hanging chandelier. The only other thing in the room is the marble fireplace. Clean and clear of all other non-nocturnal distractions. We christen the house and throw a

Christmas party for around 30 friends. I do my very best impression of Martha Stewart on MDMA. Actually, I have a little

Obsession: a borderline crush on the UK version of Martha, Kirstie Allsopp. I religiously watch her cute little Christmas shows, admire her ample bosom, and fabulous enormous cocktail rings. Inspired by her tips, I order garlands of beer hops to trim for the arches and doorways: they look amazing but stink up the house, crumbling everywhere and leave sticky marks all over the floor for months afterwards. I hang mistletoe and holly branches over the fireplace and neatly rack up little lines of coke on the green marble mantle. The tree is a 12-foot fresh spruce decorated with vintage 60's chic baubles and trinkets collected from Spitalfields Market and intricate strings of antique chandelier pieces hanging off like frosty crystal water droplets. The fridge is stocked with cases and cases of Moët, and I've made all the canapés from scratch. Dressed in a backless cream cashmere jumper covered in silver sequins, (let's just take a moment to enjoy this memory of when going bra-free was a viable option and didn't require renovation-level scaffolding and a pulley rigging system...), a vintage Mexican full circle festive skirt, hand-painted in multicolour swirls and trimmed with beads and sequins. The skirt is a total showstopper. I wish I still owned it. Kurt Geiger high-heeled, red glitter, Dorothy from Oz slippers. And an oversized red silk rose in my hair.

Dealer Number One dropped off nine grams of coke and two grams of MDMA. He also pays a business visit to a few party guests. He has a lot of loyal customers in this group. An unexpected snowfall outside creates the perfect 'white Christmas' atmosphere and inside, the conservatory continues with the 'white Christmas' theme. The party goes on until the next afternoon, snowed in on the outside and snowed up on the inside. Our dear friend Chris - an exceptional singer in an excellent band that Rich booked at his

12 Bar club night, he reminds me of a young Bruce Springsteen; they become fast friends and he is one of the funniest, nicest and equally fucked-up guys we know - bunks down for a 24-hour session. Endless stupid jokes that are only hilarious to people in the bender bubble. Everyone else lived in walking distance of home, but the train lines were down, so Chris was here for the long haul. But another lovely little surprise guest comes wandering out from my walk-in dressing room, fresh as a daisy after sleeping a solid ten hours curled up in a corner on a nest of vintage furs. It was like she stepped out of the wardrobe and into this mess, like a reverse Narnia.

Drug benders and all-nighters always seem like the most excellent idea at the time. Until I have to go run the club and Rich has to DJ without any sleep, still fucked and coming down. It's not so funny once you realise it's a terrible idea, it's far, far too late and you're too wired to get those few hours of precious, elusive sleep you need. Instead, you watch the clock, counting down the minutes and seconds you have before you have to go back to work, exhausted and fretful. 'Til you have to go and do it all over again. It's snowing still, fluffy, deep and not going anywhere. A total delightful surprise as I was getting out of the cab: a little rectangle of white paper caught my eye. I had been sitting on a drug wrap. I grabbed it and head into the club. Everyone had left London to travel home to their families for Christmas. So the club isn't busy. I can tell it will be cruisey. It's odd: I can feel the atmosphere in the club and gauge how the night is going to be. Ninety per cent of the time, it's precisely as predicted. It's that shifty ten per cent you have to watch out for. You pray everything will run smoothly when you're feeling fragile and strung out. Like now.

Looks like I wasn't the only one overindulging in the Christmas spirit. I shove the heavy door into the kitchen through to the dingy little toilet out the back to check out what treasures are in my cab wrap, but the kitchen door is jammed shut. I push again, and it gives a bit. A body is holding the door closed. I push again, trying to force it. I call for security on the radio. Best case scenario is a customer wandering into a restricted area and is leaning against the door, making a phone call, away from the music. Worse is a more curly situation. Someone passed out drunk against the door. An OD. A robbery. Heart-racing business. I give it another hard push. The door flies open, and I fall into the kitchen! One of our club promoters is standing there, looking sheepish, skittish, and greasy. Bones, full bird carcasses, and fatty chicken skin litter the ground. His face is covered in grease. Promoters ducking into a quiet spot to do a line, yeah: but hiding, jamming the door closed, eating all the leftover poussins (it's a young chicken. I had to ask when they threw the word around casually at the menu tasting) from the corporate Christmas party earlier in the evening! He'd stood against the door ravaging all six of them in a Discovery Channel-style feeding frenzy. Both of us are totally silent and don't know where to look. Security runs through the door, slipping in the chicken slime. I can't help but stare at the pile of debris, worthy of a pack of starving lion cubs. I breathe an inward sigh of relief. This is the best-case scenario. Even better is that the 'found' cab wrap has a fluffy gram of okayish quality coke. I can't wait to tell Rich. He'll enjoy the poussin story as much as the coke score!

NYE – Eve

This is a particularly bad hangover. Cocktails after work, then a night of dinner and drinks at the house of dear friends of ours. Too much fun. Too much cheer. Bottles and bottles of wine over a delicious meal, great conversations, and a secret line or two in the loo. Mrs is not a fan of drugs but Mr is, leaving sneaky little lines for after-dinner digestion in the bathroom behind a gorgeous original Peter Blake artwork, a naked lady on a swing in a tool belt.

(The secret must have come out. We popped round a few weeks later, and the bathroom handle and lock had been taken off the door.) Then on our bikes for a wobbly ride down Kingsland Road to our home sweet home. A six-pack of beers and finishing up a wrap of coke just to round the night off and sober up a little, followed by a Valium chaser to get to sleep.

I have a new marketing assistant, starting today. Who the actual fuck begins work on the day before New Year's Eve? But she was keen to get started, so... I said I would be in at 10am. I wake up at midday and open the pretty cellophane-wrapped present from last night's mini dinner party hostess with the mostest. I pop the heart-shaped ginger cookie into my dry, dry mouth to try and soak up the wine, successfully shower, sitting on the floor without passing out, and carefully build up my armour of normality. Perfect hair, carefully applied makeup and a distracting outfit. Always heels. Hungover people don't wear heels. It's my disguise.

But this one is bad. Real bad. Deathly Hallows bad. Eight out of ten bad. I stop the black cab to vomit burning ginger biscuit, acidic white wine and bubbly mixed with putrid bile onto the curb just outside Liverpool Street Station. I arrive and can't deal with meeting the new person in the hot, claustrophobic office, so I go straight to the empty restaurant. I wrap myself up like a burrito in a large white tablecloth and sleep on the banquette seating. Sleep to get away from the pain and over-familiar discomfort. Mac, the venue manager, wakes me up just before a viewing for a private party hire starts and I go down to meet the new person. I go behind the bar to make a vodka lemonade. I would never drink this lollipop liquor by choice. It's a medicinal remedy. The alcohol will stop the shakes, and the lemonade starts the hangover recovery. Still wrapped in the tablecloth, no shoes, and makeup smeared from my face-down coma nap, I greet the new girl. She looks suitably horrified. Turns out this is one of the hangover challenges I didn't win. I usually do. Hide it from the rest of the world. Rich is my only real ally. My secret partner in cover-up crime.

Do you wonder how I manage a deep-running drink and drug habit? It's easy now that I have some money in my pocket and no boss.

Health

I book in to see the very posh celebrity health guru Dr Joshi. Famous for treating everyone from Princess Diana to Gwyneth Paltrow and her red-carpet circled bruised back. I avoid telling him about the drink and drugs, just focusing on the symptoms and outcomes of the two offenders: never how I got them. Tired, lethargic, sluggish, gross skin, anxious, exhausted but can't sleep. Bloated. Getting a bit fat.

Solution:

Cupping, acupuncture, colonic irrigation, nutrition plans, detoxing, osteopath sessions. Powders, tonics, pills, and potions. I do feel better. Imagine how out of this world I would feel if I actually followed his plan for longer than 21 days.

Home

Loading the dishwasher, washing, folding, putting away clothes, keeping a house clean and tidy is impossible when you have a secret hobby that is totally draining. If people popped round and I was left in control of the house, they'd see a candidate for the biggest hoarder in London, bottle and bad life-style edition. I also promised Rich if we moved in together, I would not be so messy.

Solution:

Booked a lovely housekeeper called Grazie. She comes for three hours every day. It keeps the chaos at bay.

Safe Place

I joined the fancy gym down the road from The Bathhouse. Went to work out once but walked right back out. I just float like a starfish in the pool which is straight out of the set of American Psycho. Modern, slick, dim lighting, black glass. I hide away and marinate, seep in the sauna, bubble away like a potato in the spa, purging toxins in the steam rooms, wrapped in the luxury robes, soft towels and Molton Brown products. Easing out of come-downs and hangovers, shutting out the world. No phone that rings non-stop. No staff with endless questions, emails of doom pinging into my inbox to punch me in the head. And best of all, I never see another soul. Alone, and I adore it.

Solution:

A very expensive exclusive gym membership, where I never once used a piece of gym equipment.

Transport

Walking is out of the question, heels etc. Riding my bike is my chosen mode of transport by a country mile. Fresh air and not having to deal with people is a plus but can be unpleasant with the shitty UK weather. The only alternative to two wheels is taxis and minicabs. Not being a princess, but the daily toll of nocturnal maximum fun times turns into next-day headaches that go hand-in-hand with nausea, so buses and tubes are out of the question. The heat, crowds, no air, and claustrophobia are a recipe for a travel-induced panic attack.

Solution:

If I can't ride my bike there, it has to be a cab.

Beauty

Hair extensions, threading, waxing, fake eyelashes, manicures, pedicures, wash and blow-dry appointments. Thick miracle night creams, serums, and deep hydrating masks, bubbly foams, and slick oils to rehydrate from the draining drink, drugs and soul-sucking ciggies.

Solution:

All the help. From all the experts. From all the products.

Cat in the bag

I would die if anyone looked inside my handbag. It's a whirlwind of truth and reflects the inner workings of my life. It's impossible to pull anything from it without a rolled-up ten-pound note which I have no shame in unrolling at any cash register and dusting off the white powder to make my purchase. Loose, maxed-out credit cards, a bottle opener, screwed up lottery tickets upcycled to old coke wraps, teaspoons – I often carry pots of yoghurt for snacks. Novelty fancy coke-sniffing spoon with a little crown in the tip that I never use but have visions of Audrey Hepburn coke-taking glamour. A few pay-as-you-go phones that I buy every time I lose my contract phone. Crushed cigarettes and a fine layer of tobacco at the bottom. Empty lighters, knickers, period liners, empty blister packs of Panadol and Nurofen, Aspro Clear that I stir into every drink, the same way someone has sugar in their tea. More receipts than any tree would like to see. Makeup floating around, knocking up against coins, coins, coins. So many coins. All gold. Enough shrapnel to buy a new Mac lipstick. Tampons that have come unwrapped in the chaos. Little purses and pouches that have been enlisted in the last round of tidy up to 'keep it sorted' drift aimlessly in orbit, unzipped and empty. It's a bag of pandemonium ready to explode and let out my secrets at any point.

Solution:

Protect the bag at all costs.

Plans

I can't make any and avoid agreeing to them at all costs, because I have no idea how bad a hangover or comedown is going to be. I wouldn't dare book anything before 12pm during the week or 3pm on the weekend. We don't finish work at the club 'til 5am on the weekends, then 'unwind' for a few hours. So the sun is usually up as we head to bed. It's a vampire life. Work takes up all my mental energy these days.

Solution:

Zero tolerance for plans, unless they are a non-negotiable necessity.

And my last, most invaluable secret weapon. A whip-smart, loyal, protective and very forgiving assistant called Miss N. She keeps me on track and in check. As best as anyone can...

I give up trying to not scare the new girl. I take a trip to my safe place and home on my bike in the freezing December air. To my favourite person. Coma couch. Filthy home delivery, Downton Abbey, my secret guilty hangover pleasure, flavoured cider over tons of ice, and an early night aided by Valium should settle the score. Fresh to fight another day!

NYE - The Actual Evening – The Bathhouse Party

Flip to the preface if you need a memory jog of the evening of doom.

In the wake after the psychotic events calmed down, I cleared up the guest-list station at the end of the night and had a quick look over the Ticketmaster pre-sale printed list of customers' surnames, ages, and postcodes. One thing deeply triggers my interest. Not one person on this list is from London. My guru, Studio 54 pseudo father-figure, Steve Rubell, coined the phrase 'bridge and tunnel' crowd: the people who travel to get to a club, not locals, once a club becomes popular. In his case, Manhattanites, and in our case, Shoreditch mafia. This means our early culture leaders who came through our doors when we first opened had officially moved on to newer underground clubs and we're filling up with customers who are led by mainstream media ...

Why the fuck am I paying 150k plus in rent and rates for a central London location? This is at the top of my new year's to-do list. Not sure what exactly to do about it but I can't stop thinking that a new game plan needs to come into play.

My dear Beautiful Reader,

I just wanted to stop the story for a second. To say something to you.

Thank you.

Thank you for listening. Thank you for letting me talk.

Thank you for continuing to read this story.

At this precise point in time, writing these words has allowed something to shift. Something deeply embedded inside of me. It's changed the direction of the outcome, the ending of this story.

The unravelling of memories and putting these words on paper has pivoted my life in a direction I never thought possible, even though I've tried many, many times before. So thank you for listening, my dear friend. Tears flow as I type. I can't tell you now, as it's not the right time, but I couldn't write another word of this story without sharing this moment with you.

It will make sense much later in the story

All my love,

T x

11

Valentine's Day

'Fully booked' doesn't even come close. We've done an early and late seating. Guests receive a cocktail on arrival and two-course meal with roaming striptease entertainment. Tickets sold out in a day, with a long waitlist. We haven't thought this through properly and taken into account that diners will want to come for pre-dinner drinks and stay for nightcaps, but we need to turn the tables and reset the restaurant between seatings. To try and accommodate the bookings, we add some extra two-top tables. It's tight. Like, breathe in tight. 'Can't you just squeeze us in?' is the catchphrase of the evening and boy, will we live to regret it. Late arrivals, early arrivals, a cramped dining room. Hot. Loud. The kitchen is struggling to keep up, and the bar is cheek-to-cheek with lovebirds, all squashed in like battery hens. Not the free-range romantic evening any of us had in mind. Sometimes you smash it, and it all comes off smoothly. You have to hustle, pump and push through service. Everyone gets in the rhythm, but tonight we never got there. Not even fucking close. Poor William took the brunt of the heat, being maitre'd. He dishes me up a harsh telling off and a slap on the wrist for pushing bookings too far. The moral of the story is 'Don't fuck with people's hallmark moments'. Later's lovebirds. I'm off on my own weekend adventure! A very rare weekend away from the club!

Oui, oui! Paris, nous arrivons! Well, once we got past my self-inflicted detaining in customs. Turns out an ornamental gun belt buckle covered in diamantés attached to a lovely snakeskin belt looks like a real pistol through an x-ray machine. After the false start, we were off.

It's freezing, Fucking icy. But so lovely. I've been to Paris a few times now, by myself and with friends at different times of the year. This is by far the most precious time. Rich surprises and amuses me with his French. This man, from the wrong side of the South London tracks, is full of cultural tricks.

We stay in the heart of the Le Marais at Hotel Caron de Beaumarchais. I adore Le Marais, with its cobbled street and ivy-covered buildings, packed with gay bars, sex shops, vintage shopping, great bars and restaurants. It's a little slice of the Baroque period. I feel like a mini Marie Antoinette. From the outside, Caron de Beaumarchais looks like an antiques shop, or museum, rather than a boutique hotel. The exterior is painted the dreamiest cobalt blue. The interior is like a parlour with Louis XV harps, writing desks with feather quills, padded wallpaper, endless marble. Antique carpets and rugs, fine art, vases, and delicate ornaments.

We wander the streets; shopping, eating, and drinking. Every moment is perfect. Rich is dressed in his winter uniform, a tight black knit jumper, heavy necklaces, navy Alexander McQueen blue silk scarf with tiny white skulls and white fringing, charms hanging down his chest and wrists stacked with bracelets and silver cuffs trimming the knit. He's got his standard style, but with a weather-appropriate adaptation for the bitter cold, a vintage fur coat and leather gloves. It's a pretty spectacular look. We stroll to Chez Julien, A postcard-perfect bistro, for dinner. Lilac walls, candle-light, fresco ceiling, chandeliers, The right amount of Parisian pretension for two little lovebirds.

On the way home from dinner, I cross the street to take a photo of the facture of the beautiful hotel against the dark night. It's so cool. Bright blue set against the Parisian grey-stone row of buildings, chandeliers lit up in the windows. Pure Paris vibes. Feeling fancy using Rich's SLR camera. Life is brilliant right now. Earlier, I treated myself to a fresh pair of Christian Louboutin Ariella Clou studded boots. Shoe perfection. I take another photo. Rich is framed perfectly in one of the windows under a chandelier. He looks so beautiful. I trot inside. It's fucking freezing. He points out a pretty vignette on the floral wall. We mill about for a bit looking at all the gorgeous items in the foyer. There's a bad smell wafting about, so we start heading for the teeny-tiny two-person elevator to go to our room, when the night manager starts yelling at us "Loo! Loooo! LLLLOOOOOOOOOO! LOOOOOOOOOOO!" And pointing at muddy footprints all over the white marble floor.

I have no idea what he's screaming about. I look down. FUCK! My new Louboutins! And that is NOT mud. I've trodden sloppy shit all over this man's creamy marble floors and rugs. Ahhhhh, right! He's screaming "POOOOOO!" I do that weird little run-hop thing trying to not to touch the ground to get away before he notices my shoes… and jump in the elevator. I've left Rich for dead. I bang on the close button repeatedly, and the elevator doors ping closed, just as Rich is trying to get in. Sorry, pal, gotta go! Rich races up the stairs. He lets me into the room and tells me off for ditching him at the lift, and I hop into the bathroom. The phone is ringing off the hook. The poor dude downstairs is freaking out about the fresh sloppy pile of standard poodle shit all over my shoes and his fucking Baroque masterpiece of a floor. I get the boot off, and he starts banging on the door. Rich is trying to tell him that it's not us, but he can hear me dry-retching in the bathroom and storms in to catch me washing the poo off my pretty shoes. The poo's jammed in, all through the metal studs. Laugh, hurgh, dry heave, laugh, hurgh, dry heave, and repeat. I would have thrown the shoes away if they didn't cost a small fortune. Fuck you, poodle. The size and texture of the poo covered so much of the bootie, it would have to be a miniature-pony sized poodle that exclusively dined on foie gras. Ugh.

It was a sheepish check-out the following morning.

On the Eurostar home, my heart hurts. The most beautiful weekend, but I question it. Am I too in love with Rich? It feels dangerous. It feels lop-sided, like I love him too much. I'm wobbly from the weight of my feelings and question his love for me.

One week after returning from Paris

yttrl buy us a puppy: a Shih Tzu crossed with a Poodle. A Shit-Poo! I call him Dollar because he likes to sleep on my fake furs, like a little pimp dog.

The week after that

I buy him a friend. A minicab driver drops me home from work. I have Dollar with me, and he asks, "Do you want another cat?" Clearly, Dollar is a dog, but yeah, sure. A little flea-covered ginger tom, the size of a teacup and stinking of old piss, gets dropped off on my doorstep the next day. Rich couldn't even manage to protest, as he was green and on the verge of passing out from a crazy weekend DJing at a Barcelona festival, as I march him round to the pet store and buy up all the products and piss pads for Dollar & Bill.

The week after that

I'm pregnant.

No wonder I've been wobbling in my love levels and harvesting affection with my domestic zoo. Hormone mayhem.

We both know a baby isn't a viable option. It still doesn't make it less devastating. I love him so much and want to have babies with him, but one day in the future. But not right now. We're under no illusions, as a pair of 24-hour party people who live in the upside-down world of nightclubs, that this could work. It's not a place for a baby. We're not ready yet. It isn't even a conversation of 'if' this is an option. It's 'How did it happen?' And 'How are we going to deal with it?'

I book into a private clinic for an abortion. I needed to get it done on a Thursday and to be back at work on Friday. We deal with it side by side. Hand in hand. And it's a stepping stone of emotional trust and a wall that is slowly starting to build around us.

My love never wobbles again.

12

Remember that NYE discovery of the 'bridge and tunnel' effect at the Bath-house? Well, I've been busy nutting away, and there's now a solid plan. It's a two-phase execution.

The first stage involves an offspring: a miniature Bathhouse. The creative concept of the Bathhouse is so well-loved, it makes sense to keep it going but in a new incarnation...The Baby Bathhouse. We'll implement it in a cool suburb, just on the other side of Dalston, called Stoke Newington. I just need to start raising capital and negotiating the lease.

The second stage is still under development and more of a long game plan that I am still figuring out.

Easter

This night is stained in my memory. It feels like a scene from a film or a movie trailer I'm watching, rather than something I'm actually living out. Rich is walking in front of me, down the Bathhouse staircase, carrying his record box. Leather jacket, big hair, walking perfection and halo of pure charisma radiating off him. I trail a few steps behind him in my fancy vintage Chanel jumpsuit from our recent trip to Paris. It's jet black with wide palazzo pants and a huge white collar. The venue is full. In slow motion, we walk across the dance floor, through the crowd to the bird-cage DJ booth. Alan Cherry Cola is playing 'Sympathy for the Devil' by The Rolling Stones. He Djs the early shift on Saturdays.

This is my last amazing memory of The Bathhouse. The very last 'best night'. Giddy at the top of a faulty rollercoaster just before we come flying down, never to come back up.

The rest of the night plays out, flowing smoothly. There's little for me to do. I hang out by the door, chatting to security, then move about the club. It's in the rhythm where it runs itself. Everyone is where they need to be, and everything is working as it should. No fires to put out or issues to get sorted. I swing by the DJ booth around 1am, to pick up Rich. He puts on an extended bootleg version of 'Move On Up' by Curtis Mayfield, and we nip out to the back kitchen toilet for a line and chat which takes under six minutes. Customers are buzzing, fucking loving it. The atmosphere on Saturdays when Rich DJs is epic. The staff are efficient yet robotic. They are all pretty new to The Bathhouse, hired over the past six weeks but friendly and never let me go behind the bar to make my own drinks. They move quickly. The bar manager, Christo, who replaced Mac after the NYE cluster-fuck has given them more shifts and phased out the older original Bathhouse bar staff due to lateness, poor cleaning and various other complaints. These new guys don't have the personality and cool style but seem to be getting through the waiting customers and don't give the venue managers any headaches.

I always look forward to going through the takings and cash-ups on Mondays after a busy weekend and equally fucking DREAD it.

Mondays after a slow weekend. Thursday, Friday and Saturday were all good with the Easter holiday. Everyone was out and about. Great numbers through the doors; the weather wasn't an issue. No major incidents, and at a glance, the booze in the cellar and bars is looking low in stock.

The takings aren't good. In fact, they're fucking terrible: almost half of what I'm expecting. I go over the till print-outs, count cash, and credit cards. Everything matches up. Christo says the customers weren't drinking, but I know that's bullshit. They were. I saw them with my own fucking eyes.

The cash takings from the door and coat-check match up to what it should be. This will directly reflect if there is a change in customers' behaviour. I check the security hourly log-report of guests' entry and exit. If they all came in later, say around 1am, then yeah; it would mean a low bar taking with a normal count of customers through the door. But it's steady and staggered through the evening.

I spend the next four days going through the reports, takings, CCTV, and orders from the past month. I check and triple check, like a dog with a bone. I won't let it go until I've worked out what the fuck is happening here.

There are two occurring patterns that, in hindsight, make what was going on glaringly obvious. The credit card takings are normal. Nothing changed there over the four weeks, but we are taking in fewer cash sales. The booze orders, both quantity and value, are still the same as they've been week in, week out, over the past few months.

I make calls and have a plan in place.

Thursday's dinner and show event is pre-ticketed and paid online, so things will run as per usual. Friday is rota'd, and the shift runs as usual, except I stay until the very end, when the bars are all cleaned down and the staff are sitting having a drink. I lock all the doors and gather my security team. I'm shaking inside, but white-hot fucking fury pushes it down. Every staff member is getting searched. Pockets, bags, and full-body pat-down. Christo says I can't do it. Yes, I fucking can, Christo. Someone is stealing my money.

One guy has seven hundred pounds; one has three hundred; and one had a thousand on them. Apparently, it's all money they arrived with, to pay rent,; a loan from a friend; and another lame hollow excuse that it's 'his cash'. The four others refuse to be searched, along with Christo. They all quit and want to be let out of the building immediately. None of them ask for their wages or pick up the money from the table that had been found on them, including Christo who was on the payroll and due two weeks' pay. They just walk out, and I have to let them.

I put the call in a few days ago to Kitty, Daisy and a select few others to come to the rescue if we had the result I thought we did. It's a mean feat to run a bar, let alone a busy Saturday night with all new staff and no management, but the detective work paid off. We made triple the bar takings from the night before and double the takes of the past four weeks.

The staff that we fired on Friday were a group of Albanians. A theft-ring with an industry hustle that's apparently on the rise. They work their way into bar-staff jobs through a manager and pretend not to know each other, saying they're from different countries in the EU. The manager slowly gets rid of the original staff. They are amicable, work hard, and never raise any problems. Like never letting me behind the bar to make my own drink. I think they're helpful, but really it's to keep me out of the bar to avoid raising suspicion. They take about half the cash sales, only ringing in a limited number of them through the register. They place the cash under the fifty-pound notes, keeping track in their head of the amount they've skimmed and they clear it out every so often into a pocket or other hiding place, before I, or another manager, do the cash lift. There's a time limit to this hustle, as all the paperwork matches up, but without the technology of a livestock balance, someone has to manually put the lack of sales to the booze stock take. The manager was involved, so the discrepancy in the stocktake was swept under the rug for a few weeks. Catching on took about six weeks: with the new management and a quiet January period, the low figures weren't that unusual. They still managed to take about 45,000 pounds. We were paying them cash at the end of the shift, at Christo's request, while he got 'all the official payroll forms sorted'. I didn't really care either way but was always happy to save a few pounds in tax. This meant he could keep the staff's personal details, names, addresses, IDs etc. under wraps. They all could walk away at any moment, and we would have no idea who they were. So it's useless to call the police, unless I wanted to admit I was paying them in cash and open that whole can of HMRC worms.

Saving pennies on tax worked out to be a stupid fucking move. An expensive mistake I wish I'd never made.

After the blow of the Albanians and their 45k scam, it was like an underground earthquake that started a tidal wave of chaos. And the waves just kept rolling in, smashing me down at every turn. There's a shift in the balance which brings a new disaster day after day.

BOOM.
Electricity bill, 17K.

BOOM.
HM Revenue & Customs bill, 120K.
BOOM.
Our credit line is cut by our booze supplier. We're now strictly Cash On Delivery.
BOOM.
My dad has a triple heart attack.
BOOM.
The cleaning company has stopped coming, and there's an outstanding 25K bill.
BOOM.
Our accountant is arrested for two million pounds-worth of fraud.
BOOM.
Two of the club nights are leaving The Bathhouse.
BOOM.
The security bill comes in at 60K.
BOOM.
We're behind a month in rent. 12K.
BOOM.
Our landlord has gone into receivership and liquidated their holding company. I'm due to renegotiate The Bathhouse lease, and this won't happen with the company in administration.

I can't breathe. I am drowning. Like I'm sliding into quicksand. The more I panic, the faster I go under. Grit sliding into my airway, filling up my lungs like the inside of an hourglass. I'm running out of time.

Rich buys me a flight out to Australia for that same night after we find out that my dad died and was revived multiple times that day. I find this out via a family friend's Facebook status update. Not ideal. I need to see my dad before I start troubleshooting.

The accountant. Jesus wept, it's like something out of a film. I just can't fucking believe it, but then you wouldn't believe it either if you met him. Chubby, with a really high voice, bumbling manner, and a brow permanently covered in sweat, even in icy air conditioning. He was the least likely candidate for multi-million-pound fraud. One of the newspaper headlines dubbed him a 'Fat James Bond'. When we first started using him, he would see us 'after hours' at a reputable firm where he was a partner, saying "It's better for you to travel across London after peak hour." How thoughtful: yep, it sure was! "If you just make the cheque out to me, as I'm a partner of the firm. It's all the same thing, just much easier for you." Yes, it's shorter to write, I guess. "Can you bring cash this time, so I can just drop it directly into the safe? The local branch of our bank has closed down." Ah, ok then...

He has a wife from Albania – this part of the world is taking a beating in this section of the book, which is a pure coincidence. He shows us pictures. She looks like a beauty pageant queen circa 1990. They met on the Internet, and the marriage was never consummated, he tells us: a detail I thought was strange to report, until later, when the case went through court. It revealed that his wife went back to Albania without him on three different occasions and came home pregnant all three times (what the fuck?). He stole 120K from a successful published author. From his church. From his invalid great uncle and his many clients. He lived the high life, which included spoils for his wife and her family, properties in her home town, jewels, designer clothing and ultra-luxe holidays. He did it all for unconsummated love.

He was 'creative' with our figures, which helped with the smoke and mirrors needed to get our first round of loans approved. He never directly took any cash from us, apart from the payments we gave him. I guess he pocketed them after our after-hours meetings. But Fat James Bond was also a totally useless accountant. He was too busy drowning in fraud to alert us to the debt spiral we were spinning ourselves into. After I called him to chase up where we were with our outstanding accounts, he turned up with a massive folder of bills. All ours. And every one of them is well past the payment-due date. We've got a nice young mum called Sharon, who's fresh out of accountant's school and off the train from Essex, to help sort the accounts.

Sharon punches away with her long nails on her little calculator. She clears her throat and optimistically announces we 'only' need 267K to get in the clear and out of this nasty mess. Gee - thanks, Sharon. I'll just get out my purse. Oh, and that's only with the bills she currently has from Fat James Bond. There's a stack of bills in the office, plus a load of other loans she hasn't take into account yet, which come to over 80K.

I need to get the funds for The Baby Bathhouse secured before I make any moves to shut down final-demand bills, negotiate the debt, and damage my credit rating. It's easier to raise capital the second time around. On paper, we're a total success but have come unstuck at the eleventh hour. I need to get this moving very, very quickly, before anyone lodges formal demands before court appearance summonses are served, and County Court judgements delivered. That's when you are well and truly fucked. They sit on a Fine and Order list for six years! I have personal guarantees that hold me liable for 70K of debt, so I need to get this up and running to service loans for The Bathhouse. You didn't think I could just walk away, did you?

It's time to sell The Bathhouse. This might sound like a shock, but the curb appeal and shelf life of a club in this industry is at a prime. The clock is ticking. The sale is part of the two-stage plan. I just have to do it much quicker and take a lot less money then I'd hoped for. It's listed on a closed market for 350K. The agent assures me there's total discretion. This type of listing works with the agent calling up other vendors with similar properties, like known hospitality investors and anyone who has registered interest in wanting a bar/club/restaurant. Everyone seems to want to own a bar/club/ restaurant, or so I get told weekly. 'Gee, I'd love to be my own boss and open a little wine bar.' 'Oh, I'd love a nightclub'. Honestly, I now understand the Devil and his deathly cuntish ways. I am now a devil, only a cunt with much better shoes.

A local competitor had offered 300K just seven weeks earlier. I wish I'd snapped it up. I laughed at the offer, thinking we were in a WAY better position after the Christmas party period. We clearly aren't.

Word spreads through the staff, promoters, and DJs like wildfire; basically anyone in a three-mile radius... So much for the discreet sale listing. It unnerves everyone. This is a vulnerable position to be in. I need to sell The Bathhouse with a strong, ongoing trade. A parade of tyre kickers march through the venue, poke through my accounts, and require long meetings to 'sell the dream'. Our nightclub is well-known enough in the industry thanks to the press cover-age, awards, and good reputation, so people are showing interest for the snoop factor but when pushed to move forward, they can't commit to an offer both parties can agree to.

Leo from Caligula had started a splinter club night, back in Shoreditch, called 'After Dark', Caligula XXX or something equally sleazy. As much as they assured me it was catering to a different, more extreme crowd than the Bathhouse clientele, they could fill both clubs with enough of a following to keep the club nights in full swing. They couldn't. Leo and Jim would scream and tear at each other at the end of the night when things didn't go to their high-achieving plan. The crowds just weren't coming, but this happens with parties when they're based on attracting cutting-edge and leaders in culture. So we part ways. It's a hard and stressful decision as we started with Caligula and they brought so, so many people to the Bathhouse from the very first day. They well and truly put us on the map of clubland. But as much as the list from NYE shows it, this demographic has found new parties and undiscovered venues not blown wide open by main-stream media. It's a spoil of success that they enjoyed and have profited from, but the industry is fickle, and it flows like this. This is how culture movements work.

The one that kinda hurt was Boom Boom. Not because they were bringing in loads of customers or cash but because they played dirty and let it get intensely personal. Well, one of them did. They also decided that they wanted to spread out and start club nights with a competitor down the road and another in Central London. Just as I did with Caligula, I made it clear this was not in the best interest of The Bathhouse, and I strongly recommended against it. I have experience as both a promoter and a club owner, so I understand the desire to expand their brand. The thing is that unless there is a massive injection of cash to sustain and promote the club nights, it will flop after the first wave of opening-night hype. The customers attending the Boom Boom night kept dropping, as they promoted so many other new venues. They spread themselves too thin. The bar takings aren't even worth opening for. We started working with another booker for burlesque dancers and performers for the other nights of the week, which Boom Boom did not appreciate. The relationship begins to sour. They pull the Boom Boom club night four hours before the doors open and arrive with a big vintage bus which they park outside our venue to collect any customers who didn't get the 'change of venue email'. Fair dues. It's an excellent idea and impressive, but it could have been left at that. We parted ways; Dave Harris in his usual professional way but the dummy-spitter promoter left comments on my Facebook wall saying he hoped I died, specifically by choking on my own vomit. He followed up by bombarding me with venom-filled DMs and emails. He took that the fact I wouldn't run my club at a loss for his creative vision so personally, I was completely taken aback. Sorry pal, it's just not going to happen. Why don't you and your blinding ego go and open your own venue and then we'll talk about hosting my creative visions and not-for-profit masterpieces at your place?

Parting ways with the club promoters is a blessing in disguise. Daisy is on board now, and we keep promoting club nights in-house. We book DJs, promote and now get to keep the door money. We keep things more in the vein of our Saturday night's music. It balances in our favour, and the extra disposable cash from the door takings makes it worth the work. We know exactly how much work is being done promoting the event, what changes we need to make, and what works, so we can continue doing it. There's no drama or the politics of working with club promoters. Love to Love now only do club nights when they have a special event, since they were also struggling to maintain club night capacity. All of this gives us the flexibility to book in any cool new club nights that approach us, as we aren't committed to a weekly promoter and club night. Being in full control of the venue puts us in a much stronger position for a sale, since we're no longer at the mercy of promoters and their club nights. I just wish we did it earlier before it got so messy. We also hire cleaning staff and manage it in-house instead of using an external company.

The next colossal task is the landlord. This plan to climb out of crippling debt is totally reliant on conjuring up a miracle with these gatekeepers. Otherwise, I won't have a club to sell. I reckon I can keep The Bathhouse running at a good level and keep the wolf from the door for a few more months so it won't affect a sale, but I need a new lease. They have gone into receivership but have agreed to meet me with the administrators and their legal team. They are sympathetic that I want to sell the business, but it's not possible without a re-negotiated lease. They want us to wait it out and negotiate with the new owners once they're secured. This could take a day or a year, which is just not an option. We go back and forth and settle on the following.

Once we find a new tenant, they will be vetted by the administrators. They will need to provide three months' rent in advance plus a 50K deposit. We need to keep up to date with the rent, but they agree to allow us to pay the outstanding rent owned with the sale of the business.

Thank fuck. It's pretty unreasonable terms from the administrators, but I can work with it. Now I just have to find someone who will fall in love with The Bathhouse hard, the same way I did. The same way the previous owner, Hero and his hair extensions, helped me 'acquire the dream'.

The stress is almost physically unmanageable. During the day at the venue, I take a break and hide in the back 'coke toilet', bite down on a scrunched-up napkin and scream, cry and head back out like nothing wrong, business as usual. And at night, get fucked to forget. To manage the stress.

'Ah want tae speak tae th' owner. Dae ye ken if th' venue is fir sale an' hoo much fir?'
The accent is so strong, I can't understand what she's saying. I ask her to repeat it. Two more times.

I believe she is saying, 'I want to speak to the owner. Do you know if the venue is for sale? And how much for?' Scottish, Liverpool or Welsh maybe. .... but I get the gist of what she's asking, and it's music to my fucking ears!

This is the owner speaking: how can I help you?
And so begins the sale of The Bathhouse.

13

Mrs Payne has the thickest Scottish accent I have ever heard. I think it's because it's a muddled hybrid with an equally strong Scouse accent, Liverpool being her home for the past 30 years. It's highly unique and totally incomprehensible. She has a few family businesses she runs with her twenty-six-year-old twin daughters: betting shops, a dog kennel, greyhound racing, and a caravan park in Liverpool. Her interest in The Bathhouse is for a project for her glamour-obsessed twins who live and die for 'The Only Way is Essex'. The Payne family are not the kind of candidate that the landlord is looking for, but they have cash and plenty of it. And the twins want The Bathhouse as much as Veruca Salt wanted a golden ticket. And with the same level of vulgarity.

The Payne family haggle the price, hard. Picking faults in every element of the business. They belittle and criticise to push the price down, wanting some bits of the business but not others. Finally, they were ready to pay the deposit. The lawyers drew up the contracts, only for a phone call the next day from Mrs Payne saying she wanted to reduce the sale price by 50K. They had a portion of the money in cash and were drawing down on various other investments to make the sale price. Mrs Payne is aggressive and as destructive as a hostile bull in a china shop. Every day comes with a new problem. The administrators are not impressed by their credentials, but it appears the Paynes can meet their set financial requirements and prerequisites. The impression I get is that the administrators are also under pressure and feel they should move the property with sitting tenants and a secured lease. We are so far along with negotiations, and they keep coming back with reasons why they don't want to pay the full asking price. They've been all smoke and mirrors throughout the negotiations, the same way I was.

After Fat James Bond was behind bars, I had a meeting with a new accountant with a much savvier financial management background, who advised I should also think about a voluntary wind up and liquidate out of my holding company. That way, we could drop the outstanding debt and lower the sale price of The Bathhouse without it affecting the director's loans and personal guarantees.

Although it doesn't sound it, this is totally above board and is a legal option for businesses to handle a 'poorly-managed' situation and still be able to continue with the business. This is exactly what my landlords have done. It just doesn't feel ethical, and it's not a decision I think I can make lightly. The deal would be voluntary liquidation with an appointed liquidator to handle the sale money and the creditor's debt. The people who have personally guaranteed debt get paid out first, then staff, and the balance gets divided between the rest of the creditors. The biggest loser in this will be the taxman. But there are always casualties of war.

The Paynes arrive with an ASDA bag filled with 25K in filthy, grubby notes. They will pay half the balance through our solicitors and then a quarter sum two weeks after the exchange, with the final quarter after six weeks of trading. It's dramatically lower than the asking price and really shit to not get it all on the contract exchange, but we make a deal that we are NOT selling the 'Business or Goodwill': we are selling them the lease. A pay-out figure. This means I won't be producing the year's accounts which are due to be lodged with HMRC. I also don't leave them with the ability to bastardise the Bathhouse concept.

At home, we isolate ourselves in a protective bubble, wrapping the precious pieces of our private life in tissue paper and tucking it away from the rest of the bullshit that comes with club life. I feed him, take care of him. I jokingly call it 'packed lunch and blowjob life'. We block the rest of the noise out, and he makes our home a safe haven away from the stress of the clubland. The club isn't discussed unless totally necessary. Calls go unanswered. We take long walks down Regent's Canal with quiet lunches at the Island Queen Pub, bike rides in Victoria Park with Dollar tucked into my front basket, loving the fresh air on his wet nose and the wind in his fur. These are priceless pockets of time away from all the madness. Things are falling apart, but we grow strong together.

All the personal trimmings and benefits that come with a thriving business are quickly stripped away. My wages are cut off. No more fat cash envelopes of door money, no funds, no housekeeper, fancy clinics or softeners to reduce the harsh reality of addiction. Any cash goes right back into paying bills and keeping the business running for the sale. Rich takes over the bulk of our home bills and keeps us in coke and booze, which now has a very different purpose. It blocks out the noise. Stops the pain. Every line deadens the worry, easing me temporarily into a place that doesn't require firefighting, without a sense of impending doom. Failure is imminent, but it's the level of degrees that are unknown that plays with your mind. But the coke allows me to work to pretend everything is ok, and all 'part of the plan'. I dodge bullets during the day, keeping the venue doors locked so HMRC can't get into the building and issue me with subpoenas. At night, I run the club on a low booze stock, not enough change floats, and reduced staff, while still making sure we are getting the maximum number of customers through the doors and money through the till to not affect the sale. The Paynes turn up randomly in the evenings to see that we're maintaining the business.

Dear Universe,
Please help me, I'm fucking drowning here. Tava

Dear Tava,
Sorry lovely, but you have to keep pushing. I suggest you put your back into it and dig your heels in. It's going to get much worse.
The Universe
PS: Never give up.

There is another whole layer of this period in our life. This part of the story is difficult to tell because it isn't actually my story. I was just a tiny character in someone else's narrative. I've been torn about how this part fits into this story. Up until now, I decided I wasn't going to tell you. I didn't want it sitting in the middle of the rest of the chaos. I didn't want to taint it. But I can't leave it out of respect for the strongest people I've ever met. It was a firm reality-check for my own problems.

There is a little boy called Josh. I met him when he was four weeks old. He looks like a real-life cherub: rosy cheeks, crystal-clear blue eyes, a lovely round face with a little button nose, soft, delicate, hair so blond it's almost white. He's a beautiful boy with a calm nature. His family adore him beyond belief. Alli and Scott, childhood sweethearts, perfect parents. Doting, proud, loving, calm, besotted with their tiny little man and to be honest, they could all use this bundle of joy after the recent passing of Alli's mum, Joan. The heart of the family. Joan was also Rich's Mum. Alli is Rich's younger sister.

Josh is Rich's nephew. We spend time together at family lunches, go over to their place for takeaway dinners and X Factor, with the volume turned way down as Josh sleeps peacefully in the next room. We hear tiny noises and gentle stirrings over the baby monitor. New baby life turns into sitting up and crawling, Smiles and milestones. Teething and colds. Happy Families. Then one day, a call came for Rich. Josh has had a cold and fevers for the past few weeks and is not himself. The GP sent Alli home a few times now, but her mother's intuition has kicked into overdrive. They take him to the A&E because she couldn't shake the feeling that something bigger is wrong. And it is.

The worst.

Josh has leukaemia; a rare type of cancer normally found in adults. Alli is devastated but is positive that the treatments will cure it and that everything will be fine. Rich goes into deep shock and falls into an unshakeable sleep. Later that day, we head up to the hospital, where they will spend the next year and six months fighting for his life.

Josh is strong, made of steel, and the doctors fight. Round after round. Alli and Scott get knocked down and get back up. Daily. They take turns sleeping and are by Josh's side 24-hours a day. Shifts of love, endlessly entertaining him in the unfamiliar surroundings. The nights are full of terror and pain, morphine, and stretches of life-stripping chemotherapy. The strength this trio processes is endless, unrelenting, and inspirational. Their husband and wife relationship turns into ships in the night, round the clock carers, and champions of hope.

My love. I can see his heart breaking. He sees his little sister as the little nine-year-old girl from his happy childhood who has already suffered through the painful loss of a mother taken way too early in their life (this suggests she was 9 when mum died). No mum to support her in her darkest hours; the comfort only a mother can give when you're now a mother yourself. Vulnerable, hurting. And the gut-wrenching fear that she could lose her baby; her smiling, happy little Josh. Alli's strength is incredible. She never lets her fear show. No moments of weakness or talk of 'what if'. It's 'what's next?' The next treatments, new doctors, special programmes, additional resources, and further research discoveries.

This leaves us with the role of taking care of them. Caring for the carers. I cook meals and also have the kitchen guys at The Bathhouse make packaged meals so Alli and Scott can have a wholesome, nutritious, comforting hot meal every night. We come up on Saturdays and spend the day with them with our meals-on-wheels delivery and fun toys to distract Josh. It turns into our version of family life. Instead of visiting their dad or Alli's house, we meet at the Royal Marsden Hospital for all our family gatherings. There are moments that are dark and sad, but one thing that Rich's family are never short of are laughs, jokes, and love for each other.

The roles shift at our house. Rich was always the pillar of strength for my worries and burdens. He supports and helps me problem solve, but now he needs me. The decision is clear about what I need to do to move forward, the grit I need to show. This business deal will push me under if I don't make a ruthless decision. Now. I focus on my love. My family. And I focus on The Baby Bathhouse.

I can't keep the wolves from the door another day. I press the button. Once the details of the sale are announced, I hand the business over to the liquidator, and the vendors find out they won't be getting money. I have worked to pay off any small businesses and individuals owed with my cash from the door money and try to leave outstanding balances with corporations and bigger companies who wouldn't feel the impact as much and could write off the loss. I start getting calls and emails. Two haunt me to this day.

A lady who had done marketing for us had slipped through the cracks, in all the chaos. Her bills went to the liquidator. I didn't get to pay her out before it was handed over, as we were hoping to move forward and use them in the future. She served me up some fucking sour home truths after an accidental 'invite all email contacts' on Linkedin a few months later. She told me I had some fucking nerve reaching out after I ruined her wedding day. The 3K I didn't pay her had been earmarked for her wedding. I was rattled. Not that it was technically loads of money, but when there's a tangible effect rather than just a pound sign on an Excel spreadsheet, it takes the wind out of you. It started planting seeds deep, deep down that I don't deserve any type of happiness, not now or in the future. But the second one is much, much worse.

The security firm we used was owned by a guy called Sam. He was from Cyprus: he was polite, kind, professional, and could see that we had a solid business. He often said he would be interested in becoming a partner. Extremely conservative, well-measured, he didn't understand our more 'colourful and extravagant' crowds. He would subtly suggest the business would benefit with the club nights running more like the Saturday music and crowd. A partnership wasn't a good match. Whenever his bills arrived, he'd say, "Don't worry about it. We can sort something out." It dragged out like this for months. I buried my head in the sand about the mounting security bill. I think he hoped we could come to an agreement about a partnership. I just hoped the bills would go away.

He never did a personal guarantee with me, meaning that the business owed him the money, not me personally. So when there was no money left in the business, and the liquidators tell him this, he phoned me hourly and turned up to the venue daily. I agreed to pay him off, but it was going to take some time. He had signed contracts, which made him personally liable to his own business commitments and personal expenses which forced him to slowly sell things off. He got money from me in 5K chunks when the business had some to spare, which wasn't often. We just didn't have the cash, but he quickly ran out of time. Legally, I didn't have to pay it, but he had taken such a beating by my mistakes (and by his) and by not making me sign a personal agreement. He had a funeral for his aunt back in Cyprus, his house was being repossessed, and he sent me an email saying he couldn't recover from not being able to support her family with the funeral contributions and was going to have to kill himself. From shame, dishonour and no self-respect left.

I would be responsible for his death.

He got his money, but it took about four years. We were both broken and burnt out by the time the debt was settled. It seems cruel that although he got his money in the end, it also almost killed him to get it.

These are mistakes I made that have buried me in shame, self-loathing and regret. I also learned something about the way I do business. It took me years to understand and admit such a dark despicable character trait that I used too often...

Even when I'm at fault, I manage to place blame on the other party. Like it was his fault: he didn't do a personal guarantee. Yep, true - but maybe if I wasn't such a cunt and terrible business person who used dissociation to step away from the fact he was a nice guy, who did me a favour... I placed the blame on him and focused on his poor business choices to justify my decision and make myself feel less guilty.

The fucking Paynes pull out of the deal. Via text message at 6am on Sunday. Sorry, but the twins are not responsible enough to have the club. The sale is off.

FUCKKKK. FUCK... FUCK, FUCK, FUCK!

I pace the backyard, chain-smoking. Talking. Negotiating. Counselling. Mrs Payne feels like the twins are spoiled brats and not grateful for the expensive, 'over-priced' nightclub she's buying them. They won't go to the management course she said they needed to complete, as part of the deal for them to take over the club. They haven't got their Personal License or done the Designated Premises Supervisor course. They're out all night and sleep all day. Well, Mrs Payne, that bit makes them ready for club life. She didn't enjoy my observation.

I remind her that the deposit she paid is non-refundable and offer to give the twins training sessions and marketing workshops. I will prepare a comprehensive hand-over manual and can arrange shadow shifts for them to learn the ropes at night.

She agrees to proceed with the sale. Today.
She pulls out two more times over the next three weeks.

The last pull-out was one that cost me a lot of money. It was actually my fault. I rocked the boat. We put a spin and a tiny 'fuck you' on our upcoming closing party for The Bathhouse ... 'Cabaret is Dead...Come to the funeral'. The press runs with it. We thought it was just a funny catch-cry and our way of saying we were stepping away from the traditional club and show element of The Bathhouse into a more drink-led experience at Baby Bathhouse.

That press release riled up the cabaret & burlesque scene and sincerely pissed off Mrs Payne.

The liquidation created a weird, still, void and bubble that lets the Bathhouse run as per normal. Well, as normal as possible under the circumstances. I'm advised to wind down areas of the business that I don't need to save on wages. Daisy is in the process of opening and renovating her own bar. I am super pleased for her but have secretly been waiting for her to hand in her notice. It hasn't happened, despite my hopes she would see the financial strain I'm under and make the transition to her venue full-time. She takes one of the most significant wages, and her role is marketing, promotions, and other tasks that mostly involve planning for the Bathhouse's future, which there isn't. The Paynes aren't taking on any of our management staff, and it seems she'll wait until the final moment before leaving for her own bar, which she has every right to, but I can't afford it. So I hand her a notice for the end of the week. I know she's upset with me. The look on her face tells me everything. She doesn't directly say anything, but she also doesn't look me in the eye anymore, and our usual cigarette breaks together have somehow stopped. I feel like a fucking scumbag dipped in local anaesthetic. Mentally, I feel the hurt, but my body is disconnected and numb. Everything she has done for me and this is how I repay her? What a fucking cunt.

I have the Paynes in the venue, doing inane tasks. Measuring for table cloths, choosing fake flowers (gross). Never once does anyone come in for actual training, shadow shifts, or stay around to learn how to operate the club. It's actually bloody difficult, like a daily treasure hunt without any map. It's a Victorian building, so the electrics and the plumbing are ancient. The air con, ice machines, and kitchen equipment are old but have quirks and tricks to keep them humming. The lighting, amps, and sound equipment aren't as simple as pressing an 'on' button. It's not like they're taking over a new venue with appliances that have warranties and user instructions.

It has taken us all this time to get in the venue's rhythm and learn her ways. Like William and I had spent the best part of last Saturday night in the cavern under the men's toilet unblocking the connecting pipe from the ladies' loo that runs through to the main sewers. We had to climb in through the manhole, down into the overflow pit and reach in the pipes to unblock whatever was jamming it up, wearing garbage bags as coveralls, feet in plastic bags, taped around our ankles, and bin bags like massive condoms for our arms. Praying none of them split. With jumpers tied around our mouths and noses like train robbers, the only thing we're robbing here is fucking turds. The ladies' toilets are blocked, and dirty water is flowing out of the bathroom and into the corridor. Mind you, there is nothing wrong with the actual plumbing. There is nothing wrong with the actual toilets. There is nothing wrong with the actual pipes. It just takes one person to shove something into the toilets that shouldn't be there. For example, a bloody sanitary pad wrapped up like an Egyptian mummy in layers of toilet paper. The next person comes and does a big disco shit and covers it with more loo paper. Flush. But it won't flush away cause the pad is blocking the S-bend now, and the loo paper-shit cycle continues until the toilet attendant gets the plunger out to get the blockage moving. This just forces it further down the pipeline until a backlog of water starts surging up and out of the toilets and the whole lower level is four inches deep in water. This will be when I'm called on the radio. All this making both the male and female toilets unusable, unless you are prepared to hitch your skirt up, take off your shoes, and wade ankle-deep through a river of defecation.

Do I need to describe the smell? Just imagine Victorian-era petrified plague-shit mixed with sloppy ripe cocaine-chemical poo. It catches in the back of your throat; a punch to the gag reflex. It has the same effect as the other type of 'surprise' deep throat. Drain rods, wire coat-hangers and plungers are all a part of our tool kit against the chaos. The problem with running a late-night venue is plumbers and electricians won't come out at 2am on a Saturday night. If, by some chance, they do come out, it will be hours later, so you've missed the window of opportunity. You can't just wait until Monday to fix it. You need to know how to get around these issues and run the club under any circumstance. Rain, shit, or shine! It doesn't matter if you have a brand spanking new venue or an ancient dinosaur. These things happen in clubland, and when they do, you better be prepared to roll up your frilly sleeves, tuck your dress up into your Spanx, and get filthy. Otherwise, you can kiss goodbye to your precious takings for the evening. Customers will leave if you can't fix the issue. You usually have 30-40 minutes before the natives get restless and start heading for the exit.

I guess my point is that it's actually hard fucking work. The glamour is minimal and the bullshit constant. The work it takes to get customers to come to the club and keep returning weekly involves a highly-detailed work plan that is executed Monday to Friday by me, Daisy, and our marketing assistant. Bookings, driving online interest, press, managing VIP bookings, flyering, social media, uploading the photos from the last weekend, tagging people. The customers don't just show up once the initial hype has worn off. During opening night shifts, the club doesn't just 'run itself'. You might get the odd shifts that you can cruise through, but it's making sure those customers you worked so hard to get through the door have a great night and in turn, spend money.

Contracts negotiated and funds are raised and secured for the new venue, Baby Bathhouse, just before I liquidated The Bathhouse. There were moments when it looked like I wasn't going to be able to keep all the balls in the air and get the funds for the new project before the old deal went sour. But this project is still on the trajectory. I hadn't had the creative capacity to even think about the design process for Baby Bathhouse (Or BBH. Can we use initials please? It's too fucking long to write.). But I've started, and it's beautiful. I know, it seems wrong that I'm allowed to start a new business after selling the lease of the old one and liquidating my debt. I don't feel great about it. I actually feel deeply ashamed. I push the feeling down, packing it on top of the other shitty things I've been doing and justify my actions with 'Everybody does it,' and 'It's just business'. It's not though, is it? It's fucked. I was just a dog. In a dog-eat-dog business cycle, but I wasn't ready to give it up. What was I meant to do with the debt I had? I have to live with my decisions and consequences daily.

The Baby Bathhouse will have a decadent Gothic atmosphere. It will still have all the luxe and grandeur of its beautiful predecessor, but to attract a slightly more discerning and mature crowd. In real speak? This means fewer drugs, less drama, customers with more money to spend who want quality premium beverages over quantity. The focus is on bespoke cocktails, private parties, and intimate club nights, rather than the higher capacity late-night club vibe of The Bathhouse.

There is an industry-wide movement towards artisans' spirits, small-batch liquor, and boutique beers which we will focus in on. The site is a long, narrow Edwardian terrace set in-between a vintage record and clothing store and a cute, old school greasy caff. Opening hours are 11am to 2am with an 11.45pm liquor licence. I'm told by the current owners it has been given a preliminary ok by the police and council to extend drinking until 1.45am. It's a smaller capacity venue, holding 150 people, with a good-sized courtyard. The entire space is spread out over four floors. The basement is the nightclub area with a quick dispense bar, the ground floor will be the cocktail parlour and main bar, the third floor is the office and storerooms, and the fourth floor is a small apartment that William and his boyfriend will live in.

QUEEN OF CLUBS

The street-facing bay windows will be hung with thick, lush, purple curtains, drapes heavy in fabric trimmed with gold tassels and branding. The exterior is painted dark charcoal with gold signage framed by carriage lanterns with imitation flame bulbs. The interior walls of the drinking parlour will be covered in our bespoke Bathhouse signature hand-rubbed tile and skeleton wallpaper. Huge gilded oval mirrors create the illusions of depth. The ceiling will have panels of padded purple velvet dotted with upholstery buttons for pinched diamond shapes to add texture, but also to minimise sound and echo issues. The seating will be bespoke church pews with rolled armrests, and peaked arches painted glossy charcoal. Small, round mahogany tables with heavy cast iron ornate legs create intimate drinking nooks. In the corner, we'll hang ornate vintage birdcages of various sizes on different lengths of gold chain. Inside, suspended on invisible wires, will be hundreds of black butterflies in mid-flight. The floor will be covered in beautiful, highly polished, black and white check porcelain tiles laid on the diagonal to create a diamond pattern.

Through the dramatic, gilded, gold leaf archway and two steps up, into the cocktail bar area. To the left, the wall will have three large art installations in deep-set gilded frames, similar to those in the old masters' section of the National Gallery. We'll light them from behind to create a striking lightbox with the anatomy skeleton from The Bathhouse Collection, but Rich had designed them with flowers, bottles of liquor, cigar and smoke rings and cool, quirky de-tails added for the signature Bathhouse macabre feel. Such awesome light installations.

The bar wraps around the opposite side of the room. The bar top is an elaborate display case built to house curios. Victorian dolls' heads, delicate doll hands and feet, tiny shoemakers' lasts, poison bottles, antique glass eyes, baby snakes in pickle jars. Each display a little ode to The Horniman Museum. The back bar is mounted with handmade, peacock, stained-glass lamps that will throw coloured stained-glass patterns over the walls.

The stairs to the basement will set the tone to follow. Deep purple walls, almost the colour of the midnight sky before it turns black. With a red neon basement sign. The underground club level is simple compared to the parlour above. The floor is polished concrete. There are two old coal vaults to be converted into private VIP chambers, with white rabbit lights in gold cages in each corner. The sound system is state of the art, as is the lighting. The room is dotted with six deep optical illusion picture frames with peepholes. If you peer through the hole, Victorian pornography or an erotic sex scene is revealed. At first appearance, the room is simple, but its hidden pleasures are there for those with an inquisitive, adventurous nature.

The bathrooms have arched doors to mirror the church-pew seating and Gothic treatment. A wall-mounted cast-iron bird fountain, converted to handwashing sinks, with a beautiful brass sparrow as the tap handle.

Out the back, in the garden, rosemary, lavender, and mature roses planted on the perimeter of the garden. White pebbles are the main ground cover with large stepping stones with African violets and Baby's Tears ferns planted in-between. Down the centre will be a cobblestone pathway flanked with Victorian street lamps. Simple, white Parisian cafe tables and chairs; striking against the charcoal cement-rendered walled garden.

We take a few days off over the festive period. Rich and I start cooking at 6am: Christmas dinner with all the trimmings, dessert, cheese boards and snacks. All portioned up into individual packages. Bon Bons, presents, mini bottles of red wine, Baileys and a tiny potted Christmas tree. Packed into a cab. Christmas this year is spent up at the hospital with the family. I found us the most ridiculous costumes. Rich's is like Snoop Dog's purple pimp velvet ensemble, with the jaunty wide-brim hat, long coat and wide-leg pants, but this one a crushed red and white velvet Santa style. I have a cutesy Mrs Santa mini dress with white tights, white fur-trimmed patent heels and white fur coat. A lovely Christmas. Spent all together, piled around Josh's bed, eating our meal in boxes on our laps.

We start the BBH build next week, but I am due at my lawyer's office to sign and exchange the contracts for the lease today... BOOMs just keep coming.

There was a fire at the venue overnight, gutting the main floor and the basement. I have no idea where I stand now. My lawyer isn't sure yet, either. The current owners think I've had it burnt down. I think they've had it burned down. Purely for insurance. The question is, who is responsible for taking care of the building and what happens to our deal?

It's confirmed that a 'lit cigarette' from the beer garden started the fire, which also burnt down the neighbouring junk shop that sits next to the BBH garden. It's all a bit suspicious. There have been complaints for years about the junk shop. There are rumours that they sell actual junk (heroin) out of the shop, but it's a bit of a fucking coincidence that the venue has a fire on the very day of exchange? The lawyers determine that it is in the best interest of the sale and exchange that the current owners and their insurance take care of all the damage and the rebuild and ensure I have the input of layout, materials and finishes.

The beautiful Baby Bathhouse phoenix rises from the ashes.

Of course, we ran over budget. Of course, we ran over schedule. And of fucking course, we ran into a million problems opening. The same old community palaver and uproar of 'We don't want a strip club in our neighbourhood' (NIMBYs are loud in this area) to the basement totally crumbling with damp, once the builders stripped away the burn damage. This needed 'tanking' which meant creating a layer of protective waterproof membrane to seal out the seeping moisture with an added false wall built three inches away from the membrane. This eats up cash. And the money quickly ran out.

Now, here's a change in tone we haven't had in a while. A piece of great news! Yeah, I was shocked too. Rich received a very unexpected inheritance and will invest in the business, which allows the last phase of decorating to happen. Partners in crime, for sure! But partners in love, and partners in business? Not a well-trodden recipe for success; at least for other couples. It's exciting, nonetheless, for Hollywood-Fucking-Amazing-Love Ltd. He has already been a sounding board in every element of creating and designing this new venue, so now this just makes it 'official'.

Opening Night | The Baby Bathhouse

I jump in a cab and race home to get showered and changed. I'm covered in paint and dirt, days' worth of building and renovation grime. The venue looks incredible, and we have guests and press arriving in 45 minutes for the launch party.

I slide the key in the door and stop to think. It would be nice if I quickly popped into the off-licence to get a bottle of Moët or Veuve to have a toast with Rich, as this is his first business venture and opening night. I turn and start to head off to the shop. Fuck. I remember I cleared out the last bit of money in my account to buy ice for the venue and only have enough in coins for the cab back to

BBH. It would have been a nice little treat. Oh well, it's the thought that counts. I swing back round to open the door, but it won't move. Huh, that's odd: Dollar's not barking. Rich must be home before me, playing a trick holding the door shut or something. There's a bang. I push the door, and my leopard-print nana shopping trolley is blocking the door. Weird, it lives in the backroom usually. Why is it here? I push again, and it moves just enough for me to be able to pop my head around the door and peer inside. All the lights are on, and the cane peacock chair that is usually further into the foyer is jamming the door closed. Fuck. I call for Dollar. He doesn't come, and I can't hear his jingle-jangle collar. He and Bill always run to the door as soon as anyone comes home or knocks on the door. I push the door open and run in. The back door of the conservatory is smashed in. A metal pipe sitting in the shattered glass.

Someone is in my house. I hear noises in the far back room, my bedroom. The door bangs and I run out of the house to call Rich. My heart is racing, as I explain. FUCK, Dollar! Where is he? Bill would have hidden, but Dollar is friendly, nowhere near as wary as Bill, who has an escape route through the kitchen window. I run back into the house for Dollar. "Dollar, come here, boy!" I make little kissy noises to try and coax him out. Rich is yelling at me through the phone to get out of the house in case the intruders are still there, but I can't leave Dollar behind. Poor little pup.

I check through the rooms. I have tunnel vision, and everything seems so loud. My heart is beating in my throat. I can hear splinters of glass pinging to the floor like melting ice. The rooms have been ransacked, with drawers emptied all over the floor. Rich's studio is still locked from the outside, but there is an open suitcase in the middle of the hallway. I walk into our bedroom and see all my jewellery boxes tipped over onto the bed. They must have been looking for real jewellery, not our costume stuff. Dollar isn't under the bed, but the back door to the garden is open. I use the torch on my phone and look around. Bill springs through the doors, purring and clearly happy to see me. But Dollar is nowhere to be found.

He's been taken.
He's gone.

I call the police and report the robbery and Dollar missing. Rich gets me to quickly hide the coke in the house in a container and chuck it in the freezer, so the police don't find it. Rich calls Number One to start asking around if anyone has picked up Dollar or seen anyone with him. I hadn't even thought of this, but it sends me into hysterics. Gangs in the area steal small dogs to act as live bait for dog fights which they film and put on the Internet. I keep looking around the house for Dollar and start noticing things. My Apple Mac is gone with all my work and photos. My iPod and the BBH iPod, three serrated steak knives from the block in the kitchen. I realise the open suitcase in the middle of the hall was there because they were preparing to use it to break down the door to Rich's studio and to make it easy to carry out thousands of pounds' worth of sound equipment and computers. My dressing room has been ripped apart, looking for valuables. In a more fruitful time, there would be thousands of pounds of cash tucked around the house, but it's slim pickings these days.

I pace the streets looking for Dollar, knocking on doors. Nothing. I head out to the backyard. The row of terrace gardens has brick fences just over 150cm high. It's pitch black, but I grab a plastic garden chair, and I climb over, start calling for Dollar, and shining the torch in all the bushes and corners. Nothing. I climb over the next fence. Nothing. The next yard. Nothing. I get to the last one at the end of the row. I heard a little tink. Fuck - my heart drops. Dollar! Tink, tink, tink. I dive in the bush. He's hiding in the corner, shaking. He jumps into my arms, licking my face, He is terrified but so happy to see me and I feel exactly the same. He is so far from home.

The fences are too high to scale for a 30cm tall pup. He was carried all this way by the escaping intruders and either wiggled free from them or was dumped.

The police arrived six hours later. They're polite and professional in taking down the details of the robbery, but it's such a common occurrence in the area, we all know it won't go any further. We had let the insurance policy slip as I had no money to keep up the payments, so the Mac isn't going to be replaced anytime soon. They seem more concerned by the fact Dollar was taken and dumped.

The launch party goes on without us, and everyone sends photos and updates. Our lovely friends, Mr and Mrs Hostess with the Mostest, come over with wine and pass the time with us while the forensic investigators go over the house for prints and evidence. The intruders were wearing woollen gloves which left fibres all over the place. They pointed out that they probably jumped over the back fence. All of the other houses in our row have bars on the windows and security gates. All the yards back onto a private alleyway running along the back of the properties for an easy escape. They'd potentially cased out the place from the alley earlier, come and looked through the windows of our house beforehand. Their intention seemed to be to get into the studio room and use the suitcase to clear it out. There was no way of them knowing what was behind the door as the curtains were drawn today. The investigators want details about the stolen knives, in case they are used in another crime. They suspect that there were three robbers, from the glove marks, and the fact three knives are missing. They think I would have disturbed them coming home. By jamming the nana shopping trolley and chair against the door, it would make a crash and alert them to anyone coming in. Lucky I stood at the door and fluffed around, after disturbing their makeshift blockade, to think about the bottle of champagne and run through the status of my bank account, so I didn't have to cross

paths with them.
Thank FUCK Dollar boy and Bill are safe.

Our home, where we escape the never-ending chaos, has been invaded. Our sense of security has been violated. Every corner of my life feels dirty now. I can't get my head around it. Strange people in our home going through our things, taking my laptop, our knives, carrying away my beloved pet.

These days, they aren't even the highs and lows of the chaos. It gets low and lower. The bad news is a daily occurrence. The question isn't if shit will happen, but how bad and what will the fallout be.

14

The Baby Bathhouse is doing well. It's never as jammed-packed as the Bathhouse was when it first started out, but this is a different style of venue with a different vibe. Drinkers fill tables on the ground floor parlour bar most nights of the week. On the weekends, there are private parties and loose club nights in the basement. We have a range of tongue-in-cheek but pretty cutting edge activities that go hand-in-hand with mid-week catch-up drinks with friends, all with a Bathhouse twist. Erotic live drawing by candlelight in the basement; a pop culture quiz; stitch-and-bitch sessions; burlesque striptease classes; tarot reading and wine tastings. On the weekends, we have DJs, live music, daytime BBQs and family fun in the gardens with drinking and a little bit of dancing. It's civilised and has a friendly drinking culture that you would think the licencing departments of the police, council, and locals would appreciate, right?

Nope.

The police have stepped up their presence on the streets of Hackney, a new initiative focusing on disorderly behaviour on the streets. Coming under this new focus are licensed venues.

No new extensions of operating hours; more stringent licensing law regulations; and licensees are being held accountable for the venue's impact on the local community. Subcommittees of neighbours' voices are recognised in the council decision-making processes for the night-time economy. I have put in the extended hours' application twice, and it was turned down both times. To try and circumnavigate the issue, I submit a Temporary Event Notices application. Any venue can have twelve issued in a year. It's a temporary licence that allows you to extend your operating hours and we really do need those extra few hours on the weekend to hit our financial targets.

I have a bit of a wobble with my two-stage plan. I jump at an opportunity which wasn't quite what I was thinking for as Stage Two, but I couldn't resist. I think it was driven by ego and the idea of opening a venue pretty much across the street from the Dragon. It's an iconic location in the middle of Shoreditch, called Herbal. It's iconic not because it's a great venue, but because it's infamous for being a total shithole, sticky, multilevel, squat-style venue with a terrible reputation for drugs, violence, and gang crimes. It has been under a constant cloud of blaze smoke and deafening drum and bass for years. It was shut down by the police and its venue operator removed. This is a big venue. With an enormous footprint in the middle of Shoreditch.

What if we created an entertainment-style complex? Café, bar, restaurant, nightclub, outdoor pool, lounge, and a few boutique accommodation rooms. Guests able to buy select curated Bathhouse items, like the bespoke wallpaper, branded Bathhouse spirits and chic deco, and our own merchandise. All under the one roof in the heart of Shoreditch. Glamorous and decadent, like Shoreditch House, which is a total success even though, before it opened, little whispers circled saying it would never work in the area. It was mocked for its elitism, but it was quickly embraced by locals, and no one can deny it's a fantastic space. I love it. What if we created a Bathhouse version, without a members-only policy, so it's accessible to everyone? There's nothing like it in the middle of Shoreditch.

The property owner is responsive to the idea and will work with us in preparing the building. It will cost a bundle, but we'll address the funds later. The police are already making it impossible for the licensed venue to reopen. I have a meeting booked with the head of licensing at the Bathhouse to give them a visual indication of the kind of sites I operate, which are a million light-years away from the old blaze club. With my plans to transform the old Herbal into The Bathhouse Quarters. Floor plans and mood boards. Business references and operating procedures. Ready to open discussions on the initial concept and ideas. They brought their legal team to the meeting and proceeded to rip down the concept, me as an operator, and clearly stated that this was NOT going to happen. They vowed to fight me at every step of the way.

So, I decided to fight them back.

They put conditions on the property and the current licence. There was strictly no dancing, DJs or live music, rendering it useless to any type of night-time economy industry, other than a restaurant. The owner and I instructed a lawyer to take the Hackney police licensing department to court to overturn the draconian policing system. We won and had all the limitations removed. I woke up the next day with a deep gut intuition and decided that I couldn't continue with this business venture. Even though we got rid of the issues, my gut is telling me it's a wrong move. Starting off any venture fighting the very organisation that will determine the future of the venue is risky. We lose the holding deposit for the venue and the legal fees spent in starting the lease negotiations. But I do feel like I won this round with the police. The idea is a solid one but just not right for me as a next move. At the present time, Shoreditch is now filled with these multifaceted venues.

It's still a concept I would love to execute one day, just not right now. I'm okay, coming to the conclusion that I don't want to move forward with it myself. I just don't like to be told that I can't do it by the police because they don't 'fancy it'. This gets me back on track for the REAL Stage Two.

Unfortunately, it still leaves me with the moaning neighbours of BBH in Stoke Newington, Hackney. The reason many people moved to the area just a few short years ago was the nightlife, the bars, the people, and the beating pulse. Then it happens one day. Instead of getting home at 7am from a night out, they find themselves getting up at 7am to get into the office for a breakfast meeting. The irreversible transition from the dark side over to the light. They still want the location and the gentrified elements of the once-frequented vibrant, eclectic neighbourhood. Just be quieter, please. Less busy, please. No noise from the pubs letting out at 11pm, please. No garbage trucks removing mountains of glass bottles from recycling bins, waking my newborn baby, please. They care about fund allocations being put into play equipment for their kids, not safer night buses to get drinkers home at night. They like the idea of a midnight nightcap in a bar but haven't set foot in a venue for about five years. But it looks great on the listing for the rental property they own. They can charge top money, thanks to the location and the entertainment amenities and excellent night transport. They vote with the voice of affluence, having long-forgotten the reasons why they first loved the area. The world of possibilities and adventure; new best friends and lovers who could be around any corner; spontaneous nights out; being able to investigate a career of creative pipe dreams. These vibrant nightspots are centres of creativity. Art, music, progressive thinking, food cultures, just experiencing life and trying on new, different versions of themselves. You try on sexuality for size. No judgement and no definitive answer required.

It's also where people get practical hands-on experience and a taste for future careers. Sound engineers, photographers, film directors, band managers, and club owners. Yes, it's a pleasure-filled playground for most, but for others, it's a place to practice their craft, make connections, get invaluable on-the-job experience, and get involved with industries that don't have a paved route straight from university. Also, at the heart of music and club cultures are creators. Fashion, art, the trend-makers. There are so many reasons why there needs to be a night-time economy. Apart from the financial benefit and practical side where money and employment are fed back into the community. But also for culture and the arts. The new round of creative thinkers need time in their playground.

The problem is that this round of people have come up through the scene and stopped living for the night. They've grown up and don't want this life anymore for themselves or anyone around them. So what about everyone else? Doesn't the next group of would-be creatives get their turn? The guy who earns his living pouring drinks behind a bar to offset his poorly-paid passion for booking up-and-coming bands. What about the girl who's behind the jump of the minicab office doing the graveyard shift so she can work for free as a stylist on magazine shoots during the day, to build her portfolio? Or the pub that's stood there for 100 years before you arrived? You used to enjoy the sunny beer garden, doing lines in the toilets on a bank holiday Sunday session. Hear a band that has changed your life. Held hands with a stranger and leave with a friend for life. These places matter. These times matter.

Instead of remembering your own pre-mortgage days, you write open letters to the Hackney Gazette. You get involved with the local council and noise-reduction committee, cosy up with the local minister, join community task forces against the night-time economy and use your newly acquired adultness to get your voice heard. The police are on speed dial, so you can report any disorderly behaviour at a moment's notice. You remain faceless but vigilant as you gather evidence in your logbook of incidences. You become a keyboard troll waging a word war on any activities past 10pm. Posting endlessly until the right people start paying attention. You sit in your front rooms. Twitching curtains in the dark and write your faceless words that will slowly bring down a culture and tradition of late nights, creativity, music and movements.

These make London the genuinely magical place it is. Where subcultures and unique diversity have always thrived. Way before you, your faceless rants and your keyboard.

So a sincere and heartfelt FUCK YOU, neighbour.

The Paynes are still nutting around in the background. Squabbling and fighting amongst themselves, irritating both sets of lawyers and exhausting the administrators. The deal is set to take place. It has gone past the point of Mrs Payne and her almost daily 'pulling out' but has been so long, it's unbearable. I've moved my office to the first floor of the BBH. It's bright and light. It even has windows! That look out over trees! And so much lovely grey East London sky... There should be a Pantone colour called 'London Sky Grey'. My window looks down onto the back alley where there's a flat-roofed shed with a mangy, ancient fox living on top of it. He must be a trillion years old, has three and a half legs, and appears to have gone a million rounds with every other animal and car in the neighbourhood. Mr Fox gives zero fucks. He looks like my soul feels. I throw scraps from my lunch onto the roof for him each day.

It's the last Saturday night at The Bathhouse before the Paynes deal is finalised. All the paperwork is in place, ready to be signed on Monday morning. Payment is with my lawyer, and I need to clear out the last bits from the venue. William is helping with the crossover, and he is not happy, and rightly so. The Paynes are total arseholes.

It's the 'Farewell Funeral' party at The Bathhouse. We've made life-sized tombstones to place around the venue, ordered meter-high blood-red roses the shape of a crucifix on easel stands and frilly maroon carnations spelling out 'RIP' to hang over the bar and DJ booth: Rich's last DJ set in the magical booth. His sets have been the heartbeat of this scene. It is the end, not only of an era of clubland for me. But a marking of our relationship and how much it has grown, at The Bathhouse. I can't imagine what this club would have felt like without his influence. I wear a long, black Morticia Addams-style dress, 50's hair, and a black morning veil. Rich was on damage-control duty today. I'd pounded myself full of so much alcohol, coke and sleeping tablets the night before, that I didn't care if I never woke up. I was shaking, hysterically crying with waves of panic attacks, the madness of my chaotic life has caught up with me, smashing me into the ground. He had to wipe me down with a wet towel, and I can't see an end to all this pain. He gives me a beer to help with the shakes and knows it's not the time for a lecture on self-care. It was looking like I wasn't going to be able to pull myself together. But I did, like I always do. At the very last minute, you would never have believed it was the same person. Smiling, perfectly turned out, all hello's and air kisses. Centre of the party. All fake and pretend, like a politician, waving at the crowd, kissing babies. A complete 180° to three hours earlier, when I was so broken I couldn't get off the floor: the beginning of a terrible comedown. Filled with shame and enough self-hatred to lock me frozen in the foetal position. Dead inside. I get through the party with more coke and more booze, and with Rich's music filling the void in my heart.

Mrs Payne is still fuming about the funeral party theme. She says it was killing off the business that they were buying. As my lawyer pointed out, again, they weren't buying our company: they were purchasing the lease off us. The twins were meant to come and flyer outside the party to give Bathhouse guests invitations to their new venture. They were calling it 'The Toy Chest'. They never showed up.

On Monday, I bring down the folder with all the paperwork required for the exchange. The Paynes call me and are now requesting an electrical certificate. Argh, fuck me! By law, we aren't due one for another eight months, and it wasn't stipulated as a condition of the sale from the lawyers as a part of the handover. Now, they won't do the exchange until they get it. I call around and find an electrician willing to come over immediately and do an electrical certificate. The issue with this is that it's such an old building and any electrician will cover their own arse and note every little thing wrong with it. I don't have anyone available to come this morning, who is a 'trusted contact' and be able to reflect 'fairness' in the report, if you get what I mean. The venue is in exactly the same position, if not better, as when we took it over: we've had work done to the main switchboard and replaced the wiring after that dick spilt a drink on the DJ equipment. As predicted, the report does come back pretty scary. I slide it into the back of the plastic folder. There's nothing I can do about it now. I go to finish the deal.

They're already in the venue with a team of new bar staff who are 'cleaning'. I'm guessing they haven't been given any clear direction, so they aimlessly walk from one area of the venue, wipe down a tile, then saunter over to another random spot. Totally pointless.

The twins are hanging tacky flashing fairy lights everywhere. Mrs Payne is sitting at a makeshift desk consisting of three dining tables pushed together. Covered in piles and piles of paperwork, several plastic bags' worth of receipts, and mounds of unpacked boxes with her credit card machines. Polystyrene and plastic wrap. It's a total mess.

The venue has a really different feeling to it. The air is different. The sound is different. The light is different. The atmosphere has shape-shifted. It's not mine any more. It's not my own beautiful creation. Not my biggest success or my most colossal failure. Not mine.

I sit at the table with Mrs Payne. She flaps and farts about, taking me through each and every item on the itinerary that isn't precisely to her liking. I explain that the kitchen equipment is old and things like the big double fridge that is used for dry storage and bench space was never a 'working fridge'. We have a full walk-in refrigerator instead. It goes on and on. I can't understand why this wasn't done days ago, as it's all signed off. I'm not sure what she's trying to achieve here. Then the penny drops. There isn't time to fix or renegotiate these items as the lawyers have signed the deals off, but there is the case of the outstanding two instalments of money she still owes after the exchange date; one payment for the liquidator of 40k and one for me, also 40k.

She runs through the list and says this is going to affect our sale price. I let her know I would prefer to have the items replaced or repaired at my expense or get the lawyers involved again, as the deal is meant to be finalised. She 'ums' and 'ahhs' and all I want is to get the fuck out of there. Then she asks about the electrical certificates. I flick through the loose pages of the last minute electrical certificate and show her the rest of the folder, which is neatly presented in plastic sleeves and dividers. She scowls at the fact it all seems to be there. I get up from the table, and I wish them luck through gritted teeth in a cheery sing-song voice and fake smile and walk through the venue for the last time. It's like pressing the rewind button of when I first entered the majestic venue. Back up the creamy marble stairs, running my fingers along the gorgeous ceramic tiles embedded with my DNA for the last time. I stop at the top of the stairs, out of sight of the Paynes. With my key, I ping off two of the beautiful mosaic tiles. The ones Rich and I did rubbings of to create our wallpaper. I put the precious tiles in my bike basket and ride home, numb, with tears rolling down my face.

Sadly and not surprisingly, this isn't the last time I have to deal with Mrs Payne. The liquidator is fuming as the Paynes refuse to pay the first instalment owed after the first two weeks have passed. They're annoyed that the electrical certificate went missing. She said she saw it in the handover folder, but then it was gone. I told her the table was such a mess, it's no wonder she had lost it. She said I had ruined the business. All of this falls on deaf ears, and the liquidator got his money. When it came to my turn to collect that last payment, I knew it was never going to be easy. She made that crystal clear. We were scheduled to go to court and before the court dates came around, she cancelled, due to 'ill health', but wrote essays to the judge, all handwritten in her spidery scrawl stating why she wouldn't pay the last instalment. I gave up trying to get it. Walking away from 40,000 pounds. Fucking hurts, but there were more pressing matters that came to a head, and I didn't have the energy to fight this particular battle any more. I think, deep down, the day I walked out of The Bathhouse for the last time, I knew I wasn't going to get a penny from that dried-up old Miss Havisham cunt.

The Paynes keep the City of London authorities very busy during their operational reign, right up 'til the venue was taken off them. The industry rumours were worse than what they were caught doing, but I have read the transcripts from the tribunal hearings, and they are pretty fucking bad. I was shocked, and it takes a lot to surprise me considering I worked for the Devil and am a bit of a horned demon myself. I can only imagine what else they did behind closed doors, considering what they got caught doing!

They didn't continue with any of our music styles or try to keep the Time Out crowd that we had cultivated into a comfortable, reliable trade, once the Shoreditch scene had moved on. They wanted the flashy kind of club that was in gangster videos. They started using R&B promoters who came with the promise of big spenders, customers who paid VIP prices and bought magnum bottles of vodka. With these kind of appealing high bar spends, comes trouble.

In a very short time they operated the venue: stabbings that the venue never reported to the police. Instead, A&E had to call them in. There was a riot with over two hundred people involved, causing eight streets in the centre of London to shut down. Multiple fights and assault charges, a known drug dealer flashing around a gun inside the venue, aiming it, pretending to take people down. A disgruntled customer driving his car into the waiting entry queue of the club, driving after the people who were trying to run away. A man beating up his ex-girlfriend until she was unconscious, while security and customers stood watching, doing nothing. Customers being attacked by two men armed with baseball bats. Police intimidation and perverting the course of justice. Gang turf wars. There were open drug deals, use of cannabis and coke in the venue in plain sight at tables. Nobody even tried to hide it during police walk-throughs. They were caught pouring non-duty import vodka into magnum bottles of Grey Goose on two separate occasions, which brought on an investigation by Weights and Measures for having illegal alcohol being poured from the bar. They found a station of funnels, decanters, crates of empty premium liquor bottles, and cases of cheap booze to fill the premium bottles in the kitchen. There were tasteless club nights called the 'Tupac Massacre' and 'Valentine Slayer'. They falsely advertised the official after-party for Lady Gaga, with her personally hosting the party with over a thousand people attending and refused to close down the event even though the police confirmed with Gaga's management that they had never heard about the party and it was not happening. Police feared a riot from Gaga's 'Little Monsters', when they realised it is a scam. It goes on and on and makes me look like a saint in comparison. The Paynes seemed to be operating straight out of a Bloods and Crip's story.

That evening, I stood in the hallway of our house and made an alarming discovery. Rich said we needed to lay off the coke and booze after I imploded before the Bathhouse closing party and I totally agree that things need to change... I crumbled by 8pm, crying, begging him to go to the shop and buy me a bottle of wine. I can't go because I'm a mess. "Just call a dealer," I pleaded. "I can't go cold turkey." Having a full-blown panic attack. I couldn't breathe. My chest felt like it was in a vice. My crying, now howling. I have tunnel vision and my head is going to explode. My throat is ripped and hoarse from all the screaming and begging. My addictions are fully hooked into me now. This isn't a fun lifestyle choice any more. I need it to live.

We decide to get away for a few days, something cheap. I find the perfect place. It's a thirty-six pounds a night accommodation and two return Ryan Air flights for less than a hundred pounds round trip. It's a place where the coke dealer isn't on speed dial and delivers to the door in less than twenty minutes. We let Alli and the family know we won't be coming to the hospital this weekend and jump on the plane to Croatia, landing in Split. We spend a few days drinking, eating, and walking the cobbled streets and nearby hills. Decompressing. We talk about what the future holds. About the Bathhouse and how it ran away from me so quickly, how I could do things differently. How we wish Rich's mum Joan was still here, and how she would have been able to help me with the accounts. We talk about how we both got a shock at how coke has elevated from 'social' use to a 'necessity', and we both agree to cut back. I agree to go to see a psychologist to help with making the changes. Now the Bathhouse is gone, it will be easier. I still have fallout and a financial mess to clean up, but the actual venue is in the past now. BBH is ticking along nicely but doesn't need the brainpower or creative drive like Bathhouse did.

We wonder if London is changing - or are we? Is there a possibility for life for us outside of this draining but still electric city? We talk about Stage Two. We talk about the abortion. We talk about the robbery. We talk about Josh and the up-coming results after this particularly brutal round of chemo. We talk about all the things that we are too scared to discuss back in the familiar space of home; all the things we don't want to address: the emotional cans of worms because we are in survival mode and just trying to manage to get through the day. It's one step at a time. One day at a time. One problem at a time.

From Split, we take a dusty drive down the quiet coast to Zadar for the next leg of our journey. We park our rental car at the wharf and drag our bags, boxes of groceries, and the fresh produce we bought from the village market. We get two casks of wine and as much beer as we can carry. At the end of the wharf, we see a little fishing boat and a man who looks like a sea captain out of a stop-motion Wallace and Gromit film. The fishing boat looks sturdy enough, and we start loading our haul onto the boat. The sea captain then unloads it over the far side into the water. Confused, I peer overboard. He has a tiny boat tethered to the fishing boat. It rocks violently each time the smallest barely-there wave hits its side. When our massive booze stash is put into it, the boat almost tips over.

He speaks no English, and we speak no Croatian. Rich is less than impressed. He hates water. He's like a south London cat and definitely not a fan of small boats. Begrudgingly, he gets in the boat, and we head out to sea. The boat is sitting so low in the water that any slight movement adds to the growing pool of salty water at the bottom. I love the fresh, salty air and striking, deep blue Adriatic Sea. We stay close to the jagged rocky shore and deserted coastline for twenty minutes, then take a sharp turn straight out to sea. The curved horizon reveals our home for the next few days, as it rises from the ocean erect and proud. A deserted island with an 18th-century lighthouse and a population of three mountain sheep as our only companions. The dealers won't be able to get me out here. Or me to them.

We unpack our things in the tiny working lighthouse. There's no running hot water, the kitchen and bathroom haven't been updated since the 1920s, and the bedroom is sparse and simple with terrazzo marble floors. The 360° view of the sea from every window is breath-taking. A brief exchange of sign language charades between the sea captain, who shows us what we need to do with the lighthouse at night. Then he's gone, heading back out to sea and leaving us to it. Surely we're not responsible enough to operate a lighthouse?

It's thrilling to me, being trapped on a deserted island with my favourite person in the whole world. We set off to explore the tiny island. The lighthouse has a paved area around it with an amazing sandstone wall overlooking the vast ocean. Super yachts and sailing boats dot the water as far as the eye can see. The wind whips the water up, but this side of the island is protected. Below the lighthouse is a sandstone jetty for little boats to pull up to and a rock alcove for swimming. The water is freezing, and the seafloor is teeming with big, black, hairy sea cucumbers. But the water is pristine. Apparently, it's one of the cleanest bodies of water in the entire world. Around a small cliff is a track leading to a miniature pine forest, no bigger than twenty metres. Tall pine trees sway gently in the wind, and the ground is carpeted with years' of fallen pine needles. The smell is divine. There is a fire pit in the middle of the mini forest. Following the path around it leads to a pebble beach with rock pools at either end. It's perfect for swimming if you can brave the icy water. The trail then follows all the way back around to the lighthouse. This side of the island is barren, with grass, sheep poop and rocks. The path then meets back up at the light-house terraced area with a huge towering pine tree and a makeshift stone out-door BBQ, which has four breeze blocks and a grill across the top. You have got to be Bear Grylls to work this crude grill.

The sunsets are like an acid light show. Trippy deep purple, fuchsia, and bright tangerine blaze up the sky and then slip into the hollow black night, dotted with the most luminous stars piercing the heavens above our heads.

It takes us a day or two to unwind and get into the swing of being totally alone, but I love it. I jump into the water any chance I get. It's so cold the air gets punched out of your lungs, sends your bum hole into your stomach but fuck me, do I feel alive. We drink white wine sangria and play strip penny can. The idea of isolation and making the most of the privacy is also thrilling. The best orgasm I've ever had was on a grassy hill on the very top on the island after an icy swim, lying on my back, looking up at the perfect blue sky as the clouds drifted by. The cold, fresh breeze itching my salty naked skin and the soul-warming sunshine glowing on my body. Maybe there's something magical about the winds of the Adriatic Sea, and if it hadn't been such a perfect day, I would have sworn

I'd been struck by lightning. It was that powerful. Kind of biblical. Perhaps that's what the prophets in the old testament were having up on the hilltops. Orgasms - not receiving the voice of God! I can see now that they could easily have been confused.

I've always loved to cook for Rich. It has been a special ritual for us. A daily offering of affection and caring for his soul. I love the cooking part, and he loves the eating part! For me, it's a really lovely act of pure love, something wholesome and nurturing. We bought fresh fish and squid from a fisherman who pulled up to the island on a little boat. I wrap the fish in pine needles and leave it to slowly bake over the fire, while I gut the squid. The squid is cooked on the grill, marinated in wild herbs collected from the island and the juice from a few enormous lemons. The fresh produce in Croatia makes even a simple salad sandwich a god-like feast. Everything is so fresh and tastes like it's on steroids. Compared to the food back in the UK, which is probably on actual growth steroids and tastes like nothing, the food in Croatia has this incredible, amplified flavour.

We while away the days, reading, sleeping, staring out to sea, gazing at the stars, talking, having sex, and eating. On David Attenborough sheep watch, a teenie lamb had joined the family of three! It is deeply restorative and proves to be a wonderful way to reconnect with each other.

On the last night at the lighthouse, we're lying in bed reading, getting ready to drift into a deep, relaxed holiday sleep when Rich's phone starts buzzing with notifications. He has thirteen missed calls, a bunch of voicemails and messages that have all pinged in at once as if a satellite was perfectly in range, sending signals to the phone. Before he gets a chance to read or listen to his messages, the phone starts ringing again. He answers, and as he listens, his expression changes. The look on his face will haunt me for the rest of my life.

15

Josh was being sent home from the hospital. The relentless rounds and rounds of treatment weren't successful. The doctors, specialists, care teams, experts, second, third and fourth opinions confirmed the same thing. He has fought as hard as his little body could fight, and it was as much as one little body could take. He'd reached his limit. The treatments were just barely holding it off, but the leukaemia had taken over his body, coming back stronger and stronger after each round of chemotherapy.

I have no idea how Alli and Scott took on these words. Seeping into their comprehension. Sifted through their souls. Their little boy, the fighter, was now terminal. The fight is over, and they were to go home. To hold onto every breath. Until the very last little breath was taken.

The experts explained that once he was home and had stopped treatment, Josh would most likely have a few weeks of 'okay' health, but without the chemo keeping the leukaemia at bay, his health will slowly decline. He would be given palliative support and pain management so he could pass away in his own home with his family wrapped tightly around him.

I can't understand it. I don't get it. I don't believe it. There has to be another treatment or some other option? They turned up every day with endless positive energy. They played the game, followed the rules. Josh battled through the long, cruel days and the impossible, dark nights. This isn't how it's meant to end!

How do they put one step in front of the other? How do you walk out of the consulting room, pack up your 'hospital home' of the past year and a half, and just walk out? How do you get in the car and drive home, put the key in the door and pretend it's life as normal?

Until it's not.

This is bravery. This is courage. This is the titanium strength of a parent's love. Unlike any other, I've known. But they did it. Together. The three of them. One minute, one step, one hour, and one day at a time. They didn't have a choice.

The sea captain came at sunrise, and we chuck our belongings in a bin bag, throw it in the rocky boat, and race towards the mainland. We drove straight to the airport. I cried the whole way there, so hard that I couldn't see the road. Rich sat in the passenger seat. Silent. Wounded, still. His head resting on the window. As soon as we landed, we went straight to the hospital.

They came home and had precious days in the backyard filled with unseasonable sunshine, laughter, and beautiful times together. You wouldn't have known Josh was unwell apart from the catheter lines. But then the pain slowly crept in, and his little body started to crumble. So they camped in the lounge room with dimmed lights, snuggled down in soft duvets, fluffy rugs, favourite films, stories, and quiet play.

Josh passes away in the stillness of the night. The trio were calm, quiet and deeply in love. Next to his Mummy. Next to his Daddy. They all slept soundly for the last time, together. Both parents saying "good night" but both knowing that it was really "goodbye" to their little boy.

I have no idea how the heart has the capacity to deal with that amount of pain. It's not in our DNA to cope with this kind of loss. The bravery needed to ensure your child doesn't see your pain or fear. Your utter devastation. A parent losing a child - it's not the way it's meant to happen. Alli and Scott are stronger, so much stronger than I can ever imagine. I am humbled by their strength and sick in my head at the cruel unravelling of this family unit. How anyone can believe there is a God in these kinds of circumstances is beyond me. Science yes, but even that failed them. But for God, allowing a little boy to die after a long, drawn-out battle with cancer? The world is cruel and unjust. And I can't see how this is fair. FUCK YOU, Universe!

We all busy ourselves with tasks. Tasks to block the pain. Tasks to divert the pain. We kick into help overdrive. Anything to not address the pain. The funeral needs lots of arranging and as 'carers for the carers', our days are filled with making beautiful hand-made programmes, getting flight-path approval for a balloon release, writing a poem for the service. Decorating the space for the reception for the celebration of Josh's life. It's colourful, positive and lovely choosing things that Josh loved. And sharing them with the people who are deeply grieving the loss of an exceptional little boy.

The pain I feel isn't mine. I grieve for Alli and Scott. One moment they were a family and the next they are a couple again. I grieve for Rich's dad Bob, whose heart is breaking and he can't hide it. The pain is too powerful. Rich is strong. Always, for everyone.

A few days after the funeral, we're back home. After dinner, he slips away into his studio with the door closed. I call out for him, and he says he'll be out in a bit. I stand at the door and listen. I can feel him sitting on the floor, leaning against the door. He weeps. Deeply. It's uncontrollable and heart-wrenching. I press my palms against the door, and I can feel his pain fill the wooden fibres with grief. He pushes pain so far down. Bottled up. The pain he hides, the pain for his little sister, pain for a little boy who didn't get to grow up, pain for his mum who never met her first grandchild, pain for his dad and another loss to rip a deep hole through his family. Rich doesn't care about his pain. His pain is the pain of his loved ones. This is what devastates him.

Life feels shaky. Unsteady. I feel like I can control and sort out physical problems, issues that need 'fixing'. But I can't handle emotion. Feelings can't be controlled or fixed or handled. They hurt to the point of being unbearable, as though you're an overfilled balloon ready to explode. The emotions are overwhelming, but we block them out at home. The same way as we always do.

Rich is drained. Physically, mentally, and emotionally. This morning, he's on an early shift at the design studio. He's pleased for the distraction and rides his fixed-gear bike across central London before the sun comes up. Rain, hail or shine, he isn't a fair-weather rider like me.

He calls. He never calls me on the way into work. There's a tremor in his voice. His breathing is different. I panic. He's been hit by a bus and knocked off his bike. He's okay. Bruised, swollen, scraped, and shaken up. Between a bus and a car. The bike is crushed The helmet deeply dented and cracked.

QUEEN OF CLUBS

Tava,

FOR FUCK'S SAKE, STOP STALLING!
It's time.

The Universe

I have been stalling, not wanting to admit it.
But the love affair is over.

16

There is a saying 'when a man is tired of London, he is tired of life'. Maybe this is true but fuck me, this cold-hearted mistress has lured me in, dazzled me blind, seduced and charmed me. She's sucked me dry, drained my soul, snatched my will to live, and brutally kicked me to the curb.

I pathetically kept coming back to her, a snivelling mess again and again and again.

Now, I am officially tired of life. So yes, my love affair with London is over. I'm leaving. Doing 40 miles an hour down the A23 and I'm not looking back. Mostly because I can't. I've packed the van so tight I'm not able to use the rear-view mirror. But metaphorically you feel me, right? No turning back.

Turning my back on the city that changed my life, changed me as a person. Because I want to change what my future looks like and I have to do it away from her. I'm scared of how it would continue for us.

And this, my dear friends, is how Stage Two begins. Well, actually it started a few miles back as we pulled out of De Beauvoir Town, handed back the keys to the letting agent, and set off. Rich and I, side by side, the road-trip music curator, navigator, snack supplier, and animal wrangler. The van is so overloaded that Dollar is sitting at Rich's feet in the footwell and Bill is on Rich's lap in a travel cage. Handsome Bill is so unimpressed with the journey that he pisses all over Rich's lap two minutes into the trip. Hot ammonia cat piss fills the van's cabin, soaks into Rich's jeans, and the car seat. But you can't even be mad at him 'cause he's just so good-looking.

Stupidly and unsurprisingly, we'd stayed up all night as a last hurrah to both London and coke. We were planning on leaving both behind. Goodbye to both our mistress and our destroyer in one swift tactical move.

But making the exit clean is waaaay more painful than necessary. A strong start to the trip. It's also pissing rain as the trucks are loaded. Hail starts as we leave town.

I still won't look back.

I need to track back a bit. I'm not really skipping a big bit of story. How we got in the transit van, ears-deep in our material possessions and fur family was just uneventful for a change. I believe it's a sign from the Universe that we're doing the right thing. Something clicked for me when Rich was hit by the bus. We had been talking about making a huge life change, but we kept putting it off. That day I realised we were spread too thin, run ragged by our own life. Dancing too close to our demons and making shitty life choices.

This part was easy. A simple exchange of 'venue for payment'; a civilised business deal. The perfect choreography of how sale and exchange should go, seamless synchronised swimming compared to the Paynes. A husband and wife team bought The Baby Bathhouse. They purchased the business as a turnkey: they just had to turn up and start trading. I'd owned The Baby Bathhouse for less than a year and kinda had enough cash to start Stage Two.

I fed my fox friend my last leftover lunch crust and walked away. Both of us slightly stronger. Still broken with deep scars that won't ever properly heal, but with the new winds of change bring hope and a fresh start.

A clean slate and some sea air.

Never in a million light years would I ever have imagined Rich leaving London. But the city was changing for us: it was losing its charm, even for a diehard, living, breathing Londoner. Our outlook was also evolving, and so was the area around us. After the break-in, everything seemed heightened. These things were always happening around us: it hadn't just started out of nowhere. I was only more aware of it. One block down, a teenage girl had been shot in the neck at a takeaway shop, waiting for her order. Acid was being thrown around like holy water, and muggings turned into knifepoint robberies which turned into stabbings. There was a riot in the streets of Hackney. I rode my bike home down a smoke-filled Kingsland Road, the street packed with police and riots trucks trying to get the gangs in balaclava masks, bandanas, and hoods under control. I weaved through fires and smashed shop fronts. People looting and fighting everywhere. Prison transfer trucks round up the gangs. It was like riding through a film set of an Armageddon movie. Five people died.

Rich had grown up in a really rough neighbourhood. He'd been through a violent stabbing a few years ago after a night out with friends, when he was followed home by a junkie. The junkie stabbed him twice, through the lung, left to die. If it hadn't been for his lifesaving hero/then-girlfriend, he'd have bled out in the street. I'm deeply indebted to her for keeping my love alive before it was my turn. Rich is tougher than nails, used to street tension and accustomed to a grittier life compared to my mellow yellow Home and Away dreamy upbringing. But his past has left him edgy, and in the time since I've known him, I can feel his angst rising, the longer we stay. There was really only one choice. Although he loves London, he is also ready to leave.

I try to imagine having a child here. And I just can't.

We have put a lot of things on hold while the Bathhouse was demanding so much of my headspace. And putting our emotion and energy into the family. Deserving all of our heart space. We needed to be in London to be able to support them and make the weekly trip up to the hospital. Now we needed to do something for ourselves. They also didn't know the level of dependency we had on alcohol and coke. This was our chance for a new, positive, healthier lifestyle. I don't want to be a vampire anymore. I wanted to live back in the light. A life that didn't revolve around night-time drug-taking, numbing-body drinking, and locking ourselves away from the day.

It wasn't just us, either. We have an awesome group of close friends. Those crazy fairies rolling around the floor of the pub and the boys in tight leather and floppy fringes. They were Rich's life-long pals, and now those crazy bitches and guys are my friends, too. And they aren't actually crazy. Just really lovely, amazing cool people who were all feeling the love-hate pull with London life. Somewhere that your money stretched further, without having to compromise on your creative dreams. E-Doggy and Daisy are leaving, as well.

What would life look like away from the streets of our now not so beloved East London? Everyone is looking for more and slowly moving away. Friends were the heart of London for me. The rent at our De Beauvoir terrace was tripled. It's ridiculous. Insane. A crazy amount of greedy landlord inflation tax. I couldn't believe anyone would pay that and the property would sit empty for ages waiting for some moron to pay it. But on inspection day, over 50 people traipsed through our place. Apparently, 25 rental application offers were made that very day, and we had three offers to buy our furniture to go with it. It really was a sweet place. Hollywood-fucking-amazing-love began here, but there were so many mixed feelings for us. Falling deeply in love together, but also our life deeply falling apart.

As far as any city outside of London goes, it has that cool factor: the lovely houses, vintage shops, fantastic music scene, beautiful bars, and bundles of culture. It has to be a do-able commute for Rich. He has officially stopped DJing and just works on producing music so doesn't need to be in London for gigs. He works in the Design Studio of The Body Shop and could get door to door in 1.5hrs. Seems like a long time but it can take an hour to get from East to West London during peak hour. With the significantly lower rent and property prices, even with the expensive train commute, it will be a much cheaper and better quality of life... As long as you don't have to rely on working here, because the wages are in line with the lower cost of living. This was an easy choice for both us.

Stage Two... is Brighton!

It's a perfect place to open a nightclub.

A perfect place to start thinking about a baby born from our Hollywood-Fucking-Amazing-Love.

Brighton has a thriving nightlife, and a vibrant club scene made up of locals, university students, weekenders, day-trippers, and holidaymakers. It's a place where people come to have a good time. When we realised that our Bathhouse customers were travelling into London to party, we looked at other larger towns and commuter cities that had a strong youth population, entertainment cultures, and lower commercial rent, and an appealing lifestyle. Brighton was the first and only real choice for us.

Rich spent lots of time here with the Mod Weekenders, DJing and visiting friends who had already made the change to seaside living. As soon as I arrived off the train for the first time, I fell in love with Brighton. The old cobbled lanes and the quirky labyrinth maze of streets. It has a rogue history full of charm. It's a hub of creativity, with kooky hole-in-the-wall bars, more beautiful old pubs than you could ever want, gorgeous Regency-era buildings, and greenery for miles, right on your doorstep. Not to forget the devastatingly handsome Royal Pavilion and everyone's favourite gaudy old Palace Pier. Everything is slower, friendlier, and less prickly than London. The clincher for me is the sea! Oh, the sea... The endless stretch of deep blue English sea and pebbly shoreline. It's moody, broody, frothy, and fucking windy most of the time, but I am thrilled to gaze at the endless horizon, rather than the glowing London city skyline of smog and steel. The wind off the water has magical powers.

We pull up in the cat piss-soaked van. The moving truck is waiting for us out front of our new home. You couldn't get further away than our east London chemical-ridden Hackney grot spot. This area of Brighton is called Hanover. It's full of unfiltered sunlight, and it's impossible to hide in the darkness here. Hanover is nicknamed 'Muesli Mountain' for its high number of organic living, eco-friendly vegetarians per capita. Standing here, ready for Stage Two, a pair of bright-eyed trying-to-be-ex-coke-heads, standing at the crest of a very steep hill, looking down over Brighton and the endless sea. We're ready for change, prepared to take a blindfolded spin around and a stab at a 'normal' life.

I've found the quirkiest, strangest, coolest place for us to call home. The lovely owners rented it out to us after two interviews. The property sits on the corner of two streets. It's unassumingly plain from the outside. It's painted pristine white in a sea of multicoloured pastel terraces and looms over the neighbourhood. Across the road from the best fish and chip shop, The Codfather (ha!), and there's a huge cherry blossom growing outside. These trees are following me!

It sat empty for five months, waiting for the right tenants to come along. I do feel a bit guilty because we did leave out the fact we had a lovely Ewok-lookalike dog and a devilishly handsome cat. Two very well-behaved adopted brothers and best friends. The problem? Our new dream home is strictly no pets allowed. I'd made a pact with myself: no more bending the rules. But this was only a harmless little evasion of truth.

The terrace is in the old fishermen's cottage area and tightly packed mixed industry live-work terraces. Woodworkers, butchers, haberdashers. Our Muesli Mountain corner terrace takes up two blocks over four levels and a hotch-potch collection of oddly laid out rooms. It was built in the Victorian era, but it's simple, working-class and sturdy, rather than ornate in design, like the traditional Victorian-era aesthetic. During the 1920s, it was a general store and later was owned by a family who won the lottery while they lived here during the '80s. They converted the basement into a pub.

Yes, there is now a miniature pub in our basement. The house is painted mostly white with brass detailing and little nautical touches. There's wooden floors, nice carpeting, and duck-egg blue painted wall panelling.

The basement/converted pub will be Rich's music studio and party room. The main floor has an odd layout. You enter through the tiny kitchen - it's a bit annoying - but the rest of the house compensates for it. From there, you go down a wonky hallway into the lounge and dining room. There's a small bathroom off to the side. It's a rabbit warren of odd spaces, with no straight walls or right-angle corners in any of the rooms. It's all wonky and slanted and utterly charming. Beautiful natural light floods into the rooms from all sides. The first floor is up the steepest steps with rope and brass railing. It leads up to a low-hanging chandelier in the double-storey ceiling skylight. To the left are a bedroom and a bathroom. The latter has a roof terrace, overlooking the multicolour houses and postcard streets all the way down to the beach. Through the back is the main bedroom. It's enormous with bay windows which have deep-set benches for looking out over Brighton. There is a staircase in the middle of the room. That leads up to a lovely converted attic: this will be my dressing room. It's advertised as a four-bedroom property. It is spacious and a bit on the excessive side for two people and our over-sized furniture. But this is what's possible when you move away from one of the most expensive cities in the worlds. The rent is precisely half of what we were paying in London. I adore the bright light and old world seaside quirks. It's charming and cosy and the most exciting place for us to build a new life.

Rich loves the daily commute back to London. Finishing tracks he's made in the studio, on his laptop, gives him so much extra time to devote to his music passion. Before, the call of the pub seemed to win over studio time. The house is all sorted, unpacked, and looks beautiful with our over-the-top house trimmings, chandeliers, and furniture. It's the cutest. Lovely velvet curtains in the bedroom (no blackout blinds here) and plants. Because plants love sunlight and the curtains aren't drawn back 24 hours a day, blocking out the vitamin D. Potted herbs in the kitchen, and bright sunny perennials rim the outside windowsills and rooftop balcony. It's well on its way to feeling like a real home.

There's an organic wholefoods store at the end of the road, a café called Fanny's, with t-shirts and mugs with their irresistible business one-liner 'I LOVE FANNY'S'. The area is heart-warming and full of life. I spend my days wandering the streets of the Old Town area of Brighton, meeting with estate agents and getting a feel for the club market. Brighton is really different to Shoreditch, Hackney, and the Bathhouse venues, where gay, straight, bi, non-binary, whatever your preference is, never really came into it. Sexuality and gender identity is not a divider in the bar and club scene in East London, but here it is. Gay on one side of the city and straight on the other. Along the seafront is a long line of big-capacity clubs, mainly student venues which are open to the early hours of the morning. Dotted through the lanes and the centre of the old town are independent pubs and small wine bars. There is the main road down from the train station all the way to the seafront, filled with chain pubs, cheesey clubs, tacky hen and stag-do venues. This takes up a solid square mile of space. The main street down to the sea isn't an area I'm keen on, and neither is the strip along the seafront. Neither is the gay area. So it leaves me a section in the middle to zero in on for my venue search.

I want a smallish venue, ideally around the 300 people capacity mark with a late drinking licence and music allowed until 5am. I don't want to pay any goodwill or venue fees, and I don't want to buy an existing venue. There are no current listings of available properties with this set of criteria. This isn't surprising as it's a really narrow search window. I reverse the hunting tactics and start looking for venue licences on buildings that aren't currently in use. This turns up a few options. It's not the traditional route. It means it probably won't be an operational space, which means none of the usual amenities like loos, a bar structure or cellars are in place, but it's easier to snap up a venue that hasn't been overexposed and a tired old drinking space. Plus, I can avoid paying 'good-will' for business trade, to get a customer base I don't want and have to pay to get into a business, only to gut it and rebuild from scratch.

My vision for this new space is to make it an interactive experience; a discovery journey for the customer, not just another drinking venue. I want to avoid the full sit-down dining restaurant this time around. I'm playing with the concept of 'things aren't always what they seem'. A small quaint storefront. An antique and artefacts store filled high with curios. Green marble plinths with porcelain cheetahs, their jewelled eyes glinting as they snarl gold teeth frozen in mid-roar. A towering taxidermy grizzly bear in a fez and a rare white male peacock with its icy white feather plumes proudly on display. An original Zoltar machine in the corner. A hand-carved great, great, great grandfather clock with all the bells and chimes. Books lining the shelves from floor to ceiling with walnut library ladders on caster wheels. With an old brass National till, the 'no sale' on display and lots of panelled etched glass cabinetry. As you step through the door, a bell attached to a gold chain will ring softly to announce your entrance. You still don't know if it's that secret club you heard about, an actual store or entirely the wrong address.

After triple checking you have the correct address, an elusive shopkeeper comes out from behind a velvet curtain and offers you access to a hidden nightclub. You pay him, and he directs you to find the entrance, reminding you that "not everything is as it seems". Then he is gone. Now tasked with finding the secret entrance to the venue, you start looking around. In the corner, an Egyptian mummy sarcophagus. It's bronze paint is flaking, rich earthy tones and shades of turquoise decorate the hand-carved surface. You push on the golden medallion around its neck, opening the sarcophagus and step into a small, dark passageway that leads you towards a bright light. Your eyes adjust to the light, and the tunnel kicks you out into the middle of the nightclub! Well, this was one concept until a guy at the local pub said he heard that another venue was planning to open a bar and restaurant with a vintage counter selling vanity sets, dresses and purses. I know this operator has loads of cash, as well, so it will be a quality fit-out. It's too close to my idea, and I couldn't risk investing the cash on a concept with a lookalike down the road.

Concept clubs need the wow factor to be executed to perfection. You can't risk any confusion or a 'who did it better'. Coming up with concepts is my favourite part of club planning. It's my dream job; well - apart from being a getaway driver for a crime ring. I would love to create venue concepts, develop and oversee the creative process, get the venue designed, built, build out the brand identity, curate the opening party, manage the launch with the PR agency, then hand it over. Ideally, sell it on and not have to do the day-to-day shift grind. Oh, maybe one day when I have a cashed-up backer, and we can flip concept clubs and bars around the world. I'll pop that on the future vision board!

Back to the drawing board for concepts, but I still need to pin down this elusive physical venue. Trawling through council building properties, I've found a site that made my tiny black heart skip a beat. It's on Kings Road, a great location. Perfection, in fact, from what I can tell on the map, which can be deceiving some times. Google street view is useless, as the street is filled with skip bins chock-full of rubble. It's set back from the sea but is on the main road that runs parallel to the water, opposite the new pier backing onto the old Lanes. It was taken back from the tenants many, many years ago, due to the building being in disrepair.

There were also rumours of it being a chapter of the Hells Angels' clubhouse, drug and prostitute den. I head down to the council to investigate. It has been assigned over to a property developer on a two-year repair deal. He's taken the building off the council at a very low price. He makes the repairs in line with the council's guidelines; once approved, he then owns the property. From what I can piece together, the finishing date must be close. I find the number for the agent doing the deal. It's a six-floor building with the ground floor shop and an underground basement space which has been derelict for seven years. They haven't been into the basement as the ceiling has collapsed. Apparently, it has a 4.30am alcohol licence. Hmm... interesting. Can I meet the new owner and do an initial viewing, please?

I pull up outside the venue. The building is covered in scaffolding and is a live worksite, but the location is fucking PERFECT. It's just in front of the historic old Lanes, a lovely cluster of tea shops, jewellers, bars, pubs and restaurants. Better still, it's directly across from the Palace Piers. I jump off my bike. The wind is so strong, I can't open my eyes. It's forcing my head down, chin tucked to my chest. Hunching against the wind, I hug my bike, so we don't fly away. I can't do anything about my black and white 50's checked circle skirt blowing up and plastered itself up over my shoulders, like an upside-down reverse superhero waist cape or a hairy-legged walking picnic blanket. Please, please, fucking please don't let anyone be around to see this undignified entrance. I stumble and pull my bike into a windbreak of a kebab shop and peek my head around the corner. Yep, the owner and estate agent are standing right there. Argh, I'm too embarrassed to come out. Cursing my skin-coloured, threadbare knickers, unwaxed legs, hairy, hairy bikini line, and the winged period pad poking out.

I can confirm I have let myself go a little since leaving the capital. I quickly straighten myself out and pretend it didn't just happen. Over-compensate with confident, firm handshakes and not breaking eye contact. It's bizarre behaviour, but I try to pretend none of us had to witness that.

The new landlord looks like he works as a deckhand on a fishing boat in his paint-covered shirt, ripped shorts and worn-down deck shoes, deep tan and floppy, blond-tipped hair. So it's strange when he opens his mouth and out comes this ill-fitting blue-blooded round plummy accent. He sounds like royalty but looks like he's been on a deserted island for the past decade with a football called Wilson as his only pal. The agent is your standard, medium-priced suited, shiny-shoed perky salesman. They both look at me like none of us are at the right meeting.

The building foreman insists on face masks, hard hats with headlights, hi-vis vests, and torches. Jesus, I'm viewing a property, not mining for coal. Turns out, I needed all the gear. There was no plumbing, no electrics. I make my way down a set of stairs covered in rubble, so it's really more of a ramp rather than a stairwell. It's pitch black, and all I can smell is wood that's been rotted through by rats' piss and poo. Mould, damp, and asbestos fill the air, and the scurry of the rats as the torchlight catches their beady red eyes glowing the dark begin to make my head swim. I swallow a squeal and hot sick from the smell, which is making its way through the mask. The false ceiling has fallen down due to rot. We climb over piles of debris in the dark. My ballet pumps and bare legs are just waiting to be punctured with a rusty tetanus nail. My eyes start adjusting to the darkness, and I can make out a long bar to the left of the space. Four little archways line the right side parallel to the sea. They're service vaults, apparently for waste, coal deliveries, etc. The agent points out there are loos at each end of the building. I'm going to take his word for it. Ugh. I fucking hate rats.

The location is perfect, bang in the middle of my desired zone. The size is perfect, 250 capacity. The price is pretty perfect, zero premium, rent of 50K per year plus VAT. The licence is totally perfect: 4:30am. The only problem? The condition of the building is FAR from perfect. The landlord is condescending and arrogant but says for the right person, he could get the venue into a clean shell. This means he'll gut it, remove the rubbish, make repairs to any damaged flooring and plasterboard the walls. Ready to decorate. Okay, now it's closer to being a workable option.

But he needs a business plan and property proposal before making a decision on the tenant.

I had toyed with the idea of a Brighton Bathhouse. Could it work down here? My gut tells me it's a no. The concept is too abstract, too gothic, too kooky. This needs to be more playful. More whimsical. It's a less culturally demanding crowd than East London and far more conservative.

As I ride away, thankfully with a bit more dignity than when I arrived, I decide I will use the business model and structure of the Bathhouse and Baby Bathhouse, business references, profit and loss predictions, and press books. It presents well on paper. But I plan to create a totally fresh new creative Brightonesque concept.

Once I get home (slowly up that motherfucker of a mountain that isn't getting any easier), I google Nick Sutton, the arrogant landlord. There was something that doesn't add up about him on our first encounter…a few clicks tells me he is a multimillion-pound property developer married to an actual real-life Turkish princess, of Ottoman decent. He owns a converted former convent-turned-mansion which sits on 25 acres of land with 13 bedrooms, two pools, tennis courts, and a helicopter hanger in Sussex. The property which is currently being rented out by Adele, while the family are away for the summer. He, of course, has a private helicopter to hang in his helicopter hanger. Looks can be deceiving, but you can't disguise a silver spoon accent and the very finest education.

Brighton has given us a new outlook as a couple. It's like we've stepped out from under a dark cloud and into the salty air and rejuvenating sunshine. We explore the endless rolling hills of the South Downs on Brighton's doorstep. The opulence of the Brighton Dome, the pavilion and King Henry VIII's spectacular history. We spend our time doing cosy pub crawls and lovely talks over pints, enjoy hours and hours walking along the promenade, bike rides along the cliffs of Saltdean. I believe the level of drinking is what would be called 'social'. The need for cocaine is replaced with the very occasional 'lifestyle' gram, purely to make use of the basement pub party room. It's for good times, rather than desperation. The draining need to balance our lives with mind-numbing substances is gone. We've replaced it with light-hearted, wholesome, 'normal' couple life.

Rich even joined a kickboxing gym. I was pretty flabbergasted. I'm not sure why I was so shocked as he had always been a runner and was conscious of keeping his weight down and physique razor-thin, but health and fitness had become important to him. His body was changing into lean muscles rather than just heroin chic. It suited him, along with the tapestry of tattoos that were slowly covering up his skin. He was happy, and I really liked it. It did get in the way of our Friday night drinks because he trained early Saturdays, but it mattered less than it would have a year ago.

We pop up to see Scott, Alli, and Bob as much as we can but dedicating every weekend to visiting had put our life and journey on hold. I think Alli feels that we aren't as supportive as we were before Josh passed away and I think it is probably true. I am deeply upset by that, but we were stuck in our own chaos. The family had no idea how deep we were in, creating our own misery and just keeping ourselves alive. But they visit and see how healthy and happy we are. I hope they understand.

I needn't have worried. Alli and Scott have a lovely ray of sunlight themselves. Alli is three months pregnant! Dark clouds which have loomed over this family are slowing parting to allow small seeds of joy and light to stream in.

Rich and I sit on pebbly Brighton Beach on the sunniest of Sundays, chatting about what the concept for the club could be. We're drinking Coronas and eating juicy local five-for-£6 oysters from the famous seafood hut, the one that has the sign saying 'I came to Brighton and all I got were crabs'! We're staring out over the sea which is framed on the left by the flashing, bright, whizzing and whistling Grade 2 listed Palace Pier. On the right is the burnt-out West Pier, an accidental sea sculpture, steeped in seaside history and wonderful bygone memories. Both are the epitome of Brighton. Beautiful. Alluring. Historic.

The concept is staring straight back at us...

17

A shimmering, spectacular interactive vintage funfair, encapsulated within a nightclub. An ode to the faded grandeur of the old West Pier and the glitz and excitement of the Palace Pier.

I'm so excited about this concept and prepare the venue proposal application for the landlord. I now knew exactly what I was putting in place. I layer this new skin over the business foundations and skeleton of The Bathhouse. The Brighton Concept... The Funfair.

We negotiate backwards and forwards. It was an awkward transition; a clunky ménage à trois with three lawyers negotiating the deal. It's a legal minefield. The council still technically owns the venue until the work is finished by the arrogant landlord. They create a crossover agreement until he becomes the rightful owner upon completion of the building works.

They all love the concept of the vintage funfair entertainment venue. I, of course, tone it RIGHT down. The arrogant landlord pulls his finger out and gives us a handover date, pending completion of the rest of the building.

I've become friendly with the arrogant landlord's builders, who do really good quality work. They put in long, solid shifts and have quoted a fair price for the building works on my portion of the venue refurb. But today, they are stony-faced; all heavy brows and no building-site banter. The arrogant landlord owes them £70,000. The builders have been asking for this to be cleared so they can pay staff and buy more materials to continue the build. But he said no, they need to keep working on the project so he can complete the building, have the council sign off, start trading and THEN he will pay their bill. They don't trust him to pay their outstanding balance. They told me a story about a local electrician firm that was shafted for an outstanding bill of £60,000 by the arrogant landlord a few years back. They had a 'hands-on' way of getting their bill paid... In the middle of the night, three men in balaclavas smashed through the door of the arrogant landlord's lovely convent mansion. Dragged him out of bed and tied him to a dining chair. One of them jammed a loaded shotgun into his mouth, one pointed a rifle at the base of his skull, and the other had a baseball bat pushed across his neck... With a clear message. "Pay your bill... Next time, we won't be so lenient. We know where your children sleep."

The Arrogant Landlord is still walking around with his head on, so I guess the debt-collecting mission was successful or it could just be an urban myth.

These builders weren't as bold as their masked friends but called me to tell me they had downed tools on the job and were cutting their losses. The next morning, twenty new workers arrive, all Polish. I mention the builders to the Arrogant Landlord, and he brushes it off saying they "weren't good businessmen."

The Arrogant Landlord seems to have had a firecracker shoved up his arse the past few weeks, making sure the building work is on schedule for the council to sign off. The new Polish guys work in shifts around the clock. Day in, day out, big deliveries of plasterboard and timber arrived while the skips of rubbish are whisked away. The Arrogant Landlord is responsive and quick to act on my lawyer's request. Things finally look like they're progressing at a good pace. The second stage of the council building work is signed off, and my portion of the lease signed, and we finally exchanged the venue contracts.

I was now in a legally binding contract and champing at the bit to start this magnificent magical nightclub!

The next day, the local newspaper has scathing headlines that make my eyes bulge. The Arrogant Landlord's property down the road from us, the Lansdowne Place Hotel in Hove, a 100-plus room hotel and wedding venue, went into receivership owing the bank nine million pounds. Days following that, another property deal of his in Cardiff for the 21-storey Radisson Blu goes bankrupt. The Arrogant Landlord's building project collapsed, owing millions of pounds to over 30 contractors and firms leaving an incomplete building and an angry mob of locals.

I feel sick. All those people and their families affected. I carry a lot of guilt these days of my past mistakes. I wanted to avoid these types of business dealings. None of this directly affects our deal. But massive, massive alarm bells start ringing. If I had known what kind of businessman we were dealing with, I would have had serious second thoughts. He doesn't even seem fazed, but I can now understand his haste to get our deal done, and the council sign-off locked in before the news dropped.

Not how I was hoping to kick off my fresh start, stage two project, but I had negotiated a small rent-free period to get the renovations done. I need to get the ball rolling.

The Bathhouse was blessed with stunning, supermodel bone structure; DNA that didn't need anything other than beautiful, decadent trimmings to tap into its historical beauty. This is a totally blank space. No bones. No personality, no hint as to what it should be or transform into. There are no secrets to listen to in the walls, but the clues were close by, on our doorstep. Inspired by the old fairground feelings, the playfulness of historic funfairs, travelling circuses, old school funhouses, beautiful freak shows, mystics, and the grand tradition of trips to the seaside towns and piers of England. So much nostalgia and whimsy to draw from. Everything that makes Brighton so loved. This was the concept that I could build up with authenticity; a story that would evolve, radiating a sense that it was always here. The creative vision came thick and fast, tumbling out of my brain and filling every inch of the space. Unlike the Bathhouse, this has other layers beyond beautiful bones. It will have interactive elements and sense of discovery that will add to the intrigue of the FunFair Club.

During the design and development process of building the club, I'm put in touch with two incredible creative masters who help bring this almost impossible vision to the next level of amazing. Paul, an artist and prop-builder from Lewes, a quiet town next to Brighton. No surprises here: he has a curled, waxed moustache. He's an artist who creates weird and whimsical vintage-style wonders. Life-sized music boxes, a steampunk xylophone truck that looks like it belongs at Burning Man Festival. Old masters-style paintings with moving eyes, just like in a Scooby-Doo haunted house. Half-finished inventions, hare-brained sculptures, gramophone lamps... So many marvellous but totally fucking bonkers creations. His studio was like an undiscovered Aladdin's cave after a eccentric explosion hit it. A master of painting and elaborate craftsmanship, he was the man to create my faded vintage funfair hero pieces, props and large-scale art installations.

The second was a set builder, James: a genuinely talented feature film set artist. Working on the epic sets of Harry Potter, the latest James Bond and a vast array of major movies made at the iconic Pinewood Studios, also travelling the world creating his incredible illusions. A genius at making the world of make-believe believable. He's so skilful that it's not 'til you touch one of his creations that you realise your eyes have been fooled. A wizard at making a plain surface transformed. From plasterboard to an aged brick wall, in a back alley off-Broadway in New York, which once had a Cats poster glued to it twenty years ago. Building up the blankness of the walls, building up our history with paint to create the illusion that the FunFair was sitting here, waiting to be discovered, for over a hundred years.

The FunFair Experience

The smell of fresh-cut grass fills your nose as you step into the entrance. A small room: a frozen moment in time; an instant flashback to one of those rare English summers from your childhood holidays. You're in the middle of a field. The floor is covered in realistic lush green grass dotted with daisies and buttercups. Hidden in the walls are atomisers subtly misting the fresh-cut grass aroma. A hand-painted fresco sky and wispy clouds wrap around the walls and dance over the ceiling. Tucked in one corner is a small wooden ticket booth, and in the middle of the space is a swing. The thick knotted rope holds up a rustic walnut swing seat. In the far corner is a hand-crafted Romany gypsy caravan with three steps up to a tiny balcony. There are flickering fringed lamps on either side of the entrance. Guests are invited to step up into the burnt orange and flaky gold-painted caravan, through thick curtains, into a small passage. A split second of total darkness, which then gives way to a wall on the left that reveals a floor-to-ceiling aquarium tank, filled with hundreds of fluttery boggle-eyed goldfish staring back at you.

The Gypsy caravan walkthrough ends, leading you to the top of the staircase. The walls are covered in red and white candy-striped wallpaper and gold-framed portraits of Victorian circus performers, which are 3D holograms. Their heads turn to follow you as you walk. At the bottom of the stairs is a wall. As you walk towards it, it plays tricks on your mind and eyes. The black and white geometric swirl is an optical illusion. As you descend the stairs, the pattern moves into a hypnotic spiral with red lighting that mirrors the shape of the swirling illusion, beckoning you to step through a black and white vortex. Drawing you into the club.

At the end of the stairs, to the right, are two double doors that open onto the main room of the club. The club has low ceilings covered in Tudor rose pressed tin panels, creating an intimate atmosphere with equally low lighting to set the mysterious mood. My beloved porcelain black and white tiles create the dance floor in a harlequin-check layout. The rest is covered in thick reclaimed timber floorboards, painted shiny black but distressed, so some of the perfection has worn away, leaving some beautiful exposed wood grain. It's as though the wood is peeping through, to tell you its secrets and the stories of all the things it has seen.

Precious gem-coloured lights and motorised mirror balls cast shadows and swirling patterns across the venue, adding depth, texture, warmth, and ambience to every surface they touch. To the left of the main room, at the heart of the black and white dance floor, is the DJ booth. It has a touch of tongue-in-cheek humour, but it's impressive and undeniably unique. A human-sized Punch and Judy theatre DJ booth, where the DJ is a master puppeteer, who turns the dancers into living, breathing puppets. Pulling strings as they mix records.

The bar runs down the left of the building with six service stations and a long station for cocktail preparation. The bar top is covered with 1131.12 pounds and pence. All in two pence piece coins. The coins were painstakingly hand-placed in symmetrical rows, glued and floated with clear epoxy resin to create a smooth bar surface. Framing the top of the bar is shot-silk, red-fringed bustle curtaining. The drinks list has bespoke FunFair cocktail creations, along with impeccable classic cocktails but garnished with showmanship like flaming cinnamon sugar and magician's flash paper. Sharing cocktails are served in small travelling magician trunks, glass skull heads, and absinthe fountains. Bar snacks include tubs of house-made alcoholic artisan flavoured candy floss, like sea salt margarita, rum and raisin, and pina colada punch. Striped paper cones of brandy and spiced buttered popcorn and brown paper bags of monkey nuts. The aroma machine in the main floor progresses through the evening, pungent stimulating scents of popcorn and candyfloss. The drinks have just the right amount of kitsch and irony without going over the top.

The back wall has a large scale art installation: the inside mechanics of a carousel called 'The Cogs'. It's self-contained, a box frame with moving cogs, wheels, levers pulleys, a plasma ball, and softly glowing coal furnace. These rotating, groaning mechanical innards offer a view behind the scenes of the carousel; past the starry lights and pretty, glittery horses. The opposite wall is another art installation called 'Meet Our Beautiful Freaks': a nod to P.T Barnum's travelling troop. It's a false wall: you can slip behind and pop your face through. Placing your head on the body of a ventriloquist with a tiny devil on his knee, or the pint-size two-foot-tall General Tom Thumb or our Bearded Lady.

Next to this installation and set in the glittery stone wall is a 'skill tester-grabber machine' in an old red English telephone box. You pop a pound coin into the slot and get three turns to move the claw and grab a prize. It's filled with clear plastic balls with either a 10, 20 or 50-pound note, mini hip-flask bottles of booze, vouchers for a lifetime membership to the club, tokens to win full-sized bottles of Sailor Jerry's Rum, the sponsors of the machine.

There are four vaults off the main area. Each one can be booked for six to twenty people with VIP packages including entry, a personal host, and bottle service in your own exclusive private seating space. All the vaults are totally unique. They're the jewels of the club.

The Ball Pit

There are two adjoining vaults. The left one is filled with over 10,000 primary coloured balls and disco lights which project zigzag patterns as you play about in a sea of balls. Floating, frolicking, and reclining neck-deep in an adult-sized ball pit-slash-miniature private disco! The right side of the vault has seating for six guests.

Broken Dreams

This dome-shaped vault is hand-crafted from thousands and thousands of broken mirror shards pieced together to create a shimmering, shining mirrored igloo. It's like sitting inside a disco ball, a mesmerising feat which took hundreds of hours to create. It's lit with a rotation wall mount mirror ball that catches the light and reflects it in each of the mirrors, creating a spectacular light show. Seating for eight guests.

Bed of Nails

The tunnel-like walls of the vault have a secret-chamber feel, recreated to look like the inside of a dungeon with moss, watermarks, and stone brick cladding. In the middle of the vault is a full-sized bed of nails with a Perspex display case on top of a tabletop with over three hundred nine-inch nails. The rotating wall-mounted light seeps colour washes slowly over the walls, from blood red to deepest green. Around the bed of nails table are amber-coloured Marcel Wanders stone stools. Seating for six guests.

The Stage

The largest of the booths is set off the dance floor, slightly raised to overlook the FunFair club. This was a last-minute addition to the venue after a secret room was uncovered during renovations. Illusion starburst mirrors are dotted around the bronzed walls, above the bench seating which wraps around the space for twenty guests. In the centre of the room is a 'life-sized' mermaid reclining on her hip, elbow, and her tail. Cast in solid brass with a glass bevelled edge tabletop, revealing the beautiful creature below.

The rest of the club seating is made up of pockets of cherry red leather chesterfield lounges and deep armchairs. Clusters of Wanders' stools in blue and red, scattered around the room to double up as seating and side tables.

Our Staff

For the hostess, I designed a ruffled neckpiece in layers of black, white and gold tulle and lace. It's worn with a white, blunt cut, fringed bob wig. These flourishes are worn with the hostess's own black outfit of choice. The combination of their personal style makes it eclectic and edgy, rather than contrived. One staff member in a mix of crop top and high waisted, wide-legged pants with stilettos, while another in vintage '80s ultra-tight mini dress, opaque tights, and twelve hole Doc Martins. With the wigs and neck frills, it's fucking awesome. The bar staff wear black and white: white shirts, black pussy-bow neckties, braces and vests. Mixed with their own eccentric pieces and accessories, its undeniably cool. The FunFair staff have tons of individuality. With their tattoos, slicked-back hair and coifs. Heavy-rimmed glasses, and dripping in that universal cool bar staff vibe you find behind cutting-edge bars round the world. It's like their unwritten style code.

Branding

Rich creates a beautiful brand. We use old lettering books of circus fonts, wood-carvings, and travelling funfair posters to build a striking and uniquely FunFair brand identity and intricate FunFair logo. It's quirky and bold as the posters once were, but Rich adds ageing effects to the creative designs, which could easily be mistaken for being over a century old. Despite this, they still have the punch to cut through social media and disruption in clubland.

Music

The music policy will be more commercial than the London clubs, but we will keep impeccable standards and a top-quality sound system. We scouted a load of excellent Brighton DJ talent and pencilled in a few resident London DJs to come down and play. But my musical secret weapon, my night club superpower, is being elusive. He wants to stay in retirement. Rich said he'll play at the launch parties and will produce Funfair mixes for us to release, but he doesn't want to be a club DJ anymore. We'll see... I have a bit of time yet to convince him. But I can't honestly see a club without him playing.

Performers

We will have roaming circus performers interacting and entertaining the crowds throughout the evening and give private shows to guests in the VIP booths. Exotic snake charmers; a rock-a-billy slick-haired sleight-of-hand magician; a third-generation sword swallower; a Guinness Book of Records holder for the most hula hoops at one time; a human dust bin who eats glass, metal, and razor blades; a Parisian sad clown striptease master. There will be a Harlequin and jester contortionist duo. A 'blockhead' - a tattoo beauty queen, who hammers builders' nails into her nose, staple guns money to her flesh and sets her body on fire. Fortune telling, tea-leaf readings, as well as aura and mystic readings. A spectacular programme of rotating performers that wouldn't look out of place in a Las Vegas theatre.

As the days draw closer to our press launch and the official opening date, so much hype is building around the club. The press is buzzing, and there's whispering around town, wondering whether the concept is going to be everything I've promised. We created a video and released it to the press and launch party guests. It's a black and white silent film. The kind where a villain with a top hat and tails ties a lady to the train tracks and everyone runs around in circles to pacey organ music. Ours is with a Brighton local, a drunk clown going around delivering invitations but failing miserably and causing total fucking chaos around town. It's hilarious and succeeds in building hype.

But along with all that anticipation, concern is bubbling: an unnerving silence. I break into the first-floor apartments above the club and discover all the building works have ground to a halt. No one comes to the site. There's absolutely no work being done; it's no closer to being an actual functional building. The Arrogant Landlord has gone totally AWOL. He doesn't answer his phone or reply to emails. Finally, I 'doorstop' him at another one of his venues around the corner. He says we can do our opening party as planned, but it needs to be low-key and not published in the press, which is totally fucking pointless for a fucking press launch! We won't be able to officially open until he has the rest of the building completed and the council signs it off. The funds have dried up for this project. He says he'll get it going again "sometime soon".

I am so embarrassed with myself, I cry out of anger right in front of the Arrogant Landlord. He looks disgusted and repulsed by my emotion but the bitter disappointment, frustration, and fear of the unknown, after working so, so hard to create this space, overwhelmed me and came out through my eyes. I'm not sad, as my tears suggest: I'm fucking furious.

I had painted every surface, smashed a million fucking mirrors, grouted tiles, stripped wood, made an actual bed of fucking nails! Sweating, covered in glitter, scraping out the back alley of human faeces, and dozens of used syringes; dehomed a mini crack den and worked like a fucking dog to make this place come alive.

Now I sit here. Alone. Nine weeks and counting with my dick in my hand* with the most astonishing, fucking staggeringly beautiful nightclub that no customers or staff are allowed to step foot into. A full set of irreplaceable management and passionate bar staff. Gone. Hired, trained and prepped for the opening, just to be let go. I know they will be quickly snapped up by another venue. Mounting bills and loans that need paying. All the rolling debt from the Bathhouse and Baby Bathhouse that needs repayments. I am heading for my very own world record of most pathetic attempt at opening a nightclub. "Venue folds before even opening". Every day I ring the lawyers and council for updates, but until this bell-end, bastard Arrogant Landlord pulls his finger out and finishes the rest of the building, we remain closed.

Finally, the council has issued him a 14-day completion notice. THANK FUCK! The landlord has to finish the building within two weeks, or he hands back the property to the council.

*With one's dick in one's hand - (idiomatic, vulgar, informal) In a state of being powerless, idle or unprepared.

18

Arse in the air, on my hands and knees, scrunched under my desk, I'm eye to eye with a 9-foot albino python. At his thickest, he is the width of my mid-thigh. I don't breathe or move. Terrified, I squeeze my bottom cheeks together to stop myself from shitting my pants in this compromising position usually saved for the bedroom. He darts out from his hiding space under my desk to the far corner of the office, then to another. He slithers into every crack and corner of the room. His tongue flicks out to taste the air with its skittish, lighting-fast random movements. The travelling vibration of the bass speakers in the club below is only adding to his frenzied state.

He's sniffing out the rats in the void under the floorboards. He eats only every so often, but the smell of fresh live rat has sparked his appetite and sent him totally fucking bonkers. His owner is trying to soothe him, but the python keeps twisting and slipping out of her hands. She's participating in a game of one-sided tug-of-war, with the slippery beast who is both her competitor and the rope. She yelps for me to fill any gaps in the floor. If he squeezes into the void, we'll never get him out. I can't see that being a terrible thing at this point. Except maybe if he found his way directly below onto the dance floor and landed on an unsuspecting dancer.

I've blocked the crack under the door, so he can't get out into the faux grass entrance and head down King Street. Again, that wouldn't be the worst outcome. So, it's me now standing on any object elevated from the ground, in my sparkly red Dorothy heels, black fishnets, and black sequin wiggle dress, with my big red silk flower pinned behind my ear in soft Hollywood wave curls. Yes, I know that snakes can climb, but he seems to be sticking to the floor for the moment. I watch sideshow circus performer D Devill, who reminds me of a more angelic version of Slash, in a sequin-spangled magician's assistant outfit and cute velvet top hat holding down blonde corkscrew curls trying to catch the bright yellow menace.

Making a fool out of us, trapping us in the small, windowless office. The snake normally hangs out in here between sessions of his snake-charming show with Ms Devill, and he has NEVER done this before. Both of us are trying to get the ordinarily gentle giant back in this travel cage. Well, one is working much harder than the other. One is covering her eyes, squealing and hoping for imminent containment. It's a complete sideshow but with no audience.

With the snake finally wrangled, I'm off to do the rounds. I have a habitual route on shift that I unconsciously follow, moving in and around the venue. Back rooms, cloak check, poking my head into the VIP rooms, behind bars, and toilets, the streets and little pockets, alleys and areas we're 'responsible for' surrounding FunFair. I stop and talk to police and licensing when they happen to 'pop by' and deal with anything unexpected that crops up. No shift is ever, ever the same. Tonight the venue is at full capacity. There is a queue down past the kebab shop, where my hairy bikini line and I hid on the first property inspection. The queue weaves past the little art gallery that has to be a front for an illegal business because I have never seen one painting leave its doors, all the way down to the entrance of my competitors' empty venues. This is a great night, apart from the possessed snake.

It feels like so long ago that I first found the venue. Despite the super-annoying temporary frustration of not being able to open the club after the pointless 'press launch', the Arrogant Landlord now leaves us alone. Once we were open, that was it. All we ever hear from him now is the rent invoice emailed monthly and a payment receipt in the post.

I pop down the illusion staircase. I love secretly listening to people 'ooh' and 'aah' as they enter the venue. FunFair is proving to be quite the little darling, with both press and customers loving the interactive elements. The dance floor is heaving to an epic bootlegged mash-up C&C Music Factory - Everybody Dance Now/ White Stripes Seven Nation Army - he couldn't resist. My clubland secret weapon back behind the decks every Saturday, which I'm thrilled about. I take over a bucket of beers to Rich, which he will steadily work his way through, and a multitude of Jagerbombs that the staff drop off intermittently through the night. His irresistible charm and quick wit have him making friends with everyone anywhere he goes. In this industry, it comes back in drinks.

I swing by to see the VIP bookings and check that they have everything they need. The booths book out months in advance, and we have strong entry guest lists every week. We've filled the gap between being a bar and a big club. It's a niche that's been waiting to be filled. An intimate club that's fun, unpretentious, and plays excellent fucking tunes. April, the bar manager, is hanging at the end of the bar near the Cogs. It's her spot. I always find her here, watching the staff and overseeing customers. But lately, she's been 'nipping out to get change' or 'borrow limes' a lot from the bar next door, staying for a drink and a chat. The problem is she stays way too long, and it has become a bit of a habit. It's the only gay bar outside of Kemp Town, and she loves it in there. To be fair, they are really cool and fun. It's annoying to find my manager spending more time at the bar next door than in my venue that she is meant to be running.

April's radio works in there. So I know she pretends to be in our club when, in fact, she's next door. I've seen her through the window which would be funny if it didn't happen all the time. We had a sit-down chat last week and fingers crossed she will be back on track. For the most part, she is great. The staff love her, the customers love her, and I really like her. She's good at her job most days. But her love of overindulging in pretty girls and drugs is becoming a problem and affecting her work. Actually, it sounds a lot like me, huh! She loves to party after work is finished at 5am, going until the afternoon, then grabs a few hours' sleep before heading back to work. She is often affected by bad lifestyle choices, but as I now know, that's the game we are in. It's hard not to work in hospitality and not 'play the game'.

There are always 'issues and firefighting'. This is a part of the daily grind of running and owning a club. I actually like this part. It turns me into a sniffer dog detective, but in the last few weeks, I was unravelling a particularly curly case. We'd been full most weekends since opening our doors with excellent bar takings. Recently, the takings have dipped slightly, which is odd. Our street team was cleaning up, and competitors were taking a mild beating. There is this one super keen flyerer who hits the street hard and pulls way more customers in than anyone else. He lures them in with his cheeky-chappie banter and playful persona. Why are the bar takings a bit low, then? Customers seem ridiculously fucked, and the club atmosphere has a mild aggressive air.

Looking around, I could see customers gurning with black-looking eyes from overly dilated pupils. I had my suspicions, so I sent out a party mole to the street to see what he was doing. Sure enough, he offered up the 'too good to refuse party deal'. It turned out my ace flyerer was catching partygoers on the street and offering them a free quarter gram of 'coke' if they went to FunFair and used his discount entry flyer. They were most likely already heading to FunFair anyway, so it was a win-win for them, discount entry and free drugs. But it wasn't coke he was giving them, but cheap as shit Meow Meow (mephedrone, sold legally online as 'bath salts'). If something or someone is too good to be true, it usually is, even more so in clubland because drugs play such a big part of the scene. If there's one thing I know, it's drugs. ... He also got grassed up by fellow flyerers after the novelty of the free drugs he gave them the first week wore off. Flyerers get paid on a sliding-scale commission basis, and he was running rings around them. But I have to admit, he was pretty smart. That small investment of cheap Meow Meow and street smarts had him creaming his street team flyerers and fucking with my bar takings because the customers were too wasted on shitty bath-salts junk to drink. This week it's back to the good vibes with no rogue drug peddling flyer entrepreneurs or weird gurning dance floor zombie monsters.

I stick my head into the ball pit to see what fresh hell is unravelling today. Everything seems relativity in control, for now. There is no doubt about it. The ball pit is an outrageous success and draws people into the club out of pure curiosity. It's a double-edged sword, though. Because it's also a royal pain in the deep dark arse. We planned to have it as a private space to prebook, like the other vaults, and use it to upsell premium drinks packages. This part is fine. It's always booked back-to-back, but the problem was people enjoy the time in the ball pit, kicking back in the VIP area with their large sharing cocktail, chilling with their bottle of Belvedere vodka then having every Tom, Dick, and Harriet crash their ball-pit party, taking over the booth, knocking over drinks, pinching their bottle of Belvedere and ruining the fun. But if we let it open to everyone in the club without a booking, it's an out-of-control orgy of WWF wrestling. It turns into general chaos. People lose their belongings and start tipping all the balls out to find their phone or wallet. Then you have people instantly complaining they came for the ball pit and it was booked, or some prick had emptied it over the venue.

It's a lose-lose, really. Fantastic concept but a ball-ache drama. We have to employ a security guard to control the space. We don't book it out now, and it has turned into a logistical nightmare. Babysitting drunk adults who have a strop when their five minutes of selfie time in the ball-pit is up. Our barback, Jay, comes in every Monday to clean it out. We have a deal. He can keep the drugs and cash, and I get the phones, and personal belongings to go into lost property. We have a little tally going, £326.23 in cash and 48 mobile phones.

I haven't mentioned lost property yet, have I? This is one of the most entertaining, weirdest windows into strangers' lives you will ever get! It's a real perk of clubland. The rule is you return as much of the stuff as you can. Wallets, keys, phones etc. Making calls to try and let people know you have their items. Good karma. Once it has been there for three months, it's fair game or off to charity. I now have an 'official' system in place. I have a logbook of things found by managers. This system isn't perfect, but it stops people from helping themselves to items in the lost property department, for the most part. For example, there was once a cute little leather jacket found on a Saturday night. It was brought up to the office. And on Monday, I took a call from a customer who described the make, size, and imperfections of the jacket. We chatted for a bit. She was super sweet and thrilled to be reunited with the coat, as it had sentimental value. It was a gift from her friend's Australian fashion label. She arranged to come and get it during the week.

The next day the jacket was gone, taken from the office. I started asking around. No one knows anything. Then right on cue, one of the bar managers walks in wearing the fucking jacket. Making it clear in no uncertain terms that the jacket is lost property and that I needed it back for the customer, she denied it and said it was hers. I said it wasn't and told her about the little details the customer had described to me. The small rip on the inside pocket, and the initials hand-stitched in a heart on the collar. Sure enough, both details were there. She said it is going to be cold going home without a jacket and that she'd bring it in tomorrow. Fair enough. But the coat didn't come back. I asked again and nothing. I texted and called to remind her to bring the jacket in. Nothing. As the shifted started, and the staff rolled in for work, so does the customer coming to collect her coat. I had to explain, mortified that I didn't have it anymore. In the middle of trying to explain the situation, the bar manager strolled in, right into the middle of my conversation with the customer, wearing the fucking jacket! I was dumb-founded. I took the jacket right off her back. She looked like I had slapped her with a wet fish. I apologised profusely to the customer for the confusion and gave back the jacket. I planned to fire Jacket Thief after the shift.

The next morning, I was going through the cashing up with April when we came across something strange. Jacket Thief had made three significant manual credit card transactions, three refunds totalling close to £1800. I called to asked her what they were and then 'let her go' for the jacket situation. She picked up the call, but the line was crackling. She said she couldn't really talk because she was in Paris with her mum (!?!). Turns out the refund was made to a high-flying bar owner who Jacket Thief and I both know. He had a fabulous venue around the corner and was asking Jacket Thief to manually process the payments, punching in the numbers rather than swiping the card throughout the night. Either she 'accidentally' did refunds instead of charging (which is impossible but I'm just being kind here and giving her the benefit of the doubt), but it's a bit odd that she's in Paris just now, huh? And lying about the jacket. And happens to know the high-flyer business owner. So even though he and his pals consumed bottles and bottles of Bollinger and Belvedere all night, he not only didn't get charged, he got paid to drink them with the money from my account transferred to him as a refund! And I paid for the liquor twice, when I first bought it from the wholesaler and now again, paying him via a refund. I call directly and politely explain this to him and ask if could he please arrange for the refund to be sent back to me or I could swing by and collect the money for the drinks, and he said, nope. Ah, okay? If cash payment is a problem how about, we do a deal, and he can just drop the stock over to replace what was drunk? Nope. This is your mistake, and you have to wear the cost of it.

This is a snidey business.

Anyway, back to the lost property. You could write a chapter on it but here are the highlights from the clubs I've worked in. A briefcase filled with your usual business stuff. An end of year report, a USB stick, lanyard with an ID swipe card, an empty lunch box, and a black rubber fisting dildo that was almost a perfectly sized replica of my clenched fist to my elbow. That was an uncomfortable pick up for both parties on Monday morning. Divorce papers. A portable but full-sized weighted piano keyboard. A bank drop bag with a full week's worth of takings from a boutique designer dress shop. It had over 8K in cash, but we found the very grateful owner and a very fired shop girl. A set of real false teeth. An uneaten family-sized Indian takeaway, complete with sides. Crutches…someone got drunk enough to walk home? They were collected on the Monday by a hopping dude who doesn't remember even leaving the club. Mortarboard, gown and a degree in Zoology. A tasty black trench that I still wear 13 years later. A set of stilts. A unicycle. Not found at the same venue. There is always weed. In all my time working in clubs, I never had to go and buy weed since it turns up weekly - always in little drawstring pouches, ready to roll with paper and tobacco. Once there was a ring that looked like a fake bobble, a prize from a gumball machine. It turned out to be an almost 2-carat diamond, a princess-cut engagement ring worth 30K. We got it back on the tearful bride-to-be's finger before the groom-to-be noticed it missing. We also had to take down from Facebook photos of her kissing another man who wasn't her betrothed, the night the ring was lost. Someone left the back half of a two-man camel outfit. Enough makeup cases to open a Sephora store. But the mundane reality is each month we would donate eight bin bags filled with coats and bags which were just left behind and never collected. That's a lot of cold walks home dressed in nothing but a booze coat to keep you warm.

The biggest surprise was the number of passports, bank cards, and driver's licences that never got collected every week. We have to snip, bin or drop them with the police.

Another perk of clubland: Drugs. At 666, there was a hardcore police-issued drug safe with procedures, policies and cataloguing. It came with a logbook, evidence bags, and a dropbox safe. The Devil was fastidious at dropping the drugs found or confiscated. He was hot on busting drugs and getting them logged, sealed, and secured but then had a paranoid moment of madness and decided that the police would use it as evidence against the club. So he did the only rational thing and opened the safe and distributed the drugs to the office staff and managers. The Devil took the pills. He liked trippy shit. Ugh, the worst. There was a story floating around from years before I started at 666, that a promoter found him wasted, crawling around the office area of the club, topless, on his hands and knees, pissing his pants and mooing like a Jersey cow. Everyone else grabbed the leftovers. I took a gram of coke and ended doing it with a boy later that week at my flat. We did one line and woke up ten hours later. Fuck knows what that was. The rest was flushed after that strange blackout, and as you know, I am not one to easily pass up free drugs.

At my London clubs and now Brighton, we have a similar collection procedure. If we find customers doing drugs in the venue or find them during a search scenario and it's a small amount obviously for personal use, we don't take the drugs off them. We eject them from the club and tell them not to return. If we catch a dealer, we will call the police. Any dealing in a club needs to be instantly squashed. It's terrible for business and a slippery slope to losing control of your own club to dealers and gangs. If drugs are found and I don't want them, or the manager doesn't want them, we put them into an evidence bag and keep it in the main safe to taken to the local station every so often. I'm hot on 'bagging and tagging' all the empty mini plastic bags and wraps I find, rather than putting in the real offenders, along with random little pills, most likely paracetamol. If you don't hand over a 'suitable' amount of evidence bags, it means either you're not declaring the drugs you find/confiscate, or you aren't vigilant with the management of drug use in the venue.

I do my rounds and the final check downstairs before I finish. April is responsible for officially running the shift and is the Designated Premises Supervisor, which means she is legally in charge of the shift, doing all the admin and the responsibility that goes along with it, I just oversee the evening. Once the customers start to disperse around 4 am, I prepare any payments I need sorted and quickly look over the takings and look through security's hourly-entry log-book so I can be prepared for Mondays meetings. I don't like leaving the club until it has that feeling of calm and a smooth downhill momentum until closing time. I feel uneasy if I go and the night hasn't naturally dissolved. This leaves an opportunity for things to kick off, like a fight or a drunk customer situation not appropriately handled.

I checked the toilets on my routine walk around before I leave to make sure loo rolls aren't jammed into the sinks, there aren't any blocked or overflowing toilets, and no one has redecorated in vomit which would set into the cement if left overnight for the cleaners to sort out in the morning. I get to the bathroom after paying Rich his DJ cash and let him know I'll be ready to leave in five minutes. He needs a million warnings that we are going. He is a fucking chatterbox, especially after an evening of beers, shots, and party lines. The club is closed, the last customers had gone, the toilet attendants have left, security has checked that the venue is empty, locked and secured the venue's fire exits, and clocked off. Now it's just a skeleton crew of staff finishing up and cleaning the bar. Everyone else is having an end of shift beer, including security, chatting, laughing, and telling stories about what happened on shift. I go to check the loo, needing to go as well as I tend to hold onto it during the peak madness-witching hours when the loos are packed with 'chatty' customers and mutter to myself how it's barbaric I don't have a toilet in my office.

One of the doors is closed. I push it open, but it's locked shut. I bash on the door. No answer. I get on the gross wet ground and look under the door. Someone is passed out, crumpled down beside the toilet and the wall. Fuck. I run to the back room and grab a screwdriver and take the lock off and pull the unconscious girl from the cubical into the middle of the bathroom and check her breathing. I lift her head and start patting her face to get her conscious. She is bare-foot, covered in sick and piss with her underpants around her ankles. She comes to. She's okay, super fucking drunk but more embarrassed than anything else. She was doing a wee, and had to vomit in the middle of the wee, then passed out mid-vomit. I clean her up, take her upstairs, give her some water, my spare ballet pumps, and call her dad to come and get her.

I storm back downstairs. The staff and security get a bitter blasting. We go over the responsible service of alcohol, the closing policy and procedures which had been totally disregarded. That girl could have been locked in the venue. Flashes of her choking on her own vomit, alone in a closed-up club terrify me. Management will be in my office Monday morning with official written warnings.

We have a duty of care and today, we failed.

Not only is it deeply disappointing that my managers and security let this potentially catastrophic incident occur right under their noses, it kinda fucks with my secret home life plan. Rich and I had an agreement. Once the club is up and running, which now it is, we're financially stable, which we are, and we have a great manager running FunFair - which we don't - we can start 'trying' for a baby. This list used to feel like an eternity away, and now we are so close, but April has shown tonight that she isn't ready to be the venue manager we'd hoped she would be. Plus, the bar managers aren't as strong as I'd like. I dread to think what would happen when I had to step away with a new baby. I need to strengthen the staff, reinforce training, and get a few solid key players slotted in to ensure that the staff structure is infallible. I'll also bring in the head of security to go over my expectations and his position as a leader of the security team. He had also clocked off and left the venue two hours before closing, which is not acceptable.

But it's a totally reasonable, achievable plan that I am committed to sticking with, because if I don't have these three elements rock solid, I can't bear the thought of having a brand new baby and juggling a venue that isn't operating like a well-oiled machine. But try telling that to my vagina.

It's the next level of wanting to 'live in his blood'. It wants to create his bloodline. I know that has a medieval, Game of Thrones sound to it, but it's the only way I can honestly describe the feeling. It's this deep need to create a baby with Rich. It's a dull but pleasing ache in my heart. More love, something even greater, deeper, an extension of the Hollywood-fucking-amazing-love we share. A drawing-in during sex. I guess it's what people call a 'maternal ticking clock'. Mine isn't as gentrified or as medical-sounding as that. It's not sparked by the cutesy babies I see in the street or soft pastel stalk-printed rugs. It is a deep, guttural lust. It's like a womb ache but in my vagina. I guess that's how my body knows to get the baby-making process started.

I need to block it out.

There are essential things that need to be done. The only thing is that I'm now motivated by an internal ticking clock.

I take on the most adorable, kind, and hungry assistant. I teach her everything I know about clubs, emptying my brain into her little notebook. Marketing, online management, social media, music policies, performers, every trick, formula, tiny detail, industry hack and secret I've accumulated over the years. As well as being a knowledge sponge, she is a mini Phil Dunphy from Modern Family. Mini P for short. Full of dad jokes, walking memes and puns. She has a crack-level addiction to croissants. She makes coming into the office a pure joy. We get loads of work done but also have a really lovely time working together. She's keen to learn about clubland, especially the marketing side. Mini P wants to move to London in the next few years and knows she needs to get some substantial experience first. She also has an excellent eye for detail and follows my exacting standards, understands my design ethic and vision for FunFair. She has exceptional customer service skills, which is a big thing. Customers warm to her in the booking process, and she makes sure that details are followed through during the evening. She is happy to come in during the weekends and look after our growing booking and parties. It's the follow-through that ensures they all run smoothly and our customers' high expectations are over-delivered from our end. She genuinely cares about FunFair and her customers. It's a rare quality, and I nurture her interest. Mini-P is a secret weapon I'm developing for the future.

I've also taken on another venue manager, creating a role that is venue co-managing, under the guise that the business is growing exponentially and there will be more demands of April. I explain I don't want to overburden her with extended demands and extra hours. Gee is a quiet, softly-spoken manager from one of the larger seafront student venues. What I hope will happen is that this will make April more accountable and give her a sense of having to prove herself in the role, now that she has a counterpart who is new and keen to please. I think managing the venue together as partners will bring out the best in both of them. They both seem pleased with their newly formed alliance.

For the most part, April is good and has a great understanding of how I want FunFair to run. I can't go firing all the managers who have drug problems because I would be left to do it all myself. And then I would have to fire myself because I'm the worst. The thing that kills me is that these kids don't know how to put the hours into the job, even if you're totally hanging out your arse and operating on no sleep. Drink the hair of the dog, show up, work hard, push through it, and die later. I learned a trick very early in my club days. No talking about my hangovers or comedowns at work or the few lines of coke I have to get through a long, late shift or if I was still awake from the party the night before. They want to party but don't want to put the hard yards in on a shift. They would be un-hireable in any other industry if they had the same work ethic.

Imagine turning up to your bank teller job an hour late, stinking of cigarettes and cider, in the same clothes as yesterday and black pin eyes from a heavy ketamine session? You'd be unable to perform your job, and there'd be no way you could expect anything but a letter of employment termination after doing this week in, week out.

19

I shake Rich, tap him, poke him, pat his knee, put my finger in his open mouth, but he won't wake up. Slumped on the couch, head tilting back and mouth hanging open, it's like he's slipped into a coma, only it's 7pm and he's totally sober. It's the deepest sleep ever. Like Sleeping Beauty deep. I can't wake him for love nor money. He sleeps well into the night, so long that the two little blue lines on the piss stick have disappeared. It makes me think maybe it's not real, and the test is faulty. One second after I came out of the bathroom, he slipped into a deep sleep. A shock-induced trance. Four sticks later and he finally wakes up. Not exactly how I'd imagine we would spend the first few hours digesting the news that we are going to be parents!

I was pretty shocked too. I know we were trying now that we achieved the three prerequisites we put in place for FunFair, but I wasn't expecting it to happen that fast. I'd imagined it would be a long, drawn-out process with a load of knee-trembling not-worrying-about-getting-pregnant sex. We had tried NOT to get pregnant for so many years. I thought it would be calculating fertility cycles, all the comedy scenes of Monica and Chandler trying to fall pregnant in Friends. Catching windows of baby-making times in broom cupboards of the hospital or fully clothed with dinner guests in the next room, having a quickie in the kitchen because the little beeping alarm goes off letting us know it's time to put a few mega minutes in against the 'ticking womb clock'.

Nope. We tried once.

I keep the news a secret for as long as possible. It's tricky in a world that revolves around partying. Friends from London were down to DJ and party at the club with Rich. I was 'working' so I could avoid them and their endless offers of MDMA to a point. I would never take it during a shift anyway but probably would have gone partying after work with them. They didn't buy it when I made lame excuses each time they nagged me to come outside and smoke. Giving up cigarettes was strangely easy. A week before we had our first and only

successful baby-making attempt, I had been at a wedding. It was a long weekend of beautiful friends and celebrations, but we smoked and drank so much that on Monday morning, I had to pull the car up on the side of the road to be sick. Smoking a brand of cigarettes I wasn't used to had turned me off so hard. I was over them. As soon as I found out I was pregnant, the little switch flipped. It was comforting and so reassuring that I no longer cared or wanted to be around drinking or taking drugs. There were no feelings I was missing out. That need was replaced entirely.

I was caring for a tiny human now.

There are practical matters that need to be addressed daily. I have to get into the office a good solid hour before anyone else, so I can throw up my breakfast into the bin next to my desk and dispose of the evidence. I have 24-hour 'morning' sickness. Random bouts of vomiting and retching like a cat with a furball is a round-the-clock pleasure. In the street. In the middle of the night when I'm fast asleep. And in the nightclub toilets while I'm working. I vomit while customers do bumps of coke in the cubical next to me. My senses are so heightened. My sense of smell and disgust levels are operating in the professional task force zone that would make a Heathrow sniffer dog proud. The smell of stale alcohol turns my stomach, and fermented fruit sends me running towards the nearest bin. I was convinced there was a case of rotten lemons hidden in our office or in the entrance lobby. I hunted, sniffed, and tore the place apart. I found a half-empty glass, that would have had a spirit and mixer in it over the weekend, that had rolled under the Gypsy caravan containing a single slice of lemon collecting fruit flies on it.

I looked fucking mental. Columbo; the rotting fruit detective.

People at work are used to me being a bit elusive, keeping my own schedule, and recovering from working the late weekend shifts by having little lie-downs on my lunch break, so this early stage of pregnancy isn't very different to my old behaviour. Plus when you're the boss, people don't really comment to your face when you're being weird. Well, Mini-P does. She wants to know everything about everything, so I try to avoid her for the moment. I can't imagine how people hold morning sickness down in 'regular jobs'. I want to wait to have the scan before I start talking about the baby.

I'm pleased it's winter so I can wear a uniform of big jumpers, leggings, and fur coats, jamming my trotters into sensible shoes. I can't bear to do my makeup or hair unless absolutely necessary, so I just look like I've let myself go. Bloated and fucked, given up the will to live. My hormones are fucking mental. I cry at the Kardashians, which I would never usually watch and I weep when the guy at Pret asks how my day is going when I grab a

coffee. I howl at the overwhelming thought of having an actual baby. I have no idea how to be or feel or act normal. Once I get past the first three months, I start to feel better, brighter, and less foul. I stop crying as a replacement for daily conversation. My stomach is back to being a gut of steel. Then annoyingly, just as I thought I had turned a corner, I start feeling worse than ever. Drained. It turns out I have anaemia and gestational diabetes. I just want to sleep. At home, Rich takes care of me. Diabetes is tricky to get used to, endless testing and strict eating schedules. It's like having a part-time job.

But I have one huge fucking pressing issue. I HAVE NO IDEA HOW TO GET A BABY OUT OF MY VAGINA OR WHAT TO DO WITH IT ONCE IT'S OUT!!! I know how to run nightclubs, not raise babies. I decide to tackle it the same way I would approach a new nightclub project. With relentless research, reading, mapping out, investigating, and going on fact-finding missions. A hunt for knowledge of 'the market'. Doing all this has soothed the anxiety beast that was growing in my mind. Learning to prepare was the best way I could make this whole new stage of our lives a manageable task. A life 'to-do' list learning curve to help transform my feelings into excitement and comfort, rather than night terrors and nail-biting.

It worked. I shared my findings with Rich: formulated ideas of how we were going to tackle the birth and a newborn. We started to enjoy every second of the adventure. It was incredible, the feeling that a tiny person is growing, who is a direct result of how much we love each other. It put a layer of wholesomeness and clarity we hadn't had before. It was a step away from club-life vices, and it was lovely. I still worked as hard and put the hours in but removing excess trimmings of that lifestyle felt good. Rich is attentive and supportive, catering to my midnight cravings for samphire seaweed and the weird intolerance that I couldn't eat the same food twice for dinner. If I could remember eating it in the past few months, it turned my stomach, put a lump of hot sick in my throat, and started phantom heartburn. So we progressed through a 360° rotation of cuisines, dishes, ingredients, and flavour profiles. Strangely, it was only dinner that flipped me out as I lived on the same breakfast and lunch throughout the pregnancy.

Through all of this, there is one thing that I can't solve...

Dear Universe,

How do I manage a newborn through those tender first twelve months and a business that can't be left alone?

I can't see an answer.

Love, Tava

The evenings are filled with long, restful sleep, something I haven't had since entering clubland, and belly watch. The street light shines through the rose velvet curtains and makes the room glow pink. The pink belly moves around and around the same time every night. A little circus show of acrobatics twists and kickflips. We joke that it's a little Pack boy from the kickflips and amount of energy the baby thrashes out. But I never let on what I really want. I block the thoughts from entering into my brain or out of my mouth in case the baby can hear me or can read my mind. I don't want the baby to be sad if it can hear me and it's not what I'm hoping for. I found myself repeating the mum-to-be mantra – as long as our baby is healthy and happy.

Ok, now let's address this elephant in the room. Me. I am not one of those women who blossoms in pregnancy with a lovely little belly popping out. I bloat and expand and fill my skin and stretch until it looks like only a pinprick can bring relief. I'm more like the Michelin Man or the Stay Puft Marshmallow Man from Ghostbusters than a baby Mumma goddess of health, grace and vitality. My enviable pre-pregnancy perfectly hung 12 DD boobs morph into a set of matronly long 16 GG milkers and my feet increase by two shoe sizes.

I've created a uniform. I tried that angle the magazines tweely suggest of wearing your pre-pregnancy clothes and making small adjustments with stretch leggings and belly bands, but I look fucking ridiculous. Like a sad toad from a Beatrix Potter story squashed into a fancy dress costume. A clown, with my hair in the vintage twists, curls and frilly, fancy clothes and sparkles that suit a much smaller frame, one with a waist and fewer chins. I decided to strip back. On night shifts at the club, I wear soft black jersey stretch bodycon style dresses and maternity tights, right up and over the belly tucked neatly under the mega knockers with fringed cowboy booties and low-key 'normal' hair and simple makeup. I still wear red lipstick but swap out the harsh Ruby Woo, which somehow washes out my skin, to the lighter, brighter orange-toned Dangerous. Adding some leopard print Air Max to convert this look for the daytime. The good news is I have settled into the hormones and don't look or feel like the Walking Dead zombie I did for the first few months.

I won't push it, but I look ok.

We're scheduled to get our check-up ultrasound and gender reveal scan. The whole of Muesli Mountain looks like an alpine village covered in snow. There's no way I'm going to miss this appointment. No cabs can get up the hill, so we trudge a mile through the snow down to the hospital. Lying down on the bed, I let the operator know that we would like to check the baby's health and development first, then learn the gender pending things are on track with the baby's health. Her exact words?.. "Yes, I know how this works. For example, 'You have a beautiful baby girl but only has one leg.'"

This is the exact type of statement I was looking to avoid.

She tells us we have a healthy little girl! I'm overwhelmed with happiness. I try to hug Rich but end up almost rolling off the bed like a slippery, jelly-smeared beached whale. Our baby is healthy! I wanted a little girl. That's all I wanted. Ever. I'm totally sure I would have been thrilled if it were a boy, but I'm beyond thrilled. It has nothing to do with colours, clothes, femininity or liking girls more than boys. All my life, I have had a premonition, who this little human is that I was going to meet. I already know her, like I knew I was looking for Rich. It's the final piece of the jigsaw to complete our love. But Rich says something that surprised us both. So much so that even the 'hard truth' scan operator says she'll give us a moment alone. He wants a boy. He wanted to play Scalextrics and was actually a bit disappointed it was a girl. I just laugh because it's so out of character. I know he just wants a healthy baby. I brush it aside with an eye roll, thrilled with our news. Healthy and a girl!

I wiped the gel off my tummy, and we leave the hospital with our little black and white images. So precious. We head through the snowy streets down to the seafront. The icy air coming off the sea and the blanket of snow covering the pebbly beach is truly spectacular. I've never seen snow on a beach before. My eyes scan the horizon.

It's like a pristine dome of reflective glass.

I feel happy. A healthy little baby. Our baby. A gust of chilly wind blows in our face, and it was as though someone had thrown a bucket of ice water over Rich. He snapped out of his trance and 'came to'. He couldn't remember what had happened, where we had been, the hospital and had no recollection of saying he wanted a boy. He was in a trance, and the wind had broken the spell. I am starting to piece together an odd behaviour pattern Rich has. When he goes into shock or emotional overload, he shuts down and either sleeps or goes into a walking blackout state. When he found out about Josh, the pregnancy, and now the news of our healthy baby, it's like his body shuts down for business, unable to process the extreme emotion, good or bad.

Mini-P is a one-woman support team and a lovely distraction in the office. She loves babies and seems more excited than anyone else about our pending arrival, which she has sweetly nicknamed 'Baby FunFair'. The staff adjustments have worked well, reinforcing the foundation we needed to be able to step away for a short spell. We have a robust business model, a steady, stable customer base, the kinks have been ironed out, and we've learned from past mistakes. I have been working hard to create a formula for her to follow so she can run the back of house without me. She's been nailing the marketing, promotions and bookings all on her own. It's a simple yet effective formula of what needs to be done and how to do it to get the constant level of customers through the club. We decided to bring in a club night promoter for Fridays to take getting customers in and booking the DJs off her hands so Mini-P can focus on Saturdays and coordinating with the mid-week promoters. For the moment, I'm still working in the office and in the club at night. I plan on clocking off two weeks before the due date and have organised cover to manage and planned with Mini-P so that everything is set up for three months once the baby is born. I have a paralysing fear that I can't step away from the business. How was I going to manage maternity leave past three months? We looked into what Rich's options were and what paternity leave he was entitled to at The Body Shop. We think it's two weeks, which is standard, but someone mentions they have pretty progressive leave options – whatever that means. It's worth looking into. He swings by HR to find out. He has a friend working there, and Rich's charming nature reaps benefits once again. He explains the situation, how it's going to be a hard time for us because I had to go back to work as soon as possible and we have no nearby family to help us. HR comes back with the most excellent news. Since he has been at The Body Shop for almost five years, he's entitled to take primary carer paternity leave as I'm employed by my own business on minimum wage, which I do for tax reasons. The stars align. The condition is that I need to take a maximum of three months leave then he can take off four months from work with full pay and an additional four weeks statutory pay. This is unheard of. The upper management is not happy and tries to refuse the leave but HR fights for him and reinforce that he is eligible to the entitlements and legally can claim them.

This is humbling, utterly excellent news for us.

Dear Universe,

THANK YOU, YOU FUCKING LEGEND!

Love,

Two eternally grateful parents-to-be XX

This flips the traditional parental roles on its head and presents an excellent opportunity and answer for both of us. There is no denying that I can't step away from the business for the traditional six-to-twelve-month maternity leave. I want to give our baby the chance to be with one of us around the clock, and it is such an exceptional opportunity for a father to spend this precious time with his new baby. Although it is traditionally the mum who spends this crucial time with the newborn, there's no reason why it has to be. We jump at it, both feeling a sense of salvation, adventure, and trepidation. I always knew that I couldn't go down the traditional paved family role route in such a non-traditional, non-female-friendly industry like clubland. There just had to be another way, and there was. He was standing right next to me. As always.

It's starting to get really uncomfortable working at night. I take it easy now on shift, but I come in to oversee and make sure the venue is set up correctly, the bookings are smooth and without any issues, and that security team is in good form. Mostly to show my face about. I guess it's my way of trying to make sure everything is 'as it should be' right up to the very last minute of stepping back. The co-management plan is working a treat. Gee has a steadying influence on April and security has stepped its game up. I won't go down to the club floor again until closing. Between 11pm - 3.30am, it's too busy and I can't risk getting knocked in the belly or pushed over in a drunk crowd. It's a minefield walking through a busy club at the best of times, but when you are as wide as you are high, it becomes a whole new challenge. It's not really much of a problem now as I increased the CCTV a few months ago, so I can watch the entire club from the office. I hang out in my office, play music, have snacks, Skype anyone in Australia, making the most of the time difference. A parade of people come in to chat. I hear a commotion fire up over the radio on Channel 2, an incident in the girls' toilets. The CCTV in that part of the club is limited to the lobby, not the loos, so I roll the recording back.

FUCK ME! This is a first!

A tall 20-something with a vast head of wavy orange curls down her back walks into view of the lobby camera, then back out of sight into the loo. There's a short queue trailing out of the bathroom door, no more than four people, waiting on three cubicles. It's pretty standard in a nightclub, no more than a few minutes' wait.

She heads back in view of the lobby camera. In the middle of the walkway, she pulls her very short figure-hugging dress up around her waist, pulls off her knickers, and squats down over the ground. A big puddle of piss pools around her. Fuck, what a tramp! She doesn't get up. Instead, she hangs there for another few seconds. The other girls waiting in the queue step back and move away in horror she pushes out a mega shit. She stands up, legs still wide apart, shakes a bit to get off the excess drips off, bends over further and then wipes her arse with her knickers and throws them into the corner of the corridor. Then she pulls her dress back down, and steps over the pool of piss with the steaming island of shit. Like it was nothing. I see her cross through the view of the other camera frames as she moves to the dance floor to join her pals.

Wow. This is pretty low, even by club standards. I once worked part-time in a strip club back in Sydney as a hostess while I was at drama school. I got the job thanks to a classmate whose husband owned the club and was a very well-established man in the strip industry. One night, he and I were chatting, and we noticed a growing unpleasant smell wafting through the venue. He thinks someone has dog poo on their shoes and the shit had been trodden through the carpet. He heads off to investigate. We quickly discovered it wasn't poo on someone's shoe. The club managers had flagged a disgruntled ex-dancer on CCTV entering the building. She went to the far end of the club carrying a large white plastic bag, that looked quite heavy and full. She put on a pair of yellow plastic washing up gloves and walked from one end of the venue, snaking through the tables to the other end of the venue, conscientiously dropping the contents of the bag as she went. Dropping it. Rolling it, scattering it around like fairy dust. The contents of the plastic bag? Human shit! They dragged her out, kicking and screaming. The owner got a dustpan and brush to clean up the mess. He taught me an invaluable lesson. He would never ask his staff to do anything that he wouldn't do himself. I also had to wonder what had happened to piss the girl off so severely she harvested her own shit for weeks?

I got on the radio and put a call out for the barbacks to get the mop, bucket, cleaning equipment, and paper towels and meet me at the lobby of the ladies' toilet.

First, I changed into trainers for maximum stability, then made my way down the illusion stairs. Security kept trying to stop me, saying it was too dangerous to go into the club while it was at full capacity and to just let the staff deal with it. Waddling down like a constipated duck, with one hand propping up my back and the other shielding my eight-and-a-half-month-old watermelon belly, I head into the club.

Wading through the dance floor, I keep parting the sea of dancers until I see the big head of lovely orange curls. I politely tap her on the shoulder. She turns with a smile, thinking I must be a handsome admirer. The element of surprise plays in my favour. I grab her by the scruff of the neck and drag her back to the lobby of the bathroom. She's tall, and in heels, so she lags behind, hobbling and bent over a bit. I am way shorter than her in my sensible trainers and dumpy little legs. I throw the big roll of paper towel for her to catch, ready and waiting by the crime scene with the barbacks, and snap at her to "Clean up your own mess, you fucking animal!"

Following my strict, systematic instructions, she picks up the poo, wipes up the piss, puts the paper towels in the bin, and flushes the shit down the toilet. I make sure she mops the floor with detergent and boiling water and covers the area with antibacterial spray before putting the yellow 'slip hazard' sign over where her poop was. I tell her to collect her sodden undies and put them in a little plastic bag, like you collect dog poo, tie it up, and take them with her.

We march her back to her friends who were half-heartedly wondering what was happening and I tell them their friend was a filthy beast who shat on the floor and was being removed because we don't allow animals or toddlers who aren't toilet-trained in our club. They look dumbfounded. Not only by her pooping on the floor, which they said was not something she would ever do, but also the very angry, very pregnant lady dragging their friend around by her pretty curls.

I head back upstairs to high fives and cheers over the radio. I feel a little bit smug, but it was an idiotic, dangerous, and stupid thing to do. But fucking priceless. I think it's time to stop working nights.

I've written a three-page birth plan, attended natural birthing classes weekly, as well as couple's weekend birth workshops, hoping for a natural birth at the hospital. I wanted a home birth, but that's not possible with gestational diabetes, and I didn't really care that much to push for it. Rich isn't at all keen on home birth. We joined the ridiculous NCT joke classes that seem to still be pumping out the same archaic birthing information from the '70s, but it was more as a means to meet local like-minded mummas. Which I have and am thrilled about it. The breastfeeding 'mentor' at NCT is horrified that we are planning to do half breastfeeding and half bottle feeding after the first few weeks feeding patterns are established. She flat out says it will never work and will only give the baby 'nipple confusion' which will cause them to starve. Luckily for us, I had studied all this information within an inch of our lives. We know we live in a world where not all mums can stay at home for an extended period with their new baby and fathers can play an equally important role as nurturer. Every choice we make needs to prepare us to have Rich be equally able to feed, soothe, calm, nurture, and read our baby's cues.

The lovely little room is ready for our lovely little lady, even though she won't officially move in here for six months The view from her window is currently an explosion of summertime cherry blossoms.

The room is full of sweet furniture we both loved making. We carefully painted and decorated everything just for her. A glossy white changing table and a deep-seated vintage upholstered rocking chair with dreamy House of Hackney black and white thick striped fabric, badgers with shisha pipes, squirrels with banjos, and possums with piña coladas. We added pale green glass knobs to the drawers and cupboards. It's more of an adorable parlour than a baby's room. In our bedroom, we attached a tiny three-sided side co-sleeping bed to our big bed so we can be right next to each other, but start with good sleep patterns. A kewpie doll nightlight and white noise machine I'm already addicted to. A lovely restored, regal vintage Silver Cross Kensington Pram awaits her precious passenger.

We are deeply in love, even more so now. This experience sends our roots deeper and deeper. Finally, we're prepared for our co-adventurer's arrival to complete our Hollywood-fucking-amazing-love story.

A week before the due date

My mum arrives from Australia. It's lovely to see her, and I'm pleased for the support. I know I will be beyond grateful after the birth for her knowledge and help, but I notice I feel reserved. I feel a bit uneasy. We have been in a bubble of two preparing for three. I haven't been close to anyone other than Rich, for many years. It takes a bit of time to get adjusted. I unravel after a few days and am happy Mum gets to experience it with us. It's a genuinely special time.

An unbearable heatwave takes over Brighton. I lie in bed and binge-watch Mad Men with two fans pointing at me, covered in wet towels. I sleep like this as well but with one of those divine, U-shaped pillows. In the middle of the night, a bubble rolls out of my vagina, and it pops. And a little gush. My water broke.

18 hours after my waters broke

I'm lying on my phone, and when I finally pull it out to readjust pillows, I see a few missed calls and texts. I have been kind of banned by Rich from taking any calls to do with work, but I call back anyway. The cleaners couldn't get into the venue. This was three hours ago. April didn't meet them at the venue to let them in for the weekend deep clean and the carpet steam cleaned. Mini P calls. She can't find April, and they need to open the venue in one hour, and the place is in a state. Gee is on leave at his grandmother's funeral, and out of the area, so Mini-P is doing the best she can to get the venue open but isn't quite sure how or what needs to get done. She knows how the place needs to be set up with the lights, sounds system, and the 'physical' venue but doesn't know how to start the tills or all the venue management elements that Gee and April take care of, bless her. She is stressed to the max. I am stressed. And in labour. Fuck you, April. You're dead meat when I find you. Mini-P has three bar staff who've arrived, but because the venue is still messy and dirty from last night, she can't see them being able to open. The cleaners have just come back, but they won't be able to open for a few hours. If Mini-P can get some help, she thinks she can swing it. She also has a hen party arriving at any moment for a life drawing and cocktail workshop. April is totally missing, gone AWOL, won't answer her phone. I call, and it goes straight to voicemail. I call Gee, apologise for disturbing him but ask him to call Mini-P and talk her through the steps and codes she needs to be able to open. I tell her to take the hen party down to our competitor and pay them to host it there, then head back and open the venue the best she can. It's the best we can do.

My contractions are building. I need to get up and walk around.

April arrived at the venue three hours later like nothing happened. Her excuse? An over-the-top dramatic rendition of a rather imaginative story. She said she was arrested on the walk to work and taken to a police holding cell. It was a case of 'mistaken identity' for a crime that was currently being investigated. She claimed she was held until they proved she was, in fact, the wrong person. Seriously. This is her story which she is ferociously sticking to. I call the local police station who say they aren't at liberty to 'discuss any arrests, holdings or ongoing investigations'. I know she knows I'd call the police station and they won't discuss anything with me, because she was in the police academy and wanted to be a detective before she realised that you can't party and be a police officer. We bite the bullet and call the head of licensing police in Brighton, not a man you ever want to flag venue issues with, and explained the situation. He agrees that it is imperative to find out as April is the DPS and licensee of FunFair. He promises to investigate and get back to me.

There were no arrests or mistaken identity, and she is lying.

Of course, we knew it was utter bullshit. The reality is she went out after last night's shift ended, had partied all day, fallen asleep somewhere, and not woken up in time for work. She slipped up in her assumption she'd be protected by police protocol. She had no clue we could prove she was lying.

My labour kicks up a notch, and I don't have time to yell at her now. I have proper intense painful contractions I need to focus on to get through each one and then a baby to push out.

Baby FunFair was coming… or so we thought.

20

It's that haunting time in the dead of night, the witching hour when the morning is so far away, and loneliness can kick in if you don't have a real reason to be awake. The taxi driver is totally silent. He seems to be driving into and over every pothole, speed bump, and moon crater known to man. There's no traffic, so we glide through the street alone. I have tunnel vision. The contractions are back-to-back now. There's a small window in between when both the contractions and the pain stop. These moments are left open for a little joke with Rich or observation that the driver could have taken a faster route. Neither man is in the mood for jokes.

We make our way out of the taxi. Rich silently carries my bag, and a nurse comes and helps me into the lift to take me to the birthing unit. It sounds like a lion's den at feeding time. Roaring lionesses and their howling prey. It's deeply unnerving. The contractions get stronger and stronger each time, and I feel like I'm ready to push soon. Between my legs feels like I'm involuntarily squeezing out a basketball. It's thick and weird like I might shit out a giant Easter egg. The pain wraps tight, as though thousands of burning elastic bands are flicking my stomach and a hot iron pressed on my lower back. They put me up on the bed for an examination. I projectile vomit from the pain. Everywhere. The nurse is not impressed and asks why I didn't request a bucket or warn them. In between the contractions, I explain that's the fun of unexpected projectile vomit. You never know when it's coming or how far it will go.

They leave me flat on my back. I feel weak, like I'm going to pass out. A midwife enters, a woman who I've met before. Unfortunately, she's not friendly, despite her hair being pulled up into playful pigtails. She tells me to pull myself together. She rams two fingers into my vagina, exhales deeply, and says me I need to go home because I'm not even one centimeter dilated. And apparently, I need to get a grip because it hasn't even started yet. She tells me to get up, and I collapse down the side of the bed and begin to pass in and out of consciousness. Rich is trying to help but doesn't know what to say or do. He said he was sure we had timed it correctly. She flatly shuts us down and says to go home. I tell them all I can't go home, that it doesn't feel right. I won't make it. They say I can go down to the birth ward, but Rich can't come. No. That's not going to happen. He isn't leaving me, and I'm not going home. I would rather wait together in the hospital halls.

I feel like such a fucking idiot. How could I have ever thought I could do this naturally? The pain is unbearable. I can only imagine the next stage up of pain is passing out completely. This woman is a total cunt. How can she hate someone she doesn't know so badly? She puts me in a room and says I need to have a shot of pethidine, which I said I didn't want, but she gives it to me anyway. She repeats robotically that I'm only in early labour, need to get a grip, handle it properly and get on top of the pain because it's going to get a lot, lot worse. She is making Nurse Ratchet look like a fucking saint. She finds a bed for me. I was half expecting her to put me in a dog kennel or outside in a manger with the donkey assistant midwife. Rich isn't feeling too well, is really tired and needs to lie down. Fuck me, who's having the baby here?!

She gives me the shot and tells him the baby won't be coming until tomorrow, and he may as well sleep, which of course he does. He sleeps for two hours until the shift changes.

His relaxing nap is rudely interrupted, eventually. I rock and pant alone. The doors open and a tall goddess that looks like Disney's Pocahontas walks in, with a small flame-haired sidekick who looks like Princess Merida from Brave. They warmly greet me. They're taking over the shift, and we are all going to birth this lucky baby together! They are super excited by my birth plan and have noted down my requests, which all look great. It was like how Snow White danced and skipped into the seven dwarfs' dark, dusty, unloved cottage, singing her sweet song as she lovingly threw back the curtains, letting in little blue-birds, trailing pretty ribbons, tiny posies of snowdrops and forget-me-nots, soft rays of warm buttercup sunlight and endless amounts of Disney hope floods the hospital room.

She does a gentle internal examination and is shocked, utterly flabbergasted. She calls for a second opinion and both agree that I am ready to push and is deeply sorry that the pigtailed birth midwife had completely miscalculated things and wrongly diagnosed me. I had a shy cervix which wasn't 'presenting in a typical way', meaning I have just done the final stage of labour alone, in the foetal position on a bed, rocking and facing the wall with my birth partner soundly asleep on the floor. I was at the very peak of the contraction pain when Pigtails said the labour hadn't even started. I knew I was tougher than that. I'm actually thrilled and re-energised.

They have to really shake him to wake him up. Fucking narcoleptic!

Mums called to quickly come to the hospital. Rich freshens himself up after his restful nap. The guardian angels kindly laugh when he goes to get changed into jeans, like after a long haul flight and you are an hour out of your holiday destination airport. They let him know there is some more grunt work to go, so stay in the tracksuit pants. They have properly read my three-page birth plan and encourage him to go about his tasks. He sets up the speaker, the LED candles, and the lavender spray, the homoeopathic remedies, and birth ball. They put mattresses on the floor, as per the plan... It's cosy and calm. And they don't scold or ridicule me and my wishes for our baby's journey into the world. I asked for the lights to be dimmed when she comes out she so could adjust to the light slowly. I'm sure it's pitch-black in the womb, and nobody likes it when the lights are suddenly switched on. If everyone can just let Rich and I talk to her so she is reassured by familiar voices and once she's out to be given straight to me... Can we stay calm, quiet? I don't want to yell or scream and upset the baby. I want to move through natural birth positions and stay off the bed and out of the birthing stirrups.

And can we listen to Fleetwood Mac's Rumours? And most importantly, I would like gas and air!

The difference that 20 minutes made changed our whole birth experience. Dark, mean, prickly, angry, and hostile to warm, kind, nurturing, positive, and respectful. Beautiful. And fuck me, this gas is the best ever. I could do anything on this shit!

I am in control, calm now I know that I was, in fact, in the peak of the labour pains and so fucking grateful of that shift change. Rich, Mum, and my two guardian angels are going to guide our baby out. We push to 'The Chain'; we squat to 'Go Your Own Way'; hunch down on all fours to 'You Make Loving Fun'; we grunt to 'Don't Stop'; breathe to 'Dreams'; hang off Rich's neck to 'Oh Daddy', and repeat the process for three hours. Now, listening to Rumours sends shivers down my spine, and makes my vagina wince.

But as hard as we try in our positive Fleetwood Mac-Disney birth dream, this little baby is stuck. She's not going anywhere, try as I might.

Things turn very quickly. She's not making it. Someone hits the emergency button, and the crash team is instantly in the room. There is no time for an emergency Caesarean section and no spare operating theatre available, which is why I was left to try and birth naturally for so long.

Dear Tava,
She's scared and tired. Keep it together,
close your eyes, and be calm for her.
Don't scream or yell, she is frightened.
I love you.
The Universe

I'm lifted back into the bed, and my legs are jammed through the stirrups. The rooms energy shifts once again. There are now 12 people in green scrubs, masks, and various uniforms. No one catches my eye as I look through my legs at them, but my guardian angels reassure me that our baby is coming, they are still here for me but will be stepping aside to let the obstetrician and doctors take over. Everything is going to move quickly now. They are all either staring down deep into my vagina or at the monitors. Beeps, buzzing, and warnings fill the room. I listen to the Universe and close my eyes. Apart from the one main voice commanding the room, leading with instructions and the replies given and decisions made, there is no unnecessary talking. I agree to do everything he says. I don't care what has to be done to me, I just want our baby out of danger. Rich is on one side, and my mum on the other with their hands wrapped around my arms.

I close my eyes for the last time, and I won't open them until you're here. I breathe deeply, inhaling the gas as I hear the sound of a chicken breast being cut with kitchen scissors. I block out all the fear.

I have a vision that fills my mind and body. I need to push past the 'black envelope' which I see behind my closed eyelids. "I know you can hear me, my little love. Everything is going to be okay. You can come to me soon, but you need to be brave." I push. Pushing through the black envelope in my mind's eye. We are back-to-back, and your neck is locked, and your chin is jutting forward. They reach inside me and pull, but you won't move. You can't. They cut more. The commanding voice tells me to push. Push as hard as I can, but it's still not enough. Your little heart rate is dropping. "You're tired. I know, my love. Be brave, my baby. Just two more pushes left in both of us. Together." The deep voice gets to work, the clunk and scrape of metal forceps and a ventouse. They're ripping me apart, and you're viciously pulled. I push through the black envelope and beyond. Your head comes into the light. You're safe now, my love. Another push and that last push smashing the envelope into pieces and you, my child, are free.

We lock eyes. I already know you.

The voice tells Rich to quickly cut the thick, gristly cord and my fragile little bird is snatched from my arms and a ribbed rod slid down your tiny throat.

You cry.
The room breathes.

She's given back to me. "Isn't she so beautiful?" Rich doesn't seem as momentarily convinced. She's covered in blood, and her skin is a midnight blue. Both he and mum are both sheet white. They look like they've witnessed a terrible accident. We're all in shock. My body is shaking uncontrollably, but our little girl is healthy. She's out. Her head is squashed from the ventouse suction cap, and she has deep cuts on her forehead from the forceps. Bruises and angry red marks cover her head and face from the force used to get her out. That will later turn to a delicate scar to remind us of her strength.

She is perfect and so, so strong.

Welcome to the world, my little Dorothy. May you lead a life filled with love, enchantment, and wonder. The strongest heroine and with the kindest, purest heart.

I lie my head back with my eyes scrunched tight. Steadily inhaling on the gas and breeze out the after-birth. I'm weeping from the overwhelming relief that she is safe. She always felt safe when she was in the womb, protected by my body, but the limbo of the birth canal trapped her in 'no man's land'. I felt her safety was out of my control but not yet in the capable hands belonging to the dozens of eyes on her crowning head. That she was in the hands of the Universe. She wasn't in, and she wasn't out. In the outside world, those dozens of eyes could protect her.

Rich says hello to his lovely little lady. Her eyes are taking him in she is making tiny baby-dragon noises. Mum and I hold hands while I have layers and layers of skin tissue and multiple cuts sewn up. The surgeon is trying to show Rich the fantastic stitching job she is doing, but he can't look. His eyes are wide, and his face glows in wonder looking at her. I've never seen anything like it. His pure joy and total overwhelm of the tiny bundle in his arms beaming back love into his face making it glow. Everyone has to make careful little steps as they move about the room, like after the snow melts and turns to black ice. It's not snow or ice their slipping and sliding about in. It's my blood.

She looks like a sweet tiny wizard. Her skin slowly turns pink, her little skull pops out of the conehead shape, and her soft black doe eyes take us in. Wrapped up. Safe.

Later, in that weird dead-of-night that usually makes me feel uneasy, I cradle the tiny bundle in my arms. I take in the vast view from the 12th floor spanning over Brighton. The water bounces back the light of the full moon. It would have been a 5-star view if I was doing a Trip Adviser hotel review. I would have had a mixed review of the service, but the view's magnificent. I make out the King's Road and imagine FunFair, in the twinkling lights. It would be smack bang in the middle of a club night, and my stomach drops at the thought of ever stepping back in there…

*Dot doesn't know anything about how she was birthed yet, not the issues or the stories and certainly not what music we were listening to. We were in the car today and Fleetwood Mac's Don't Stop came on my Spotify Daily Mix. She pipes up totally out of the blue. "So, how many people were in the room when I was born, Mum?" WTF! I knew babies could hear from the womb!

21

I don't sleep for another three days. Since my water broke, that means it's going on five days. Every time I close my eyes, I panic and jolt awake. I worry if I sleep, I will die, or Dorothy will die. My mind stuck in the birth, a nightmare loop gripped in the fear I won't be able to push through the black envelope and never wake up. I lie on my back with Dot in her usual spot for the past nine months. I worry that I will jolt and send her flying across the room or I'll fall asleep, and my arms will let her go, and she'll roll off the bed. I tuck her into a swaddling wrap and tie it behind my back, this homemade sling works for both of us. I feel like she is still in my stomach. A recreated womb. I wish I could get in there with her. I close my eyes, and I feel all the familiar lumps and bumps that were hidden under a layer of belly skin. What I was convinced was her knee was actually her little bottom. And where her head was, in fact, her back. It's bizarre. All of it blows my mind.

"So, this is the kitchen. We'll make meals for you here when you start eating. This is the lounge room, where we hang out and like to watch TV. This is Dollar, he's your dog!" We welcome her to her new home, giving Dot a little guided tour of the house. The book we've decided to follow is called The Baby Whisperer. It suggests talking to our baby as a person, a human. I really like the way it puts things. I explain where we're going, how things work, who this is. We talk to her, so she knows what's happening. I find it reassuring, like I'm repeating back to myself the 'plan' and it fills the weird gap between the disconcerting silence and not really being one for cutesy baby talk.

I time each breastfeeding session with military precision, keeping a feeding log of which boob, the time it started and ended. It allowed me to start making up a feeding pattern, understanding my body and also to notice her little habits in how she feeds. I follow the routine to the letter, noting down every little detail in my note-book. If nothing else, it keeps me focused and stops me from freaking out. So I keep following the plan and the book. As a result, from studying her so carefully, I'm able to read her cues, guiding her into her sleep routine and feeding patterns from the way her face and body move and her little meeps and cries. They signal what she needs. She is a little riddle that I was slowly working out. Of course, there are growth spurts, cluster feeds that send us into a sweaty spin, and my drained boobs are like turned out pockets. Running around the house, snapping, crying and wondering what the fuck is wrong, but the more we follow the routine, the more we find our groove.

Rich is now also the swaddling master of the house and confident co-pilot. We know what she needs to be doing at any given moment. She is like clockwork. We keep her sleep environment varied between the cot, pram, and Moses basket in the living room, so she was happy and adjusting to different background noises and soundscapes. Dot is a baby who was as comfortable in her buggy having a nap in a busy café or pub as she was breastfeeding in total silence at home or the busy, noisy world around her. It was a fool-proof system for us to follow those first few months. That way, Rich could have Dot clocked by the time I went back to work. I also had a deep, driving fear that I wasn't going to be able to make the transition of me going back to work so early but with the three of us following a book carefully, it gave me a sense of being able to stay on top of the unknown.

She is a perfect baby. I love being a mum so much. And I adore seeing Rich become the most amazing father.

But we've found a few small kinks in the 24-hour baby chain.

KINK ONE - Rich is totally incapable of functioning at night or on any reduced sleep. We laughed before Dot arrived, saying how good we'd be on limited sleep, thanks to our vast experience as '24-hour party people'. Experts in late nights, DJing, and running clubs 'til daybreak would have prepared us for being able to handle sleepless nights? Nope. Rich can't wake up, and if he's woken up, he's snappy and pretty useless. It pissed me off that he just couldn't pull himself together, so I take back all the night-time duties. I have infinite patience for this tiny human, but we work it out with me sleeping in her room and drifting in and out to the soothing upstairs-downstairs dramas of Downton Abbey during night feeds. It fucking sucks but my body just seems to be in tune with hers, anyway. I instantly wake up the moment she even moves a millimetre.

KINK TWO - I am having a weird emotional overload. It's like a wall of responsibility and how dangerous the world is comes crashing down on me and I must protect my little love from danger. I almost throttled the cab driver on the trip home from the hospital. He wasn't speeding or driving carelessly, I was just paranoid about the precious, fragile, priceless little Faberge egg in the car seat. All the terrible human behaviour I have seen in clubland. It's utterly terrifying now I am a protector. I check her breathing every time she sleeps, watching her miniature chest rise and fall, my hand in front of her mouth to feel for the sweet little breath. Checking the room, body and water temperature like I have OCD. My eyes can't move away from the CCTV baby monitor. My internal mother's intuition switch has been flipped. HARD.

KINK THREE – A daily drain on every single thing I do, from taking a step or rolling over in bed to going to the toilet. It puts a layer of 'yuck' on everything, pain mixed with, what the fuck now?! I try not to let it shit all over my beautiful new baby time, but it's hard. Introducing FRANKENVAGINA. My poor, poor pretty little pre-birth vagina is gone, may she rest in peace. In her place is a wounded, ripped, crude beast. A savage survivor. After pushing for so long, there was permanent damage to the passage. An avalanche of injuries. Starting with the stitches after the episiotomy, the official name for the widening of the birth passage in delivery, that was the cutting that sounded like meal prepping chicken breast. The stitches fell out, leaving the wound half-open, spreading from the side of the vagina to butt cheek. This then became infected. My body goes into repair mode, and a thin skin membrane called a skin bridge starts growing over the base of my vagina. It looks and feels like the skin of a drum or like someone's wrapped a layer of plastic wrap over it. It's like I'm weeing on a pranked cling-filmed toilet. It ended up ripping, which was super sexy as you can imagine, and as painful as it sounds. I'm close to closing up shop forever. Every day is filled with dread and unshakable constipation. All the little everyday routine tasks of caring for a baby make me grit my teeth in discomfort.

It is a clusterfuck of problems. The general rule is that pushing a baby out should be kept to two to three hours. Mine went well over that. I officially have a rectocele posterior vaginal prolapse. Basically, everything has collapsed internally, mashing my bladder down into a kidney shape, squashing my bowels into my vaginal wall, and creating a bulge in the passage. I have to wait two and a half years for my operation with the NHS. I waited so long it was passed over to a private hospital, but I was never in a position to actually have it before then, as you can't lift more than 5kg and can't be properly mobile for eight weeks. It has mixed results for such a significant operation. How is it even an option with a small child to lift, a business to run, and no family to help?

After the GP reads the birth notes, he refers us to a birth counsellor. She's an independent midwife who assures us that ours wasn't a typical birthing scenario. She promises us that the treatment from the pigtailed nurse will be looked into. I should never have been left to push for so long: that's what caused the avalanche of injuries. The birth goes to a review board. We're offered counselling, but neither of us wants to talk about it anymore. I take away the little positive pockets of joy from the birth and leave the rest of it as unfortunate circumstances.

She said it's good to talk about it, so we can be prepared for the next birth but fuck that, I'm NEVER having another child. End of. Both of us feel exactly the same. It's never changed to this day. We have our Hollywood-fucking-amazing-love family, the three of us. That ticking clock, the profound need to make a child with the love of my life never, ever returns. Not once. I never have the womb-shaking pull again. It just goes back to the regular wanting to live in his blood.

I have no idea how I am ever going to be able to work like this. I struggle to walk long distances. Stairs make me wince. I can't wear heels, and any uneven surface terrifies me. I panic at the thought of slipping; the type where one foot slips out, your legs come apart, and you need to stop yourself from doing the splits. That is my greatest fear. I cautiously shuffle along, aware of my own body in a way I've never been before. With each step I take, I'm reminded of the battle wounds. I can't lift anything anymore. That's a significant problem for someone who has to shift cases of beer, boxes of flyers, and generally packhorse around. Dashing up and down illusion staircases, climbing ladders with abandon during the day, ducking and diving through the dance floor obstacle course, hich teems with lurching drunks, and skating across slippery floors at night are all unofficial parts of my job description.

A few months before my due date, I naively and ridiculously suggested that we have a family meet up in Ibiza five weeks postpartum, as my brother is 'eloping' to Santorini and the rest of the family wanted to meet Dorothy. It seemed like an excellent suggestion to meet in the middle. Sun, sea, and Balearic paternity leave. Luckily, Dot is a dreamboat, and our routine is transferable, but honestly, it's a daze. The three of us take family naps, laze about, feed, eat, and repeat. It's lovely relaxing with my parents and siblings in a rambling white-washed private villa with pockets of palms, day beds, and a sparkling pool. The usual family bullshit and squabbles kick off from time to time, but it's nice to be in a family atmosphere having lots of hands to help, and the beautiful villa is big enough to give everyone space.

Ibiza is incredible. I can't believe I've never been here before. It's not how I would have imagined it at all! There is so much more to the island than clubbing. I think Rich has a pang of envy when everyone else goes to Pasha but the idea of a night on the tiles at the superclub makes my womb shiver, boobs weep tears of milk, and my knees knock. For me, this holiday is a no-plan, slow stroll, ice cream and fish-lunch kind of vibe only. One thing I didn't anticipate was having the continued rollercoaster of postpartum emotions. It's similar to the first few months of pregnancy, mixed with the feeling that a veil of imminent danger has drawn close. I'm scared. Scared of the world. Scared of how sensitive I am. Is this who I am, now that I'm a mother? I wish I knew back then it was all hormonal and things would settle down. Then I could have been less terrified of being so terrified. Here is a perfect example.

While we were in Ibiza, Mum offered to take Dot for the afternoon so we could hang out and relax. I hired a '70s vintage Mini Moke without a roof. It's pretty much a sardine tin on wheels, and we piled in, drove back by the villa on the way to the beach to show my parents. Cruising through the orange orchards dripping in ripe fruit, down the dusty, deserted roads and the brightest bluest sky, one of my siblings has a speaker in the back blaring Ibiza classics with the wind whipping up my hair. Loving life. We pull up, and my mum quickly points out this isn't proper behaviour for two new parents, let alone my sibling in the back with no seat belts. I could wipe out a whole family. This would typically run off my back with a 'Whatever, Mum' but at the beach, while the others swam in the sea, sunned themselves and sipped rosé, living their best life, I sat in the toilets and wept. I called my mum, desperately wanting to apologise and over-explain. Weeping eyes and leaking breasts. I just wanted to go home and hold my baby.

My mum didn't need an explanation. We are all adults, but I had bouts of this crippling self-doubt and anxiety. It came in waves and would disappear just as suddenly. Granted, it wasn't the best, safest car-hire choice but I guess Mum was flexing her own 'mum-safety muscle'. I realise the vast responsibility I have for a tiny human and not just me and Rich. That is a mega thing to get used to. Oh, and just to clarify, the sardine tin car was never meant to take our tiny human. There was a very, modern, air bagged, air-conditioned car for her.

Being in Ibiza leaves me with a taste to return to the magical island. The sunny weather and chilled-out island life bring out the best in Rich. He seems to unravel in the sunshine and truly relax. He is a warm climate creature. It still baffles me that he hates the cold so much, even though that's what he was born into. After dinner, I swing in a hammock, the CCTV baby monitor resting on my chest listening to the lovely little breathing, my post-baby fat poking through the hammock holes like a strung ham. I look up at the stars that are so much brighter here than in the UK. The air is warm and sweet with orange blossoms. It's one of those holidays that makes you wonder whether you could run away and start a new life. A bit of me wishes Rich and I came out here in pre-baby days to party, DJ or do a club project, but visiting as a new family, we're experiencing a different side to the beautiful island, rustic dining, striking craggy rocks, shimmery sea and blazing sunsets, and the warm-hearted magic feeling that pulses through the island. I genuinely believe there is magic in the air here. The three of us are so deeply in love already, it's such a special time to be in an idyllic location.

A Balearic bubble of newborn baby bliss.

The perfection of the holiday is punctured with the reality of my own clubland responsibilities. I get a phone call from the Arrogant Landlord. He cuts to the chase. Put simply, our basement nightclub is ruining his serviced apartment business above, and if I don't fix it, he will revoke our lease. I dare not tell him I'm out of the country, chilling out in a private villa in Ibiza or god forbid, that I've even been off having a baby. Although the club is being handled by my business partner during my maternity leave, it's like being called out by a headmaster for ditching school, but I'm not actually doing anything wrong. I just have inbuilt guilt for not being at the club, and those scared waves roll right in. I tell him I'll come to his office on Monday. Luckily, I'm booked on a flight back late Sunday.

The midnight flight from Ibiza to Stansted is packed with all the mess heads still awake from a solid shift of pill-popping and MDMA dabbing at Amnesia. They check straight onto the flight, avoiding the 'couple with a baby' like the plague. She is perfectly well-behaved while the other passengers crumble from holiday bender comedowns around us. She was so content on the flight she didn't even get through the feed, falling asleep, leaving me with one full, aching boob, throbbing, lactating, making white tide mark rings on my soaking wet vintage batik dress. I dared not wake her up to finish and fix my discomfort, risk her kicking off to feed her in the very unmanageable feeding position which we have seemed to have landed in. I didn't fancy getting my mega knocker meals-on-wheels out. It's not just a simple case of whipping it out and latching on. It's a two-handed job of holding her in the feeding position with one hand and holding back the bulk of the breast away from her tiny face to stop it suffocating her. I am all for public breastfeeding, but our style is more of a crossed-legged yogi position of perfect balancing, positioning, and the milk god stars aligning. Dot is half-breast fed and half-formula bottle-fed, despite the NCT feeding 'cow' saying it wasn't possible. These days, I think it's actually encouraged as a good feeding option. The milk flow has adjusted itself and takes into account the bottle feeds as long as we keep them around the same time every day. The body is truly amazing! And in no way is there ANY nipple confusion or any lack of bonding. Getting us ready for the back to work feeding transition.

The Arrogant Landlord has an office on the grounds of his mansion's 25-acre property. It's a converted barn next to the towering convent with tight security and lots of assistants milling about. He is pleasant enough on arrival, but as we go into the office and sit around the board table, I draw blanks. I have forgotten how to do this. I feel like I shouldn't be here. I feel raw and fragile. My head is filled with cotton wool, and my tongue flops around my mouth like it's had an accidental jab of local anaesthetic during a tooth filling, He instantly drops the nice act. He's sincerely pissed once he gets talking and I don't need this to progress further. It needs shutting down immediately. My baby-brain switches gears and I start being able to speak with a mild level of authority on how I will address the issue with a matter of urgency. He puts a spreadsheet on the table listing sound complaints, claiming his guests heard music and felt vibrations up to the 3rd-floor apartments until 5am. I glance over his detailed list of complaints, immediately at a glance a few dates ring alarm bells. We don't open past 2am mid-week.

I reassure him that the issue has my full attention, but I'll need a few weeks to handle everything. I begrudgingly go straight into the office and watch the CCTV for those dates. April had a lock-in. Drinking my booze and 'playing' DJ with the staff and a load of their friends on those dates. One went until 6am after having closed down the club at 1.30am. The Friday promoter brought in a huge bass system and piggybacked it to our sound system, which is a BIG, HUGE fucking no-no. The sound IS travelling up into the landlord's apartments. I can understand why he's pissed. I'm pissed.

And just like that, I'm back at work, unofficially and I have a shit list to work through. Well, I say I'm back... My body is kind of here, but fuck knows where my brain is. It keeps checking in and out. So I crack on praying my brain will turn up soon...

First on the agenda

Soundproof the venue. I call a few companies that specialise in noise reduction to look at the place and what solutions we can install.

Secondly, fire April. Yes, yes, yes, I know. I know April should have been gone after 'mistaken identity gate'; i.e. lying about being arrested, but I have been otherwise engaged keeping a tiny human alive. I'm on it now. She's gone, and I feel like a right cunt because she had a lovely dinner gift voucher for Rich and me at The Grand's posh restaurant down the road and a gift for Dot. Argh, that's the problem with April. She's a kind, good-hearted person but makes ghastly work choices.

Back in the office, Mini P is a saving grace along with her hard and fast Pret croissants and coffee mainlining. It's like I've never left, but now there are lovely pockets of time set aside. Rich and Dot come in for feeds, we sit down in the empty club, I do the crossed-legged breastfeed in the stage booth and catch up on the news of their day so far. How her morning nap went, poo consistency, what's going down in the land of daddy day-care café life. I just want to go home with them. It feels so rushed. Too soon to leave her. I want to stow away in the cosy buggy and have Rich push us both back home up the mega hill. At the same time, I'm so grateful that Rich has this precious time with Dot.

One of the sound proofers comes back inside from the fire exit. He's looked through the venue, measuring everything up and presents us with a quote for 45K to seal and soundproof the venue. The sound is escaping through the two fire exits at the back wall of the club. The air ventilation also leaks noise into the back alley, which travels into the apartments above. The wall behind the DJ booth has a steel frame running through the building which conducts the bass. I get that it's a lot of work but fuck me, that's expensive. I politely thank him. He leaves, and I chuck the quote into the nappy bag. I can't afford that.

Rich explains the concept of how sound travels, what sound waves need to be blocked, and how soundproofing works. He had done it to his home studio back in De Beauvoir. This was the same principle but on a much, much larger scale. Fuck that. I'm not paying 45K. I'm going to do it myself. I study sound-proofing on the weird, wide and wonderful Internet. Hallelujah for YouTube tutorials. What did we ever do without them?! I laugh with Mini P about how I've learnt to raise a baby and how to run a club from them. I joke, but it's actually kind of true.

I have a builder come and build a false wall behind the DJ booth and pack it full of sound-absorbing insulation, have a cover made over the ventilation shaft with two-stage chambers to defuse the noise and still allow airflow. I order 50 sq. metres of industrial soundproofing 'egg box' acoustic foam, buckets of foam glue, staple guns and Stanley knives, and set about creating sound locks in the exits. They are covered all over in the egg box foam tiles, and the doors on the other side are sealed so they can open and close in an emergency, but when they are closed, they create a total soundproof airlock. When you stand in them, there's an unnerving dead silence. I line the air vent with the soundproofing foam and cover the ceiling in the ladies' loos and lobby with the same, as there is an apartment directly above. Finally, I surround the interior of the DJ booth with it.

Oh, and I have the promoters come and remove their big-arse bass bin speakers before I list them on eBay. A secure box goes around the amps and sound system, complete with a lock. No more unauthorised DIY DJ sound adjustments. We are now on sound lockdown! I create a document with all the installations, modifications with images, audio tests and recordings we've completed with the apartment manager and a sound engineer present. We're all clear in every level of the building. I send it off to the Arrogant Landlord.

I'm covered in a fine layer of semi-permanent glue and bits of black foam are stuck to my hands, which won't come off even after multiple showers. I almost died a few times from non-pleasure seeking asphyxiation in the fire exits from the glue and sprays, oozing blisters on my hands from thousands of staple guns squeezes and have a crick in my neck from doing the ceilings. It took two weeks and 6K and a begrudgingly satisfied landlord.

22

I'm heart-explodingly obsessed but am physically broken. The birth has left every inch of my body wrecked. Every drop of energy and goodness went into getting that little baby out safely. Never in a million years would I change that and I'd do it again for her, but it shows that you can be so prepared, yet nothing can prepare you for what actually is in store. I've lost my confidence in myself, my body, and my personality. I can't exercise to lose the baby weight, so I stay a big, bloated size 16, never going back to my pre-baby body, which used to float between and 10 and 12.

I do the internal exercises from the physio to try and stop the prolapse from progressing further. I know what you're thinking: 'Eww gross'. Yes, sadly, I agree. Do I piss myself? No, this type of prolapse affects my bowels. Can I still have sex? Yes. Surprisingly. Am I disgusted by it? Yes. I feel like there is a secret in my pants. And not a cool, sexy one. It's definitely a dirty one: a secret that has stolen my carefree nature, lust for life, and my normally unshakable self-confidence. Not my confidence in being a mother or a partner or the owner of a business. It's the part that makes me, me. I just kinda pave over it with nonde-script clothes, supportive structural underwear, and tights to hide away the hideousness I feel. I don't want to attract attention with fancy outfits or bold looks.

I realise that the person I was, before having a baby, is gone. But I get to hide behind the most beautiful, smiling sweet-natured, heart-melting baby. She is the perfect disguise.

I feel really embarrassed and ashamed of myself but cover it well with 'mum-life' tasks, jobs to do, hide my body away for good. Fade into the background. But I feel saddest for Rich. This experience changes the girl he fell in love with, inside and out. Disappeared for a very, very long time. In spite of everything, he never once falters in his affection, love or attention. His love is like a little anchor that keeps me from drifting further into a sea of self-pity.

We're out having cheese and wine at 10 Green Bottles in the lanes of Brighton with friends. It's a lovely wine bar with great staff, posh wines, and a slightly older crowd. I nip to the loo. Dot is asleep in her pram, next to our table. It's not busy yet, as it's only about 5pm. I'm having a nice time. We don't really see people at the moment, since I haven't been feeling great, but it's nice to go out and feel 'normal' for a bit. On the way back from the loo, I pass by a group of 40-something guys who are drinking a few tables down from us. One of them stops me and says, "Excuse me, can I tell you something? You really remind me of a film star." Haha, I think to myself: that's sweet. In the past, I'd been likened to Zooey Deschanel a few times, with my long hair and heavy fringe and twee little 50's dresses, but I don't have any extensions in at the moment, so it can't be her. He continues, "I just want to see if my mates can guess..." So I stand there, and he says, "Hey guys, doesn't she really remind you of someone...? You know that actress in that Stephen King movie?... You know... Kathy Bates... in Misery!"

They all roar with laughter and slap him on the back while I stand there. My heart feels like it's been punched. I think it actually broke a bit. Not that I ever needed validation from anyone, let alone a prick with a dick, but the humiliation was brutal because that was precisely how I felt with my dull shoulder-length hair, overweight and big round face. But to be so boldly mocked in front of a semi-circle of jesters, him holding court, setting me up for the blow. I felt like a 10-year old being taunted by the cruel older kids at school. The fucking WORST thing is I felt like I had scrubbed up okayish today, considering how gross I was feeling, that I was covering my battle wounds. I'd squeezed and poured myself into some sausage-skin Spanx, and a stretch French Connection black dress that hides a multitude of sins, with an Yves St Laurent leopard-print scarf. I was frozen, horrified, embarrassed, and so ashamed of what I looked like now. I stutter, and stammer in a whisper, "I've just had a baby, you fucking prick," and walk back the table, crying. Rich jumps up and goes flying towards them. He fucking rages and grabs the cunt by the throat and slams him up against the wall of wine bar, lifting the guy's feet off the ground. His face goes red. You don't fuck with South London. I think he's actually going to strangle the prick until our friends jump in and pull him off.

Hollywood-fucking-amazing-love isn't always pretty, but it's always fucking loyal.

I push through the club shifts in flat shoes and a uniform of 'theatre blacks'. I don't want to be seen any more, at work or in my personal life. I want to blend into the background. Other than having to physically take it easier, I truck along. Otherwise, it's business as usual. Mini P and I re-evaluate the promotion planning to keep the customers rolling in, drinking up and dancing the night away. We weather the inevitable ups and downs that come with club life, while plotting how to tackle the changing seaside seasons. Summer is hard for clubs. Everyone wants to drink in the sun all afternoon, so by the time we open at 10pm, the only thing on their minds is grabbing a kebab and stumbling home to pass out. We need to make the club irresistible to compete with the allure of afternoons spent in sunny beer gardens.

Heavy rain is a nightmare for street teams, but settling snow is the worst. It keeps everyone from venturing into town from their cosy local pub. That generally cold, slightly miserable drizzle that's the staple British weather is excellent for business. Not too hot, not too cold, juuuusssst right. We tackle new venue openings that look like they may be a threat to business head-on. Our method of attack is to ramp up our online presence. We checkmate promoters at their own games. We look after DJs, staff, and club nights, making sure our house is in order, so no one wants to stray to greener grass.

Another venue owner is trying to pinch my precious Mini P, who is now in charge of her very own marketing and promotion manager and office assistant, but to no avail. Thank god! We firefight negative online reviews and reward customers who leave good ones. Our little black book of entertainers grows and grows to keep it cutting edge. Everything from mind-readers and fire-eaters to chainsaw jugglers. We hone in on securing big events, corporate functions, Christmas parties and weddings, and branch out into really cool, creative and alternative hen do's and bridal parties. We book in groups of hens, utilising the empty venue before opening it to the public by offering the groups private workshops and masterclasses, like striptease and feather-fan dance, hula-hooping, pin-up hair and makeup, erotic games, and cocktail making. Once the club opens, they get a private area and hostess service. It's really well received and gets booked out quickly.

We bring in a new round of promoters. Now that I'm back at work and Rich is on paternity leave, he isn't DJing at the club. He does create an incredible summer mix for us to use for promoting the venue. We hand Saturdays over to a promoter. Although we lose the door money, they bring in a high-spending glamorous crowd who arrive earlier in the evening. We don't have to directly pay the entertainers, and we've negotiated with the promoters to carry the cost of them, instead. They pay all the promotion costs, including DJs and street teams. So it actually comes out in our favour, as long as they put the work in. This requires a close relationship, constant check-ins and regular updates of how the weekend is looking. While we may lose a large part of creative control, we still guide the way they design and promote. The downside is that the music is a lot more commercial and they won't change their music policy. But you have to weigh up what you are willing to let go.

Handling promoting in-house for a single club night takes a team of one full-time, one part-time and a few online guest listers. They reach out to their own contacts and the club's target demographics online, befriend them, and get them excited to come to the club and be added to the guest list. Then, there's a street team of 6-10 people on the night. During the week leading up to a club night, one person does shop drops with flyers and posters, while teams of twos canvas universities, shops and during summer, the seafront. That's not including the time it takes to design and create the ads, posters, social content and flyers, then getting them listed in gig-listing magazines. Instagram is on the rise, and Facebook has just changed their algorithms. Unless you pay and 'boost' all your posts, they don't get seen. This is a massive game-changer for an industry which has run on free marketing with a free, wide reach to customers for so long. We still do these things to keep the club in people's minds, but the promoters do the nitty-gritty grunt work to get the bodies through the door at their event. It gives Mini P and me time to work on various avenues of increasing revenue, like curating a 'Freaks & Darlings' show for the Fringe

Festival and a travelling off-shoot of our beloved club!

Spring and summer in Brighton are bustling with so many events and enquiries for bookings. We just can't cater to them all, thanks to our solid trade. We have a brainwave: Travelling FunFair. A pop-up mini version of our much-loved club with an interchangeable mobile unit that can be used as a stand-alone cocktail bar or an all-singing, all-dancing, travelling circus. Our talented, zany curly moustache artist Paul applies his talents to it to create a gorgeous masterpiece. Hand-painted tassels, trimming, and bustle curtains: it's a total showstopper. The Travelling FunFair has a roller deck filled with performers, bespoke cocktail menus, pastel flag bunting, bales of hay for seating, candy floss machine, and frosé dispenser. With DJs and a mobile sound system, it's perfect for a festival-themed field wedding or a bar at a food festival. It turns out to be really popular, and another great little side-hustle for FunFair. Being able to tap into off-site business opportunities with our existing customer base is good for business.

Rich is on the last two weeks of his paternity leave. It's gone by in the blink of an eye. Our little girl is already eight months old. She's sitting, crawling, weaning, winning hearts, itching to stand and smashing milestones down like they're feathers. She makes parenting an enchanting adventure with her eagerness to embrace life with an open heart. We make the most of the last few weeks and head to Australia for my mum's 60th and for Big Nanny and the extended family to meet Dot. Rich has never been to Australia. My mum and Dad are still renting the most amazing tiny boathouse in Palm Beach. We decide to hire a beach house just across the water on Mackerel Beach to host Mum's party and have a base camp for family visits. It's in a national park, right in the middle of lush Australian bushland. A deserted beach, wallabies, iguanas, and all the mozzies in the world. Pure Summer Bay Home and

Away vibes. Dot is one of those babies who has 24-hour charm. You can see Rich's charisma beaming out of her little heart-shaped face already, with the same infectious smile and hypnotising icy-blue eyes. She relishes in the loving family attention. Rich is blown away by Sydney's beauty. I had also forgotten what a stunner of a city it is. Also, it was nice being surrounded by family again. But as we've established time and time again, clubland keeps on spinning. And there is no rest for her residents.

Two phone calls change the course of our life's direction; one that we thought we'd solidly planned.

Call one: Chief of Police. Brighton Police Station

We had landed and arrived at our Airbnb in Kirribilli, a neat little art deco apartment looking across the stunning Sydney Harbour and laughing Luna Park, before heading down to 'Summer Bay'. Rich and Dot are asleep after the long flight. I'm dazed and jet-lagged, but it's too hot and bright for me to sleep. Plus I know full well the curse of an 'afternoon' nap that turns into a deep sleep that, in turn, means being wide awake at midnight. At least those two are synced up. I get to battle the 'lag' alone. I absent-mindedly answer the call, not expecting the crime of the century to unfold into my lap. We're being investigated after an 'anonymous package' was dropped in to Brighton Police Station: a ring binder containing fifty A4-sized screengrab printouts of patrons in our club taken from our Facebook page, our weekly club photography with the FunFair logo neatly tucked in the corner, placing them at the scene of the crime. The photos are marked up with red circles around the faces of underage customers. With the name and age of each person noted on the side of the page. There are over one hundred underage customers in total.

It turns out that some enterprising young genius has totally fucked us over, producing more than one thousand fake IDs for the local Sussex kids. He was so good at the forgery, he got to Spain via Gatwick Border Control with one of his masterpieces on a family vacation and was caught on the way back into the country. Apparently, he used a fine layer of virtually undetectable film with a tiny mark adjusting the date to make the underage owner of the passport over 18. It was so well executed, it passed through half a dozen passport checks in the UK and Spain. The police are pissed. I mention that his fakes must have been exceptional if they can get past officials, but this is dismissed. The chief of police tells me that after the envelope drop, we were tested by underage 'test purchase agents', accompanied by undercover police agents and failed on three accounts. Fuck. Two minor agents gained entry, and one got served alcohol. Okay, fair enough. (FUCK) Due to the severity of the case, my license is going to be reviewed. The venue will remain closed until the hearing, BUT if I wanted to keep my venue open, there is an opportunity for me to cooperate with the police.

These are their conditions. First, fire my current security firm, which I don't have a problem with as this falls on them. There's footage of security talking and laughing as the underage police agents just walk in. Security didn't even check any IDs at 10.15pm when we'd only just opened. They were pretty much the first customers into the club. Second, fire the bar staff who served the undercover police test agents. We sent them over to a friend's pub to work and paid their fine. Our staff work in a busy, fast-paced environment. They need to know security has done their job of checking ID on the door. Thirdly, we need to install an ID facial recognition scanner and programme that they can rent to me (funny that). And lastly, I will need to be interviewed by the local paper with pre-arranged questions and my answers, given to me by the police, letting everyone know we had dropped the ball but are so, so grateful for the police department's rigorous new policies, leniency, and protection of venues like us.

It's funny how the fooling of two different countries' national border control wasn't mentioned in the article I was quoted in. The fake ID forgery was totally out of our control, but it opened us up to be investigated, and we failed pretty miserably. The fact that security didn't pick up on the undercover police accompanying the underage test dummies makes me wonder what the fuck they were doing. Undercover police stick out like sore thumbs. Nothing changes. There still exactly the same as they were on my first encounter at 666: always about 20 years older than our regular customers, in puffer jackets that they keep on instead of placing them in coat check, baggy jeans, and stupid, clunky hiking boots with red laces. They drink Coke. Like reluctant dads chaperoning teenage daughters to a Taylor Swift concert. You can spot them a mile away.

I have to admire the little dude who pumped out these stellar IDs. It would be hard to not be secretly proud if you were his parents. But there's a bigger mystery in all this. Who the fuck did the 'anonymous letter' bomb drop to the old Bill?

Call Two. An offer of 500K to buy the FunFair Club

This is an intriguing call. Oh, and half of it is in cash. As lovely as that sounds, there's a big problem with cash. Well, apart from the fact it's probably illegally-earned money, and illegal for me not to declare it. So if you don't pay the tax on it, it's hard to spend. Especially in the way I would want to be able to spend it, from a sale. A weekly cash envelope of door takings is one thing, but a massive amount like that is different. Plus, I hadn't even thought about selling Fun-Fair. Yet.

These two phone calls open up a conversation between Rich and me that never in a million years did I ever think we'd be discussing.

It wasn't me who asked the question. On a small wooden ferry, going back to Mackerel Beach after a special day spent on a family friend's luxury yacht under the pink salmon sky, he asks,

"Why don't we move out here?"

I never thought I would hear those words from Rich, but the beautiful country and buzzing city has really blown him away. Moving would mean a better life for Dot. But it's not that easy. England is my home now and has been for years. I would never have a child with someone and one day say, "Oh sorry, but I need to move back to my country." England is my country. It makes sense to me. I don't know if I want to leave the UK. I feel like that's where I belong, although I can't deny there is a pull-push with Australia, purely for my family, that never disappears. But England always won. It felt like I found my real home, that I was meant to be born here, not Australia. The English sense of humour, slightly stand-offish nature, and outlook: I like it. I like who I grew into living there. But now that we have a child, it's near impossible not having family close by. This would also never be a decision that would be mine. Because I know how hard it is leaving family, friends, and life as you know it, behind. It's too much to ask of a person, and I'd never ask that of Rich. It worked for me but for lots of people, moving to another country isn't such a positive experience. But here I am. On a holiday thinking, yeah we could run away…

Back to reality. Gee, our manager, is moving out of clubland and into insurance. It turns out anyone good gets out of the game, moves to bigger corporate chain clubs or opens their own venues. I'm a bit gutted about it. He was stable, which makes a really nice change from the usual types you wind up with. It's hard to find people who are happy to work vampire hours and not be villains. So I settle and hire a manager that I don't love. He's a bit too much of a 'Slick Rick' for my liking. We'll see how it goes. His references speak highly of him, and he has substantial club experience. It's in chavvy clubs, but that's okay. He might warm on me.

I meet the buyers with the flash cash offer. It doesn't feel like it will be an easy sale. They have a very different story now that we meet face to face. They don't have any cleared funds, meaning they would need to sell assets or remortgage properties, which isn't easy in this financial climate. They had some cash but not nearly the amount they implied they had. It's certainly not enough to make me consider such a poorly presented offer. They were looking to pay off the balance over time. Zzz ... please. The big numbers were just to get my attention, which to be fair, it did. They wanted to plant a seed, and although I am not going to sell the club to them, I am going to sell the club.

And we are going to move to Australia.

These two calls shifted me. I am sick to the back teeth of the high stakes drama that comes with clubland. The way things can just turn on a pin at any time; never being able to switch off. It's bone-achingly stressful, back-breaking hard work. An industry built on shifting sand. But it's also what I know. I never thought there was an option to cash my chips in and walk away from clubland. Be normal. What would I do without a club? It is who I am...

Because we haven't drawn large sums of money out of the club or taken massive wages, we live a pretty regular life for the amount of stress and responsibility that comes with running a club. Rich still works full-time. I take the weekly cash door money and a minimum wage. We have a part-time nanny, now that Rich is going back to work, and house cleaner who comes twice a week. We take a few nice holidays a year, and I like to buy organic produce when possible. We have a very comfortable life, but that's the extent of the 'lavish' living. It's not the crazy, high-flying nightclub mogul life you would expect, to make the insane bullshit worthwhile. I feel like I'm on a hamster wheel, spinning and working to pay wages, give the taxman his cut, repay loans, pay business rates and crippling interest, just so I can take out more loans, keeping the scrambling steady and constant. My debt makes me want and need more debt. But its packaged as 'growth, success and expansion', not debt. I now understand what 'working for the man' means. It's not an actual boss: it's a slave to the 'big business corporation and government'. My life is just to service loans and pump money back into the local community, keep people employed and fatten up big businesses, never quite getting ahead. Just keep my head above water; play my part in turning the wheels of a small business that is a part of a broader broken economy and it fucking sucks. All the while, the police and council don't want there to be a night-time economy past 10pm. I want to get off the wheel, but every single day the club and her demands come first. Non-stop calls, emails at all hours of the day and night, putting out constant fires, and endless organising. Day shifts and night shifts. As much as I try to step back with managers, it is such a high-maintenance, high-risk business model that it needs constant attention.

Rich knows, even if we have plans, if something happens at the club, it will take priority. That's why we had to make sure he was going to be super-connected with Dot. Financially, we are no better off than if we were both working in good highish-level full-time roles.

The only thing we have more of is shit-loads of stress. Having to be available to a club 24 hours a day takes its toll, especially now that there is a baby in the mix. We have rolled our profits and investments from the Bathhouse to the Baby Bathhouse and into FunFair. But there is one 'club mogul' trait. The cost of our mutual pre-baby coke habit over 5 years comes to well over 200K, and god knows what it would be if you added to the tally our individual drug consumption before we met (which makes me physically sick as I just worked it out now, using pretty conservative calculations).

But to sell FunFair and not roll the profits back into another business will be a life-changing payout for all the work and investment over almost seven years. It's not quite early retirement, but it's pretty good for a 30-something who left school at 16 and isn't an heir to a trust fund.

I list the club with an agent and start the 'courting process'. Selling the dream. Again. It's easy with a beautiful, busy club like FunFair. It is still in good shape. It has excellent customer traffic and is well known. Everyone from my competitor down the road to a retired couple swing by and put in offers. I'm not in a rush, so I don't snap them up. They are all almost 100K off the asking price of 400K.

In six weeks, Slick Rick manages the following…

He genuinely pisses off the club promoters, irritates the new security firm, annoys and antagonises Mini P, the bar staff, the customers, the bar next door and pretty much the greater population of West Sussex. He is smooth as silk with me. Nothing is a problem. "These are just teething issues, trust me." "Trust me" was his catch-cry, and it couldn't have been further from the truth.

Every time the night report pings in at 5am, it wakes me up with 'The Fear': either with reports of low takings if I wasn't at the club for a mid-week event, or full of some extraordinary tale which unfolded in the two hours after I've left for the night.

Pretty sure he was skimming the tills and door takings. It magically went back to the regular takings after two weeks, as soon as I mention the drop. Now that I look back, he didn't realise how closely I watched and calculated the cash and started looking into stock orders and till reads. So he started a new angle. 'Borrowing' stock (booze) from the bar next door, selling it during the shift and pocketing the profit. Then he'd replace the 'borrowed' stock with bottles from my wholesale stock order, recording the liquor disparity down as inflated 'wastage, spills, DJ, and staff drinks'.

There were allegations of serious sexual assault on a customer after she had left the club with Slick Rick. I learned about that after receiving an evidence request by the police. Four legal proceedings were officially lodged over the next three months, which coincided with his reign. Three of them were women. One customer losing her finger, which he denies, but I found it wrapped in plastic cling film, hidden in the deep freezer, still with the pastel pink acrylic nail attached. One customer 'breaking' her leg on the dance floor but still managing to walk home and back again in the morning to collect her car from outside the venue. We caught her leaving the venue, talking to Slick Rick, and coming back on the outside CCTV camera. And another woman 'breaking her ankle' in the Broken Dreams vault. The CCTV shows her dancing, drinking on for another four hours and kissing Slick Rick after the venue closed. I think he is grooming people to advance with legal proceedings against the club and me and then planning to take a cut of the compensation pay-out.

The fourth legal case was a staff member who was severely electrocuted in the club while stapling Christmas fairy lights into the Cogs mechanical art installation, while he was really drunk. He was thrown across the room, knocked out, and the staple gun melted the nerves in the palm of his hand. Slick Rick told him to sue me. The staff member said he would never sue me because Slick Rick knew he was drunk, wasn't rota'd on, nor fit to work. He was just doing Slick Rick a favour. He shouldn't have been stapling live wires, and that only shows how drunk he was. He tried to sue me three months later.

Weird drug issues started happening. One of the security guards came into my office totally off his head one night shift deep in the K-hole after being given a wrap of 'coke' by Slick Rick. Suspicions that he decanted cheap liquor into premium bottles, à la Mrs Payne (Bathhouse days) style. He didn't turn up with the Travelling FunFair bar as arranged for the super important University Freshers' Fair, a captive audience of customers for the next year. We cleaned up the previous year, pulled out all the stops, and reaped the rewards in loyal customers for a solid year. His absence meant we missed all this trade, leaving other clubs to pick up all the students. He brought in an after-party promoter who is a front for drug dealing and gang meetups. And his last big 'fuck you' was starting a 40-person brawl on the street after the club closed for the evening. A 40-person fight that was still in range of our CCTV. I had to watch, mortified, when the police came to the office to view the footage.

Reports of 'incidents' trickled in slowly during his last week working here. The rest came to light over the next few months, long after he was gone. He had a very, very busy six weeks. The shortest managerial reign but the most destructive manager to date. I fire him and run the venue myself with the help of Mini P. Brighton let out a collective sigh of deep relief when he left the city.

As much as I didn't want to take over his role and manage the club myself, I had no other choice. The man was pure poison. If the destruction he left in his wake wasn't bad enough, it was brought to my attention that a set of potential buyers I was successfully wooing at the club ended up staying back after I left one night after 3am-ish. Slick Rick asked them to stay for an after-hours lock-in, gave them free drinks, and made inappropriate comments about the female buyer's tits. Argh.

But I don't plan on managing for long because I will get these buyers across the line. I need to be in control of every aspect of the club, leaving nothing up to chance and no one to spoil the delicate deal that's going to get us out of club-land for good.

23

I tuck Dot tighter into the buggy with her fluffy blanket, give her a reassuring little smile, and pull down the weather shield down, so she's protected. We're being followed. As I walk home from the club, a car ominously creeps a few metres behind us. I swing around and take a photo of the car and licence plate, then take a sharp turn off the pavement onto the cobbled pedestrian street. Now they can't follow us in their car. Dot and I navigate the labyrinth of winding old lanes which have so many forks, twists, and turns, it will kick us out on the other side of Brighton and we'll be able to continue home without them knowing where we live.

They're big guys. I noticed them across the road, yesterday, in their pulled-down baseball caps and hoodies, hanging by the club door, waiting for me to leave. I feel them several feet behind me when I go to Pret for coffee and again when I head to pick up change from the bank. I have 2K in cash in my bag to switch to coins and small notes for the club cash registers: they could be planning to rob me, but they just hang behind. The next day, they're standing in the doorway, and I have to ask them to move to get in the club door. My heart slams against my chest, but the fucking idiots, these poor excuses of stand-over men, gave the game away when one of them turned up in a work hoodie under his coat. They got aggressive and brazen when I blew their cover. I shield Dot behind me in the pram, and they puff their chests up and stand an inch away from my face, doing their best to intimidate me.

It's the security firm that I fired for the underage ID scam: muscle who didn't work in my club but to scare me into paying my bill. That's why I didn't recognise them straight away. The thing is, security all have the same sort of look. Slapped-faced henchmen following a lady with a baby: that's brave. Absolute heroes! I'd be scared if they weren't thick-as-shit knuckleheads. I'd disputed their bill and not paid after we were told to fire them by the police. I contacted my lawyer to look into a possible breach of contract case before I pay the firm's outstanding bill. Maybe I should add intimidation and stand-over tactics to the list of grievances.

Our nanny is lovely but utterly unreliable, due to a series of intense health issues that keep unfolding each week. I chose her for her warmth and her life-long career in childcare. She's a grandmother figure, and she's so lovely I can't fire her. I end up taking on another incredibly sweet nanny who has a relaxed-aunt vibe. We met on the baby circuit. She's agreed to help me for a few afternoons before she moves to Australia. Dot is turning two next week and trying day-care two afternoons a week. It's hit and miss. Some days she likes it, some days she fucking hates it. Once I've dropped her off, I stand outside and listen to her. I can tell from the way she cries whether or not she's going to settle down after a few minutes. If she doesn't, I just walk in, get her, and we go to work together. I don't want her to be anywhere she doesn't want to be. She's a tiny human, and she doesn't need to feel sadness or separation just yet. There is plenty of time to find out that life is full of these fucked-up feelings. So the rest of the week, she comes to the office with me.

She hangs in the doorway, secured in a bouncing harness, while Mini P and I work on this season's marketing plan. We turn on the disco balls and the nightclub light show, a hypnotising private baby sensory session, while I do the booze stock take. Conduct bar staff interviews while walking along the promenade, pushing her to sleep for her afternoon naps. She sits on Mini P's lap, tucked into the desk, bashing her computer keyboard as they edit photos and upload them to social media. She never touches the ground in the club. God forbid she picks up a pill, an old wrap or a bit of broken glass. The reality is that it's fucking hard; like harder than I ever imagined. This wasn't the quick sale we hoped for. It was six weeks, which turned into six months. On top of the day-to-day duties my knee-high assistant and I take care of, I do night shifts, as well. We're home from the office by 5pm to feed, bathe, and get Dot ready for bed. I get dressed, prepare and eat a quick meal for Dot and me, and leave Rich's portion out for him. I get ready to go to open the club, as Rich leaves work at The Body Shop, a train from London Bridge then a cab from Brighton train station. We catch up on a call when he is in the cab. I wait by the door, he gets out. A quick kiss hello, a hug goodbye, and I jump into the waiting taxi and head back to the club to do it all over again.

The sale drags on. And on. And fucking on. We are still in negotiations. Time has a very different way of marking itself now. It's not parties, holidays, deathly hangovers, or cool outfits that spark my memory now. It's in front of me. It transforms, growing, unravelling the unique magic of our child. A personality. Favourite new games and new words. Discovery and wonder. Angry red gums from erupting milk teeth. Nappy rashes, night terrors, and fevers. Watching tiny fingers come together to a pick a blade of grass for the first time and inspecting it with unwavering curiosity. Funny, quirky habits that Rich and I love telling each other if it happens on the other one's 'watch'. The world from the knee-high view is a fun place to be a part of. The security and stability we all feel in our home routine, the love that develops between us. A triangle. You can see time tick by now, reflected in the life of our child.

Dot is a walking and talking miracle. She looks like a tiny life-like doll. Wise beyond her years. I adore every little thing about her. I used to believe you can have it all: a progressive work-life while being a nurturing parent. It wasn't until I actually had a child that I realised I'd set the bar of self-expectation too high. Unless you have round-the-clock help and professional care, it's impossible. But I give it all a good crack. Perfect partner. Wonderful mother. Focused businesswomen. I am so sleep-deprived that I have to settle on ensuring that no one dies. At home or work, it's a good, realistic daily benchmark to work towards. I remember to book the broken vagina in for sex a few times a week, so that keeps the fire burning at home. I do my best half-awake effort at work. We're not focused on creating cutting edge, experimental pop culture movements in clubland now. We concentrate on substantial trade, getting bodies through the doors, and turning over good money. We need to maintain a steady business until the club is taken over by the new owners. It's not the time to experiment. Just make sure we're hitting targets. Our goal is to keep it warm for the new blood. Customers only care if the music is good, the venue is cool, and the drink prices are competitive.

I would guesstimate I'm functioning at a quarter of full capacity. During the week, I am on Dot night-time sleep duty. She still wakes up a few times a night for bottles, a lost dummy, nightmares or soothing, all the regular baby business. Rich has to get up at 5am for work during the week. On the weekends, he is totally in charge of Dot, apart for a few hours when he goes kickboxing, and he also helps get the change from the bank and other weekend club errands. Rich has really stepped up into being a great night watchman. I think his night-time tolerance has grown with his love for Dot. It's pretty hard not to drag yourself over scorching coals for that smiling little cherub face. It makes my work at the club possible. And I try to get some sleep in between the madness.

My short-term memory is so non-existent, it's becoming dangerously unreliable. I can't concentrate. By the time I finish a sentence, I've forgotten what I was saying in the first place. I drop, smash, and break crockery every day, like there's a Greek wedding in my kitchen. I trip, bump, and knock into corners of doors. I shouldn't be operating heavy machinery. Some of the things are funny, and cliché tired-working-mum behaviour but it starts to develop into pretty bad and borderline dangerous. I end up in tears of frustration by how overwhelmed I am at our situation. And the tiredness feels like it's killing me. I fear something terrible is going to happen due to my exhaustion. I just want to get the sale over with, so we can start a life where I don't need to be distracted and drained. I can't wait to just be a mum first and whatever I choose to come second.

This month has been particularly hard. All December, we've hosted Christmas parties during the week, as well as our regular programming. It's four weeks of round-the-clock work. Here are a few examples in this month alone of why I won't be winning Working Mother of the Year:

I tied Dollar up outside Pret while I went to get the morning coffees. I went into work as usual. At the end of the day, I called him, when Mini P said that I didn't bring him to the office today. FUCK! I run back to Pret. I had left him tied to the fence, and he had been taken to the local vet. The next week, I do exactly the same thing but this time, three hours passed before I realised Dollar was still tied up outside Pret.

Dot managed to lock herself in my bedroom. I'd closed the door so she wouldn't go down the stairs while I went to grab a nappy and some wipes from her room. In a split second, after I shut the door, she somehow turned the pretty complicated, stiff lock and I had to call the fire brigade to come and climb in the tiny second-storey vent window. It was just like that Diet Coke ad, except it was a child, not a kitten in a tree. They were all young and fit, and the guy who climbed into the tiny, oddly-angled bay window had to take his protective trousers off and go through in his undies. Dot enjoyed the whole experience of mummy playing games under the door, trying to get her to pass me the key, and loved the fire-truck tour after. Mummy was less excited but pleased she had a bra on, which is a rare occasion when indoors these days.

For a pretty experienced, pre-baby enthusiastic home cook, I have thrown out more saucepans in a month than anyone would use in a lifetime, I have a new talent of boiling water totally dry. Scalding the pans till the non-stick bubbles and peels off. Burning anything that enters the oven. Set fire to everything that dares to be grilled. The fire alarms go off daily, which set off the crying-baby and barking-dog chaos. I don't have any saucepans left. Each time Rich comes home, there are charcoaled pots and pans cooling down on the doorstep before they go in the bin. My not-so-subtle message that it's takeaway again tonight. In a rare, successfully not 'charcoaled' basic meal of chicken drumsticks and a sad little salad, halfway through eating my dinner, I realised I was using the chicken bone as a greasy utensil instead of my knife, pushing food onto my fork with it and trying to cut up my salad with the bone. The delirium is real.

Dot refuses to get into the pram and wants to walk everywhere. Until she doesn't. Then she flat-out refuses to take another step, so we still 'need' the pram and we still use it for transporting shopping, baby bags, laptops etc. Up the mega hill. I struggle to carry her over any distance, thanks to the fun and oh-so-practical prolapse.

We head out, off to work, down the hell-raiser hill. One hand holds Dot's lovely squidgy little digits, and one hand guides the buggy down. We get near the bottom of the hill, and she trips. My reflexes kick in, and I let go of the buggy to catch her. My non-agile post-birth gait is too slow to also catch the runaway buggy. It flies down the steep hill, picking up speed and momentum, crosses through four busy highway lanes, weaves magically through the traffic as cars honk, dodge and beep until it slams to a stop at the gutter. My bag, Dot's toys, blankets and baby bits go flying in the air like an exploding Mothercare piñata. Not one person stopped or came over to help. No one in the cars could have known there wasn't a baby in there. They just beeped and honked at the inconvenience. Two thoughts: thank fuck Dot wasn't in the runaway pram and thank fuck Dollar wasn't tied to it.

Off to do errands, I drive down the hill only to realise the guy behind me is madly beeping at me to stop the car. I stop and jump out. What's up, fucko? I had left my full mug of coffee on the roof of the car, while I was loading Dot and the bags into the car and drove off! It wasn't even a plastic travel cup. No, I'd left the danger-red Pantone 186 coffee cup I'd gotten Rich for Christmas on the roof. I'd driven about a mile away from the house before I worked out why he was tooting at me. This mishap was in the more amusing camp. I air-cheers'd the guy, took a sip of the coffee, and got in the car.

I am drained but determined. There is an end in sight. I see it as a mental and physical challenge we can get through as long as we stay focused and stick to the routine.

JUST DON'T LOSE THE DOG OR THE BABY

But this one was the scariest. It was a sign that I was indeed operating on borrowed time, pushing my body too far. I woke up on New Year's Day with a pounding headache and wondering how I could have let myself get so, so fucked up when I have a baby to look after. I can't remember what I did? I can't even move. It feels like a pre-baby De Beauvoir MDMA-coke-bender-binge-drinking-for-days-hangover-come-down paralysis. Then I remember that I didn't even have a drink last night. I was totally sober but fluey. I'd worked the NYE party, and during the evening, started to feel really, really run down. I call out to Rich. I can't get out of bed. Seriously. It's funny for a moment, like it's the next level to my working-mum tiredness. That is until we both realise I ACTUALLY can't get up. Now we're both fucking terrified.

I get him to pull me up to a standing position, and I tried to walk, but my whole body drops to the ground like a sack of potatoes. My eyes won't focus properly. I have no control over my body from the neck down. I can't move it. I'm not in pain, other than feeling fluish. Rich calls an ambulance. The paramedics check my vitals, which are all stable, but they decide I need to go to emergency. Getting me off the second floor with the narrow staircase and dogleg corridors that won't fit a stretcher is a problem. They get a mobility chair, a sort of seat-thing they can carry, and the three of them lift me up and put me on it. I feel like I'm blind drunk. The room is spinning and all I want to do is lie flat and be still on the ground. They violently jolt the chair, jerking it back, like kids do, to trick each other at school. I dive off the chair and throw my body onto the safe ground. Facedown. Everyone just stares at me. They have no idea what just happened. I snap at them – "why did you do that?!?" They still just stare. The chair didn't move. Not even a millimetre. It was my mind or body playing tricks on me. My brain waves are short-circuiting. Glitching.

I spend the first 24 hours in ICU going through a series of tests. I worry that something had ruptured during the birth or that my birth canal was infected and rotting. They rule out both possibilities and say it could be a stroke. They wheel me off for an MRI. Rich and Dot leave, as we're told that we shouldn't have a child in the area as their immune systems are not strong and severe infections and viruses are being treated in the ward.

I stare at the ceiling. With a blinding headache from the fluoro lights that are always on in the ICU. I have to have a nurse slide a flat bedpan under my bum when I have to piss. Lucky I don't ever shit these days. This is the first time I've been thankful for my extreme constipation. They wheel me through the different wards. The metal beads on the hair extensions I just had put in need to be removed before I go in for the MRI. If not, apparently, my head will explode. What a fucking shitter, a complete waste of money and lovely hair extensions. They take me into the stroke ward. A 34-year-old in a stroke ward. I feel so alone and helpless. Soon we will have family support for these kinds of situations.

It kinda feels like someone has hit the 'pause' button on my body and forced me into a non-negotiable rest. My brain isn't running away to 'Fear Town' yet. It's too tired and worn down to even pack a bag. I'm started on a broad spectrum treatment in case it isn't a stroke and to start treating an infection, if it is one. I start to get movement in my hands and feet. They go through a process of elimination and strike out a stroke, which I am over the moon to hear. It's confirmed as acute Labyrinthitis, an infection in the inner ear that causes severe vertigo. Along with walking pneumonia and physical exhaustion. Thank fuck it's nothing serious. Two more days pass before I can stand up, then I get to wobble home like a drunken sailor on his sea-loving legs. I'm back at work two days later to open the club after NYE. The doctors tell me I have to slow down. I am pushing my body too hard. I'll rest when I get this deal done.

I have finally locked down the buyers Slick Rick was making crude breast comments to. The group of friends have put down a non-refundable deposit. A couple and two of their single friends: 'The Gang'. They pool together a cash deposit, remortgaging their properties, and borrow money from relatives. Not ideal, but they are committed now. So I keep working, keep pushing to keep this club going strong. I keep running a nightclub with a baby on my hip. It's taking so long, she's a proper walking-talking toddler, who is in full swing potty training and asking 'but why' to everything. Knowing that Rich's spouse visa is ticking away, our deadline for moving to Australia is nearly within sight. A fresh start, blue skies, and new opportunities, and I am taking one for the team. I might be totally, utterly fucking exhausted but it's for our family and a different life. Life miles and miles away from the shadows of clubland.

Mini P hands in her notice. I'm not surprised, but I am utterly devastated. I knew it would be happening soon. She plans to leave in two weeks. She has a job and a flat in London to move into. Although I'm super pleased and couldn't be more excited for her, I have to remind her that her contract actually states she needs to give four weeks' notice. She asks for a favour to leave early, but I really can't do it, as much as I want to. Advertising the role, doing interviews, training, and a handover isn't possible in two weeks. Especially when I'm already managing both the venue alone at night and running the office by day. I was hoping we could time it closer to the sale exchange. We get in an argument on the phone, and both end up crying. I really need her, and instead of being honest, I get angry and frustrated that it's not going the way I need it to. I regret it now. I handled it really poorly. Like I did with Daisy. She doesn't know about the sale and I can't tell her why I need her to stay, as I can't risk people finding out about the deal before I'm ready. I can't risk the same panic that sur-rounded The Bathhouse when the news spread that we were selling. There are already whispers, and it sends vultures to my door, picking off my staff and promoters. Any disruption to the current business model can massively affect the sale price. Mini P leaves two weeks later.

We smooth it out by the time she finishes, but I'm sad. Mini P is the best co-worker I have ever had or will have - along with Kitty and Daisy. The office has lost its warmth, croissants have lost their shine, and I'm alone, apart for my tiny knee-high sidekick.

'The Gang' are nice. Eager and keen to do 'spot checks' on the club and see that I am running it properly until the handover. I see them every weekend while they are painfully still trying to refinance their flats and borrow more money from the bank and friends. I can see them assessing the headcount, the vibe, and watching the staff. Every week, the venue continues to do well, except the week after NYE when I was in the hospital. Regardless of me being flat on my back, the first Saturday after the festive period is always quiet. I told this to them and said it'd be better not to open, but they didn't want to give the wrong impression to customers. So I opened, and they saw for themselves how there were only thirty people in the club. Brighton was a ghost town, as students go back to their hometowns, and our competitors' venues were shut. Every other time they made their research (drinking) trips, they get the full banging club experience, the direct result of weeks and weeks' worth of work. They will be running the club themselves without any managers, which is a good idea. Being hands-on keeps things tight.

Running the night shifts isn't the hard part. The part I always found the hardest is staying awake past 1am without coke, but that's my kryptonite. The night shifts are a series of tasks and problem-solving. It's labour intensive, but most people pick it up quickly once they're shown how to handle the problems that crop up and the quirks of a venue. There is a sweet spot in the night when you have the customers in the venue and off the street. You know how many people are in for the night and you have them safe in the club. Issues rarely occur inside the venue. Between CCTV, the managers, and security, any potential problems get nipped in the bud and removed through a discreet exit. But the street is no-man's land. Open to the public, anything can happen. The police watch everything. Things can kick off with people walking by, who don't have anything to do with your customers or club, but if shit happens on your patch, it's your responsibility. Entry and exit need to be quick. Clean. Quiet. The nights are never, ever dull.

Marketing and promotion are the sides that require tactical industry experience and insider knowledge. It's not the kind of role you learn on the job, if there's no one around to teach you. You can't make mistakes or do trial and error with a nightclub. That sort of approach will quickly damage your business. Everything needs to be spot-on every time you open your doors and charge people entry. You have to meet their high expectations and exceed them. Mini P and I created a manual and a very concise how-to for when I was on maternity leave. I'll be giving this to The Gang as a guidebook for how to recreate the club nights and marketing strategy we currently use. The Gang said they'll want to do all the music programming, booking, marketing, design, and promotion themselves. I suggest keeping in touch with someone who is social-media savvy and has industry insight, but they are confident in their collective skill set. They really want to apply their own creativity and take wages out of the business. That old chestnut. I totally understand the temptation, but they will need to get learning - and fast. I learned on the job but was lucky to have that creative drive and obsession with music, art, and creating 'atmosphere' already in me. Let's hope they have the sixth sense, too.

I encourage The Gang to come to the office during the day and begin learning the ropes while the solicitors start the sale proceedings. They don't. Instead, they keep coming down during business hours to drink. I see them looking around, soaking it up. They hold each other's hands, close their eyes and sing Jess Glynn's 'Hold my Hand' and dream of what it's going to be like being your own nightclub boss. They're on the wrong side of the bar to get any real idea of what it's like. It's about unblocking toilets and fixing sound equipment with a dance floor of people booing at the silence; fixing air-conditioning; finding out that some fuckwit filled up your commercial bin, so now you have a club full of rubbish and nowhere to put it. It's about vomit, drug overdoses, and the pig DJ who spat in a customer's face for making a bad song request. It's working on getting customers through the doors, not just for a one-off party, but every single week. It's about never being able to switch off. Firefighting, every damn day. But I smile and sell the dream.

I guess I make it look easy. They must look at me and think 'Well if she can do it with a baby in tow, we can definitely do it as The Gang.' One of them worked in a pub before: no one else in the group has any relevant music, creative or design experience, and they all lack the insight into the existing customer bases age, culture or demographic. They're a good ten years older than our average customer. This is why Mini P was such a lifeline for me. She was our age-perfect customer demographic. She knew exactly what our customers wanted.

But they're just keen to get stuck in. What they overlook are the hours and the ten-plus years of experience I've clocked up in the industry. I'm a certified expert if you consider Malcolm Gladwell's theory that it takes 10,000 hours to master something. I have surpassed that several times over. I may not be an expert in the business elements of my operations but nightclubs and creative direction, I do know. I don't guess: it's a calculated formula. The Gang sits there, sipping on drinks, thinking they are next in line for the crown, but it doesn't quite work like that. You can't just sing 'I'm ready for this!' But I'll let them off tonight. They're celebrating paying another instalment for FunFair.

We are SO close.

I've been thinking about the future. What does it hold for me? I don't know who I am or what I am away from nightclubs. It's been my identity for so many years now, I have no idea what life will look like once I finally step away. I complain about the daily grind and the police and council's constant changing of the goalposts, but I love the creative boundary-pushing. I love curating magical moments in time. I love the art, music, and design, the parties and events. There is so much I adore about this world. A space where I didn't have to be accountable to the police and the strict general 'clubland' rules. I dream about this place; a creative space, a chameleon venue, a blank canvas with great bones that doesn't require the scattergun approach to generate the general footfall traffic of customers, but a 'space' for special events, high-concept seasonal ticketed parties, art shows, creative collaborations, pop-up museums, and installations. A totally evolving space that could move and change with trends, tastes, whims, and programming.

A place to host master classes, creative workshops, a food and drink learning annexe and a studio for us to do creative direction consulting for other businesses and activations. Taking the elements that work from the industry and the parts that I love doing, the pre-booked events and the ticketed shows. It shifts the model from nightclub entertainment and bar and evolves it to Events: creativity. This could work in Sydney. It would smash East London or LA, but I think maybe Sydney will get it...

I am also mapping out a crazy idea for a book. A contemporary take on Martha Stewart's first book, 'Entertaining'. From cocktails to spirit infusions to laying a table. Recipes we developed, worked with and on. From hosting Christmas dinner to a faultless juicy roast dinner for 4/8/10 or 12 people. Wine guides, cheat sheets, dinner party dynamics. Hangover tonics, come-down survival and how to have a house party without making enemies of your neighbours.

Tips, hints and hacks you need to know about being a modern host. A traditional hardcover book, really beautifully designed, shot and illustrated with cool collaborations, from mixologists to artisan chutney makers to florists. With an online component or an App with music playlists that Rich will produce and do DJ mixes for different vibe parties, dinners or festivities. With the digital element, it means you can use it anywhere without lugging the physical book. Accessible if you were on an Easter break and cooking up a holiday feast in a country house. Or a friend's party and they don't have a banging playlist. The digital portal will also have a design section... customisable invites and party stationery. Ones to print for more formal occasions or fun Instagram tiles and invite GIFs you can make personalised and send over social media and DMs. Seamless hosting. All in one place, curated rather than having to trawl the Internet... I imagine it's the kind of cool glossy book that would make the perfect house-warming or Christmas gift.

It has been a week filled with lawyer meetings and structuring the sale terms. These are the good type of lawyer meetings, apart for the extraordinary bills. Otherwise, it's a nondescript week of regular clubland chores, which I happily work through, keeping Dot in a hard and fast supply of ice-cream and icy poles because she's been a little teething, dribbling monster all week, poor thing. Rich takes a day off to help with her so I can crack on at work. I have a new surge of energy, knowing that this will be someone else's to-do list soon. I get distracted by loads of ideas about the future. I feel like we can finally get excited and start planning the move to Australia. So it's a pretty standard day when the knock on the door comes. Apart from the fact it is raining as hard and harsh as razor blades. The angle of the rain felt like slices on your skin. I open the door, after a loud knock cuts through the rain outside. There's a soaking-wet man in a suit that would have been smart this morning, water running off his chin, and a useless umbrella with the fabric ripped off its frame by his side, standing at the door. He asks for me by name. I confirm that, yes, that's me. He hands me a thick posh envelope with a coat of arms on the top right corner and my name and the club's address written neatly in the middle. The rain has made the pen ink wash out into a pretty unintentional watercolour wash. He walks away, his head down to shield himself from the pelting rain. He throws the umbrella into the curb and runs down the road out of sight. Only lawyers and the court hand-deliver letters.

A bolt of lightning strikes through me the split second I open the letter. I read it again. I call up my business partner, neither of us entirely understanding the meaning of the letter's contents. I call my Brighton lawyer, and he clarifies, and it was worse than I could ever have imagined. I put on my coat, leaving my handbag, scarf, hat, gloves, laptop and the work I was doing just before the knock came. I take my phone and keys. Lock the club. I stand on the street in the biting rain and howl like a cut beast. I had never felt this level of pain before, like I'd been hit by a semi-trailer. I call Rich, who is at home with Dot and tell him what happened. He told me to come home, right now. I'm sorry. I can't. I hang up and walk across the road, hitting the ignore button each time Rich calls. Walking down the promenade, heading along the shore to Rottingdean, the chalk-white cliffs.

Everything is gone. Every penny, every hour I have ever worked. Rich's money, my parents' money, my money, my business partner's money. All the money I owe people and the money I owe the bank. The money from the sale. Everything. Gone. Our future. Dot's future. There is no future for our family. All of these years, all taken away from me. I have no skills to recover from this, nothing to show for the work I have done. What I have put Rich

through. We have no money to emigrate now, and nothing here to rebuild. Everything I have ever worked for is gone. Everything I have sacrificed as a mother. For nothing. As a partner. Only to destroy his life. All the things we put off 'til we had the cash: a home, a wedding, being happy, living a normal life. The final reward from the work we have done. A life without the chaos. I have fucked it all up. Our future rested on my shoulders, and now it's gone.
We have nothing. I am nothing.

(ping) Please, I'm begging you. We need you. Come home now. I love you. Please x

I turn around and walk home in the razor-blade rain. Thankful for each slice it takes from my face and ice flakes gnawing at my ungloved hands.

At home, Rich's words are surprisingly calm and pragmatic. Supportive. But I see the flashing pain in his eyes. His face shows me panic, and he is scared. His words do not. It's not the loss of the money: that hasn't sunk in for him, yet. He's still saying "We'll work it out. We always do." It's my behaviour that's scaring him. I can't work it out this time. I can't be here the moment that he realises the extent of the damage and how this will affect us; when he works out our soon-to-be financial devastation can't be 'worked out'. I can't bear to even think about his pending pain. The shame is toxic. Putrid. The betrayal is crippling. There are no tricks left or plays to be made. No coming back from the letter. It's checkmate. Game over.

I have been possessed. A caged animal, looking down the barrel of the gun that's going to end my wild life as I know it. I have nowhere to go and no other escape routes. I can't be me right now. In my own brain. Inside my own skin. I sweat. I itch. Shake. I can't do this.

He gets me to drink some water, in between sobbing. He doesn't know what to do. I sit and rock. Howl. Weep. I grip the heavy pint of water because my life depends on it. I want it to explode in my hand. It doesn't, so I smash it on my head. Cracking it on my skull, over and over again. Until it registers in Rich's brain what I am actually doing, and he fights my arms down to stop the destruction. I want my body to hurt and release the pain inside. To even it up. The bolt of lightning opened up a section of my brain, heart and spirit that has never been called on before. I have a direct channel to death. He is waiting on the end of the line for me. As though he was always there, but now I wanted to talk, and he is ready to listen. The only person who will understand. It's a conversation with Death that I start playing over in my head. A loop. It is only a matter of time before I meet him. Not if, but how will we meet?

These are thoughts I've never said out loud: not then and not now. As far as either Rich or the Doctor knew, "I have been thinking about killing myself", not the details or the thought process or the feelings. It's a secret that fills my mind. I leave the room to think about it if Rich is home, just in case he can read my mind, which sometimes he can. I think about when I can do it, so I am alone at home. But I am always either with Rich or with Dot. I think about the club. For some reason, it feels too cold. I hide away, and I sit on the soft sheepskin rug in my bedroom. I can feel Dot; her calm, beautiful presence humming through the walls, soundly sleeping in her cot. I calculate her age: she won't even remember me. The pain won't be too bad for her if I do it while she's this young. She will have everyone else's memories of me to grow up with. And the pretty pictures of us. But I don't know if Rich can take another loss.

I will slice my wrists with the deboning knife, cut through the small heart tattoos on each of my inner wrists up through the soft white skin on my arms. It will be over then, but not too quick because I deserve to hurt. I deserve to suffer... But the mess. Who will have to clean up the carpets and rugs? I think of what that would do to a little person's life. No. I hide the knife away. I think about stepping into traffic, but there's no guarantee I'll die, and I could hurt other people in a car crash. I pray for a vicious cancer to fill my bones. I will my heart to stop beating. I use a secret browser on my computer so Rich won't see the search history. I google the most painless, cleanest way to die. I find there are special bags you can order to stop you breathing, but I can't bear the thought of how that would affect the person who found me. I decide drinking and prescription drugs are the answer. It's obvious, isn't it? But I need to get the drugs. We don't have anything in the house anymore. I start googling how to buy them online, what pills work or if over-the-counter ones will do it. Then in a moment of clarity, I work out that I actually can't afford to die. Not in a 'the world can't be without me' sort of realisation. Like financially. How will Rich work and look after Dot? Even if I'm gone, the problem remains, and Rich doesn't have the skills to deal with the letter alone. Because there is no 'fix'. Abstract problem-solving is my part of our joint skill-set, not his. We have no money now. We just paid an outstanding solicitor's bill from our last sale. Our credit card is maxed-out from putting Rich's immigration paperwork fees on it; our accounts are overdrawn; and our credit line is poor.

Every penny we have is in that business. There's no life insurance pay-out, even if I make it look like an accidental overdose. My parents have just suffered a financial hit in the stock market crash, which wiped them out. They are bankrupt and on a pension. No one in my family has money. Someone will have to 'deal' with my body. I guess they'd want to cremate me and send the ashes home. That costs money. The logistics of a grieving family who don't even have the money to buy a bus ticket, let alone flights for someone who killed themselves outside of their home country.

Without a single penny to even clean up my final mess. Fucking pathetic.

The pain that my suicide would inflict on Dot and Rich outweighs my own selfish pain. I'm not allowed to do more damage.

I have to keep fighting.

I had forgotten these thoughts. Erased them from my surface memories. Pushed it deep down. My eyes are burning with acid hot tears as I typed that. It flowed from a tight, trapped, closed part of my brain; it kicked my heart and punched out of my fingers into the keyboard without thinking. Just telling you. My thoughts. I can't really find the right words to tell you the way I felt, but this is what I thought would be the only option. To stop it all. I had blanked out that period. And ashamed that I thought that I could do that to them. We are a triangle. They can't live without me, and I can't live without them. Not now and not in a trillion light-years.

This is that part of the book that I never want my mum to know about. Not the drugs or stupid behaviour. The darkness. This is my secret. Even now, from Rich. This will hurt him, but I think he knew, but not to the extent of the planning process. And that I will need to be honest and have a very frank conversation about my mental health with Dot, when she is old enough to know about this section of our lives. But it happened. And this is the ramifications of real actions. I could leave it out; tell you I was 'depressed', but is that what the world needs now? More covering-up of real issues that push us back into the dark, away from the light? I felt I was so alone in my pain, but maybe being honest will let someone else know that they are also not alone…

I sat quietly, just like every other mother with their child, in the waiting room, jiggling the buggy. People always give us a knowing, reaffirming smile when they look at Dot. She beams at everyone, a real heart-warmer. I do that grateful 'thanks for thinking my baby is cute' face. I hear my name called. I wheel the buggy to the window so Dot can look outside and play with her toys and so she wasn't looking at me. I'd chosen a GP I didn't know. I cry and purge out the bare, stripped-back minimised problem, whispering my neatly packaged emotions as best as possible. The objective is to stay out of a mental hospital and keep my child safe with us, but enough details told to get what I needed …The extreme financial pressure, crippling depression, and suicidal thoughts. The doctor prescribes me 40mg citalopram to take daily, and propranolol four times a day, and wants me to see a psychologist. It's useless unless they have 500K they can give me.

I walk away with prescriptions to live, not die. The doctor won't give me the Valium I requested. He gives me short scripts to limit how many tablets I receive at a time. I take my medicine as directed, and promise Rich I won't 'do anything'. I add a self-medicating layer of alcohol and coke to the Doctor's treatment plan when I have to work at night in the club, still keeping my promise to Rich, but just enough of my old friends to numb the pain. It means I can function in the outside world, still turn up and play the final game. Balancing dangerously on a thin wire with two fates on each side. I wobble and sway emotionally but crash through daily life now with a robotic, dead nature. I am physically alive, but black inside. It's the exact zombie combination I need to get through the next barrage of apocalyptic devastation. I am a soldier. Dead eyes. Dead heart. I am conditioned, prepared for the fight, and I won't give up until we're on the other side.

There are two apparent sides to my personality now. Dead eyed soldier at work, and at home, my only laser focus is to care for my family. Putting one foot in front of another, to love and take care of my baby, our earth-shatteringly divine child... I hold her close and tend her needs just like any other doting, obsessed mother. And a dedicated 'wife'. Rich viciously loves, protects and supports me, keeping our triangle of love secure. It's the opposite of the business version of me. Our fort of defence built unshakably at home, allowing me to start fighting my greatest battle in clubland...

24

What was in the Letter?
Here is the breakdown. It was relevantly long and was not clear what it meant without legal interpretation into non-lawyer-speak for me. So this is the bare bones.

THE LETTERHEAD
From a law firm I have never had any previous dealings with, but was honoured with a Royal Warrant Appointment (they are the royal families' legal team, so already we are dealing with the highest legal defence in the country. Strong start for them; appalling for me. The local Brighton legal team I was using for the sale had no idea how to try to fight it. I had to call on our old Wimple Street London legal firepower.

ON BEHALF OF
A property company that I have never heard of from China with an outpost based in London (The Chinese) A quick Google sent shivers down my spine. Multi-billion dollar international investors.

REGARDING
Forfeiture of the Head Lease, occupied by Charter House LTD (The Arrogant Landlord - Nick Sutton) and the termination of the sublease basement and ground-level 12a Kings Road occupied by Me LTD (My company)

Dear Casualty (Me LTD)

We are writing to inform you that the head lease, on the address above, has been breached, resulting in termination. Effective immediately, deeming the sublease of Me LTD automatically terminated. The head lease is in arrears, and the outstanding balance of Me LTD rent is also in arrears of £205,000. You may apply for relief of forfeiture, with compensation of £205,000 or you will need to vacate the premises in 14 days and revert the property to a clean shell state.

PS You're fucked.

Yours Sincerely, The Chinese

The Law
The termination of a head lease automatically terminates any sublease. Sub-tenants can obtain relief against forfeiture of the head lease.

If the head lease is forfeited because the tenant has breached its terms, the underlease will end automatically. As an alternative, a subtenant may be able to agree with the property owner that if the head lease is forfeited and the underlease falls away, the property owner will grant a new contract to the subtenant and they obtain relief against forfeiture of the head lease.

Clear as mud? Here are three months of digging out the Arrogant Landlord's limited companies, contracts, legal team finding case studies of similar scenarios, rental invoices and receipts. Fact-finding to get to the bottom of what-the-fuck was going on. But the above law doesn't sound so bad, does it? I thought, oh well we can claim compensation... But nope: it was ME to pay the compensation!

What does this mean, in a nutshell, please?
The Arrogant Landlord has broken his lease with the new building owner, the Chinese. I can stay and arrange a new rental contract, BUT I must pay compensation to the new landlord/building owner, the Chinese. Which is the outstanding rent I have ALREADY paid to the Arrogant Landlord that he, in turn, hasn't paid on to The Chinese. So, in theory, paying my rent over 2.5 years, twice. The first time around, that was never paid on and is sitting in the Arrogant Landlord's pocket. I need to pay the Chinese 205k in a lump sum, or I'll be kicked out of my venue. And I will have to spend about 25k to remove my Funfair fit-out and with new plasterboard walls, white paint and the venue set to neutral.

How is this possible?
We signed a lease with the Arrogant Landlord. We were NEVER a sub-tenant. So how are we a subtenant renting from The Arrogant Landlord, who is renting from the new owners, the Chinese. We have never heard of them, let alone signed any contracts with the Chinese...

Yes, but a few months after we signed a lease with The Arrogant Landlord, he created a shell company called Charter House Ltd. and leased himself the apartments on floor 1-5. Sold the entire building to the Chinese. With himself and ME Ltd. as 'sitting tenants'.

Creating a new structure of property hierarchy:
Building owner and current landlord – The Chinese
Head lease apartments floor 1-5 - The Arrogant Landlord - Charter House Ltd.
Sublease ground floor and basement - ME Ltd.

We were never told of the sale or the shift in lease terms, as it is totally inadvisable ever to take on a sublease, as they have very little legal protection. Such as this.

Yes, but we paid our rent and have receipts to prove it...
All this time. For over two years. The Arrogant Landlord collected my rent. Issued me a receipt and never paid it on to the head lease Chinese landlord. 205k. All the time knowing that he would collect my rent for as long as possible, while the Chinese didn't kick him out or alert us to the fact that our rent was never paid over to them.

How did he do it?
When The Arrogant Landlord sold the building, he created a new limited company, but with a very slight name change on the invoice, so we weren't aware or didn't notice it went from Charter House Ltd. to Charter Apartments Ltd. The terms continued as per our agreed lease. We were invoiced for the rent, we paid the rent, and a rental receipt was issued. If I were late on the rent, he would call to chase it; if there was a problem, like the sound issue or he wanted to come down for drinks, he would email or call. We were never given a new lease to sign, taking us from tenants to sub-tenants, but by paying the rent, we silently agreed to the new terms, even if we were not privy to the changes.

What does this mean to the club?
The only options are paying the 'unpaid' rent again, to compensate

the Chinese, even though the landlord has taken our rent and not paid it. Or fight it in court, but the judge will rule that we compensate the Chinese and also pay their legal costs. Or hand back the keys, walk away and turn our backs on our investment in 14 days.

What does this mean to the sale?
Basically, it is dead in the water. But the part that has double-fucked me is that I have spent The Gang's deposit. Paying my old security firm from The Bathhouse. It is non-refundable - yes, but nobody would or could have imagined that this million-to-one scenario would occur. So because the law falls on the side of the Chinese here, I do technically owe the back rent to the Chinese, so if we don't pay it and walk away from the venue in 14 days, that would mean that The Gang was legally entitled to get their non-refundable deposit back. Because there is no 'venue' to buy or sell, if we 'walk away'... There is also the matter of the mounting tax bill I had planned to clear with the sale money. Plus, the meter is running on our expensive law firm to try and get the best result, or at best salvage something out of the Chinese Vs Arrogant Landlord Vs Me. Plus there is also the lawyers that started on drawing up the Funfair sale. This is adding up to be an eye-watering legal bill.

What does this mean for me?
I'm fucked as it stands now. Feet-set-in-concrete fucked. No-coming-back-financially kind of fucked. And possible further litigation and court proceeding from the knock-on effects of this fuck-over. Bankruptcy.

Why did they let the bill build-up to 205k before even contacting us? This is the burning question for me. Why did the Chinese and their solicitors leave it so long to alert us to the fact that the rent wasn't being paid, so we could deal with it before it got so out of control? They said they were letting it resolve itself. And allowing him to make the payment. But two fucking years? Never once letting us know our business and livelihood was in jeopardy. I think they wanted it to happen. I also believe if we pressed this harder or took it to the court, that this is a powerful defence point.

So, from the beginning?
I believe that The Arrogant Landlord had planned to do this from the very beginning. Getting us to use our funds to renovate the ground floor and basement of the building. Selling the building, keeping himself as a tenant, and with us as a sitting tenant and diligently collecting my rent, liquidating the shell company at the last minute so he can walk away with the profits from the initial building sale to the Chinese and milking our monthly rent payment for as long as he could before the Chinese kick us all out. Him knowing that we legally don't have a leg to stand on because we were unknowingly bumped down to a sub-tenant and gave us no rights, but all the responsibility for the rent he had been keeping. And he just liquidated the business, so he is not personally or professionally liable for taking my rent and not paying it on. Knowing that the Chinese will come after me for the rent he kept. But the bone-wrenching frustrating thing is, he is untouchable.

Surely this is illegal?
What he has done is all 'legal'. Just. It is tactical, deceitful and a formula he appears to be operating under. I think if it was done as a 'one-off'. It's legal or wouldn't arouse suspicion from 'higher authorities' (I don't even know who that would be). But I'm still suspicious. The fact he runs shell company businesses, and phoenix business deals, makes me wonder what is going on behind the scenes. Is there some sort of fraud going on? Or is it more borderline: just ruthlessness and callousness? He is listed on over 97 director posts in Companies House. Along with his Turkish princess. This is how they stay in a mansion with a heliport. Live a

life that people can only dream of because they destroy everyone else's lives, businesses and dreams.

It is watertight. We get expert council, consult lawyers who specialise in this kind of immoral phoenix business ventures. But he crosses the T's and dots the I's. No wonder someone put a shotgun to his head.

Is there an upside, silver lining or a solution... Something? Regardless of the fucking cluster fuck of an arse-raping the Arrogant Landlord has done and the Chinese recording it, rubbing salt in it and posting in on YouTube. The one good thing I do have is Funfair. And it's a good business. Still. And even if I don't make a penny off it, the buyers are still keen-ish.

I should have gone to the press, calling him out in public. Pushing for more regulation around 'sub-leases', but we wanted to try and get the sale done, as the Gang was still keen. It seemed like the best solution at the time. But mentally, I wasn't in a great place as we have established, thanks to this prick. But now I wish I or someone could put a loaded gun to his head and made him pay back my cash, so we can just go back to the original sale plan.

The Gang has been told about the complications with the lease, and we get our lawyers to start talking to the Chinese legal team about what a new contract would look like if we were to sell the existing business. The Gang pay us for Funfair, then we pay the rent arrears to the Chinese, and then we walk away. Because if we don't sell the business on, the Chinese won't be able to get any money if we just close the business and walk away. This would mean I walk away with nothing. But no further legal action.

It is so messy and fucking cruel. Being so close to the sale.

Inches away from stepping into the light and out of the shadows of clubland. We were so close, I could taste the freedom with the tip of my tongue. And now the very best I can hope for is to walk away from this final deal, not owing someone who can afford to chase me for it or court proceedings to recover costs from me, personally.

What do you do now?
So, I make it sound like walking away with nothing is really the most likely and the only option. Yeah, it is. But the reason why I can do it now, where before it was the most life-devastating soul-crushing news? Is because of Rich. Never once has he blamed me. He is frustratingly angry. He is deeply fucked off, south London cut-snake fury, but it's not at me, which was my deepest fear. He has said from the day it happened that we just need each other. As long as we are together, we will be ok. It's just money: we can make more. When you think about what other people go through, like Alli and Scott and the loss of their son, this is nothing. You can replace cash, but you can't replace a loved one or each other. And I actually believed him and that he genuinely believes this. It is this unconditional love and optimism in a fucking horrible circumstance that gives me the strength to keep fighting.
Because if we can just get away with just a little money, we can make it work. The three of us. Start again, with nothing, but together. In a new country. Away from clubs. We wanted to leave it behind, and nobody could have seen this coming. There were red flags for the Arrogant Landlord's previous practice, but this high level of fraudulent business tactics was impossible to predict. I thought we had a watertight lease. But clearly, it wasn't enough. Its robbery in plain sight. But legal. He is so smart. Too smart for me. And he won.

Two big life lessons learnt during this period. The first one is Never Give Up. We've said it so much that you will hear Dot parroting this like a tiny superhero. We might not be able to find her favourite soft toy, Llama, or if I say something can't happen, she rattles out our family motto ... 'But Mummy, we NEVER give up.' It's pretty inspiring to be coming out of our child's mouth, her not knowing the origin of the expression and the meaning it has to Rich and me, and her wholeheartedly believing in it already. The second isn't a neat social media catch-cry: it's more of a relationship mantra between Rich and me that is remembered and practised in actions; not said out loud. Turn to each other, not on each other. It's so easy to get angry, frustrated and lash out at our partners when times are hard, place blame, point fingers and yell. Rich's humility showed me that by loving each other unconditionally and supporting each other, it allowed us both to push through. It's protective, vicious love that keeps our bond so tight. Love each other hard. Not snapping and blaming, turning on each other. But turning to each other with support, kindness, love and patience. Building each other up. It is the reason we came out the other side. Together. Stronger.

Did you deserve this? I feel like people think this and don't say it, but I mull over it daily.
There is a part of me that thinks I deserve this. For mistakes made in the past. That it's karma. Maybe it is... or perhaps it's the Universe with a fucked-up bullshit lesson. But I can't even be bothered to talk to her at the moment to ask. Maybe because I put so much coke up my nose in the past? Fucked people over. Perhaps because I wasn't careful with my money? Or maybe it's not anything, other than I got fucked. Plain and simple. I lost this round to the cunt of the century.

How did you manage?
I would be embarrassed to say this to anyone who has lost a loved one, but it's a grieving process for me. Denial - it's not happening. It's my club. They can't do this to me. Then anger: I want to smash

the Arrogant Landlord's posh-twat little face in with a baseball bat and burn down his mansion, to bargaining with the Chinese... How about we call it even? The outstanding rent arrears can be written off as an unfortunate event for us all: you let me sell the club, and I keep my profits..? Then back round to depression (we've covered this in the last chapter)... and finally, acceptance. If I can just walk away with my family, I will be ok.

Dot and I have a daily survival routine.
On the days we don't go into the office, it looks like the below. I am careful to not let Dot see me crying or feel the distress. Rich takes over on the weekend.

Morning
We wake up when we want, have breakfast. Play. Take Dollar for a walk. Watch cartoons. Start the day-to-day club-running phone calls and emails.
Dot naps. I cry and make the calls where I know I either have to yell at people or concentrate and make decisions, without the chaos that surrounds a 2-year-old Tasmanian devil while I'm on the phone.

Afternoon
Dot's afternoon nap. I lie on a mattress on the floor next to her as she sleeps. Her rhythmic breathing is soothing and I try to be close to her peace. I sleep when she does, to press pause in the pain.
We go to the park, the seafront or for ice-cream or see her little NCT friends, pretend we are ok. We do work chores, go to cash and carry, get change. See lawyers.

On the weekend, I will go into the club until 4am or 5am. Rich will have Dot, and I balance on a drug and booze wall, of not too much and just right to get through it. I can't stand setting foot into the venue. I fucking hate it. But it has to be done, and I have to pretend nothing is wrong and it's business as usual. Tits and teeth and the very essence of Never Giving Up....

Rich and Dot let me sleep till 1pm Sundays. The afternoons are for a family activity. Pub lunch or the seafront stroll. Even though I feel utterly fucked and wrung out from working the night before, it's a pocket of perfection. A little daisy growing in a corner of hell.

Always lock your doors (if you can't pay your bills).
Money is becoming a problem now. The sale has dragged on so long, and on top of fees surrounding the Chinese legal battle, I have bailiffs coming to the door at home and the club during the day. I had avoided opening the door when the bell rings for months: it's easier at the club. I always keep the venue secure, even when I'm inside, and can see who's at the door on the CCTV cameras. Anyone with a clipboard is 99% of the time looking for money. I have been hiding out of sight at home. One of them is particularly unrelenting. She came really early this time and rang the bell. I was half-asleep in the kitchen, making Dot porridge. The side gate creaks open. I froze, and we locked eyes as the doorbell is ringing through the house. Dollar starts barking. She had security with her. Fuck, the side door's not locked. Eyes still locked, I move first, run to secure the door, but she's right there. Closer than me and turns the handle. It opens, and she is walking into the kitchen before I could get there first. By law, if the door is unlocked, she is legally allowed to enter the premises. Fuck. I had to let her walk through the house and list down the items and their values. I tried to say most of the items were Rich's, my 'flatmate', so the rules are it couldn't be listed, but she states clearly we were de facto and living together with a child. So it was both of our belongings to go on the seizure list. She notes down everything from the vintage silver cross pram (the rule with baby/kids' stuff is they can only

take double or spares, because we have a stroller and the higher valued item is listed) to Rich's studio equipment, to the Flemish chandelier. Everything. Dot's screaming to be fed her breakfast, porridge burning on the stove, setting off the smoke detectors and alarms. Dollar is shaking from the chaos of strangers stomping through the house and taking photos with a flash. I have 7 days to clear the outstanding debt, or they will return with a van and remove our possessions to settle the balance. Fuck. And they did. The doorbell spiking my nerves, I forgot they were coming, caught up with all the other bullshit 'stuff' going on in our life. I run to the window and spy through the velvet curtains in my bedroom. A huge removals van waited outside our house. I don't answer the door, but they call up into the house from the street. They have a warrant issued by the court to enter the property and remove the items.

I had to tell Rich, call him at work. I have been trying to hold down a few other problems apart from the main Chinese issue. I didn't want to totally overwhelm him. He says he has some cash hidden in the house for an emergency, which I didn't know about, that I can use to pay them off. He is fuming at me. It was the start of our 'getaway' family money. He makes me promise that I have to be honest with everything, every single thing now. We need to be tactical. No secrets. I think he regrets saying that now. His stomach drops when he sees my name flash up on incoming calls and texts with the daily new bullshit decisions that need to be made, and the waves of devastation that roll in. Steady, solid and unrelenting with each call and ping.

Do we have a deal then?
Because I have kept going, making sure the club is 'business as usual', the sale has stayed warm. The Gang was STILL raising funds, anyway, our lawyers explain the situation with The Chinese to the Gang and their legal team and they turned the sale on its

head, and used our fucked-up situation to their advantage and dropped their offering price. Which, of course you would do, if your lawyer was any good and is precisely what I would do if I were in their position. The Chinese came back and said they would consider the Gang as new tenants and agree to issue a new licence, but would have the operating hours, drinking and live music licence restricted and need to close the venue at midnight. Which is fucking ridiculous and our lawyer fought it back to 2.30am for last entry, which the Gang is happy with. They still reduced their offer. I get it up a bit further by adding the Travelling Funfair pop-up bar to the deal, which we were hoping to sell as an individual unit. But it gets the deal across the line, but it is a fucker as I was going to sell it to raise some cash.

What is the outcome?
We have negotiated with the Chinese the balance of rent due down to £148,000. The one tiny thing that lessened the blow is that my parents get the money back I owed them. I don't get Rich's money back, but the shame of not being able to pay my parents, after they had lost everything in the GFC crash, was devastating. So with the bank loans, legal fees, and personal guarantees, I walk away from rolling-over profit and debt of 3 nightclubs, across from the Bathhouse, Baby Bathhouse, FunFair and the Travelling FunFair, 10 years of solid grind, all for the princely sum of £7000. It wouldn't even cover the taxi fares I spent over that time to get in and out of work. A career that has pretty much left me insolvent.

The last week of Funfair
Dot and I have a case of unrelenting gastro, and it is vile and vicious. Dot is in pieces. It's a tag-team 24-hour vomit fest. Tapping each other out on who's turn it is to purge. Like a couple of little and large WWE exhausted wrestlers, we lie together on the mattress. I can't sleep: I have to watch her round the clock. She has been vomiting in her sleep, doing that terrifying scary silent

vomit choke, so I need to make sure she doesn't roll onto her back. It hasn't got Rich yet, and we are keeping him away so he can keep working, as he's freelance now, having left The Body Shop so he can make as much money as quickly as he can. No sick pay or security, but higher-paying jobs. And I also need to contain the illness so I can get better for the weekend to run the club and he can stay healthy to take over weekend Dot duty.

The last Saturday. Before the sale.
It's busy, I'm knackered and wiped-out from the worst week with gastro and finished up the legal negotiations. The finish line is so, so close. I have a few excellent core staff who have really helped me in the past few months. Earlier tonight, I marched out a shift manager who had been with me for a few months. She really wanted to open her own fetish nightclub, so I gave her some training, She was also really hard-up with cash, had a pretty sad story, so I helped her out by paying a month's rent and spotting her money before wages were due. Females in the club industry at venue management level are few and far between. She was with me for less than 3 months and got pinched by a competitor, but the condition was that he also wanted my bar staff. He had heard that I was selling, so she agreed. That morning, she changed the Facebook Funfair staff group to the competitors' Seafront (Traitors) Nightclub group, and she told the staff that I had sold the club, none of them had jobs, she was going over to the competitors' Seafront (Traitors) Nightclub, and it was arranged that they were all coming. They were to work tonight and walk out at the end of the shift. My excellent staff called me to ask if this was the truth and let me know of the mutiny. I called everyone except the ring leader and said it was business as usual, I was selling the club, yes, but the new owners want all our existing staff, which was true. With a sale, I try and keep as many as the staff as possible, but we are not 'selling' the staff as a part of the deal: just wanting to hand over the venue with a reliable team. We always pitch it as a positive

change for the staff. They all turned up to work, and once she got in, I removed her from the Facebook group, got her keys back and told her to leave. Clubland, dishing me up some last minute fuckery and fire-fighting. It's the last Saturday of the club, and we will be signing the paperwork to close the sale on Monday. I made my way home, shattered, broken and exhausted. I must have passed out and smashed my head on the floor of the kitchen.

There is another ridiculous hold-up, and the Chinese's lawyers kicked off with a new, unreasonable 11th-hour condition that my lawyer needs to fight. It holds the sale up. Again. Fuck. I have to work another weekend, and I am actually going to have a mental breakdown. I have mentally clocked out.

Dear Tava,

FUCK OFF UNIVERSE!

- Ok, sorry

The real last Saturday. Before the sale.
I don't believe this will ever end. I open the club up, then hide for the whole shift in the office. Lie on the couch with the lights out and watch Game of Thrones. Winter is indeed coming, for all of us... Scoffing down soul-soothing hot chips and socially unacceptable garlic sauce from the kebab shop next door. Then down again at closing time to lock up. Ironically, the takings are no different than if I'd run around busting my gut. It wouldn't be good if I did it as a long-term management plan, but it was a good one-night-only reprieve to let it twirl along without me, while I have a rest, distracted by the sister fucker, broken Bran, and heads on spikes.

The last day.

The date has been confirmed, and all the solicitors agree it will be sale exchange today. I sit in the office with the very excited Gang. I sit in the club, totally run out of small talk. Waiting for the green light. Nothing till 6pm and my lawyer called and said the Gang's lawyer hasn't got their paperwork across the line today, so I can't give them the keys. I walk home. We are so close, but at any moment, the deal could go south. It jerked backwards and forwards, round and round and side to side, like the waltzer on the seafront. I constantly have that feeling of hot sour sick in the back of my throat these days. It's been a year-long grind with the Gang and 6 months of torture with the Chinese. But as I now know, like the day the letter came to the door, it takes one thing to change the course of your life. And there was still time for a nasty surprise or more life-fuckery to crop up.

The real last day.
I've agreed to meet the Gang at the club at 2pm. The way the deal is structured is the money goes from the Gang's law firm to my law firm; our lawyer takes their fee out of it, pays out any personal guarantees, and the outstanding rent compensation directly to the Chinese's lawyers. The Chinese didn't trust me not to take the sale payment directly from the Gang and fuck off, not paying them or my legal fees. Because you know what, I totally would have done that, too. Once all the funds are where they need to be, and the paperwork is exchanged, the venue will officially be the Gang's. But not until all the pieces of the puzzle are in place. Another afternoon of awkward small talk. I have shown them how the venue works, keys, codes, exits and gone over the hand-over file. The passwords, the marketing manual and the instructions to the CCTV. You name it, I have covered it off. Manuals for the manuals. Lists, instructions with photo reference of how to do everything 'Funfair'. I wish them luck, hand over the keys and walk out.

It's surreal. The bubble of surrealism is popped a moment later. The Gang is calling. I'm not 30 seconds away from the building. Fuck.

Them: Hello?
We can't get into the computer.
Me: Hiiiii? The instructions are on page one of the manual. You just hit enter to 'wake' the screen up. This part is not password-protected. Hmm not even at page one of the manual and there's the first call…

I keep walking. I feel like Kevin Spacey in the last scene in The Usual Suspects, his character, Keyser Soze, walks and returns to the 'real him' with each step…. I have to stop myself from running. Not sure what I'm running from, but it's a burning instinct. I expected to return to 'myself' as I walk home. For it all to be different. It's not, and neither am I.

How do you pack down life after 13 years?
With lots of walking around in circles, sitting reading old cards, love letters and pouring over every memory. Procrastinating and crying. Drinking wine. Me packing the boxes and Dot unpacking the boxes when my back is turned. Suddenly everything seems precious and worthy of 'the memory box'. The nannies, housekeeper and preschool went the week we got the letter of doom, due to zero cash flow. So the house is in a right state, it's hard to know where to start, and now that we have little money we need to be ruthless about what we can take and what has to go. We have had to reduce from a full shipping container to a shared one: a quarter of the space. 20 boxes and no large furniture. Three lives into 20 boxes. I spend the next 3 weeks selling everything we own, like a possessed doomsdays' believer. Baby accessories are really easy to sell second-hand because we brought all the best brands. Clothes, shoes and handbags, anything designer that can make

decent cash. The rest are job-lot sales. All my fancy dresses, beautiful party clothes. I fucking hate them. Mocking me on their hangers, perfect in their crisp dry-cleaning bags, a neat row of reminders of the person I used to be. Who dared to dream and hope for a fabulous future, full of success. Living a pretty fucking spectacular life. Carefree, ignorantly happy. Slim as fuck. I will never wear them again. I want to bin the evidence of my demise, not that I have anywhere to wear them out of clubland or that I could even fit into them with my current self-soothing five-a-day diet of cheap wine, takeaway from the Cod Father, chocolate, bread and toddler leftovers. I sell what I can, saving a few key outfits for Dot for when she's older. I pack, wrap and box up our belongings to ship. Selling anything not tied down. Rich parts with his beloved record collection: 10,000 pieces of vinyl, spanning 25 years, and loyal Technics record decks, to raise cash for flights. I have a little secret cry. He's had one of them since he was 15, when he was a skinny little kid. He bought one of the decks, and his friend down the road brought the other one. They would walk to each other's place, taking turns to carry the deck to the other house, so they could DJ with them as a pair, not being able to afford the set himself. I know what they mean to him. And what parting with his history and his passion means. His strength of character through all of this has floored me. So much personal sacrifice for our family.

In his design day job, he has been doing as much overtime and long hours, scratching every pound together to add to a very minimal getaway fund. Every pound counts, adding to the sad but growing little money pile. We're moving in with Rich's dad, into a very compact 2-bedroom bungalow for the next 8 weeks to save money, tucking away what we would have been paying in rent and for Rich's longest goodbye to London, along with his vast collection of life-long friends and to spend time with his family. Rich sees someone every night, but I only want to see a few special people. In both London and Brighton, I have made beautiful loyal-as-fuck friends that are closer than family now, and I don't even say goodbye to some. It's too hard. Dot and I go to visit Daisy for a weekend in her lovely chocolate-box cottage in the middle of beautiful gardens in Margate. Daisy has done so well with her venue and clubland has worked out better for her. Totally shocking, Daisy is now sober, and she seems very happy. Which is a fucking bizarre and crazy concept to me: we have always been a friendship based on drinking. But it's actually very nice to see her. It's calm. The next weekend is our afternoon farewell drinks in London: my most beloved venue, the Commercial Tavern. It's like all the most aesthetically beautiful things in the world came together and exploded inside a pub. So many memories in this place. From the 666 days, sitting outside having beers, to late-night dates with Rich. I love it here.

For the most part, I don't tell people we got fucked over by the Arrogant Landlord. Even if I do, they don't understand what it fully means to me. They just say "oh fuck" and "wow, that's a shame, but you can do another venue." Not understanding the devastation, the financial ruin. So I focused on the 'we're moving to Australia for a better life for Dot'. Which is partly true. Not that I'm actually fucked and lost everything I've ever worked for. And I don't even have a penny to do anything else. And pretty grim hope for the future because there aren't a lot of job listings on seek.com calling for ex-wild-west clubland entrepreneurs. Or postings on LinkedIn for getaway drivers, which is my fall-back career choice.

I can't look...but I just can't look away...
I watch from afar, in my dressing gown, obsessed with the Funfair social media platforms. The Gang had a bustling first few 'launch' weekends, which would be expected, as there is the follow-through of customers that have been at the end of our marketing cycle and pre-booking booth and guest list. Now they should be working on the next round of seasonal marketing, thinking past the first few weeks when they have all the friends coming down and the initial

hype. They just seem to be promoting a Halloween party, not all the other nights surrounding it, as well. But they have Christmas coming up, which is a tremendous fool-proof money-making period. They have clicked into the premium position on the clubland seasonal calendar. It's what happens after this period that will show what they are made of. Understandably, they wanted to put their 'stamp' on Funfair, which they said from the beginning, and is what a lot of people will want to do, but it baffles me a little as they paid for an existing brand and customer base. We handed over material that we had designed to carry them during the cross-over, 'til they found their own designer that they wanted to work with, as Rich did all of our design. But they didn't get a designer. The 'creative' one in the Gang took the role of 'designer'. Flyers and social media posts which were done in Word (?!), with stock images that had copyright watermarks embedded into them. With the type plonked on. The opposite of what we had been doing. The Funfair brand we created was slick, cutting-edge and really fucking cool. They were naming them things like Cheesy Fridays and Saturday Shemozzle (I had to google it to find out what the fuck a shemozzle was – 'a state of chaos, confusion, a muddle'), they used clip art images of a wedge of cheese and wording like 'cheesy pop' and 'classic 80s'. This is not the language used in current clubland: it's really dated, and not what people loved Funfair for. It is pretty tragic, and it's heart-breaking to see what they are doing with the club. And their investment. They are also starting to position themselves as a gay club, but just because some of the Gang were gay, it didn't mean that it is the recipe of success for a gay club. They went to press saying they were the premier lesbian and gay club of Brighton but still the same beloved Funfair. They had a solid base to run from, but they did the clubland kiss of death: CONFUSION. They 'trial and errored' music policy, design, the visual identity and language used online and shifted the club position' in real-time, for everyone to see. Experimenting is a balancing act: it's necessary to create new movements in pop culture but it's not done with

1980's disco catch-cries and clip art... It gave a confused image of what the club was, who it was for, and what the fuck it is. People are fickle and don't like to be fucked with on their Saturday night out. They didn't follow the formula I'd left them with. I could see from what they were doing online that it was totally random. I was told they didn't have the manpower hitting the street with flyerers; they didn't have the online presence; and they didn't continue with the creative concept of The Funfair as we created it. Unless they quickly slot it into a version that worked for them and smashed the living days out of it, they won't last 6 months. Clubland is harsh and demanding of its residents. They paid good money for a solid concept and should have continued it. Not play Russian roulette with creative ideas. They have put their houses on the line for it. They wouldn't go to a casino and gamble their house away: I can't see why they would do it so easily with wanting to 'have a go' with trying to work out how a nightclub works, with no experience. They should have followed the formula for a year, assessed the market, learned the ropes and then started on implementing changes once they have a full overview and learned what makes a club work and what the customers wanted. A result of their trial and error and inexperience, unfortunately, the customers start to drop away.

But I can tell you that every time they came down, it was full and busy. And from our misfortune with the Chinese, they paid half the going-rate for Funfair...They saw it with their own eyes: I know how to run and keep a club busy. Sadly, the club concept fell away with their watered-down, confused version of Funfair and the customers stopped coming. You don't just push a button or turn a key. They didn't find out how to run the club. They spent their time checking that I was running the club properly before it was theirs. Instead of coming into the office during the day to see how to get the customers through the doors. It's as simple as that. It's sad, but it's the harsh truth.

25

The intense heat pushing me into the earth, forcing my body to move slowly. Dragonflies dart and dance about my head. Sweat driving out the toxins. Egg foam turns to tadpoles that turn to frogs. As the wet season rolled in over the lush rice paddy terraces, we couldn't be further away from clubland if we tried. And we did try. Mornings spent on long, black sand beaches and wild frothy surf: me, staring blankly at the horizon, Rich training and working out. Dot building endless castles and enchanting cities in the sand. Uninterrupted time together. No phone or emails. Disconnected. Afternoons of tropical storms, thunderous lighting shows and family naps. If you took a snapshot and ask a random stranger what was happening in the picture, it would be a happy family enjoying a family holiday in paradise. The reality is, it's a happy family yes; but one biding their time, having run away from chaos, nervously waiting before they hit the shores of a new life in Australia. Where it's cheap and warm, and your money goes much, much further. We also need to rest, recoup and rebuild. And it helps that we can do it all on 40 pounds a day. We had a few days of accommodation pre-booked, then starting looking around and found a private villa with a pool and have simple meals.

After we walked away, with only just enough money to start a new life in Australia, we decided that we needed to regroup, mentally, physically and as a family. We stop in Bali for 3 months. A shimmery silver lining to a very dark cloud. With the money Rich saved before we left, the cash from the items we sold in the UK, and Rich doing a few remote freelance design jobs while we are in Bali, it was actually better for us to live here in the 'holding period'. Cheaper than staying in the UK and cheaper than moving to Australia in the peak holiday periods of Christmas, when the job market grinds to halt from the first week of December to the first week of February. We have to hit the ground running, getting straight into work, as we won't have enough cash to last more than a few weeks in Sydney.

The villa was on the outskirts of Ubud, in the cool, lush tropical mountains. A tiny self-contained walled compound in the middle of rice-paddy fields, off a dirt road with an ancient temple at one end and a grassy field filled with goats, chickens and a horse at the other. The four-walls compound making up the perimeter walls of the villa, rimmed with palm trees, heady frangipanis and clumps of towering bamboo. It has two bedrooms, but Dot sleeps in with us on a little day bed. Only the bedrooms have four walls and doors; the rest of the rooms - kitchen, bathrooms and living area - are all open-plan onto a courtyard filled with stepping stones, thatched-roof day beds, a babbling brook that runs through the tropical garden, pooling at a pond filled with giant lotus leaves and flowers, home of two snappy turtles and a plunge pool. Open to the fresh air, frogs, critters and mother nature. Sleeping to the soothing tropical rain is hypnotic and the remedy for my insomnia. We eat simply. Rich works out with a Thai boxing trainer, and I slowly came off the antidepressant medication and try to unravel, after the rollercoaster of clubland. It helps and is such a fantastic experience for Dot, loving that we were all together hanging out, everyday swimming, visiting the terrifying but cute monkeys, watching the world and nature go by as we stand still. I wish we could hide here forever. I try, every day, to feel better. Then I remember we are not staying here, in paradise, in our bubble of pure perfection. Then the slow wave of impending doom creeps into the pit of my stomach: I am going 'home'.

Bali has magical powers. It's like it forces you with its heat and humidity to slow down. It calms with its peaceful island energy. It disarms you with the kind, beautiful people that call it home. It secretly whispers to your soul with its street offerings, prayers and incense snaking through the air. Traditions seep into your being. It reminds you that the world and its creatures are magic, with her lush forests, mesmerising flowers, turquoise butterflies and naughty little monkeys. It is a multidimensional lesson that money isn't everything and happiness can be a choice.

Bali put what I have, right in front of me. With no distractions or filters. I have nothing, but I actually have everything. The heart of a fucking incredible man and the joy, love and wonder of our child. Enough money to move to a different country and take respite for 3 months on a tropical island. Bali helps, but it doesn't totally fix or erase 13 years of chaos in three months. But it supports us to soften the blow and prepare us for the next stage.

Rich works daily on building my portfolio, a calling card for my work as a creative director for hire. A visual collection of all the clubs, the marketing, the brand identity, the elaborate events, sponsorship deals and party collaborations. Along with the reams of press clippings. He lays it out carefully and beautifully. It's curious to see my career displayed in a 40-page book. Its fills me equally with pride and sadness. So much success and so much failure.

Our time on the zen island goes way too quickly: by the time I was feeling relaxed and getting into island life, it was time to leave. Our time was gloriously uneventfully gorgeous. Except entering and leaving the country. Airport and customs are still a recurring ball-ache for me and my poor travelling companions.

ARRIVAL

We get picked off to be searched. Into an interview room and our bags thoroughly examined. It wasn't a random selection. Questions are raised why I have 18 hardcover books in my bag. (Apparently, this is how drugs are smuggled.) They haven't quite understood my answer: "They are for research and reference for a book that I was starting to write about 'entertaining'. Being the hostess with the mostest? You know, cocktails and canapés? Recipes?" Each book is inspected page by page, x-rayed, spines cracked, and drug tested. Rich is also using this inopportune time to flag a question about this 'book'. Firstly, how is a dyslexic going to write a book? I don't know yet, what's your point? Perhaps you could turn your focus to working on getting a 'job' that will put food on the table as soon as we arrive in Sydney, please? As a dyslexic unpublished author with no literary contacts, who is good at drinking, writing a book about parties sounds fun. But it is a passion project, not a job. And we need jobs. Secondly, I need to use this time to build my portfolio, line up interviews and research the Sydney market. Usually, I would push back, but he has a point. Begrudgingly, I put my book to the side and start looking for 'normal' work.

DEPARTURE

I wake up in the dead of night, sat bolt upright and ran out to my computer to check our flight itinerary. The flight was at 12 midnight, last night: not 12 midday today. We had missed our flight. FUCK! We run around, pack our bags and make a mad dash to the airport. We max out the last of Rich's credit card with new flights that we just can't really afford. As we go through passport control, we knew we had overstayed by three days, but we were told 'just have some cash on you to, get them to look the other way'. We were taken into an interview room again and asked why we overstayed 33 days. Oh fuck. Yikes, I didn't realise it that long. We had had a bit of experience in the past 'paying' on the spot fines direct to police with traffic issues. And the Internet seems to suggest you just need to pay a 'cash fine' on departing, so I didn't think too much about it just prepared with the equivalent of £50 in a pocket. This is a lot more official than I was imagining. The head of passport control, in his super-smart military uniform, demands to know why we overstayed and that we need to pay £5000 in fines. Which we don't have. The airline customer service tries to help and says, this particular immigration officer is very strict and doesn't let anyone get away with it but that he can come and see our bank balance, and pull out that amount we owe and if not, then as close as possible. And he will decide if we can board our plane. I pull out the maximum that the cashpoint lets me. Its only £150. We go back, and he says it not enough. We ask to speak to the Australia consulate, and he said they have no jurisdiction with illegal over-stayers. The only option is we pay the full fine, or we don't leave Bali. And every day we stay over is another day added to the fine, or get detained in the detention centre. We get marched back out to a holding pen. Dots getting hot, tired and super grumpy: rightly so. Rich is worried and I know he blames my 'relaxed, don't worry about' it attitude that gets us in trouble too often. I have been running thought the scenarios. I go back in. Tell him that we only have this money and this is it, we are deeply sorry. He doesn't care. "Get out 'til you get the full amount, call your family - whatever you need to do." We go back and forward for 2 more hours. We can't miss this flight: we have no more back-up cash. And I can't hand over the last 2k we have. I get Rich and Dot, and we go back into his office, and I have an idea. I realise he won't take the money directly from me as a payoff. We sit down at his desk and ask to speak to him as a last plea. Dots still crying, and his irritation is rising. I get the massive wedge of Indonesian Rupiah cash and place it on the table and slide into the centre of his desk. Bow my head slightly.

"We ask for leniency and are sincerely apologising for our wrongdoing, we respect the culture and rules. And we will never disrespect them again." Hi picks up the phone and speaks in Indonesian and all I hear is the word 'baby'. He was calling the consulate in Jakarta. He said we are irresponsible and the baby is screaming. He takes our passports. Tells us to get out. We all stand up, the pile of cash is left on the table, and we are marched to a tiny corridor, given our passports. He barks "NO SMILES" and pushes us all through a back door which slams behind us. We are kicked out into the duty-free shopping area, on the right side of the passport control with minutes to catch our flight.

Thick metal bars on all the windows. This is 'home' for the foreseeable future. No escape. My chest can't expand to get the air I need to keep my emotions level. Prison? Not exactly. But I do feel trapped. I go into the bedroom to cry: I don't want to seem ungrateful. This was our new home. It's hard to be truthful here without hurting anyone's feelings, as the flat was kindly arranged as a landing pad for us. Mum and my sister trying to make it homey for us. Dot loved her room, Mum had been collecting beautiful little bedding and cheery cushions to make it sweet for her. Family donated furniture. I look at the flat, and it is the physicality of my failing. My fall from grace and this is what it looked like in four walls. Bali was dreamy, but not the reality of what starting again looks like. This is.

The building is sitting on the curb-side corner of two main highways. Yellow brick 60's block, it was booked in for a total renovation but we needed to move in now, so the landlord gladly put it off. With peeling wallpaper, yellow paint, thick layers of dust on the broken curtains and blinds. Sprayed on lumpy ceiling, so when the upstairs neighbour - who is renovating round the clock - chips away at my soul with each tile he removes, the bobbly-spray ceiling bits fall like cement hailstones. The carpets are over 30 years old: they are threadbare, with holes, stains and with the crumbling underlay that poofs up clouds of dust with any movement with an impact higher than a footstep. Spurring black mould in our bedroom cupboard. The kitchen is cobbled together with old 70's cabinets and broken drawers. The peeling bench laminate has deep cracks with old food baked in.

Wasps - furious inhabitants - nest on all the front windows. Armies of ants protect their territory. Each morning we come into the kitchen, all the surfaces are black and moving like the tide. No amount of cleaning or bug-spray fixes it. New ones return overnight. It is above the shared garaged of the block so that every time the door is buzzed open by the other tenants, it rumbles, shaking the bed and wakes us up. The constant noise and pollution of the 24-hour highways and higher rent than our beautiful Brighton terrace. All of this would have been manageable, but it was its location that haunted me. Not the highways. Or the crumbling interior. It was across the road of the house I owned with my ex-boyfriend. Where I decided that I would leave to follow my heart to pursue a life of adventure, chase my giddy dreams and to track down Hollywood-Fucking-Amazing-Love. I did track it down and had his child, and this is what I brought him to. The exact location where

I decided Australia was no longer for me. I can see the property, through the bars on my kitchen windows as I do the washing up and wasps head-butt the glass. The supermarket is the same one I use to use, walking the aisle, willing a life of excitement. The chemist is the one I brought the pill from. The same doctor I now take Dot to. The petrol station, I would fill my car and daydream about what else is out there... The same bottle shop that used to be a place visited for a special occasion bottle of bubbly: now it's a daily visit for 'necessary' wine, what's on offer that doesn't taste like cats' piss or smell like ammonia. The same greasy MSG-laced Chinese restaurant, with the same sweet couple STILL working there. A daily reminder of my failure, how far I have come to have not achieved anything. I have come full circle. It's so very far from the homecoming I would have planned. You know the one when you're thin, rich and fabulous and you go to a school reunion or bump into an old boyfriend or arch frienemy and fucking smashing the granny out of life? Like Beyoncé's Coachella Homecoming..? Well, this is the polar opposite of that.

My beautiful portfolio is met with 'owws, ahhhs and wowwwws. What an incredible body of work, what an amazing career you have had'. And tumbleweeds. No work. Everyone echoes that Sydney hospitality, bars, nightclubs and events have suffered diabolically since the lockout laws, restricting the operating hours of venues and alcohol sales. That vibrant city we visited over 2 years ago was wiped out with the new regulations. Kings Cross is dead. Sydney is a ghost town after 9pm. Big hospitality operators are moving into 'family-focused' restaurants. Small operators were flocking into fringe suburbs.

I had my sights set on one fantastic 'big operator', applied for a creative director role and got hit with a firm 'No thanks. You don't have any relevant Sydney experience.' Which kinda shocked me.

QUEEN OF CLUBS

Great ideas are great ideas, no matter where you are in the world.... Aren't they? Nope, not here. Sydney has a very particular 'attitude' that has taken me aback. I have never felt more like a round peg in a square hole.

It's as if Australia has been frozen in time. Its toxic masculinity is, laughably, still rife. It feels like perhaps this pretty city, with its crisp, clean beaches and shimmery harbour is more superficial style over creative substance. It feels cut off from big ideas and original thinking. Disconnected from the world's cultural progress. Like it stands alone in the same bubble that made me feel claustrophobic and isolated all those years ago, and it hasn't changed or evolved with the rest of the world. Knocking down 'tall poppies' and stifling individuality appears to be a national past time here now.

Rich thrives. My love hits the ground running in Australia. Because he's excellent at his job, he has a highly desired skill-set and is charismatic and easy to be around, so getting work is no problem for him. He is booked solid every day from day 2. Thank fuck. He keeps food on the table, a roof over our head and cheap wine in my glass.

Dot is living her best life. Spending days down at Palm Beach with Nanny and Pop Pop. It's magical, and the very reason we wanted to moved here. They go on sunsets walks, breakfast on the beach. Feeding the ducks, spotting seals. Having her grandparents to play, entertain and share the delight in her elaborate sandy games. It's everything I could hope for our little girl. She blossoms in the sun, sea and fresh air. We have her in a little preschool, around the corner from the prison flat, that seems to be quite nice. We spend our weekends at the swimming pool next to Luna Park in the cool, the shadows of the iconic bridge, and going on walks around the pretty harbour. It's brain dead but beautiful. Kind of what the doctor ordered but it's a hard beige-coloured pill to swallow.

Every day I feel like I'm living a double life. In cultural witness protection. Nobody knows our previous life back in the UK, and fewer people care. Since we've moved back to Australia, I've stopped telling people what we did or trying to explain the magnitude of what went down. If you tell the stories in isolation and not part of a big picture, it sounds arrogant and a little boastful. I can see their eyes glazing over. Australia can't seem to digest anyone a bit different. So, I stopped talking. Stopped being that girl. Nobody cares about her. That girl who owned all those amazing nightclubs. Because the truth is, I don't anymore, and the more I explain how cool and crazy it was, the more desperate, pathetic and washed-up I sounded. And how lost and lonely I felt. I am living in Groundhog Day, surrounded by a black cloud of failure, shame, and hopelessness. Back living in the very street that I left behind in Neutral Bay over 13 years ago. I push on because I don't have a choice.

I have been putting my portfolio under the nose of anyone who stands still for just a moment. It finally looks like I might get a break.

A small hospitality group need some fresh creative ideas, a couple of their venues refurbished and their social media and branding sorted. They say their staff aren't hitting the mark and they want to be more competitive to the big operator I tried to get work with. Ok – fantastic: this is right up my ally. I love the idea of being to elevate their group for them. After the meeting, I worked overnight with Rich, creating a mini-pitch for creative concepts and an excellent strategy for their venues. I get the job and an attractive salary to go with it. I really want to be good at this job. I want this to work. To just slip into Sydney life. By the end of the week, I have a full overview. The 360° circle of bullshit continued, and I was now working for a new version of The Devil. Fuck, this is not good in the first few days. From the CEO: "You need to push your co-workers down if you want to get ahead here. You need to tell us if people aren't doing their job properly, how you could do it better and we will get rid of them and give you a promotion." When I said something like 'in my venues, we found that customers love/engage/respond well to 'blah blah blah/good, solid creative idea...'; when I suggested something that worked flawlessly in my old venues, I was met with "Tava - you don't own any venues anymore, so that's not relevant. We just want to hear what would work here, not what has worked in the past for you." It's a cruel environment, and I'm slipping into a septic, vile coma of pig headed misogyny. It's suffocating.

Every reason I was pushed to leave Sydney, all those years ago, is now part of my daily life. I clearly don't know how to fit back into the workforce. And these guys had no idea what they are doing with daddy's trust fund money, other than losing the property portfolio hand-over-fist. They are angry, chronic cokeheads. Breeding a vile, toxic, blame and bully culture in their business, making it impossible to do any productive work. One of the girls in my team sits in her car crying before starting work, and a chef broke down the other day, saying he can't stand the mind games any longer. They fired me on the day before my 3-month probation. And I couldn't have been happier.

From this stifling, harsh reality and horrible introduction to Sydney's work culture, I go down the project route. Being freelance is much more brain-friendly for me. Cut out the bullshit.

I am a mother first. That was the deal now. I am a mum, and I won't be apologising for it like I had to over the past 3 months. Or making excuses for it and also hiding the fact I was a mother to get the stupid job done. I haven't been through hell and back with Funfair to just do it again. I won't be busting my balls or putting other people's dreams first. Our family is my priority. Rich took the lead during the early years with Dot, and now it's my turn.

This is an outstanding feeling to have. I will only do work that allows me to leave on time. Don't work excess hours and juggle my work around being a mum. Because this whole idea of 'supporting working mothers' is actually bullshit. I quickly learn these are buzz words to trick mums into thinking they can manage it all. Then feel like massive failures. This crappy little job did three great things for me that I can thank those coked-up cocks for...

1. A reminder: I am a Mother first. No ifs or buts.

2. Gave me 'relevant' Sydney experience. Which is total bullshit but people now felt more secure to book me as I had 'local' market knowledge.

3. Propelled me to the first of many freelance experiential Creative Director projects.

Oh, one last big thing... It gave me a significant tax return. A chunk of money I sorely needed.

I start working on two creative direction projects. Designing a pop-up bar for a new spiced-rum brand to take on the road to events and festivals. A rebranding project for a cocktail bar. I was putting one foot in front of the other. What starting again was meant to look like. But as soon as things started looking up. FUCKING BOOM. Our Little Lady isn't doing well. She's grizzly, lethargic, and poorly behaved. Like a delayed 'terrible 2's… She turns 3 in a few days. She's off her food. Irritated and just not well. We visit the doctor, and they say there is nothing wrong with her. We're sent away. She sweats through the night but no temperature. She cries often and wants to sit on my lap. It is so out of character. She has always been our bubbly, bright, independent little girl. Highly advanced. Speaking in complex full sentences, totally toilet trained by 2.5. A happy little girl with beautiful manners and high curiosity. She had been sleeping through the night since Bali, now she's is waking up every 2 hours. We try to work out what's happening. I ask the preschool, but because they have so many new and causal staff they say, yes she's not eating much food, as per usual and taking herself off for naps during the days and crying a lot, asking for mummy. This is NOT her usual behaviour, why didn't they tell me this? Well, we don't really know her, so we don't know she's not herself… For fuck's sake! Next day, on her birthday, Rich takes her to the Hello Kitty cafe so I can set up the house for her birthday party. He calls, she is sheet white and says she feels really sick and is crying. When they get back, the party is set up: all the family is here, pastel bunting, streamers and helium unicorn balloons filled the fugly flat; a big 3-tiered Disney princess cake by a kind aunt, and so many presents. It's a 3-year-old's dream. She walks in, looks around, bursts out crying, walks into her room and sleeps. She wakes up and comes out; she seems a bit better but then goes and lies down again on our bed. She calls to me, 'Mummy come here, I'm scared'. I was right next to her. 'I can't see you, mummy'. I am right in front of her direct line of sight. Her vision is dropping in and out. It's a Sunday, so we call an out of hours doctor in case we don't make it to the medical centre before it closed. Mum drives us. I have to carry her. Her little head and shoulders are stiff, and she can't look down. By the time we are seen by the doctors, Dot's neck is now stuck up, and her vision is affected by the bright lights. The doctor said she has a terrible ear infection. Gives us antibiotics. We have a tense conversation where she sees I am not satisfied with the diagnosis. She states that ear infections can be very unstabling for a child. We go home. We're not convinced. Everyone leaves, worried for our tiny beauty. A knock on the door. It's the on-call doctor. She looks at Dot and in her ears. "I don't want to worry you, but I think there is something very wrong here. It's not an ear infection, you need to take her to emergency now." Rich and I get in a cab to the hospital. Her neck is now totally immobile. They think it's a bladder or a kidney infection. They take blood, but we will need to wait 3 hours for the results, but it's not a bladder or urinary tract infection. She is starting to deteriorate while we wait for the blood results. Her body is aching, and she's whimpering now. We go through family history with the doctor, and we have to say what we are both thinking but don't want to say out loud in case it makes it real. The high white blood-cell count can also be an indication of particular cancers. This is exactly how Josh was presenting before he was diagnosed. Rich and I never say it out loud to each other, but we think it. Please, I fucking beg you - not Dot, too. Parades of doctors, specialists and heads of departments come through to see her. She is treated for meningitis, rare blood diseases and a wide but blind net of treatment is put into an IV. Not because of incompetence, but because it is still a mystery. Her body giving no clues to what is wrong, other than deteriorating. She is so small. And so scared. And so brave. She is slipping out of our grip. I leave the room to cry, so she doesn't see me. I am terrified. Nothing can happen to her, that's not the fucking deal here! The doctors have confirmed it's not cancer or leukaemia, which is the biggest relief. It's short-lived because it doesn't stop her melting away in front of our eyes.

She keeps saying she just wants to go home, that she is feeling better. "See Mumma, I can move my neck again." She tried, but she can't, then she cries with the fear she can't control her body and the pain of trying. She is so smart she has clocked that the nurses in the uniforms are the ones to be scared of: they poke and prod, give her needles and change drips, they have so much to do and are always so professional but rushed, whereas the doctors and specialists, in 'regular clothes' talk and soothe first. They take the time to play games, make her laugh and ask her funny questions. She can't eat or swallow solid food now; they are putting it through the IV. She is put in an isolation room, in case of rare infectious diseases. There are no answers. In 24 hours, she is unable to walk from the pain and unable to control her bladder or bowels. She is back in nappies. In 48 hours, the side of her beautiful little face and eye have dropped like a stroke victim, and the open eyes pupil is a tiny pinprick in size. Her neck is stuck looking up and to the side, as if she looking at the sun. Her fragile body twisted and her muscles locked. She is in agony from the weight of her own body. I go round collecting pillows and make a round-circle nest for her. My heart. My family. I can't be without you. Three is our magic number. Please, I fucking beg you universe, not this. Not her. Rich and I hold each other in the hallway when Mum takes care of Dot, so we can get a coffee from the parent's room. Two ghosts clinging to each other. Our mouths telling the other one everything is going to be ok. The doctors will work it out. But these words were said without conviction. We have been here before. We are helpless. She can't be held anymore, and her bones ache, but she won't let me leave her side: we have to be touching, but she needs space in her pain. Endless Pepper Pig on my laptop is the only momentary distraction to the pain. I have to turn and move her body for her. She is in a deep trance, not awake but not asleep. There is no peace in her stillness. She looks like a tortured angel on a fluffy cloud in her white pillow nest, on a big adult hospital bed in a tiny-child hospital gown and little fingers gripping her pink teddy with her pale blue nail polish painted ready for her little birthday party. Surrounded by drips and monitors. It's an adult's ward, so everything is too big for her: pulse clips, blood pressure bands. Making every task clumsy and creating an unnecessary fuss. We dread the high-pitch beeping that means the drip is blocked and has to be reinserted into her delicate skin. I quickly try and make sure there are no kinks in the tubes, or she's lying on it… Sometimes it stops, and if it doesn't, she starts crying and begging for nobody to touch her arm even before the nurse enters the room. It's fucking heart breaking. Rich can't sleep here: there isn't space. But he is by her side when he is, and is the one who notices the dramatic deterioration overnight. Things are going too slow. We go through a channel that allows you to 'officially' escalate medical treatment for an independent assessment in the case of an emergency and consult with a higher department. The treatment we were receiving was impeccable, but it was too slow. They agree. They say that parents are the indicators of the severity of illness in a child. We desperately feel we are running out of time. And we ask the doctors to move faster, for decisions and treatments to happen quicker. The time this is taking and the way she is crumbling, she won't be here in another 24 hours. Finally, a paediatric anaesthetist and the specialist team put Dot under for the MRI and lumbar punch. It's a training hospital: I get this is all a part of the necessary learning process, but it's painful when it's your child. She refused to lie on the bed, so Rich has to hold Dot to try to keep her calm and still her, but she screams and begs to go home, terrified by what's happening. The two men in blue caps and blue face masks in scrubs and gloves, trying to hold her down and cover her face. I'm scared, so imagine a little child! She's desperately moving her aching, locked body when the trainee anaesthetist tries again and again, but keeps missing her mouth and nose to get the mask. He grabs the back of her head with both hands - she hits him off with more power than I would've have imagined her body was holding. The teacher anaesthetist has to step in: she is fighting with every ounce of strength left in her body to get away. I'm on the ground, trying to stroke her hair and calm her panicking body trying to climb away. "Mummy! daddy! PLEASE don't do this to me, stop! Stop them! STOP IT!" She starts screaming with fear, but no noise is coming of her mouth. "Be brave my baby - everything is going to be ok. Nothing's going to happen, bubba. Try and relax: trust me, baby…" The fear in her eyes and stiff body is haunting. Her little body drops limp, losing the fight with the anaesthetic and she goes into the artificial sleep, with my 'reassurance' the last thing she hears and Rich looking deep into her terrified eyes. She is wheeled away from us. We hold each other, our bodies shaking together with my violent sobbing. Her pain and terror cuts through both us.

Dot has a large abscess growing between her throat and her spine, and she has a life-threatening infection in her lymph nodes. The abscess is crushing the spinal cord and closing over her throat, affecting the movement and blood flow in her body to her brain. The infection is taking over her blood. It's the worst-best news we could ever hope for. Terrifying that she is days away from it travelling to her heart, which is fatal, but the treatment can be started immediately. Officially, she has a Parapharyngeal abscess, Torticollis and Horners Syndrome.

6 Hours Later

We are in an ambulance, being transferred to the new specialist children's ward, where the medical treatment will be completed. Dot and I are both lying on the gurney, being pushed through the quiet halls in the middle of the night. Dot whispers, "Look, mummy…" She moved her neck one centimetre with a massive smile on her face. "I can move my neck a little bit." I have never been so fucking happy in my life for a tiny little miracle. Sobbing with happiness and relief, I can't hug her 'cause she's still in agony. I call Rich. Our little girl. This second we know she's going to be ok. This means she is responding to the treatment. If it didn't work, they would need to operate to remove the abscess through her spine. It's as scary and as high-risk as it sounds. There was a split-second thought that flashed through my mind on the second day: there was a possibility we're going to leave the hospital, and our heart wasn't coming with us if they didn't hurry up. And I was right.

The rate she was crumbling in front of our eyes. The question marks from the doctors. The fear in Rich's face. My mum's silent but terrified support. Our baby's poor, tiny body locked and riddled in pain. The doctors don't know how this happened or how long it was going on for. The abscess was enormous, so it has been growing over a decent period. They were astounded at how well she handled the pain, once they knew what she was dealing with and what her little body had been through. Dot's body had been ravaged with infection but she never had a temperature above 36.8, even though she was drenched with fever, which is kind of anatomically impossible. And this is something we need to be very cautious of in the future; a non-presenting fever. The doctor from the medical centre asked if I could come and speak to her. She apologises and was deeply upset that she missed such a deadly infection. I can't even begin to count our blessings.

She is the heart of our tiny family. Back where our heart belongs, between Rich and me. Our Hollywood-Fucking-Amazing-Love story doesn't exist without her.

It felt like we have had the rug ripped out, again. How dare you even think about being happy or how can you even think you can start again? Just when we began to lead a 'normal life' away from clubland. But, I realise this is not rational thinking. We are not victims here. We have our beautiful little girl. Other parents didn't

QUEEN OF CLUBS

have the outcome we did, showing us what to be grateful for. This is the beauty of life. What love is actually about and how fucking lucky we are. It keeps me thankful for our beautiful family unit on the one hand; and on the other hand, holding me fucking terrified that at any point devastation can still knock at my door, or be waiting for me around any corner. Reinforcing that we aren't safe and or away from the traumas of the past. It follows close behind us, ready the moment we let our guard down.

I take the next few months to nurse Dot back to full health, and start taking care of mine for the first time in a very long time... and it feels good. It's time to start getting a grip on myself, physically. I also see a doctor for a full check-up, as I still feel physically wrecked, drained and no better than Funfair times. I think I have depleted any energy reserves and serotonin levels from years of drug and alcohol use and I have been running on adrenaline for so long. Turns out I have hypothyroidism; an alarming underactive thyroid. Tiredness all the time, excessive weight gain, depression, slow movements and thoughts, brain fog, poor memory and concentration. Muscle aches, weakness and cramps. Thin, brittle hair, flaky nails and skin. All-round shit heath and crappy body. Yes! I was pleased to hear this. Slowly the weight drops off with the medication, and the energy is increased, so I can start to exercise a bit. Slowly losing the coat of shame and self-doubt that came with every extra kilo added to my body that never left me after pregnancy. The doctor said it's almost impossible to lose it with unmedicated hypothyroidism. It's time to stop hiding my physical issues. I even start to look into managing life with the prolapse. Diet, things that irritate it and managing crippling constipation. Not just ignoring it or pretending it's not there, but what I can do to live with it as she's not going anywhere till I get surgery to be sliced open again and rebuilt.

26

I am consciously making a choice to be happy. Telling myself I am, until it's true. And no surprise, the Universe rewards me for working on my admittedly average attitude, trying to adjust my wonky mindset and started presenting me with things I never thought possible. Like I was actually allowed to be happy. It was ok to be happy. And rays of warm sunny hope started seeping in. Mum has brought me over a big dusty box from storage. My memory box from before I left Australia for England, over 15 years ago. I open the lid. On top of the pile is a stack of actor's headshots: a girl. Black and white photos of a youthful, fresh-faced actress with dreams of Hollywood and stars in her eyes. An acceptance letter from The Lee Strasburg Theatre Institute acting school to go to study in New York. An overwhelming bolt of realisation strikes me. I have been on the most soul-shaking, bone-aching journey, weathering my fair share of emotional and physical battle scars. But I am still standing. Standing in the very same place I first dared to ask the Universe for Hollywood-Fucking-Amazing-Love…. Well, technically across the road, but you get what I mean.

This is a love story. Our love story.

Imagine if I had chosen NYC instead of London all those years ago…

I've never known Rich to be so obsessed with the minute-by-minute weather report. The drive to Palm Beach is slow in the torrential rain. He is so fidgety. It's magically stopped for our after-dinner walk and drinks, allowing the sky to put on her Milky Way show, ripping through the black sky, I have on a beautiful dress Rich brought me from Bali. Floor-length, black, flowy '70s gypsy-style, with a thigh-high split and cut-out ornate embroidery, lacing up through the front and with balloon sleeves. Flat black suede strappy sandals, salty wavy hair from a gorgeous swim earlier. A gardenia pinned in there. I annoyingly tread in a cold deep puddle up to my ankle bone, and my left shoe squishes as we walk down the road to Barrenjoey House for nightcaps. Dot's staying back with Nanny and Pop-Pop.

Rich is quiet as we walk, hand in hand. The restaurant is closed for a private party. He is super pissed off. So, we cross the road to walk on the wharf, to look at the stars. It's covered in a layer of rancid seaweed and sand flies after king tides. Fishermen gutting and beheading their fish and police checking out a suspicious car. It's funny, 'cause it's usually totally deserted at night. Equally miffed, Rich steers us down to the beach. The beach from my endless summers as a child, where the Universe told me to take a chance and open my own club. The beach we got the ferry from: this very wharf, when we decided to move to Australia and now the beach where our daughter spends her days running up and down in the warm golden happy sunshine. We take off our shoes and walk. Argh, it's started spitting and the wind is whipping the sand, my hair and the dress in every direction. Rich stops us and points out the grinning moon behind the clouds. He holds both my hands. "I know we have been through a lot, and I know things have been hard for us, but we are stronger, together because of it. I love you so much. I have always loved you. I love our family. I love you more than ever, and I know the time is right, now." I cry. My signature happy-tear mess cry. He fumbles in the sand and gets down on a half-knee-kinda-stance as a wave comes in. 'So will you..? Marry me?"

Blab. Snot. Sob. 'YES!'

"Can I get up now? I'm getting soaked."

And puts on the most beautiful, diamond ring.

The most imperfect-perfect engagement. To the most perfect man. In the most perfect location. We toast and have champagne with Mum and Dad and tell Dottie the news. It's so, so special. I do this weird cry-laugh for another 4 hours. Embarrassed by the attention and elated with the love. He did well, considering his plans were scuppered at every single turn. I'm laughing at this now: poor fucking guy. This beach means so much to me, and he knows that. Last year, he arranged a dreamy midnight picnic after a long boozy Valentine's dinner at Barrenjoy House, on the beach with champagne, candles, a fluffy rug, cushions, music and a full moon turned it right on. We walked down the beach from the restaurant to discover it all set up on the sand waiting for us (thanks, Mum). It was truly spectacular, but I cried myself to sleep that night because I thought he was actually proposing and it was just so, so perfect.

Tonight, it was perfect in every single way.

Beautiful, pure and honest love.

The shift in mindset that we were allowed to actually be happy. We had suffered enough, and the future was ours to live out how we wanted now. Things started to happen. I received a substantial payment from a big creative direction job - and my tax return in the same week. I am landing some interesting creative direction projects now. All the lovely things and significant life experiences that I knew were gone when our money was taken from us. Things that we never thought possible, after losing every penny we had worked for. I want to do something amazing for us with this chunk of cash.

We run away to our happy place. Los Angeles. Our city of dreams. We stay in the Hollywood Roosevelt, go vintage shopping, take Dot sightseeing and hang by the iconic pool. Rich catches up with his LA pals. Dot and I hang about, in our matching heart-shaped sunglasses, living out our best Lana Del Ray dream life and eating banana splits in bed. It's Hollywood heaven. Then off for the next leg of the adventure...

Tears pool in my eyes. I try not to blink and tilt my head up to stop them rolling down my face, ruining my makeup. I dab it with a tissue. The most perfect sky and soft, rustling green leaves. Waiting, counting bars in the music. This is the moment I have asked for. Everything that I have dreamt of. I take a step closer. From the bright desert light into the cool darkness. My eyes take a minute to adjust. Tears that I can't stop. I let them roll down my cheeks. This time it is the tears of a girl who found her boy. Tears of a girl who got her deepest heart's desires. Universe, I thank you for allowing me to experience one of the most beautiful moments in time. I slowly walk behind Dot. She makes my heart want to explode with joy. She takes one step, carefully chooses the perfect specimen, then throws one red rose petal from her little satin basket. Taking her flower-girl duties so seriously. 'Til she arrives at Rich. She beams, "Daddddyyyyyyy!" and jumps into his arms. Pachelbel's Canon in D fills the tiny church and adds to my emotional overload. I am so filled with emotion: it is toppling and bubbling out of my body. Rich also looks a little overwhelmed. Not emotional: more like shit just got real. I grip my flowers tight, still crying. I always knew that I would be emotional. But I can't stop my face exploding with all the feelings. I sob ecstatic tears. I have a wet soggy tissue scrunched in my hand. I don't know what to do with it, so I pop it into Dot's little petal basket. The ceremony starts. "We are gathered here today..." but it's shut down as quickly as it began with a very loud scolding: "Oi MUM! This is NOT a bin!!!" Dot picks the soggy wet tissue out of her little basket, disgusted at me and marches off and gets rid of it... The Reverend is dressed in a smart '50s rock-a-billy style suit, black-rimmed glasses and slick back hair. You can tell he doubles up as 'Elvis'. He croons his way with the speed of a cattle auctioneer through our vows. Never taking a pause for air. The words are jammed up in the back of my throat. Both my hands in Rich's. The chapel is empty. With only our tiny girl by our side. These are such private personal words that I never felt they could be shared: the emotion and the sentiment is only between us. It feels too private. Offering up your heart to this person. For me, it was never a commitment that was meant for an audience. Words to honour. A moment in time to stop and say: it was always you, and it will always be you. Forever, yes.

We were always happy never to marry; happy to keep living as 'boyfriend and girlfriend' 'til we were old and grey. After losing our money, we never thought it would be an option, anyway. Weddings seem like a financial excess: so much money for one day. But the idea of eloping to Las Vegas captured our heart and was the only way it made sense to us. Three of us. In love. Forever. 'Til death do us part. We slide on our matching rings, which we bought in a Hollywood vintage store. Thick ghetto 'gold' bands. One side says LOVE, the other side says FUCK. $9. Perfect. I do have a very fancy double finger ring coming from a jeweller in NYC. For me, I decided that an amazing wedding ring on my finger is a 'forever memory', rather than a pretty expensive dress folded in a box for the rest of my life. When we decided on Vegas, it had to be The Little Church of the West.

A tiny redwood chapel with bell tower, stained-glass windows and shingle roof. A 1940 replica of a pioneer town church. Massive double doors open to a tiny chapel with a few rows of wooden pew seating and hanging bronze gaslight chandeliers, vintage electric church candles on each side of the aisle, set on a grassy patch with big leafy trees. A pocket of nostalgia; the oldest building on the flashing, heady Las Vegas strip. Rich has a mod-style light grey suit with a button-down collar shirt, handmade black floral tie and hankie; fingers, wrists and neck in trademark silver. My devastatingly handsome groom. Still that fucking cool boy that I fell head-over-heels in love with, but so grown up now. He had my whole entire heart forever from that very first day. Our little flower girl is as cute as all the buttons in the world in the dress she picked out in LA. It's spectacular: layers of frothy, pale pink tulle and a little gold lace top. Gold glitter jelly shoes. She had a baby's breath flower crown, which she prefers to carry, rather than wear it on her head, and a matching pom-pom, round bouquet. Rich painted her tiny nails pale pink while I got ready. She looks delicious, like a sugary cake ornament. She's so sweet, calling it 'our wedding day'. I wear a simple, long kind of geometric lace, floor-length, figure-hugging dress, a load of cleavage with a nipped-in waist (thanks to the addition of corset and spanks underneath), with a fishtail-kick at the bottom. A handmade, gold metallic leather flower half-crown; long straight hair with my heavy fringe; bright red Mac Lady Danger lips, with a beautiful floor-length veil trailing behind that my Mum made for me. The most incredible killer sky-high stack '70s gold heels, with lightning bolt straps, by Terry De Havilland, and a round bunch of blood-red frilly carnations, dusty pink sweet peas, anemones with black centres and crimson petals. I had both Dot's and my bouquets made with vintage posy holders. My flowers were meant to be a sweet little '50s neat posy, not flashy, but it was so big... Everything seems bigger in America. They are glorious. A blue glass evil-eye pinned into my flowers from my very superstitious sister-in-law and a brooch with pearls from my mum. I treasure these thoughtful gifts. I know it is hard for my mum, and other family members, to not be here, but we didn't want a fuss made over our wedding. We wanted it to be uncomplicated and simple. The outfit finished off with a dusty pink pouch purse with floor-length fringing. This is the best outfit I have ever worn in my life. Everyone talks about a dream wedding dress, but mine was 'a wedding look'. All the elements making up my dream outfit. I daydreamed of finding my dream man, but never the dress and all the trimmings. So this is a real treat.

We book a car to drive us around, instead of getting Ubers. A stretch limo turned up, much to Dot's delight, continuing the 'everything is bigger in the USA' theme, after our very short, and very sweet, lightning-speed wedding ceremony. We jump in and head to the historic Neon Bone Yard, an open-air museum full of all the old vintage Vegas casino signs. We have our photos taken in a private area of the museum with what will turn out to be the biggest surprise of the wedding day - our photographer, a native Las Vegan. Dot runs around in front of the camera against

QUEEN OF CLUBS

the backdrop of the iconic Lady Luck sign, glitter horseshoe and towering pastel letters. It's a dreamy colour pallet of golden pinks and cool greys during the 'magic hour' of the desert sunset. Rich grabs us some pre-mixed margaritas, to have in our flash transport, then it's on to downtown, walking around the old district of Vegas with its vintage flashing lights and gritty backdrops. Downtown side streets with peeling street art, abandoned movie theatres, while we chat and walk around with these vistas and a kaleidoscopic story-filled backdrop unfolding behind us. The photographer captures the precious moment. The photos are a mix of natural, candid images, snaps our personalities and his signature style of spotlight and long exposure to create high-contrast stylised images. I am blown away when the contact sheet arrives a few weeks later. It's us. Captured in little frames. The love and fun. But his signature-style ones look like an editorial shoot that could be mistaken for a White Stripes album cover, or a Tarantino film poster, These are the best wedding photos I have ever seen. And we're in them. I'm fucking thrilled! There was a time after Dot was born that I felt like I was never going to get close to looking and feeling like my old self again, and these photos meant more to me than I imagined. I look beautiful. And happy. And in love. Not the clubland-girl kind of pretty, but adult beautiful. The beauty of my daughter is an extension of our love. The beauty in my husband is a reflection of how I have loved him all these years. This is true beauty. And I see it in myself here. With them. Captured in these photos.

This is what Hollywood-Fucking-Amazing-Love looks like.

A divine luxe wedding dinner for three, starting with oysters, king crab, caviar and prawns. Popping a bottle of Laurent-Perrier Rose to toast. Then filet mignon, shoestring fries with a smoky Pinot Noir. For Dot, olives to start with, fish and chips for her main meal and a lemonade: her choice for her 'best-ever meal', bless her. After dinner, Rich plays Claude Debussy's Clare De Lune for me, transfixed by the hypnotic dancing fountains and the light show of The Strip, all from our lounge room. We had the wedding feast laid out in our own private dining room, in our very own penthouse. This is where we really treated ourselves. The penthouse suite in the Bellagio with the fountain-facing view for the next four nights. Bar, dining room, lounge room, 3 bathrooms and a bedroom. I never want this day to end. Ever. Dot and I finish with a sofa jumping, table-top dancing party, 'til we all fall asleep in the giant bed. The most cherished day of my whole entire life. I loved the day Dot was born, but this one was more fun for me and because we shared it together, it makes it so special. Purest of love and total opulence. It's an outstanding combination. The next leg of our trip is for our little Dot. Disneyland! To be fair, I think we enjoyed it as much as she did! What a dreamland. It is as magical as we hope for. I always wanted to go as a child but never did. I got a baby brother instead.

Epic love life. Check.

Giddy with our loved-up USA experience, inspired to keep moving to the light, we move out of the barred-windowed, double-exposure highway flat that was on the 'wrong' side of the Harbour Bridge for people like us. We move to Camperdown, on the edge of the city. It's gritty and with bundles of urban charm. It reminds me of Hackney. Rich finds us a big 'New York' loft-style apartment in a converted, long, industrial, hallway entrance, open-plan 2-storey high ceiling with a mezzanine. So much space. It has a massive rooftop with views spanning the whole city; a pool, gym, bbq areas and tennis court. We hosted the most epic celebration of our professional party lives up on the rooftop, A 'farm in the city' party for Dot, getting a pony, a baby llama and calf into the goods lifts.

It was the first eviction notice we have received for a party, which is pretty ironic! Thank god they turned the eviction around, because we love it here. It was the best move for us as a family. Lots of people more like us; creative thinkers, cultural diversity and young families. It's not as judgemental as the other side of the Sydney Harbour Bridge, which is very generic and up its own arse for no reason, which is not our vibe at all. It feels too fake. Next year, Dot will go down the road to a great little school. For now, she is in a new fantastic preschool that we trust and feel confident in.

We are going through a learning curve with her at the moment. In her early years, it was hard not to be that proud, boastful parent, 'Oh my baby is doing this, she's started that, milestone this, yadda yadda.' She smashed them. She did everything early and with ease. She made us look like excellent parents. But Dot has started having really advanced emotions and fears. We got trapped in the goods lift of the apartment block, and it was stuck, bouncing between floors. It didn't help that her slightly older cousin was saying, "Don't worry, Dot. You won't die: if it falls, it will just break your legs." He was probably right, but it didn't help Dots out-of-control fear. This incident seemed to trigger escalated anxiety, well beyond a typical 4-year-old. So much so that, as parents, we couldn't soothe her. She has big feelings of empathy, wants insight into human behaviour well beyond her age, and a keen interest in how and why things happen. A high vocabulary from an early age, understanding words and just throwing them casually in a sentence in the correct context. From about Bali time, when she was 2.5 years, you could have very complex conversations with her. She could do funny random things, like whistle like R2D2, and make astute observations of things happening around her that an adult would miss. Lots of little things that made life with her so, so cool. Every day is a random surprise of what she's learned or thought of. She picks up words in other languages and uses them in sentences. She has a ridiculous long-term memory, remembering things from 8-months old. We address the anxiety with the preschool, and they also suggested that they think she is gifted. An example they used was that she was building a sensory museum with light reflectors and prisms during her free playtime. She's four! I had been working on a creative-direction concept for a sensory museum and quickly showed her my concept boards, which she remembers 4 weeks later. After testing, turns out she has an IQ of 98%, exceptional abstract thinking, complex emotional understanding and highly empathetic, well beyond her years. A tiny genius. A great thinker and feeler. Which is why the anxiety had started so early. It's crazy. She has a low-functioning working memory, and we need to watch out for dyslexia in the future. I have both of these exhausting, challenging 'traits' but without the certified genius part. Dot's huge heart, thoughtfulness and the way she thinks about the world is extraordinary. She is one of these special people who will make the world a more beautiful place. But I'm also pretty astounded that she has come from us. Two people who have put our brains and bodies, pre-baby times, through hell. We worried that it could affect our future children, but in fact, we are blessed with the total opposite. It's like a perfect storm; the collision of two obsessed creatives. My favourite reply after we told a few people is Kitty's. She kills me. 'Well, sweetheart, she didn't lick it off the floor, did she?"

Outstanding home life. Check.

My unusual and pretty unique career as a project-based creative director started out in Australia, mostly with hospitality and lifestyle industries, branding and bar design. But it has shape-shifted into a more niche, specialised market. Conceptual Ideation and Experiential Activations.

On paper, my work officially looks like this.

A dynamic creative, with a strong focus on forward-thinking concepts, uncovering trends, creating community and cultural movements, strong messages, imagery and unforgettable brand atmosphere. With precision and balance, knowing that incredible ideas need to translate into brand exposure and awareness – and ultimately to increase revenue and strengthen customer loyalty.

What the fuck does that actually mean?

Big picture thinking. I get booked to come in and create fuck-off amazing ideas that allow customers to connect and interact with a brand. Create ideas for parties, festivals, art shows and installations, formulate collaborations, photoshoots, immersive 'museum', concepts for AR/VR reality games and apps. Like all the installations, parties and events I did with my nightclubs, without the day-to-day running of my own clubs. Just the ideas and creative part. Ideally, I would love to create these concepts and experiences as purely 'interactive art', but so far these all live and breathe because of commercial marketing budgets, as I don't have the backing to start my own venture as planned, but this is a pretty good compromise as far as a 'job' goes.

I usually come in like a creative Mary Poppins when a company hasn't got the resourcing to do the project in-house, or they need to pitch for new business. Then I leave again when the idea is nailed. It swings between feast or famine. It flips between juggling high paying, multiple projects at the same time, then flops to no work at all. But being project-based, it means that we can control a comfortable balance between family life and work.

I am non-negotiable with my working hours: when I'm not working, being present and engaged parents is our priority. If I was working full-time in an agency, as a Creative Director, this is the kind of position where you are expected to work through the night on pitches and 'urgent' deadlines. So this suits me: I love and am obsessed by creating ideas, but I don't care about climbing the bullshit corporate ladder. These type of projects are massively dictated by financial year-end, budgets, elections and holiday periods. One minute I'm being flown out to work on a sensory museum experience for an artisan liquor brand; the next, working on a multi-billion-dollar project on what the future of tourism Australia looks like (for a huge casino group), to curating an art installation to celebrate the release of a rare wine collection. To ideating a mini-festival inside a major festival and designing a VIP-guest experience for the most well-known watch company in the world, at the most prestigious car race in the world. Then I have 4 weeks of no new work. And repeats like this all year. Through my winning streak, I can charge $2000 a day, and nobody blinks an eye. When the industry is quiet, I use the time to make new contacts. I hit the street a bit like a 1970's door-to-door salesman, setting up 'meet-and-greets'. This is where I will send a creative agency a love letter and my portfolio of work. We then meet up have a chat: it's like a first date. People always respond well to my experience, and I love to chat about my work. We get all excited about the projects we could work on together. It feels a bit soulless and draining, as you don't walk away with any new projects then and there, but it's an essential creative mating ritual. Putting the time in while nothing is going on makes me the first person they call when an exciting brief lands on their desk that needs big thinking.

Happy work life. Check

Life's looking good, huh!? ...

This is where I planned to end the story up, all neat and tidy

Perfectly gift-wrapped.

Hollywood happy ending. Fade to black.

...and they lived happily ever after.

The End.

I really wanted to have a feel-good ending. 'This is what life is like when you exit clubland...' What happens to the girl who dedicated over a decade to 'the night'? When the disco ball stopped spinning, the lights are turned on, and the DJ has played his last song? Well, they lived happily ever after, of course!

But there is a secret. A push-pull. An underlying self-saboteur; the devil in my ear just won't go away. The itch that still has to be scratched.

There has been no magic reset button, that I desperately crave. It wouldn't be honest or true to the full journey out of clubland. I would be giving you the social media 'best life' full-face-tune-filter ending.

You, my dear friend, deserve the truth.

If we let the story run a few months longer, you get to the real ending. It's messy, it's certainly not pretty, but it's real, and there can be beauty and freedom in the truth.

We are conditioned to want things to be perfect, but life isn't perfect, and neither am I.

27

The real ending.

All those years and years of unhealthy lifestyle habits, self-medication, hazards of the industry and addiction. These run deep. My secret push-pull? Drinking. It takes a very different shape now that I am away from clubland, for a few reasons. I'm a mum. So it's not about bars, nightclubs and all-night benders kind of drinking but there is a lot of leeway for an acceptable level of alcohol. Mum-drinking. Prosecco at picnics, family-friendly pub lunches with wine and all the kids running around. Gin and tonics after the bath and bed. Pints and mini golf. All the wine. There is this level of acceptance and entitlement for mums to drink.

Jokes about mummy medicine. Parenting with a Negroni in your hand is totally socially acceptable. I'm not saying it's right, but just look at social media feeds, and you'll see what I'm talking about. It's happening, and I get behind it. I actually don't know one non-drinking mum who doesn't open a bottle of wine at 6pm.

Another contributor that reshapes the way I drink now is that Australia has extremely strict liquor laws and anything past two glasses of wine and decibel levels above whispering will get you removed from any licensed venue. Rich and I seem to give off red flags to security because we look 'different' to your normal Sydneysiders, even if it's just a low-key night. So we don't really get baby-sitters to go out, 'cause when we do, it doesn't end well. Booze shops also shut early, mostly around 8pm, so you have to be organised and get your wine in advance. So you might grab a few bottles to last the whole weekend, but they are hard to not drink, sitting there. When they wink at you from the shelf - all shiny and full of wine, when you promised yourself you weren't going to open another bottle tonight. If I had to put a bra on, go outside, walk to the shops, I wouldn't bother, but it's just sitting there... Teasing me, wanting to extend the good times. And the last significant new change I have learnt about my drinking is now creativity is my commodity, and I charge for it, without the total self-indulgence of being self-employed and doing things at my own speed. After one drink, alcohol turns off the creative part of my brain, they can't co-exist. If I drink and try to 'be creative', then look at the ideas the next day, they're total dog shit! I can't drink and be creative. It's one or the other. I can't work hungover, so when you get paid to come up with fuck-off amazing ideas by the end of the day, this is just not acceptable. I never drink more than a glass when I'm working a creative direction project. So my drinking takes a new form. I fall into the 'weekend-fun mum' with late-afternoon, socially acceptable drinking. Then home after mum-duties are done, and once Dot is in bed, it's a heady, steady red wine and Netflix session. Like a fancy, premium liquor, adult version of teen binge-drinking and blacking out. But it's not intentional. I don't technically sit down and aim to drink to blackout: it's just how my body is reacting now. I think before, when I used to take coke, it fights off the effects of the alcohol and now, with my continually trying to keep weight off with no carbs, unbalanced keto diet and intermittent fasting, then booze on top - it just hits me, like a hard black wall. Blackout. I haven't been able to transition over a

decade of unhealthy drinking habits into a new social norm. These old habits that are so far ingrained I can't seem to remove them, even if I try to break the cycle fully. I manage to keep my creative mind operating while I'm on the job, It's irritating and distracting but can hold off the want and need to drink during the project and then I have my drinking escapism in blocks. There seems to be no healthy balance that I can control.

As far as drug status goes? Surprisingly quiet. I am sick to the back teeth of it. By the end of it, I used coke in club life as a tool to stay awake, to feel 'normal'; like people use coffee in an office job. It's an occupational hazard that I'm pleased to kick to the curb, plus I'm not interested in the terrible quality, cut with meow meow 0.6-gram bag of 'cocaine' in Australia that costs $300. That's just fucking ridiculous, by anyone's standards, especially an ex hard- core devotee. Everyone knows you never buy only one bag, and because it's cut with the shit mephedrone, it's also sending everyone a bit fucking mental. The strange thing is that I always just assumed that it was the coke that I was addicted to. But I've been hoodwinked by grape varieties, regions, small-batch liquors and a well-dressed addiction, a charade in product knowledge and disguised in the top-shelf beverages.

I am trying to be ok. Put old habits behind me. 'Just get over it. You've left it all behind now', as one of my family members told me. I try. I expected that as soon as I handed back my keys to clubland, touched down from zen Bali, back to Australia, it would all be ok. I wanted to be ok. The terror followed me, itching in the pit of my stomach. The truth was that writing these words has shown me that I am not really ok. I am in a post-trauma shock haze, so many terrible things happening back-to-back over a long period of time.

tProtected in alcohol. To feed my pain, shame and keep the cycle of self-destruction going.

I expertly shoehorn my drinking in between being a lovely mum, overcompensating on the weekend, up early making nutritious breakfasts, MacGyvering Barbie hammocks and princess Lego castles, doing crafted birthday cards, planting seedlings, long scooter sightseeing walks, bake-offs, extended learning, art galleries and museums: that's not to say it's without a dusty little hangover and a remedial lunchtime Bloody Mary, but I am a dedicated, obsessed and doting 'tiger' mum, and that between being a focused creative director, and an exceptional wife, packed lunches and fuck-off amazing dinners. I love my role as a mother and wife. I am far from a drunk sitting alone on a park bench with a paper bag.

I do get some clanging, motherfuckers of hangovers. But it's a smoothed out, non-noticeable drinking pattern that steps up a notch with any milestone moments, achievements, extended family fuckery or stressful situations. Good or bad, I deal with it all the same way I have done for over a decade. I drink. I drink to forget my worries. I drink to feel good. I drink to switch off. I drink to unwind. I drink to numb any pain. I drink to ease the everyday blah. I drink because red wine tastes fucking delicious and margaritas make my pants wet. I drink to smooth out the bumps. I drink because it's really fun. I drink because that's what I do and what I've always done. It's who I am. And I drink to forget the itch that creeps into the pit of my stomach. The downside is that it gets out of hand, sometimes. Badly. And I'm starting to get scared. I know I have an unhealthy relationship with drinking.

I don't really make new friends because of it, or socialise with work colleagues. I can't be trusted to drink with 'new people'. Most creative agencies have significant drinking cultures, and I always seem to work on 'booze brands'. I got really close with a particular team but never went out for drinks with them. One work friend keeps nagging and nagging me, and now I just joke "Oh, I can't come drinking with you 'cause I really like my work and that will never continue if we go drinking together." I joke, but it's true. I'm deadly serious. I can't be trusted to locate my 'off button' after 2 drinks. I don't trust myself to not do something really, really stupid. This isn't clubland, where everyone gets drunk and it's totally normal to drink, get wasted and take drugs at work. If you don't, it's weird, and there's a level of mistrust. Night life after-work drinks means you pop out for one and could return 48 hours later, but the most annoying thing about it is forgetting your sunglasses for your epic walk of shame. This is sensibleville. I'm now an 'adult' and work on creatively demanding projects, in between all these 'weekend drinking incidents'. Nobody would have any idea this happens once I clock off. It's my secret.

I keep thinking of other ways to handle it. Controlling it. Negotiate with it. Reading books about it. Research. I do try, but seem powerless to make any changes. I know life is always going to have challenges and celebrations in both work life and home life. I need to learn to deal with it in a different way, not the bottom of a bottle or raising a glass. But old habits die hard and are almost impossible to break. Although I do try, but always fail. It's in my DNA. That pull-push of drinking is like the tide for me. If I'm not drinking, then I'm thinking about when I can drink. And when I am drinking, I'm thinking about the next drink I'm going to pour. Then I think that I want to stop drinking after this drink. Then I don't drink, and I think about drinking. Then I drink. It's a pattern. A cycle, a dance and we go round and round. It happens daily. Even if I wanted it to stop, it's out of my power.

Like I can't control the sun and the moon, that's the universe's job.

Highly functioning Alcoholic. Check.

A huge, daily struggle is that I don't just 'fit back' into Australia. I desperately try. But it's a struggle, and I have changed. It seems exactly the same as the day I left, 15 years ago. Rich and I made the decision to move here on a glorious two-week holiday. We were so grateful to have an escape plan in place, after it turned to shit for us in the UK, to have Australia to run to. But me expecting there to be an 'ok' switch proved problematic. I expected it to be a warm and smooth transition back in.

The same week Rich and I left for our wedding, my parents separated after 40-plus years of marriage. As an adult, it had an unsettling effect on me. The family we moved here for, gripping so tight to the idea of this amazing family unit that was going to make our life so wonderful, just doesn't exist with us in it. It feels like a handful of marbles thrown high up into the air, and desperately trying to catch them all on the way down. It's impossible. It has changed everyone as individuals and shifted the entire family dynamic. It creates a new energy of friction and aggravation. The reason we chose to move to Australia was my family, and a better life for Dot, and this was dismantled. What I craved when it was just the three of us together in Brighton: it was uncomplicated and straight-forward in that we didn't have to deal with other people's drama, opinions and bullshit that comes with extended family life. But raising a child is challenging with no 'village.' I dreamed for a family life of friendship, love and support. Maybe I romanticised it from afar, and the thought of the idyllic family life we had when we were younger. Before things got so complicated by life, and now I guess family 'from afar, the grass seems greener' is very different to being in the middle of it.

It's fucking messy and makes me question my sanity, self-worth, personal boundaries and moral compass daily.

Unhealthy drinking triggers. Check

Where is Rich in all this? Right next to me, but drinking isn't a problem for him. He can handle his alcohol and could stop any day. Neither of us says it, but I know we both think it... What happens if we take away the very thing our relationship was built on?

I mostly manage to control and hide my 'uncontrollable' drinking into the social disguise of 'acceptable', but things like these happen every so often… and I had a big pile of stories to choose from.

When most people would think it's time to stop drinking.

Rich and I get tickets to the Jet 10th anniversary concert of Get Born, the album. A rare-as-fuck mum and dad night out on the town. Dot's at Nanny's for a sleepover, and I don't have a creative direction project on. Look out. Margaritas with dinner, squishy concert beer, a pint in each hand, bar crawl home. Drunk as fuck. Deadman walking drunk. Some guy looks at Rich the 'wrong way'. This happens a lot in Australia with drunk pig men everywhere. It's usually a variation of a Gallagher joke, which typically rolls off his back. The guy says something other than the usual bullshit: Rich gets up close to him. I can't hear, but he says something back, an inch from the guy's face, then walks off to the bar. I glare at the pricks. I didn't hear the exchange between Rich and them, but the guy laughs, and it pisses me off because I think he is still taking the piss out of Rich.

SNAP.

I smash the end off my pint glass, bashing it against the edge of the table and hold my jagged weapon an inch from the guy's face. He is not laughing any more. I calmly let him know "I'll glass" him if he doesn't shut the fuck up. I'm grabbed and dragged out by security. They push us down the road before the guys call the police. I am so protective of Rich, always, but I have no idea why I did it. A fucking one-women western bar brawl; an unlikely gunslinger in her very late 30s and in a fancy paisley Coco Fennel dress. I never have 'glassed' anyone in my life. I didn't even know that I knew how to knock the end of a glass off. My body wasn't in control, nor was my mind. I just saw RED.

Then smash. My anger and hate were terrifyingly so close to the surface: ready, waiting, wanting to fight. I feel like the dead-eyed soldier from clubland, just sitting there ready to attack when called on. Picking the bits of glass shards and wiping the blood off my hands so we can go to the next bar. Not ever mentioning that I was a possessed psychotic smashing the glass and threating to cut them. I was blind drunk. A walking, talking blackout. This was a Wednesday.

When I would have imagined that I would have stopped drinking.

There was no special occasion for the drinking, other than unwinding on a Saturday. A few cocktails at happy-hour after visiting the Rolling Stones exhibition. Wine with dinner. A bottle of Moet and beers during the evening watching Netflix. I go to bed drunk, so

I take a few Ambien sleeping pills, left over from a USA trip, to ensure I can sleep to ease the next day's hangover. I woke up a few hours later, hot, confused by a vivid life-like dream. I'm coming out from our recycling room in our apartment hallway, and I'm naked. Our front door is locked. I came out for fresh air. SNAP. I come too, and it's not a dream. FUCK. I'm in the hallway. FUCK. I'm totally naked. Blackout drunk. Desperately banging on the door to get in. Confused and disorientated. No idea how I got out here...Why am I naked!? Thank fuck! The front door opens: I rush over to get into our apartment to hide, but I can't get in. I'm being blocked. violently pushed back into the hall. He fights me out and slams the door. ... What have I done?!? It's not my door; it's a neighbour. The doors all look the same. I go back to our front door and start banging, again. Louder. Crying. Knowing that Rich can't hear knocking on the door inside the warehouse apartment. He sleeps like a log, and I will be here 'til he wakes up in the morning and realises I'm gone. I think I could go outside and try to climb up to our first-floor balcony, but that means going out on the main road, naked. And the fire doors will close behind me, with no keys to open them or anything to prop them open with to get back in if I don't make the climb. I bang with all my might 'til my knuckles are raw and split. Try to cover up my horrendous nakedness. He opens. THANK FUCK. I sob with relief. Rich is confused. I try to explain what happened, but I don't know. Bewildered, I just went out for fresh air... Trying to piece it together, there's a loud bang on our door. 'OPEN UP, IT'S THE POLICE!' Still naked, I hide behind the kitchen bench and poke my head around. Rich opens the door, and the police shine their torches in. Our neighbour had called the police saying a naked, crazed lady was trying to break into his apartment. 'Yes, that's me. I'm ok, I was just 'sleepwalking and been drinking.'

I'm far from ok.

When I did stop drinking.

It was a regular Sunday. Pub lunch and wine. With a sibling, who needed a sympathetic ear as the cousins played together, the adults ate, drank and talked. Back to the warehouse for a few sunset rooftop drinks, swim, then back to the apartment for nightcaps. I didn't have to work tomorrow, and Dot was at vacation care before she starts school in a few weeks. So it didn't matter if I had a hangover. The next day, I am paralysed from alcohol poisoning. I beg Rich to help me. "Sorry, but I have to go to work'. I can't get up to make Dot a packed lunch. The room's spinning. Holding back vomit. I can't drive and would be so over the limit. Rich said to call my mum but I can't: I don't want her knowing. I have to stay lying down. Dot starts running about the house. My eyes are closed to try and block out the pain. I can hear cupboards opening and closing, taps running, little bare feet darting around. Back by my side "Don't worry, mummy. I'll take care of you." She got a flannel, sick bucket and a towel, tucks a blanket over me and carefully strokes my face, putting the damp cloth on my forehead.

"Don't cry, Mummy. It will be ok."

An act from the purest heart, beautiful kindness and utter selflessness that soothed the most horrendous shame-filled selfish beast. It crossed me over the ever-looming invisible line. I don't deserve her, and she doesn't deserve this.

This is what my rock bottom looks like. It's putrid and vile. The itch in my stomach. My no-return.

The moment my heart broke.

The relief I felt on this day, that it was finally over, was utterly overwhelming. Humbling. On my knees for the last time. This is the reset button. The new journey. The freedom and peace I craved. I didn't know how to find it, because I was holding onto the habits and behaviour of the past.

I will never take another sip.

My last link to clubland cut.

Forever.

My Dear Beautiful Reader,

This journey with you has changed my life.

*Today, on my 40th turn around the sun, this much I know:
I have learned that you can travel around the world and end up exactly where you started, but that doesn't mean it's the end. It is the shelter from the storm until you're ready to start a new adventure. I've learnt that I am like Jon Snow and the bitter disappointment of an ending. Being sent back to the Knight's Watch. Back to where he started. After all that. For nothing. But they didn't say he couldn't walk past the wall, to start a new splinter story on the other side... I've learned that you have to follow your heart, chase your dreams, show up and fuck-up, but never, ever give up. It was messy, wild and hard. And it hurt deeply but fuck me, was some of it fun. That being a mother is the highest honour given in life, that I will never take a liberty with it again.*

That I am a creative imaginer, an ideas man (lady) not the great business mogul Girlboss that I tried so hard to be. That I tried and I failed. But I'm proud that at least I did try when lots of people might not dare. I have learnt that I wasn't able to decode the trauma alone that was hidden behind a mask of addiction without a saint-worthy psychologist to hold up the mirror and let me see it for myself. I knew I found the right one when her eyes didn't fully bulge out of her head with the naked hallway story. She kinda smirked, slowly nodded and said 'wow'. Like she was impressed at my level of commitment to the chaos. Tears pool in her eyes when I whisper out the secrets of my lowest pain, toxic shame and deepest regrets. Non-judgemental empathy is a potent healer. I learned that emotional honesty can bring peace to the gnawing, terrifying feeling in the pit of my stomach.

That I made mistakes, for which I am deeply and genuinely sorry, but it's now time to stop torturing myself. But promise to make more mindful decisions, with my eyes wide open from now on. I found out the painful way, coming back into a fully-grown family unit, after being away for so many years, that it's almost impossible to stay sane and you sure-as-shit better have a rolling weekly appointment in your google calendar with your therapist to deal with the family drama. Our version of Keeping up with the Car-Crashians (TM Rich Pack), I've learned that if my mum can start a new life on the other side of her smashed-down dreams of a perfect white-picket-fence family life, then she is 'tough enough' to read this now. I know that my home is where my heart is, and my heart is my husband and my child. Not a location on a map or the city where I was born. I've learned that nothing is better than an uninterrupted 8 hours sleep in freshly washed, decent thread-count sheets. It is equally life-affirming when the sleep comes because your child stays in her own bed, after 5 years of broken sleep, as it is to not being a sleepless-raging-24-hour-cocaine-zombie-clubland-resident.
Both are truly precious.

I've learned that you, my dear beautiful friend, have shown me how to stand in the light and that it's finally time to let go of the liquor bottle I have held on too tight for support. This is where the new journey starts.

But lastly and most importantly, I know that Hollywood-Fucking-Amazing-Love truly exists and it demands you travel the world to find it. Break your vagina for it. Lose yourself only to find a newer 'softer' imperfectly perfect version of yourself. To love viciously, without question, can bring both soul-soothing comfort and knee-knocking, heart-pounding excitement.
It's not a myth or rumour: it's an actual fucking truth.

I thank you from the bottom of my little black heart for being here with me. Unravelling this journey, helping me to learn all this.

Goodbye, my dear, dear friend. I miss you deeply, already,

Tava xxx

QUEEN OF CLUBS

epilogue

Dear Universe,
So is this how it ends?

Dear Tava,
No, this is the beginning.
Now you tell the world our story

QUEEN OF CLUBS

TAVA O'HALLORAN

the end...

I may have walked away with 'nothing' from clubland…

Except for these words.

QUEEN OF CLUBS

notes

Listen
The Queen of Clubs soundtrack, mixed by Rich Pack.
soundcloud.com/qoc_soundtrack

Queen of Clubs: Behind the Scenes | Pre-Order Now.
Released on 1st October 2020
Photos and candid interviews with its incredible clubland residents and characters.
amazon.com/author/tavaohalloran

Queen After Clubs: Rock Bottom | Pre-Order Now.
Released on 1st January 2021
Unravelling the chaos to finding freedom.
Sobriety was only the very tip of the iceberg…
amazon.com/author/tavaohalloran

Shop
Queen of Clubs Merch
We have taken the incredible, macabre wallpaper Rich and I made (by rubbing the Victorian tiles with charcoal at the Bathhouse, creating the iconic backdrop to wild parties and club photography) as inspiration for our Limited Edition, Queen of Clubs Merch Range. From canvas hi-top trainers, to poster prints, to journals

to beautiful cushions and bespoke rolls of the iconic wallpaper available for your home.
www.tavaohalloran.com/shop

Sensory Journey
I have curated, designed, and hand-poured a Queen of Clubs candle. Recreating our story

Top Note - Tobacco Flower.
Naivety and kaleidoscopic adventures.
Hopes, and dreams.

Heart Note - Full Bloom Blood-Red Rose.
The most profound love affair.
Smoky hypnotic Nag Champa.

Base Note - Gunpowder Flint.
Rock bottom despair and the darkest night.
Unwavering resilience, grit and strength.
*also available in a room spray.
https://www.tavaohalloran.com/shop

AR
Real-World Augmented Reality Launch Party Filter
We created a virtual world that you enter via an Instagram filter portal into the Queen of Club's launch party, accessible anywhere in the world. A shimmery disco ball-filled book-signing room and glamourous selfie feature.
@QOCbook

Need help?
If you feel you might need some help with drug and alcohol addiction, don't wait until your version of rock bottom. If you have googled 'Do I have an addiction?', taken online quizzes on acceptable levels of drinking or done deals with yourself over how much

or when you drink, it's an issue you don't need to continue. I wish I hadn't wasted almost ten years of my life negotiating with the bottom of the bottle.

Visit your doctor for a chat about making changes, or there is a ton of information online to get your journey started at recovery.org.uk https://www.recovery.org.uk/

Anti-Social
In my personal life, I stopped posting on Instagram when I was bouncing around rock bottom. I couldn't fuel the gross-dysmorphic-split-personality-online-phenomenon. Only posting the beautiful aspects of my life; my wonderful cherub child and handsome cool husband, the pretty food I cooked and heady cocktails I sipped, while I was a fucking mess behind the scenes, naked in hallways, vomiting and retching till my teeth turned to chalk.

Professionally, now that Queen of Clubs is a self-published project, it's kinda the obvious choice to transition back onto the social media platform. A double-edged sword to expand the world of QOC further, to be able to talk and engage with you about the book, creativity, addiction and love. And as an entrepreneur, use it as a natural tool. But it feels disingenuous: I can't go back to sharing and engaging on Instagram now, throwing my Kindling content to the Zuckerburg antisocial forest fire.

I still want to talk and share with you! But not on a platform that is full of fake news and unpredictable algorithms. I will always do commercial work around social media with my creative direction clients: that's my day job, but in my personal life I'm certainly not doing this to be an insta-infamous poster girl.

So, I have made a decision, and I don't know if it's really stupid, but it feels right. I will have a Queen of Clubs profile on a few social platforms as a 'landing page' for people who are seeking us out, share our launch party AR filter, to find people who would love the story and redirect readers. This is more of a signpost and waving to new people, letting them know where we are gathering online.

If you fancy joining this alliance of like-minded people, message me if you have a question. Enjoy curated high-quality original content, behind the scenes and insight to Queen of Clubs, creativity, music mixes and interviews. Q&A's, inspiration, courses and blogs. From chasing dreams and outwitting gatekeepers. How to self-publish your own story and what makes great design. To thoughts on addiction and the benefits of being a non-drinker without the 'woo-woo' bullshit. Super varied and a breather from Instagram.

I'm looking to connect genuinely. On a platform that is real. With people who want only to be there. No fake news. No mind numbing soul-sucking scrolling. No face-tuning, no sunsets or photos of my coffee, gripped by fingers full of rings and a perfect mani. No rubberneckers at a car crash or shit-stirring trolls.

But there still could be a few memes, right?

Come join us in the member's area, its free!

www.tavaohalloran.com

See you in there!
T x

Printed in Poland
by Amazon Fulfillment
Poland Sp. z o.o., Wrocław